S0-CQT-066

The 70-290 Cram Sheet

This Cram Sheet contains the distilled, key facts about the Managing and Maintaining a Microsoft Windows Server 2003 Environment exam. Review this information as the last thing you do before you enter the testing center, paying special attention to those areas where you feel that you need the most review.

HARDWARE DEVICES AND DRIVERS

1. Windows Server 2003 controls whether users can install signed device drivers, unsigned device drivers, or both. The three choices for the Unsigned Driver Installation Behavior policy setting are Silently Succeed, Warn but Allow Installation, or Do Not Allow Installation. From the Hardware tab on the System Properties window, the choices are Ignore, Warn, or Block.

2. USB supports a maximum of 127 devices connected to one USB host controller (root hub) with no more than seven tiers (seven layers of USB hubs daisy-chained together). You can use no more than 5 external hubs in one physical chain of hubs. Each device can be no more than 5 meters away from the port of the hub that it is connected to.

3. From the Network Connections window, you can join multiple network connections to form a network bridge by first selecting each connection in the Network Connections window and then clicking the Bridge Connections option.

4. You can make changes to the binding order of protocols and you can modify the network provider order for the installed network adapters by clicking the Advanced Settings menu option from the Network Connections window.

5. The Authentication tab of a network connection's properties sheet is where you can enable or disable IEEE 802.1x authentication, which is enabled by default. You can select the Extensible Authentication Protocol (EAP) to be used on the system from the EAP Type drop-down list box as follows: MD5-Challenge, Protected EAP (PEAP), or Smart Card or Other Certificate (default). The Advanced tab is where you can turn on or off the Internet Connection Firewall (ICF) feature and the Internet Connection Sharing (ICS) feature.

6. If Windows Server 2003 is installed with just one CPU present (a uniprocessor system) and you later want to add one or more additional processors (to create a multiprocessor system), you must use the Hardware Update Wizard to install a new hardware abstraction layer (HAL) to enable support for multiple processors.

SERVER STORAGE

7. Basic disks use partitions, not volumes, and they can store up to four primary partitions or up to three primary partitions and one extended partition with logical drives.

8. Dynamic disks use volumes, not partitions, that you create from unallocated space. You can create up to 2,000 dynamic volumes on one dynamic disk. The 5 types of dynamic volumes are simple, spanned, striped, mirrored, and RAID-5.

9. You can use either the Disk Management console or the diskpart.exe command-line utility to work with disk storage.

10. Only Windows Server 2003, Windows XP Professional, Windows 2000 Professional, and Windows 2000 Server support dynamic volumes.

11. You can convert a basic disk to a dynamic disk and retain all data on the disk. However, you cannot revert a dynamic disk back to a basic disk without first deleting all existing volumes (and data). You must first back up the data on the dynamic disk and then you can restore the data from backup onto the new basic disk.

12. Administrators can use the fsutil.exe command-line tool for managing disk quotas, managing mount points, and performing several other advanced disk-related tasks.

13. Using the diskpart.exe command-line tool, you can extend a basic partition, but it must be formatted as NTFS, it must be adjacent to contiguous unallocated space on the same physical disk, and it can be extended only onto unallocated space that resides on the same physical disk. You cannot use Disk Management for this task.

14. Spanned volumes cannot be mirrored or striped, and spanned volumes are not fault tolerant.

15. Striped volumes cannot be mirrored or extended (spanned), and striped volumes are not fault tolerant.

16. Boot volumes, system volumes, striped volumes, mirrored volumes, and RAID-5 volumes cannot be extended (spanned).

17. The boot partition or volume is the drive letter where the Windows Server 2003 operating system files are stored, such as the `c:\windows` folder. The system partition or volume is the drive letter where the system's startup files are stored, such as `ntldr`, `ntdetect.com`, `ntbootdd.sys`, and `boot.ini`. The boot partition or volume and the system partition or volume can be one and the same, such as the `c:` drive.

18. `Defrag.exe` is a command-line version of the Disk Defragmenter tool.

19. You cannot install Windows Server 2003 on a dynamic volume that was created from unallocated space on a dynamic disk. The Windows Server 2003 setup program recognizes only dynamic volumes that contain partition tables. Partition tables appear in basic partitions and in dynamic volumes only when they have been converted from basic to dynamic.

USERS, GROUPS, AND COMPUTERS

20. The LDAP distinguished name must be unique throughout an Active Directory domain. For example, the distinguished name of a computer named `station01` located in the `Sales` organizational unit, which is part of the domain named `amazon.com`, is `CN=station01, OU=sales, DC=amazon,DC=com`.

21. Active Directory under Windows Server 2003 supports four levels of domain functionality: Windows 2000 mixed, Windows 2000 native, Windows Server 2003 interim, and Windows Server 2003. The Windows Server 2003 domain functional level supports Windows Server 2003 domain controllers (DCs) only.

22. To add support for Windows 9x and Windows NT 4.0 computers for accessing Active Directory resources, you can install the Active Directory client software so that they can access resources stored in Windows Server 2003 Active Directory domains.

23. Either one or both of the following error messages indicate that you need to reset the computer account:

    • The session setup from the computer DOMAINMEMBER failed to authenticate. The name of the account referenced in the security database is DOMAINMEMBER$. The following error occurred: Access is denied.

    • NETLOGON Event ID 3210: Failed to authenticate with \\DOMAINDC, a Windows NT DC for domain DOMAIN.

24. Groups that are designated as security group types contain security descriptors that assign access permissions on resources for users who are group members. You can also use security groups as email distribution lists.

25. You can change the type of a group from security to distribution or from distribution to security at any time, provided that the domain is set at the Windows 2000 native or the Windows Server 2003 domain functional level. You cannot change group types under the Windows 2000 mixed domain functional level.

26. You can assign security groups universal scopes only when the domain functional level is set at Windows 2000 native or Windows Server 2003. You can assign distribution groups universal scope at any domain functional level. Universal groups specify permissions on resources spread out over a domain tree or throughout an entire forest.

27. The `csvde.exe` command-line tool exports data from Active Directory and imports data into Active Directory using the comma-separated values (CSV) file format. Programs such as Microsoft Excel and Microsoft Exchange Server administration utilities can read from and write to CSV files. This tool is Microsoft's *preferred* method for automating the creation of user accounts in Active Directory using a bulk importing procedure.

28. To control the number of cached interactive logons (CILs) for domain-member computers running Windows Server 2003, Windows XP, or Windows 2000, you can configure the group policy setting named Interactive Logon: Number of Previous Logons to Cache, from the Default Domain Security Settings console, under the Local Policies node, Security Options subnode. The minimum setting is 0, which disables CILs. The maximum setting is 50. The default setting is 10.

29. You can protect both local and roaming profiles from being permanently changed by users if you simply rename the `ntuser.dat` file to `ntuser.man`. This configuration is called a mandatory user profile.

NETWORK RESOURCES AND TERMINAL SERVICES

30. Under Windows Server 2003, the default share permissions are Everyone:Allow Read, not Everyone:Allow Full Control.

31. You can only publish shares in Active Directory from the Shared Folders snap-in.

32. Under Windows Server 2003, the default NTFS permissions are Administrators:Allow Full Control, System:Allow Full Control, Users:Allow Modify, and Creator Owner:Allow Full Control.

33. Members of the Administrators group inherit unlimited NTFS disk quotas by default. You assign disk quotas on a per-user, per–drive-volume basis. You cannot assign disk quotas to groups.

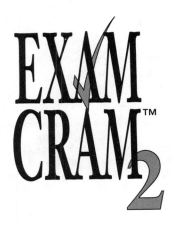

Managing and Maintaining a Windows® Server™ 2003 Environment

Dan Balter

CERTIFICATION

MCSA/MCSE Managing and Maintaining a Microsoft Windows Server 2003 Environment Exam Cram 2 (Exam 70-290)

Copyright © 2004 by Que Certification

International Standard Book Number: 0-7897-2946-6

Library of Congress Catalog Card Number: 2003100987

Printed in the United States of America

First Printing: October 2003

06   05   04   4   3   2

Trademarks

All terms mentioned in this book that are known to be trademarks or service marks have been appropriately capitalized. Que Publishing cannot attest to the accuracy of this information. Use of a term in this book should not be regarded as affecting the validity of any trademark or service mark.

Warning and Disclaimer

Every effort has been made to make this book as complete and as accurate as possible, but no warranty or fitness is implied. The information provided is on an "as is" basis. The author and the publisher shall have neither liability nor responsibility to any person or entity with respect to any loss or damages arising from the information contained in this book or from the use of the CD or programs accompanying it.

Bulk Sales

Que Publishing offers excellent discounts on this book when ordered in quantity for bulk purchases or special sales. For more information, please contact

U.S. Corporate and Government Sales

1-800-382-3419

corpsales@pearsontechgroup.com

For sales outside of the U.S., please contact

International Sales

1-317-428-3341

international@pearsontechgroup.com

Publisher
Paul Boger

Executive Editor
Jeff Riley

Development Editor
Susan Brown Zahn

Managing Editor
Charlotte Clapp

Project Editor
Elizabeth Finney

Copy Editor
Kris Simmons

Indexer
Heather McNeill

Proofreader
Katherin Bidwell

Technical Editors
Edward Tetz
Jeff A. Dunkelberger

Team Coordinator
Pamalee Nelson

Multimedia Developer
Dan Scherf

Interior Designer
Gary Adair

Cover Designer
Anne Jones

Page Layout
Bronkella Publishing

CERTIFICATION

Que Certification • 800 West 96th Street • Indianapolis, Indiana 46240

A Note from Series Editor Ed Tittel

You know better than to trust your certification preparation to just anybody. That's why you, and more than two million others, have purchased an Exam Cram book. As Series Editor for the new and improved Exam Cram 2 series, I have worked with the staff at Que Certification to ensure you won't be disappointed. That's why we've taken the world's best-selling certification product—a finalist for "Best Study Guide" in a CertCities reader poll in 2002—and made it even better.

As a "Favorite Study Guide Author" finalist in a 2002 poll of CertCities readers, I know the value of good books. You'll be impressed with Que Certification's stringent review process, which ensures the books are high-quality, relevant, and technically accurate. Rest assured that at least a dozen industry experts—including the panel of certification experts at CramSession—have reviewed this material, helping us deliver an excellent solution to your exam preparation needs.

Best Study Guides

We've also added a preview edition of PrepLogic's powerful, full-featured test engine, which is trusted by certification students throughout the world.

As a 20-year-plus veteran of the computing industry and the original creator and editor of the Exam Cram series, I've brought my IT experience to bear on these books. During my tenure at Novell from 1989 to 1994, I worked with and around its excellent education and certification department. This experience helped push my writing and teaching activities heavily in the certification direction. Since then, I've worked on more than 70 certification-related books, and I write about certification topics for numerous Web sites and for *Certification* magazine.

In 1996, while studying for various MCP exams, I became frustrated with the huge, unwieldy study guides that were the only preparation tools available. As an experienced IT professional and former instructor, I wanted "nothing but the facts" necessary to prepare for the exams. From this impetus, Exam Cram emerged in 1997. It quickly became the best-selling computer book series since "...*For Dummies*," and the best-selling certification book series ever. By maintaining an intense focus on subject matter, tracking errata and updates quickly, and following the certification market closely, Exam Cram was able to establish the dominant position in cert prep books.

You will not be disappointed in your decision to purchase this book. If you are, please contact me at etittel@jump.net. All suggestions, ideas, input, or constructive criticism are welcome!

Ed Tittel

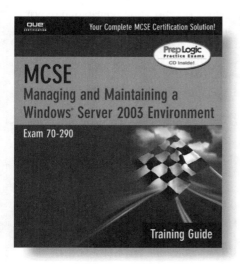

I dedicate this book to my lovely wife, Alison, and my darling kids, Alexis and Brendan.

❧

About the Author

Dan Balter is the Chief Technology Officer for InfoTechnology Partners, Inc., a Microsoft Certified Partner company. He works as an independent consultant and trainer for both corporate and government clients and has worked with several different network operating systems throughout his 20-year career. Dan takes pride in turning complex, technical topics into easy-to-understand concepts. Dan is a Microsoft Certified Systems Administrator (MCSA) and a Microsoft Certified Systems Engineer (MCSE). He specializes in Microsoft networking technologies, firewalls, VPNs, and other security solutions in addition to designing and implementing messaging and business solutions for large and small organizations.

Dan is a coauthor for the best-selling books *Exam Cram 2: Windows XP Professional* and *Exam Cram 2: Windows 2000 Professional* published by Que Publishing. Dan frequently speaks at conferences across North America, including Advisor DevCon conferences and *Windows & .NET Magazine* Connections conferences. A graduate of USC's School of Business in 1983, Dan has authored more than 300 video– and CD-ROM–based computer training courses, including instructional titles on installing, configuring, and administering Windows 95, Windows 98, Windows NT, Windows 2000, Windows XP, and Windows Server 2003. He is also a featured video trainer for courses on Microsoft Exchange Server, Microsoft Outlook, and Intuit's QuickBooks small business accounting software. Dan is the video trainer for *ExamBlast—Windows Server 2003*, *ExamBlast—Windows XP Professional*, and the *QuickBooks Pro* training series on video and CD-ROM from http://www.BlastThroughLearning.com.

Dan and his family live in the Santa Rosa Valley area in Southern California, near the city of Camarillo. Dan lives with his lovely wife, Alison; their 7-year-old daughter, Alexis; their 4-year-old son, Brendan; and their golden retriever, Brandy. When he's not writing, researching, or consulting, Dan enjoys traveling with his family, swimming, playing basketball, rooting for the L.A. Lakers, going for long walks, listening to music, and exploring new age spirituality. Dan can be contacted via email at Dan@InfoTechnologyPartners.com.

About the Technical Editors

Edward Tetz graduated in 1990 from Saint Lawrence College in Cornwall, Ontario, with a diploma in business administration. He spent a short time in computer sales, which turned into a computer support position. Since then, he has been performing system administration and LAN support for small and large organizations. In 1994, he added training to his repertoire. He currently holds the following certifications: MCT, MCSE, MCDBA, CTT+, A+, CIW MA, CIW SA, and CIW CI. He has experience with Linux, Apple Macintosh, IBM OS/2, Novell NetWare, and all Microsoft operating systems. Over the years, he has delivered training on many Microsoft products through Microsoft's CTEC channel. He currently works as a consultant for IMP Solutions in Halifax.

Over the years, he has worked on many titles with New Riders Publishing and Que Publishing. He enjoys working with Jeff Riley and the rest of the crew at Que.

When not working, he spends time with his wife, Sharon, and their two daughters. He can be reached at ed_tetz@hotmail.com.

Jeff A. Dunkelberger, MCSE, MCT, is currently a Solution Architect in the Hewlett-Packard Enterprise Microsoft Services practice, where he works with HP's large Federal government and commercial customers, helping them solve their business problems with Windows and Exchange solutions. Most recently, Jeff completed a special assignment as the Lab Master on the design and delivery team for the HP Windows 2003 Academy series. HP's Windows 2003 Academy program is an intense, practical field-training exercise attended by hundreds of HP's Windows consultants around the world.

Jeff completed his master's degree in business management at the McGregor School of Antioch University and acts as a technical editor for several computer-book publishers. He lives in the Washington, D.C., suburb of Alexandria, Virginia, in a very small house with his attorney wife, two dogs, and three cats, and he can be reached at jeffd@hp.com.

Acknowledgments

Endeavoring to author a book is a daunting task at best; accepting the challenge to write a technical guide covering all the ins and outs of a new network server operating system seems near impossible at times, while impending deadlines loom overhead. Of course, it's the family who bears the brunt of the burden with Dad staring at two different computer monitors while tinkering with yet a third one off to the side! My darling wife, Alison, has always encouraged me and supported me: Thank you so much for always being there for me; I love you more than words can convey! To my two beautiful children, Alexis, age 7, and Brendan, age 4: I love you both and I appreciate you both so much. Thanks for being patient with me while I was working on this book!

I offer my sincere, everlasting gratitude to both Mike Smith at InfoTechnology Partners, Inc. and Alan Sugano at ADS Consulting Group, Inc. for being instrumental in helping me complete this book. Mike researched and assisted me in writing numerous questions throughout this book. Alan is largely responsible for the content of Chapter 8 on disaster recovery techniques and procedures. Thanks, guys; you both did a tremendous job! I also owe a lot of gratitude to Aaron Spurlock and Marty Bouillon for assisting me with most of the questions and answers for the two practice tests in the back of the book. Thank you so much, Aaron and Marty; the book would not have been completed on time if it weren't for both of you!

All our lives seem to be so hectic; where would we be without the help and support from our loved ones, our friends, and our distinguished associates? To our nanny, Sonia Aguilar; her husband, Hugo; and their kids, Claudia, Gaby, and Huguito: Thank you so much for taking such great care of our kids. We are very fortunate to have you all in our lives! To Edie Swanson, our office manager: Thank you for taking such good care of our business matters and, often, our personal matters! To Tim Leonard: I really appreciate your advice, your assistance, and your friendship; thank you very much! To Dan Holme: Thank you for your friendship, your advice, and your support; knowing you really means a lot to me! I'm grateful for everyone in my local Business Networking International (BNI) group; you all make a terrific extended family!

To Greggory Peck, thanks for partnering with us on Blast Through Learning (`http://www.BlastThroughLearning.com`). I appreciate your patience with me, and thanks for just being an incredible friend! A ton of appreciation has to go to Scott McIntyre, Navin Jiawan, Derek Melber, Jeremy Moskowitz, Don Jones, and Mark Minasi: I really appreciate all your friendships; you guys all provide me with a lot of inspiration to always keep learning and to be the best author, trainer, and consultant that I can be! To Ron Sharpshair: Thank you for all your guidance, wisdom, and advice that helps to make me a stronger and better person each and every day! Also, to Rev. Irma Oestmann and everyone associated with Unity Center Church: Thank you for always being my guiding light and assisting me in staying on the spiritual path.

Finally, to Dawn Rader and Ed Tittel at LANWrights: It's been GREAT working with you; I hope to work with you on other projects in the future! Thanks for having a lot of patience with me, Dawn. To Jeff Riley at Que Certification: I've enjoyed getting to know you over the past several months, and I appreciate all that you've done for me! To everyone else at Pearson Education: Thank you for the terrific ongoing relationship that my wife and I have developed with you over the last several years. Okay, so now: When's the due date for the upcoming Windows "Longhorn" Exam Cram 2 book...?

Contents at a Glance

Table of Contents

We Want to Hear from You!

As the reader of this book, *you* are our most important critic and commentator. We value your opinion and want to know what we're doing right, what we could do better, what areas you'd like to see us publish in, and any other words of wisdom you're willing to pass our way.

As an executive editor for Que Publishing, I welcome your comments. You can email or write me directly to let me know what you did or didn't like about this book—as well as what we can do to make our books better.

Please note that I cannot help you with technical problems related to the topic of this book. We do have a User Services group, however, where I will forward specific technical questions related to the book.

When you write, please be sure to include this book's title and author as well as your name, email address, and phone number. I will carefully review your comments and share them with the author and editors who worked on the book.

Email: feedback@quepublishing.com

Mail: Jeff Riley
Executive Editor
Que Publishing
800 East 96th Street
Indianapolis, IN 46240 USA

For more information about this book or another Que Publishing title, visit our Web site at http://www.quepublishing.com. Type the ISBN (excluding hyphens) or the title of a book in the Search field to find the page you're looking for.

Introduction

Welcome to the 70-290 Exam Cram 2! Whether this book is your first or your fifteenth *Exam Cram 2* series book, you'll find information here that will help ensure your success as you pursue knowledge, experience, and certification. This book aims to help you get ready to take—and pass—the Microsoft certification exam "Managing and Maintaining a Microsoft Windows Server 2003 Environment" (Exam 70-290). This introduction explains Microsoft's certification programs in general and talks about how the *Exam Cram 2* series can help you prepare for Microsoft's latest MCSE and MCSA certification exams. Chapters 2 through 9 are designed to remind you of everything you'll need to know to pass the 70-290 certification exam. The two sample tests at the end of the book should give you a reasonably accurate assessment of your knowledge—and, yes, we've provided the answers and their explanations for these sample tests. Read the book, understand the material, and you'll stand a very good chance of passing the real test.

Exam Cram 2 books help you understand and appreciate the subjects and materials you need to know to pass Microsoft certification exams. *Exam Cram 2* books are aimed strictly at test preparation and review. They do not teach you everything you need to know about a subject. Instead, the author streamlines and highlights the pertinent information by presenting and dissecting the questions and problems he's discovered that you're likely to encounter on a Microsoft test. *Exam Cram 2* authors work hard to bring together as much information as possible about Microsoft certification exams.

Nevertheless, to completely prepare yourself for any Microsoft test, we recommend that you begin by taking the "Self Assessment" that is included in this book, immediately following this introduction. The self-assessment tool will help you evaluate your knowledge base against the requirements for becoming a Microsoft Certified Systems Administrator (MCSA) and a Microsoft Certified Systems Engineer (MCSE) for Windows Server 2003 under both ideal and real circumstances.

Based on what you learn from the "Self Assessment," you might decide to begin your studies with some classroom training or some background reading. On the other hand, you might decide to pick up and read one of the many study guides available from Microsoft or third-party vendors, including the award-winning *MCSE Training Guide* series from Que Publishing. We also recommend that you supplement your study program with visits to http://www.examcram2.com to receive additional practice questions, get advice, and track the Windows Server 2003 MCSA and MCSE programs.

This book includes a PrepLogic Practice Exams, Preview Edition CD-ROM. This software simulates the Microsoft testing environment with similar types of questions that you're likely to see on the actual Microsoft exam. The CD-ROM gives you the option to purchase additional questions (with answers) from the PrepLogic Web site. We also strongly recommend that you install, configure, and play around with the network operating system software that you'll be tested on: Nothing beats hands-on experience and familiarity when it comes to understanding the questions you're likely to encounter on a certification test. Book learning is essential, but without a doubt, hands-on experience is the best teacher of all!

The Microsoft Certified Professional Program

The Microsoft Certified Professional (MCP) program currently includes the following certification titles, each of which boasts its own special abbreviation (as a certification candidate and computer professional, you need to have a high tolerance for acronyms):

➤ *MCP (Microsoft Certified Professional)*—This is the entry-level certification title from Microsoft. Passing any one of current Microsoft certification exams qualifies an individual for the MCP credential. Individuals can demonstrate proficiency with additional Microsoft products by passing additional certification exams.

➤ *MCSA (Microsoft Certified Systems Administrator)*—This exam is for anyone who possesses a high level of networking expertise with Microsoft operating systems and software products. This credential is designed to prepare individuals to manage, maintain, and support information systems, networks, and internetworks built around the Microsoft Windows Server System and Windows XP and Windows 2000 desktop computers. New MCSA candidates must pass four exams to become certified. Microsoft currently offers two tracks for the MCSA credential—MCSA on Windows 2000 and MCSA on Windows Server 2003. The exam requirements for attaining each MCSA credential are detailed in Tables I.1 and I.2.

 Required core exams that are also available as elective exams can only be counted once toward a candidate's certification. An exam may count as fulfilling a core requirement or it may count as an elective, but the same exam cannot count as both a core exam and as an elective exam.

Table I.1 MCSA on Windows 2000 Exam Requirements	
Client Operating System Exams	
Candidates Must Pass One of the Following Exams	
Exam Number	**Exam Title**
70-210	Installing, Configuring, and Administering Microsoft Windows 2000 Professional
	OR
70-270	Installing, Configuring, and Administering Microsoft Windows XP Professional
Networking System Exams	
Candidates Must Pass Each of the Following Two Exams	
70-215	Installing, Configuring, and Administering Microsoft Windows 2000 Server
70-218	Managing a Microsoft Windows 2000 Network Environment
Elective Exams	
Candidates Must Pass One of the Following Elective Exams (or Candidates Must Pass Two of the Following CompTIA Exams)	
70-028	Administering Microsoft SQL Server 7.0
70-081	Implementing and Supporting Microsoft Exchange Server 5.5
70-086	Implementing and Supporting Microsoft Systems Management Server 2.0
70-088	Implementing and Supporting Microsoft Proxy Server 2.0
70-214	Implementing and Administering Security in a Microsoft Windows 2000 Network
70-216	Implementing and Administering a Microsoft Windows 2000 Network Infrastructure
70-224	Installing, Configuring, and Administering Microsoft Exchange 2000 Server

Table I.1   MCSA on Windows 2000 Exam Requirements *(continued)*

Elective Exams

Exam Number	Exam Title
70-227	Installing, Configuring, and Administering Microsoft Internet Security and Acceleration (ISA) Server 2000, Enterprise Edition
70-228	Installing, Configuring, and Administering Microsoft SQL Server 2000 Enterprise Edition
70-244	Supporting and Maintaining a Microsoft Windows NT Server 4.0 Network
CompTIA A+ Exam and CompTIA Network+ Exam	Passing both of these exams qualifies as having passed one Microsoft elective exam.
CompTIA A+ Exam and CompTIA Server+ Exam	Passing both of these exams qualifies as having passed one Microsoft elective exam.

Table I.2   MCSA on Windows Server 2003 Exam Requirements

Client Operating System Exams

Candidates Must Pass One of the Following Exams

Exam Number	Exam Title
70-210	Installing, Configuring, and Administering Microsoft Windows 2000 Professional
	OR
70-270	Installing, Configuring, and Administering Microsoft Windows XP Professional

Networking System Exams

Candidates Must Pass Each of the Following Two Exams

70-290	Managing and Maintaining a Microsoft Windows Server 2003 Environment
70-291	Implementing, Managing, and Maintaining a Microsoft Windows Server 2003 Network Infrastructure

Elective Exams

Candidates Must Pass One of the Following Elective Exams (or Candidates Must Pass Two of the Following CompTIA Exams)

70-086	Implementing and Supporting Microsoft Systems Management Server 2.0
70-227	Installing, Configuring, and Administering Microsoft Internet Security and Acceleration (ISA) Server 2000, Enterprise Edition

Table I.2 MCSA on Windows Server 2003 Exam Requirements *(continued)*	
Elective Exams	
Exam Number	**Exam Title**
70-228	Installing, Configuring, and Administering Microsoft SQL Server 2000 Enterprise Edition
CompTIA A+ Exam and CompTIA Network+ Exam	Passing both of these exams qualifies as having passed one Microsoft elective exam.
CompTIA A+ Exam and CompTIA Server+ Exam	Passing both of these exams qualifies as having passed one Microsoft elective exam.

 If you are already certified as an MCSA on Windows 2000, you can expedite the certification process for becoming an MCSA on Windows Server 2003. Just pass a single upgrade exam—70-292, "Managing and Maintaining a Microsoft Windows Server 2003 Environment for an MCSA Certified on Windows 2000." Once you've passed this one upgrade exam, you're certified as an MCSA on Windows Server 2003.

➤ *MCSE (Microsoft Certified Systems Engineer)*—Anyone who has a current MCSE is recognized as possessing a high level of networking expertise with Microsoft operating systems and products. This credential is designed to recognize individuals who have the skills to plan, design, implement, maintain, and support information systems, networks, and internetworks built around Microsoft Windows Server 2003, Windows XP, Windows 2000, Windows NT 4.0, Windows 9x, and the Windows Server System family of products. The road to becoming an MCSE can start by attaining MCSA credential. New MCSE candidates must pass seven exams to become certified. Microsoft currently offers two tracks for the MCSE credential—MCSE on Windows 2000 and MCSE on Windows Server 2003.

New MCSE candidates who are not already certified as MCSEs or MCSAs on Windows 2000 must pass seven tests to meet the MCSE requirements. It's not uncommon for the entire process to take a year or so, and many individuals find that they must take a test more than once to pass. The primary goal of the *Exam Cram 2* test preparation guides is to make it possible, given proper study and preparation, to pass all Microsoft certification tests on the first try. The exam requirements for attaining each MCSE status are detailed in Tables I.3 and I.4.

Table I.3	MCSE on Windows 2000 Exam Requirements
Client Operating System Exams	
Candidates Must Pass One of the Following Exams	
Exam Number	**Exam Title**
70-210	Installing, Configuring, and Administering Microsoft Windows 2000 Professional
	OR
70-270	Installing, Configuring, and Administering Microsoft Windows XP Professional
Networking System Exams	
Candidates Must Pass Each of the Following Three Exams	
70-215	Installing, Configuring, and Administering Microsoft Windows 2000 Server
70-216	Implementing and Administering a Microsoft Windows 2000 Network Infrastructure
70-217	Implementing and Administering a Microsoft Windows 2000 Directory Services Infrastructure
Networking Design Exams	
Candidates Must Pass One of the Following Exams	
70-219	Designing a Microsoft Windows 2000 Directory Services Infrastructure
70-220	Designing Security for a Microsoft Windows 2000 Network
70-221	Designing a Microsoft Windows 2000 Network Infrastructure
70-226	Designing Highly Available Web Solutions with Microsoft Windows 2000 Server Technologies
Elective Exams	
Candidates Must Pass Two of the Following Elective Exams	
70-219	Designing and Implementing Data Warehouses with Microsoft SQL Server 7.0
70-028	Administering Microsoft SQL Server 7.0
70-029	Designing and Implementing Databases with Microsoft SQL Server 7.0
70-056	Implementing and Supporting Web Sites Using Microsoft Site Server 3.0
70-080	Implementing and Supporting Microsoft Internet Explorer 5.0 by Using the Microsoft Internet Explorer Administration Kit
70-081	Implementing and Supporting Microsoft Exchange Server 5.5
70-085	Implementing and Supporting Microsoft SNA Server 4.0
70-086	Implementing and Supporting Microsoft Systems Management Server 2.0
70-088	Implementing and Supporting Microsoft Proxy Server 2.0

Table I.3 MCSE on Windows 2000 Exam Requirements *(continued)*	
Elective Exams	
Exam Number	**Exam Title**
70-214	Implementing and Administering Security in a Microsoft Windows 2000 Network
70-218	Managing a Microsoft Windows 2000 Network Environment
70-219	Designing a Microsoft Windows 2000 Directory Services Infrastructure
70-220	Designing Security for a Microsoft Windows 2000 Network
70-221	Designing a Microsoft Windows 2000 Network Infrastructure
70-222	Migrating from Microsoft Windows NT 4.0 to Microsoft Windows 2000
70-223	Installing, Configuring, and Administering Microsoft Clustering Services by Using Microsoft Windows 2000 Advanced Server
70-224	Installing, Configuring, and Administering Microsoft Exchange 2000 Server
70-225	Designing and Deploying a Messaging Infrastructure with Microsoft Exchange 2000 Server
70-226	Designing Highly Available Web Solutions with Microsoft Windows 2000 Server Technologies
70-227	Installing, Configuring, and Administering Microsoft Internet Security and Acceleration (ISA) Server 2000 Enterprise Edition
70-228	Installing, Configuring, and Administering Microsoft SQL Server 2000 Enterprise Edition
70-229	Designing and Implementing Databases with Microsoft SQL Server 2000 Enterprise Edition
70-230	Designing and Implementing Solutions with Microsoft BizTalk Server 2000 Enterprise Edition
70-232	Implementing and Maintaining Highly Available Web Solutions with Microsoft Windows 2000 Server Technologies and Microsoft Application Center 2000
70-234	Designing and Implementing Solutions with Microsoft Commerce Server 2000
70-244	Supporting and Maintaining a Microsoft Windows NT Server 4.0 Network

If you are already certified as an MCSE on Windows NT 4.0, you do not need to pass an elective exam to attain the MCSE on Window Server 2003 credential. You need to pass only six exams, instead of seven. The core exam requirements are the same for MCSEs on Windows NT 4.0 who want to become certified as MCSEs on Windows Server 2003 as for new candidates; the MCSE on Windows NT 4.0 credential qualifies as an elective exam.

Table I.4 MCSE on Windows Server 2003 Exam Requirements	
Client Operating System Exams	
Candidates Must Pass One of the Following Two Exams	
Exam Number	**Exam Title**
70-210	Installing, Configuring, and Administering Microsoft Windows 2000 Professional
	OR
70-270	Installing, Configuring, and Administering Microsoft Windows XP Professional
Networking System Exams	
Candidates Must Pass Each of the Following Four Exams	
70-290	Managing and Maintaining a Microsoft Windows Server 2003 Environment
70-291	Implementing, Managing, and Maintaining a Microsoft Windows Server 2003 Network Infrastructure
70-293	Planning and Maintaining a Microsoft Windows Server 2003 Network Infrastructure
70-294	Planning, Implementing, and Maintaining a Microsoft Windows Server 2003 Active Directory Infrastructure
Networking Design Exams	
Candidates Must Pass One of the Following Exams	
70-297	Designing a Microsoft Windows Server 2003 Active Directory and Network Infrastructure
70-298	Designing Security for a Microsoft Windows Server 2003 Network
Elective Exams	
Candidates Must Pass One of the Following Elective Exams	
70-086	Implementing and Supporting Microsoft Systems Management Server 2.0
70-227	Installing, Configuring, and Administering Microsoft Internet Security and Acceleration (ISA) Server 2000, Enterprise Edition
70-228	Installing, Configuring, and Administering Microsoft SQL Server 2000 Enterprise Edition
70-229	Installing, Configuring, and Administering Microsoft SQL Server 2000 Enterprise Edition
70-232	Implementing and Maintaining Highly Available Web Solutions with Microsoft Windows 2000 Server Technologies and Microsoft Application Center 2000
70-297	Designing a Microsoft Windows Server 2003 Active Directory and Network Infrastructure
70-298	Designing Security for a Microsoft Windows Server 2003 Network

If you are already certified as an MCSE on Windows 2000, you can expedite the certification process for becoming an MCSE on Windows Server 2003. Just pass two exams—70-292, "Managing and Maintaining a Microsoft Windows Server 2003 Environment for an MCSA Certified on Windows 2000," and 70-296, "Planning, Implementing, and Maintaining a Microsoft Windows Server 2003 Environment for an MCSE Certified on Windows 2000." Once you've passed these two upgrade exams, you're certified as an MCSE on Windows Server 2003.

Once you become an MCSA on Windows Server 2003, you can upgrade your status to the MCSE on Windows Server 2003 credential by passing the remaining exams required for MCSEs. You may take either a Windows Server 2003 networking design exam *or* a Windows 2000 networking design exam to satisfy the MCSE on Windows Server 2003 design skills requirement.

➤ *MCSD (Microsoft Certified Solution Developer)*—The MCSD for Microsoft .NET credential reflects the skills required to create multitier, distributed, and Component Object Model (COM)-based solutions, in addition to desktop and Internet applications, using new technologies. To obtain MCSD certification, an individual must demonstrate the ability to analyze and interpret user requirements; select and integrate products, platforms, tools, and technologies; design and implement code; customize applications; and perform necessary software tests and quality assurance operations.

To obtain the MCSD for Microsoft .NET credential, an individual must pass a total of five exams: four core exams and one elective exam. The requirements for obtaining the MCSD for Microsoft .NET credential are summarized in Table I.5.

Table I.5 MCSD for Microsoft .NET Exam Requirements	
Core Exam: Solution Architecture	
Candidates Must Pass the Following Exam	
Exam Number	**Exam Title**
70-300	Analyzing Requirements and Defining Microsoft .NET Solution Architectures
Core Exams: Web Application Development	
Candidates Must Pass One of the Following Two Exams	
70-305	Developing and Implementing Web Applications with Microsoft Visual Basic .NET and Microsoft Visual Studio .NET
70-315	Developing and Implementing Web Applications with Microsoft Visual C# .NET and Microsoft Visual Studio .NET

Table I.5 MCSD for Microsoft .NET Exam Requirements *(continued)*	
Exam Number	**Exam Title**
Core Exams: Windows Application Development	
Candidates Must Pass One of the Following Two Exams	
70-306	Developing and Implementing Windows-Based Applications with Microsoft Visual Basic .NET and Microsoft Visual Studio .NET
70-316	Developing and Implementing Windows-Based Applications with Microsoft Visual C# .NET and Microsoft Visual Studio .NET
Core Exams: XML Web Services and Server Components Development	
Candidates Must Pass One of the Following Two Exams	
70-310	Developing XML Web Services and Server Components with Microsoft Visual Basic .NET and the Microsoft .NET Framework
70-320	Developing XML Web Services and Server Components with Microsoft Visual C# and the Microsoft .NET Framework
Elective Exams	
Candidates Must Pass One of the Following Elective Exams	
70-229	Designing and Implementing Databases with Microsoft SQL Server 2000 Enterprise Edition
70-230	Designing and Implementing Solutions with Microsoft BizTalk Server 2000 Enterprise Edition
70-234	Designing and Implementing Solutions with Microsoft Commerce Server 2000

➤ *MCAD (Microsoft Certified Application Developer) for Microsoft .NET*—The MCAD credential provides industry recognition for professional developers who build powerful applications using Microsoft Visual Studio .NET and Web services. MCAD candidates are required to pass two core exams and one elective exam in an area of specialization. Table I.6 details the exam requirements for earning the MCAD credential.

Table I.6 MCAD for Microsoft .NET Exam Requirements	
Core Exams: Web or Windows Application Development	
Candidates Must Pass One of the Following Four Exams	
Exam Number	**Exam Title**
70-305	Developing and Implementing Web Applications with Microsoft Visual Basic .NET and Microsoft Visual Studio .NET
70-315	Developing and Implementing Web Applications with Microsoft Visual C# .NET and Microsoft Visual Studio .NET

Table I.6 MCAD for Microsoft .NET Exam Requirements *(continued)*	
Exam Number	**Exam Title**
70-306	Developing and Implementing Windows-Based Applications with Microsoft Visual Basic .NET and Microsoft Visual Studio .NET
70-316	Developing and Implementing Windows-Based Applications with Microsoft Visual C# .NET and Microsoft Visual Studio .NET
Core Exams: XML Web Services and Server Components Development	
Candidates Must Pass One of the Following Two Exams	
70-310	Developing XML Web Services and Server Components with Microsoft Visual Basic .NET and the Microsoft .NET Framework
70-320	Developing XML Web Services and Server Components with Microsoft Visual C# and the Microsoft .NET Framework
Elective Exams	
Candidates Must Pass One of the Following Elective Exams	
70-229	Designing and Implementing Databases with Microsoft SQL Server 2000 Enterprise Edition
70-230	Designing and Implementing Solutions with Microsoft BizTalk Server 2000 Enterprise Edition
70-234	Designing and Implementing Solutions with Microsoft Commerce Server 2000
70-305*	Developing and Implementing Web Applications with Microsoft Visual Basic .NET and Microsoft Visual Studio .NET
70-306*	Developing and Implementing Windows-Based Applications with Microsoft Visual Basic .NET and Microsoft Visual Studio .NET
70-315*	Developing and Implementing Web Applications with Microsoft Visual C# .NET and Microsoft Visual Studio .NET
70-316*	Developing and Implementing Windows-Based Applications with Microsoft Visual C# .NET and Microsoft Visual Studio .NET

*Note: Exams 70-305, 70-306, 70-315, and 70-316 can be used as valid elective exams only if they are not used to satisfy the core exam requirement.

➤ *MCDBA (Microsoft Certified Database Administrator)*—The MCDBA on Microsoft SQL Server 2000 credential reflects the skills required to implement and administer Microsoft SQL Server databases. To obtain MCDBA certification, an individual must demonstrate the ability to derive physical database designs, develop logical data models, create physical databases, create data services by using Transact-SQL, manage and maintain databases, configure and manage security, monitor and optimize databases, and install and configure Microsoft SQL Server. To become an MCDBA on Microsoft SQL Server 2000, an individual must pass a total of three core exams and one elective exam. Table I.7 outlines the exam requirements for becoming an MCDBA.

Table I.7 MCDBA on Microsoft SQL Server 2000 Exam Requirements	
Core Exams: SQL Server Administration	
Candidates Must Pass One of the Following Two Exams	
Exam Number	**Exam Title**
70-228	Installing, Configuring, and Administering Microsoft SQL Server 2000 Enterprise Edition
70-028	Administering Microsoft SQL Server 7.0
Core Exams: SQL Server Design	
Candidates Must Pass One of the Following Two Exams	
70-229	Designing and Implementing Databases with Microsoft SQL Server 2000 Enterprise Edition
70-029	Designing and Implementing Databases with Microsoft SQL Server 7.0
Core Exams: Networking Systems	
Candidates Must Pass One of the Following Three Exams	
70-290	Managing and Maintaining a Microsoft Windows Server 2003 Environment
70-291	Implementing, Managing, and Maintaining a Microsoft Windows Server 2003 Network Infrastructure
70-215	Installing, Configuring, and Administering Microsoft Windows 2000 Server
Elective Exams	
Candidates Must Pass One of the Following Elective Exams	
70-216	Implementing and Administering a Microsoft Windows 2000 Network Infrastructure
70-293	Planning and Maintaining a Microsoft Windows Server 2003 Network Infrastructure
70-305	Developing and Implementing Web Applications with Microsoft Visual Basic .NET and Microsoft Visual Studio .NET
70-306	Developing and Implementing Windows-Based Applications with Microsoft Visual Basic .NET and Microsoft Visual Studio .NET
70-310	Developing XML Web Services and Server Components with Microsoft Visual Basic .NET and the Microsoft .NET Framework
70-315	Developing and Implementing Web Applications with Microsoft Visual C# .NET and Microsoft Visual Studio .NET
70-316	Developing and Implementing Windows-Based Applications with Microsoft Visual C# .NET and Microsoft Visual Studio .NET

Table I.7 MCDBA on Microsoft SQL Server 2000 Exam Requirements *(continued)*	
Exam Number	**Exam Title**
70-320	Developing XML Web Services and Server Components with Microsoft Visual C# and the Microsoft .NET Framework
70-015*	Designing and Implementing Distributed Applications with Microsoft Visual C++ 6.0
70-019*	Designing and Implementing Data Warehouses with Microsoft SQL Server 7.0
70-155*	Designing and Implementing Distributed Applications with Microsoft Visual FoxPro 6.0
70-175*	Designing and Implementing Distributed Applications with Microsoft Visual Basic 6.0

*Note: Exams 70-015, 70-019, 70-155, and 70-175 are scheduled to be discontinued after June 30, 2004.

➤ *MCT (Microsoft Certified Trainer)*—Those with the MCT credential are recognized as qualified instructors for delivering training courses based on Microsoft Official Curriculum (MOC), including Microsoft Developer Network (MSDN) courseware. MCTs must possess both technical knowledge and instructional ability. Therefore, it is necessary for an individual seeking MCT credentials (which are granted on a course-by-course basis) to pass the related certification exam for a course and complete the official Microsoft training in the subject area and to demonstrate an ability to teach. MCT status must be renewed annually.

A candidate can satisfy the teaching skills criterion by proving that he or she has already attained training certification from CompTIA, Novell, Caldera, Cisco Systems, Citrix, or Oracle or by taking a Microsoft-sanctioned workshop on instruction. Microsoft makes it clear that MCTs are important cogs in the Microsoft training channels. Instructors must be MCTs before Microsoft will allow them to teach in any of its official training channels, including Microsoft's affiliated Certified Technical Education Centers (CTECs) and its online training partner network. An MCT candidate must also possess current MCSE, MCSD, or MCDBA certification before he or she can apply for MCT status.

NOTE

Microsoft has announced that the MCP+I and MCSE+I credentials are to be discontinued because the skill set for the Internet portion of the program is included in the new MCSA and MCSE programs. Therefore, this book does not provide details on these tracks here; you can go to **http://www.microsoft.com/traincert** if you need more information.

After a Microsoft product becomes obsolete, MCPs typically have to recertify on current versions. (If individuals do not recertify, their certifications become invalid.) Because technology keeps changing and new products continually supplant old ones, this requirement should come as no surprise. It also explains why Microsoft announced that MCSEs had 12 months past the scheduled retirement date for the Windows NT 4 exams to recertify on Windows 2000 topics.

The best place to keep tabs on the MCP program and its related certifications is the Web. Currently the URL for the MCP program is http://www.microsoft.com/traincert. But Microsoft's Web site changes often, so if this URL doesn't work, you should use the Search tool on Microsoft's site and type in either MCP or the quoted phrase "Microsoft Certified Professional" as a search string. This search will help you find the latest and most accurate information about Microsoft's certification programs. If you are already an MCP, you have earned access to the MCP Secured Site, which is open only to skilled technology pros who have passed at least one Microsoft certification exam. MCPs can log onto the MCP Secured Site by visiting https://partnering.one.microsoft.com/mcp. You must use a .NET Passport account to log onto the MCP Secured Site.

Taking a Certification Exam

After you prepare for your exam, you need to register with a testing center. Each computer-based MCP exam costs $125, and if you don't pass, you can take each again for an additional $125 for each attempt. In the United States and Canada, tests are administered by Pearson VUE and by Prometric. Here's how you can contact them:

➤ *Pearson VUE*—You can sign up for a test by calling 800-837-8734 or via the Web site at http://www.vue.com/ms.

➤ *Prometric*—You can sign up for a test through the company's Web site, http://www.2test.com or http://www.prometric.com. Within the United States and Canada, you can register by phone at 800-755-3926. If you live outside this region, you should check the Prometric Web site for the appropriate phone number.

To sign up for a test, you must possess a valid credit card or contact either Pearson VUE or Prometric for mailing instructions to send a check (in the United States). Only when payment is verified, or a check has cleared, can you actually register for a test.

To schedule an exam, you need to call the appropriate phone number or visit one of the Pearson VUE or Prometric Web sites at least one day in advance. To cancel or reschedule an exam in the United States or Canada, you must call before 3 p.m. Eastern time the day before the scheduled test time (or you might be charged, even if you don't show up to take the test). When you want to schedule a test, you should have the following information ready:

➤ Your name, organization, and mailing address.

➤ Your Microsoft test ID. (In the United States, this means your Social Security number; citizens of other countries should call ahead to find out what type of identification number is required to register for a test.)

➤ The name and number of the exam you want to take.

➤ A method of payment. (As mentioned previously, a credit card is the most convenient method, but alternate means can be arranged in advance, if necessary.)

After you sign up for a test, you are told when and where the test is scheduled. You should arrive at least 15 minutes early. You must supply two forms of identification—one of which must be a photo ID—to be admitted into the testing room.

All exams are completely closed book. In fact, you are not permitted to take anything with you into the testing area, but you receive a blank sheet of paper and a pen or, in some cases, an erasable plastic sheet and an erasable pen. We suggest that you immediately write down on that sheet of paper all the information you've memorized for the test. In *Exam Cram 2* books, this information appears on the tear-out sheet (Cram Sheet) inside the front cover of each book. You are given some time to compose yourself, record this information, and take a sample orientation exam before you begin the real thing. We suggest that you take the orientation test before taking your first exam, but because all the certification exams are more or less identical in layout, behavior, and controls, you probably don't need to do so more than once.

When you complete a Microsoft certification exam, the software tells you whether you've passed or failed. If you need to retake an exam, you have to schedule a new test with Pearson VUE or Prometric and pay another $125.

The first time you fail a test, you can retake the test the next day. However, if you fail a second time, you must wait 14 days before retaking that test. The 14-day waiting period remains in effect for all retakes after the second failure. Once you pass an exam, you may not take that exam again. Registration for prerelease (beta) exams is by invitation only, and these exams may be taken only once.

Tracking MCP Status

As soon as you pass any Microsoft exam, you attain MCP status. Microsoft generates transcripts that indicate which exams you have passed. You can view a copy of your transcript at any time by going to the MCP secured site and selecting the Transcript Tool. This tool enables you to print a copy of your current transcript and confirm your certification status.

After you pass the necessary set of exams, you are certified. Official certification is normally granted after six to eight weeks, so you shouldn't expect to get your credentials overnight. The package for official certification that arrives includes a Welcome Kit that contains a number of elements (see Microsoft's Web site for other benefits of specific certifications):

➤ A certificate that is suitable for framing, along with a wallet card and lapel pin.

➤ A license to use the MCP logo, which means you can use the logo in advertisements, promotions, and documents and on letterhead, business cards, and so on. Along with the license comes an MCP logo sheet, which includes camera-ready artwork. (Note that before you use any of the artwork, you must sign and return a licensing agreement that indicates you'll abide by its terms and conditions.)

➤ Access to the *Microsoft Certified Professional Magazine Online* Web site, which provides ongoing data about testing and certification activities, requirements, changes to the MCP program, and security-related information on Microsoft products.

Many people believe that the benefits of MCP certification go well beyond the perks that Microsoft provides to newly anointed members of this elite group. We're starting to see more job listings that request or require applicants to have MCP, MCSA, MCSE, and other certifications, and many individuals who complete Microsoft certification programs can qualify for increases in pay and responsibility. As an official recognition of hard work and broad knowledge, an MCP credential is a badge of honor in many IT organizations.

How to Prepare for an Exam

Preparing for any MCSA– or MCSE–related test (including Exam 70-290) requires that you obtain and study materials designed to provide comprehensive information about the product and its capabilities that will appear on the specific exam for which you are preparing. The following list of materials can help you study and prepare:

➤ The Windows Server 2003 product CD-ROM. This CD includes comprehensive online documentation and related materials; it should be one of your primary resources when you are preparing for the test.

➤ The exam preparation materials, practice tests, and self-assessment exams on the Microsoft Training and Certification site, at http://www.microsoft. com/traincert. The Exam Resources link offers samples of the new question types on the Windows Server 2003 MCSA and MCSE exams. You should find the materials, download them, and use them!

➤ The exam preparation advice, practice tests, questions of the day, and discussion groups on the http://www.examcram2.com.

In addition, you might find any or all of the following materials useful in your quest for Windows Server 2003 expertise:

➤ *Microsoft training kits*—Microsoft Press offers a training kit that specifically targets Exam 70-290. For more information, visit http://microsoft. com/mspress. This training kit contains information that you will find useful in preparing for the test.

➤ *Microsoft TechNet CD or DVD and Web site*—This monthly CD- or DVD-based publication delivers numerous electronic titles that include coverage of Windows Server 2003 and related topics on the Technical Information (TechNet) series on CD or DVD. Its offerings include product facts, technical notes, tools and utilities, and information on how to access the Seminars Online training materials for Windows Server 2003 and the Windows Server System line of products. Visit http://www. microsoft.com/technet and check out the information for TechNet subscriptions. You can utilize a large portion of the TechNet Web site at no charge.

➤ *Study guides*—Several publishers—including Que Publishing—offer Windows Server 2003, Windows XP, and Windows 2000 titles. Que Publishing offers the following:

➤ *The* Exam Cram 2 *series*—These books give you the insights about the material that you need to know to successfully pass the certification tests.

➤ *The MCSE Training Guide series*—These books provide a greater level of detail than the *Exam Cram 2* books and are designed to teach you everything you need to know about the subject covered by an exam.

Each book comes with a CD-ROM that contains interactive practice exams in a variety of testing formats.

Together, these two series make a perfect pair.

➤ *Classroom training*—CTECs, online partners, and third-party training companies (such as Wave Technologies, New Horizons, and Global Knowledge) all offer classroom training on Windows Server 2003, Windows XP, and Windows 2000. These companies aim to help you prepare to pass Exam 70-290 as well as several others. Although this type of training tends to be pricey, most of the individuals lucky enough to attend find this training to be quite worthwhile.

➤ *Other publications*—There's no shortage of materials available about Windows Server 2003. The "Need to Know More?" resource sections at the end of each chapter in this book give you an idea of where we think you should look for further discussion.

This set of required and recommended materials represents an unparalleled collection of sources and resources for Windows Server 2003 and related topics. We anticipate that you'll find this book belongs in this company.

About This Book

Each topical *Exam Cram 2* chapter follows a regular structure and contains graphical cues about important or useful information. Here's the structure of a typical chapter:

➤ *Opening hotlists*—Each chapter begins with a list of the terms, tools, and techniques that you must learn and understand before you can be fully conversant with that chapter's subject matter. The hotlists are followed with one or two introductory paragraphs to set the stage for the rest of the chapter.

➤ *Topical coverage*—After the opening hotlists and introductory text, each chapter covers a series of topics related to the chapter's subject. Throughout that section, we highlight topics or concepts that are likely to appear on a test, using a special element called an alert:

This is what an alert looks like. Normally, an alert stresses concepts, terms, software, or activities that are likely to relate to one or more certification-test questions. For that reason, we think any information in an alert is worthy of unusual attentiveness on your part.

You should pay close attention to material flagged in Exam Alerts; although all the information in this book pertains to what you need to know to pass the exam, Exam Alerts contain information that is really important. You'll find what appears in the meat of each chapter to be worth knowing, too, when preparing for the test. Because this book's material is very condensed, we recommend that you use this book along with other resources to achieve the maximum benefit.

In addition to the alerts, we provide tips that will help you build a better foundation for Windows Server 2003 knowledge. Although the tip information might not be on the exam, it is certainly related and it will help you become a better-informed test-taker.

> This is how tips are formatted. Keep your eyes open for these, and you'll become a Windows Server 2003 guru in no time!

> This is how notes are formatted. Notes direct your attention to important pieces of information that relate to Windows Server 2003 and Microsoft certification.

➤ *Exam prep questions*—Although we talk about test questions and topics throughout the book, the section at the end of each chapter presents a series of mock test questions and explanations of both correct and incorrect answers.

➤ *Details and resources*—Every chapter ends with a section titled "Need to Know More?" That section provides direct pointers to Microsoft and third-party resources that offer more details on the chapter's subject. In addition, that section tries to rank or at least rate the quality and thoroughness of the topic's coverage by each resource. If you find a resource you like in that collection, you should use it, but you shouldn't feel compelled to use all the resources. On the other hand, we recommend only resources that we use on a regular basis, so none of our recommendations will be a waste of your time or money (but purchasing them all at once probably represents an expense that many network administrators and would-be MCSAs and MCSEs might find hard to justify).

The bulk of the book follows this chapter structure, but we'd like to point out a few other elements. Chapters 10 and 12, "Practice Exam 1" and

"Practice Exam 2," provide good reviews of the material presented through-out the book to ensure that you're ready for the exam. Chapters 11 and 13, "Answers to Practice Exam 1" and "Answers to Practice Exam 2," offer the correct answers to the questions on the sample tests that appear in Chapters 10 and 12. Appendix A, "Suggested Readings and Resources," offers you several books and Web sites that contain useful information on Windows Server 2003. Appendix B, "What's on the CD-ROM," and Appendix C, "Using the *PrepLogic Practice Exams, Preview Edition* Software," provide helpful information about the material included on the book's CD-ROM. In addition, you'll find a handy glossary and an index.

Finally, the tear-out Cram Sheet attached next to the inside front cover of this *Exam Cram 2* book represents a condensed and compiled collection of facts and tips that we think are essential for you to memorize before taking the test. Because you can dump this information out of your head onto a sheet of paper before taking the exam, you can master this information by brute force; you need to remember it only long enough to write it down when you walk into the testing room. You might even want to look at it in the car or in the lobby of the testing center just before you walk in to take the exam.

How to Use This Book

We've structured the topics in this book to build on one another. Therefore, some topics in later chapters make the most sense after you've read earlier chapters. That's why we suggest that you read this book from front to back for your initial test preparation. If you need to brush up on a topic or if you have to bone up for a second try, you can use the index or table of contents to go straight to the topics and questions that you need to study. Beyond helping you prepare for the test, we think you'll find this book useful as a tightly focused reference to some of the most important aspects of Windows Server 2003.

The book uses the following typographical conventions:

➤ Command-line strings that are meant to be typed into the computer are displayed in monospace text, such as

```
net use lpt1: \\print_server_name\printer_share_name
```

➤ *New terms* are introduced in italics.

Given all the book's elements and its specialized focus, we've tried to create a tool that will help you prepare for—and pass—Microsoft Exam 70-290. Please share with us your feedback on the book, especially if you have ideas about how we can improve it for future test-takers. Send your questions or comments about this book via email to feedback@quepublishing.com. We'll consider everything you say carefully, and we'll respond to all suggestions. For more information on this book and other Que Certification titles, visit our Web site at http://www.quepublishing.com. You should also check out the new *Exam Cram 2* Web site at http://www.examcram2.com, where you'll find information updates, commentary, and certification information.

Thanks for making this *Exam Cram 2* book a pivotal part of your certification study plan: best of luck on becoming certified!

Self-Assessment

The reason we include a self assessment in this *Exam Cram 2* book is to help you evaluate your readiness to tackle MCSA and MCSE certification. It should also help you to understand what you need to know to master the main topic of this book—namely, Exam 70-290, "Managing and Maintaining a Microsoft Windows Server 2003 Environment." You might also want to check out the Microsoft Skills Assessment Home Web page—http://www.msmeasureup.com/test/home.asp—on the Microsoft Training and Certification Web site. But, before you tackle this self assessment, let's talk about concerns you might face when pursuing an MCSA or MCSE credential on Windows 2000 or Windows Server 2003 and what an ideal MCSA or MCSE candidate might look like.

MCSAs and MCSEs in the Real World

In the next section, we describe the ideal MCSA and MCSE candidates, knowing full well that only a few real candidates meet that ideal. In fact, our description of those ideal candidates might seem downright scary, especially with the changes that have been made to the Microsoft Certified Professional program to support Windows Server 2003, Windows XP, and Windows 2000. But take heart: Although the requirements to obtain MCSA and MCSE certification might seem formidable, they are by no means impossible to meet. However, you need to be keenly aware that getting through the process takes time, involves some expense, and requires real effort.

Increasing numbers of people are attaining Microsoft certifications. You can get all the real-world motivation you need from knowing that many others have gone before, so you will be able to follow in their footsteps. If you're willing to tackle the process seriously and do what it takes to obtain the necessary experience and knowledge, you can take—and pass—all the certification tests involved in obtaining the MCSA or MCSE credentials. In fact, at

Que Publishing, we've designed the *Exam Cram 2* series and the *MCSE Training Guide* series to make it as easy for you as possible to prepare for these exams. We've also greatly expanded our Web site, `http://www.examcram2.com`, to provide a host of resources to help you prepare for the complexities of Windows Server 2003, Windows XP, and Windows 2000.

The Ideal MCSA or MCSE Candidate

To give you an idea of what an ideal MCSA or MCSE candidate is like, here are some relevant statistics about the background and experience such an individual might have:

 Don't worry if you don't meet these qualifications or even come very close: This world is far from ideal, and where you fall short is simply where you have more work to do.

➤ Academic or professional training in network theory, concepts, and operations. This area includes everything from networking media and transmission techniques through network operating systems, services, and applications.

➤ Two or more years of professional networking experience, including experience with Ethernet, Token Ring, modems, and other networking media. This experience must include installation, configuration, upgrading, and troubleshooting experience.

 The Windows Server 2003 and the Windows 2000 MCSA and MCSE programs are much more rigorous than the Windows NT 4.0 certification program; you really need some hands-on experience if you want to become certified. Some of the exams require you to solve real-world case studies and network-design issues, so the more hands-on experience you have, the better.

➤ Two or more years in a networked environment that includes hands-on experience with Windows Server 2003, Windows 2000 Server, Windows 2000/XP Professional, Windows NT 4.0 Server, Windows NT 4.0 Workstation, and Windows 98 or Windows 95. A solid understanding of each system's architecture, installation, configuration, maintenance, and troubleshooting is also essential.

➤ Knowledge of the various methods for installing Windows Server 2003, Windows XP, and Windows 2000 operating systems, including manual and unattended installations.

➤ A thorough understanding of key networking protocols, addressing, and name resolution, including Transmission Control Protocol/Internet Protocol (TCP/IP), Novell NetWare's Internetwork Packet Exchange/Sequenced Packet Exchange (IPX/SPX), and Microsoft's NetBIOS Extended User Interface (NetBEUI).

➤ Familiarity with key Windows Server 2003– and Windows 2000 Server–based TCP/IP utilities and services, including Hypertext Transport Protocol (HTTP—used for Web servers), Dynamic Host Configuration Protocol (DHCP), Windows Internet Naming Service (WINS), and Domain Name System (DNS), plus familiarity with one or more of the following: Internet Information Services (IIS), Internet Protocol Security (IPSec), Internet Connection Sharing (ICS), Internet Connection Firewall (ICF), and Terminal Services.

➤ An understanding of how to implement security for key network data in a Windows 2000 Server or a Windows Server 2003 environment.

➤ A general working knowledge of Novell NetWare network environments, including IPX/SPX frame type formats; NetWare file, print, and directory services; and both Novell and Microsoft client software. Working knowledge of Microsoft's Client Service for NetWare (CSNW), the Gateway Service for NetWare (GSNW), the NetWare Migration Tool (NWCONV), and the NetWare Client for Windows (XP, 2000, NT, and 98) is helpful.

➤ A good working understanding of Active Directory. The more you work with Windows Server 2003 or Windows 2000 Server, the more you'll realize that Microsoft's latest server operating systems are quite different from Windows NT Server 4.0. New technologies such as Active Directory have really changed the way Windows is configured and used. We recommend that you find out as much as you can about Active Directory and acquire as much experience using this technology as possible. The time you take learning about Active Directory will be time very well spent!

To meet all of these qualifications, you'd need a bachelor's degree in computer science plus three years' work experience in PC networking design, installation, administration, and troubleshooting. Don't be concerned if you don't have all of these qualifications. Fewer than half of all Microsoft certification candidates meet these requirements. This self-assessment chapter is designed to show you what you already know and to prepare you for the topics that you need to learn.

Put Yourself to the Test

The following series of questions and observations is designed to help you figure out how much work you must do to pursue Microsoft certification and what kinds of resources you can consult on your quest. Be absolutely honest in your answers, or you'll end up wasting money on exams that you're not yet ready to take. There are no right or wrong answers—only steps along the path to certification. Only you can decide where you really belong in the broad spectrum of aspiring candidates. Two things should be clear from the outset, however:

➤ Even a modest background in computer science will be helpful.

➤ Hands-on experience with Microsoft products and technologies is an essential ingredient in certification success.

Educational Background

The following questions concern your level of technical computer experience and training. Depending upon your answers to these questions, you might need to review some additional resources to get your knowledge up to speed for the types of questions that you will encounter on Microsoft certification exams:

1. Have you ever taken any computer-related classes? [Yes or No]

   If Yes, proceed to Question 2; if No, proceed to Question 3.

2. Have you taken any classes on computer operating systems? [Yes or No]

   If Yes, you will probably be able to handle Microsoft's architecture and system component discussions. If you're rusty, you should brush up on basic operating system concepts, especially virtual memory, multitasking regimes, user-mode versus kernel-mode operation, and general computer security topics.

   If No, you should consider doing some basic reading in this area. We strongly recommend a good general operating systems book, such as *Operating System Concepts* by Abraham Silberschatz and Peter Baer Galvin (John Wiley & Sons). If this book doesn't appeal to you, check out reviews for other, similar, books at your favorite online bookstore.

3. Have you taken any networking concepts or technologies classes? [Yes or No]

If Yes, you will probably be able to handle Microsoft's networking terminology, concepts, and technologies. (Brace yourself for frequent departures from normal usage.) If you're rusty, you should brush up on basic networking concepts and terminology, especially networking media, transmission types, the Open System Interconnection (OSI) reference model, and networking technologies, such as Ethernet, Token Ring, Fiber Distributed Data Interface (FDDI), and Wide Area Network (WAN) links.

If No, you might want to read one or two books in this topic area. The two best books that we know are *Computer Networks* by Andrew S. Tanenbaum (Prentice-Hall) and *Computer Networks and Internets* by Douglas E. Comer and Ralph E. Droms (Prentice-Hall).

Hands-On Experience

The most important key to success on all the Microsoft tests is hands-on experience, especially when it comes to Windows Server 2003, Windows XP, Windows 2000, and the many add-on services and components around which so many of the Microsoft certification exams revolve. If we leave you with only one realization after you take this self assessment, it should be that there's no substitute for time spent installing, configuring, and using the various Microsoft products on which you'll be tested. The more in-depth understanding you have of how these software products work, the better your chance in selecting the right answers on the exam:

1. Have you installed, configured, and worked with the following:

➤ Windows Server 2003? [Yes or No]

If Yes, make sure you understand basic concepts as covered in Exam 70-291. You should also study the TCP/IP interfaces, utilities, and services for Exam 70-293, and you should implement security features for Exam 70-298.

If No, you must obtain one or two machines and a copy of Windows Server 2003. (A trial version is available on the Microsoft Web site.) Then, you should learn about the operating system and any other software components on which you'll also be tested. In fact, we recommend that you obtain two computers, each with a network interface, and set up a two-node network on which to practice. With decent Windows Server 2003–capable computers selling for about

$500 to $600 apiece these days, this setup shouldn't be too much of a financial hardship. You might have to scrounge to come up with the necessary software, but if you scour the Microsoft Web site, you can usually find low-cost options to obtain evaluation copies of most of the software that you'll need.

➤ Windows 2000 Server? [Yes or No]

If Yes, make sure you understand the concepts covered in Exam 70-215.

If No, you should consider acquiring a copy of Windows 2000 Server and learn how to install, configure, and administer it. Purchase a well-written book to guide your activities and studies (such as *MCSE Windows 2000 Server Exam Cram 2*), or you can work straight from Microsoft's exam objectives.

 You can download objectives, practice exams, and other data about Microsoft exams from the Training and Certification page at **http://www.microsoft.com/traincert**. You can use the "Exams" link to obtain specific exam information.

➤ Windows XP Professional? [Yes or No]

If Yes, make sure you understand the concepts covered in Exam 70-270.

If No, you should obtain a copy of Windows XP Professional and learn how to install, configure, and maintain it. Pick up a well-written book to guide your activities and studies (such as *MCSE Windows XP Professional Exam Cram 2*), or you can work straight from Microsoft's exam objectives, if you prefer.

➤ Windows 2000 Professional? [Yes or No]

If Yes, make sure you understand the concepts covered in Exam 70-210.

If No, you should obtain a copy of Windows 2000 Professional and learn how to install, configure, and maintain it. Pick up a well-written book to guide your activities and studies (such as *MCSE Windows 2000 Professional Exam Cram 2*), or you can work straight from Microsoft's exam objectives, if you prefer.

Use One Computer to Simulate Multiple Machines

If you own a powerful enough computer—one that has plenty of available disk space, a lot of RAM (at least 512MB), and a Pentium 4-compatible processor or better—you should check out the VMware and Virtual PC virtual-machine software products that are on the market. These software programs create an emulated computer environment within separate windows that are hosted by your computer's main operating system—Windows Server 2003, Windows XP, Windows 2000, and so on. So on a single computer, you can have several different operating systems running simultaneously in different windows! You can run everything from DOS to Linux, from Windows 95 to Windows Server 2003. Within a virtual-machine environment, you can "play" with the latest operating systems, including beta versions, without worrying about "blowing up" your main production computer and without having to buy an additional PC. VMware is published by VMware, Inc.; you can get more information from its Web site at **http://www.vmware.com**. Virtual PC is published by Connectix Corporation; you can find out more information from its Web site at **http://www.connectix.com**. Microsoft recently acquired the Virtual PC technology from Connectix Corporation. For more information on this acquisition, you can go to **http://www.microsoft.com/windowsxp/pro/evaluation/news/windowsvpc.asp**.

For any and all of these Microsoft operating systems exams, the Resource Kits for the topics involved always make good study resources (see Figure SA.1). You can purchase the Resource Kits from Microsoft Press (you can search for them at **http://microsoft.com/mspress**), but they also appear on the TechNet CDs, DVDs, and Web site (**http://www.microsoft.com/technet**). Along with the *Exam Cram 2* books, we believe that the Resource Kits are among the best tools you can use to prepare for Microsoft exams. Take a look at the Windows Deployment and Resource Kits Web page for more information: **http://www.microsoft.com/windows/reskits/default.asp**.

2. For any specific Microsoft product that is not itself an operating system (for example, SQL Server), have you installed, configured, used, and upgraded this software? [Yes or No]

If Yes, skip to the next section, "Testing Your Exam Readiness." If No, you must get some experience. Read on for suggestions about how to do this.

Experience is a must with any Microsoft product exam, be it something as simple as FrontPage 2002 or as challenging as SQL Server 2000. For trial copies of other software, you can search Microsoft's Web site, using the name of the product as your search term. Also, you can search for bundles such as BackOffice, Enterprise Servers, Windows Server System, or Small Business Server.

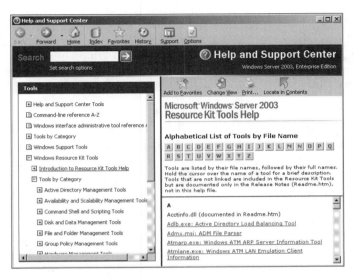

Figure SA.1 Viewing the alphabetical list of tools for the Windows Server 2003 Resource Kit.

If you have the funds, or if your employer will pay your way, you should consider taking a class at a Microsoft Certified Training and Education Center (CTEC). In addition to classroom exposure to the topic of your choice, you get a copy of the software that is the focus of your course, along with a trial version of whatever operating system it needs, as part of the training materials for that class.

Before you even think about taking any Microsoft exam, you should make sure you've spent enough time with the related software to understand how you to install and configure it, how to maintain such an installation, and how to troubleshoot the software when things go wrong. This time will help you in the exam—and in real life!

Testing Your Exam Readiness

Whether you attend a formal class on a specific topic to get ready for an exam or use written materials to study on your own, some preparation for the Microsoft certification exams is essential. At $125 a pop—whether you pass or fail—you'll want to do everything you can to pass on your first try. That's where studying comes in.

We include two practice tests in this book (Chapters 10 and 11, "Practice Exam 1" and "Practice Exam 2," respectively), so if you don't score very well on these tests, you can study the practice exams more and then tackle the test again. We also have practice questions that you can sign up for online through `http://www.examcram2.com`. The PrepLogic CD-ROM in the back of this book has sample questions to quiz you on; you can purchase additional practice questions from `http://www.PrepLogic.com`. If you still don't hit a score of at least 70% after practicing with these tests, you should investigate the other practice test resources that are mentioned in this section.

For any given subject, you should consider taking a class if you've tackled self-study materials, taken the test, and failed anyway. The opportunity to interact with an instructor and fellow students can make all the difference in the world, if you can afford that luxury. For information about Microsoft classes, visit the Training and Certification page at `http://www.microsoft.com/traincert/training/find/findcourse.asp` for locating training courses offered at Microsoft CTECs.

If you can't afford to take a class, you can visit the Training and Certification pages anyway because they include pointers to free practice exams and to Microsoft-approved study guides and other self-study tools. And even if you can't afford to spend much money at all, you should still invest in some low-cost practice exams from commercial vendors. The Microsoft Training and Certification "Assess Your Readiness" page at `http://www.microsoft.com/traincert/assessment` offers several skills-assessment evaluations that you can take online to show you how far along you are in your certification preparation.

The next question deals with your personal testing experience. Microsoft certification exams have their own style and idiosyncrasies. The more acclimated that you become to the Microsoft testing environment, the better your chances will be to score well on the exams:

1. Have you taken a practice exam on your chosen test subject? [Yes or No]

   If Yes, and if you scored 70% or better, you're probably ready to tackle the real thing. If your score isn't above that threshold, you should keep at it until you break that barrier.

   If No, you should obtain all the free and low-budget practice tests you can find and get to work. You should keep at it until you can break the passing threshold comfortably.

 When it comes to assessing your test readiness, there is no better way than to take a good-quality practice exam and pass with a score of 70% or better. When we're preparing ourselves, we shoot for 80% or higher, just to leave room for the "weirdness factor" that sometimes shows up on Microsoft exams.

Assessing Readiness for Exam 70-290

In addition to the general exam-readiness information in the previous section, there are several things you can do to prepare for the Exam 70-290. As you're getting ready for the exam, you should visit the *Exam Cram 2* Web site at `http://www.examcram2.com`. We also suggest that you join an active MCSE/MCSA email list and email newsletter. Some of the best list servers and email newsletters are managed by Sunbelt Software. You can sign up at `http://www.sunbelt-software.com`.

Microsoft exam mavens also recommend that you check the Microsoft Knowledge Base (available on its own CD as part of the TechNet collection, and on the Microsoft Web site at `http://support.microsoft.com`) for "meaningful technical support issues" that relate to your exam's topics. Although we're not sure exactly what the quoted phrase means, we have also noticed some overlap between technical-support questions on particular products and troubleshooting questions on the exams for those products.

Go Take on the Challenge!

After you've assessed your readiness, undertaken the right background studies, obtained the hands-on experience that will help you understand the products and technologies at work, and reviewed the many sources of information to help you prepare for a test, you'll be ready to take a round of practice tests. When your scores come back positive enough to get you through the exam, you're ready to go after the real thing. If you follow our assessment regime, you'll not only know what you need to study, but you'll know when you're ready to set a test date at Pearson VUE (`http://www.vue.com`) or Prometric (`http://www.prometric.com`). Go get 'em: Good luck!

Microsoft Certification Exams

Terms you'll need to understand:

✓ Case study
✓ Multiple-choice question format
✓ Build-list-and-reorder question format
✓ Create-a-tree question format
✓ Drag-and-connect question format
✓ Select-and-place question format
✓ Hot area question format
✓ Active screen question format
✓ Fixed-length test
✓ Simulation
✓ Adaptive test
✓ Short-form test

Techniques you'll need to master:

✓ Assessing your exam readiness
✓ Answering Microsoft's various question types
✓ Altering your test strategy depending on the exam format
✓ Practicing to make perfect
✓ Making the best use of the testing software
✓ Budgeting your time
✓ Guessing as a last resort

Exam taking is not something that most people look forward to, no matter how well prepared they might be. In most cases, familiarity helps offset test anxiety. In plain English, this means you probably won't be as nervous when you take your fourth or fifth Microsoft certification exam as you'll be when you take your first one.

Whether it's your first exam or your tenth, understanding the details of taking the new exams (how much time to spend on questions, the environment you'll be in, and so on) and the new exam software will help you concentrate on the material rather than on the setting. Likewise, mastering a few basic exam-taking skills should help you recognize—and perhaps even outfox— some of the tricks and snares you're bound to find in some exam questions.

This chapter, besides explaining the exam environment and software, describes some proven exam-taking strategies that you should be able to use to your advantage.

Assessing Exam Readiness

We strongly recommend that you read through and take the self assessment included with this book. (It appears just before this chapter.) It will help you compare your knowledge base to the requirements for obtaining MCSA and MCSE certification, and it will also help you identify parts of your background or experience that might be in need of improvement, enhancement, or further learning. If you get the right set of basics under your belt, obtaining Microsoft certification will be that much easier.

After you've gone through the self assessment, you can remedy those topical areas where your background or experience might not measure up to those of an ideal certification candidate. But you can also tackle subject matter for individual tests at the same time, so you can continue making progress while you're catching up in some areas.

After you work through this *Exam Cram 2* series book, read the supplementary materials, and take the practice tests, you'll have a pretty clear idea of when you should be ready to take the real exam. Although we strongly recommend that you keep practicing until your scores top the 75% mark, 80% is a good goal, to give yourself some margin for error in a real exam situation (where stress will play more of a role than when you practice). After you hit that point, you should be ready to go. But if you get through the practice exam in this book without attaining that score, you should keep taking practice tests and studying the materials until you get there. You'll find more pointers on how to study and prepare in the self assessment. At this point, let's talk about the exam itself.

What to Expect at the Testing Center

When you arrive at the testing center where you scheduled your exam, you need to sign in with an exam coordinator. He or she asks you to show two forms of identification, one of which must be a photo ID. After you sign in and your time slot arrives, you are asked to deposit any books, bags, or other items you brought with you. Then, you are escorted into a closed room.

All exams are completely closed book. In fact, you are not permitted to take anything with you into the testing area, but you are furnished with a blank sheet of paper and a pen or, in some cases, an erasable plastic sheet and an erasable pen. Before the exam, be sure to carefully review this book's Cram Sheet, located in the very front of the book. You should memorize as much of the important material as you can so you can write that information on the blank sheet as soon as you are seated in front of the computer. You can refer to that piece of paper anytime you like during the test, but you must surrender the sheet when you leave the room.

You are given some time to compose yourself, to record important information, and to take a sample exam before you begin the real thing. We suggest that you take the sample test before taking your first exam, but because all exams are more or less identical in layout, behavior, and controls, you probably don't need to do so more than once.

Typically, the testing room is furnished with anywhere from one to six computers, and each workstation is separated from the others by dividers designed to keep anyone from seeing what's happening on someone else's computer. Most testing rooms feature a wall with a large picture window. This layout permits the exam coordinator to monitor the room, to prevent exam-takers from talking to one another, and to observe anything out of the ordinary that might go on. The exam coordinator will have preloaded the appropriate Microsoft certification exam—for this book, that's Exam 70-290, Managing and Maintaining a Microsoft Windows Server 2003 Environment—and you are permitted to start as soon as you're seated in front of the computer.

All Microsoft certification exams allow a certain maximum amount of testing time. (This time is indicated on the exam by an onscreen timer clock, so you can check the time remaining whenever you like.) All Microsoft certification exams are computer generated. In addition to multiple choice, most exams contain select–and-place (drag-and-drop), create-a-tree (categorization and prioritization), drag-and-connect, and build-list-and-reorder (list prioritization) types of questions. Although this format might sound quite simple, the questions are constructed not only to check your mastery of basic facts and figures about Windows Server 2003, but also to require you to evaluate one or more sets of circumstances or requirements. Often, you are asked to give more than one answer to a question. Likewise, you might be asked to select the best or most effective solution to a problem from a range of choices, all of which are technically correct. Taking the exam is quite an adventure, and it involves real thinking. This book shows you what to expect and how to deal with the potential problems, puzzles, and predicaments.

Exam Layout and Design

Historically, there have been six types of question formats on Microsoft certification exams. These types of questions continue to appear on current Microsoft tests and they are discussed in the following sections:

➤ Multiple-choice, single answer

➤ Multiple-choice, multiple answers

➤ Build-list-and-reorder (list prioritization)

➤ Create-a-tree

➤ Drag-and-connect

➤ Select-and-place (drag-and-drop)

The Single-Answer and Multiple-Answer Multiple-Choice Question Formats

Some exam questions require you to select a single answer, whereas others ask you to select multiple correct answers. The following multiple-choice question requires you to select a single correct answer. Following the question is a brief summary of each potential answer and why it is either right or wrong.

Question 1

> You have three domains connected to an empty root domain under one contiguous domain name: **tutu.com**. This organization is formed into a forest arrangement, with a secondary domain called **frog.com**. How many schema masters exist for this arrangement?
>
> ○ A. 1
> ○ B. 2
> ○ C. 3
> ○ D. 4

The correct answer is Answer A because only one schema master is necessary for a forest arrangement. The other answers (Answers B, C, and D) are misleading because they try to make you believe that schema masters might be in each domain or perhaps that you should have one for each contiguous namespace domain.

This sample question format corresponds closely to the Microsoft certification exam format. The only difference is that on the exam, the questions are not followed by answers and their explanations. To select an answer, you position the cursor over the option button next to the answer you want to select. Then, you click the mouse button to select the answer.

Let's examine a question where one or more answers are possible. This type of question provides check boxes rather than option buttons for marking all appropriate selections.

Question 2

> What can you use to seize FSMO roles? (Choose two.)
> ❑ A. The **ntdsutil.exe** utility
> ❑ B. The Active Directory Users and Computers console
> ❑ C. The **secedit.exe** utility
> ❑ D. The **utilman.exe** utility

Answer A and B are correct. You can seize roles from a server that is still running through the Active Directory Users and Computers console, or in the case of a server failure, you can seize roles with the ntdsutil.exe utility. You use the secedit.exe utility to force group policies into play; therefore, Answer C is incorrect. The utilman.exe tool manages accessibility settings in Windows Server 2003; therefore, Answer D is incorrect.

This particular question requires two answers. Microsoft sometimes gives partial credit for partially correct answers. For Question 2, you have to mark the check boxes next to Answers A and B to obtain credit for a correct answer. Notice that choosing the right answers also means knowing why the other answers are wrong.

The Build-List-and-Reorder Question Format

Questions in the build-list-and-reorder format present two lists of items—one on the left and one on the right. To answer the question, you must move items from the list on the right to the list on the left. The final list must then be reordered into a specific order.

These questions generally sound like this: "From the following list of choices, pick the choices that answer the question. Arrange the list in a certain order." Question 3 shows an example of how they appear in this book; for an example of how they appear on the test, see Figure 1.1.

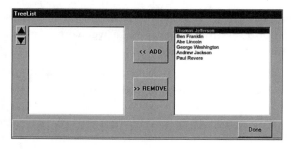

Figure 1.1   The format for build-list-and-reorder questions.

Question 3

From the following list of famous people, choose those who have been elected president of the United States. Arrange the list in the order in which the presidents served.

- ○ Thomas Jefferson
- ○ Ben Franklin
- ○ Abe Lincoln
- ○ George Washington
- ○ Andrew Jackson
- ○ Paul Revere

The correct answer is

1. George Washington

2. Thomas Jefferson

3. Andrew Jackson

4. Abe Lincoln

On an actual exam, the entire list of famous people would initially appear in the list on the right. You would move the four correct answers to the list on the left and then reorder the list on the left. Notice that the answer to Question 3 does not include all the items from the initial list. However, that might not always be the case.

To move an item from the right list to the left list on the exam, you first select the item by clicking it, and then you click the Add button (left arrow). After you move an item from one list to the other, you can move the item back by first selecting the item and then clicking the appropriate button (either the Add button or the Remove button). After you move items to the left list, you can move an item by selecting the item and clicking the up or down arrow buttons.

The Create-a-Tree Question Format

Questions in the create-a-tree format also present two lists—one on the left side of the screen and one on the right side of the screen. The list on the right consists of individual items, and the list on the left consists of nodes in a tree. To answer the question, you must move items from the list on the right to the appropriate node in the tree.

These questions can best be characterized as simply a matching exercise. Items from the list on the right are placed under the appropriate category in the list on the left. Question 4 shows an example of how they appear in this book; for a sample of how they appear on the test, see Figure 1.2.

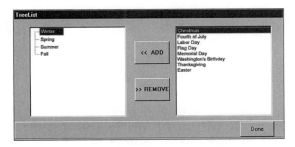

Figure 1.2 The create-a-tree question format.

Question 4

> The calendar year is divided into four seasons:
>
> Winter
>
> Spring
>
> Summer
>
> Fall
>
> Identify the season during which each of the following holidays occurs:
>
> Christmas
>
> Fourth of July
>
> Labor Day
>
> Flag Day
>
> Memorial Day
>
> Washington's Birthday
>
> Thanksgiving
>
> Easter

The correct answers are

➤ Winter

Christmas

Washington's Birthday

➤ Spring

Flag Day

Memorial Day

Easter

➤ Summer

Fourth of July

Labor Day

➤ Fall

Thanksgiving

In this case, you use all the items in the list. However, that might not always be the case.

To move an item from the right list to its appropriate location in the tree, you must first select the appropriate tree node by clicking it. Then, you select the item to be moved and click the Add button. Once you add one or more items to a tree node, the node appears with a + icon to the left of the node name. You can click this icon to expand the node and view the items you have added. If you have added any item to the wrong tree node, you can remove it by selecting it and clicking the Remove button.

The Drag-and-Connect Question Format

Questions in the drag-and-connect format present a group of objects and a list of "connections." To answer the question, you must move the appropriate connections between the objects.

This type of question is best described using graphics. Question 5 shows an example.

Question 5

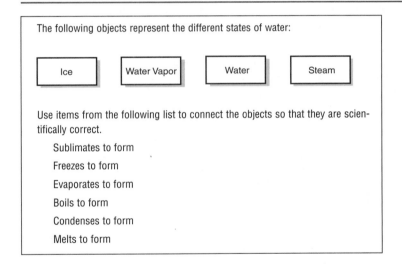

The following objects represent the different states of water:

Ice   Water Vapor   Water   Steam

Use items from the following list to connect the objects so that they are scientifically correct.

Sublimates to form

Freezes to form

Evaporates to form

Boils to form

Condenses to form

Melts to form

The correct answer is

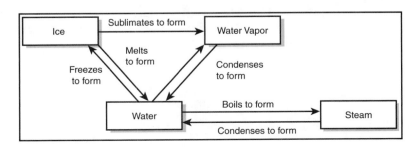

For this type of question, it's not necessary to use every object, and you can use each connection multiple times.

The Select-and-Place Question Format

Questions in the select-and-place (drag-and-drop) format present a diagram with blank boxes and a list of labels that you need to drag to correctly fill in the blank boxes. To answer such a question, you must move the labels to their appropriate positions on the diagram.

This type of question is best described using graphics. Question 6 shows an example.

Question 6

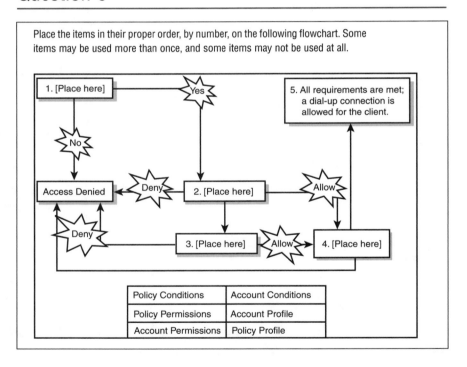

Place the items in their proper order, by number, on the following flowchart. Some items may be used more than once, and some items may not be used at all.

The correct answer is

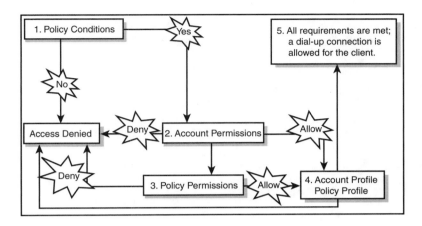

Design Exam Question Formats

The Windows 2000 MCSE track first introduced Microsoft's design series of exams. For the Windows Server 2003 MCSE track, design exams continue to be a core part of the curriculum. For the design exams, each exam consists entirely of a series of case studies, and the questions can be of six types. The MCSE design exams for the MCSE on Windows Server 2003 include the following:

➤ 70-229—Designing and Implementing Databases with Microsoft SQL Server 2000 Enterprise Edition

➤ 70-297—Designing a Microsoft Windows Server 2003 Active Directory and Network Infrastructure

➤ 70-298—Designing Security for a Microsoft Windows Server 2003 Network

For design exams, each case study or "testlet" presents a detailed problem that you must read and analyze. Figure 1.7 shows an example of what a case study looks like. You must select the different tabs in the case study to view the entire case.

Following each case study is a set of questions related to the case study; these questions can be one of six types (which are discussed in the following sections). Careful attention to the details provided in the case study is the key to success. You should be prepared to frequently toggle between the case study and the questions as you work. Some of the case studies include diagrams, which are called *exhibits*, that you'll need to examine closely to understand how to answer the questions.

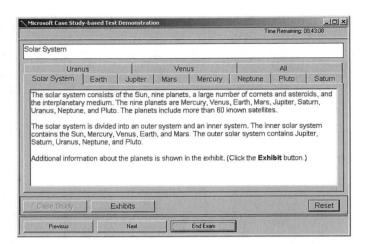

Figure 1.7   The format for case-study questions.

After you complete a case study, you can review all the questions and your answers. However, after you move on to the next case study, you might not be able to return to the previous case study to make any changes.

For the MCSA and MCSE core exams and the upgrade exams, the same six types of questions can appear, but you are not likely to encounter complex multi-question case studies. The MCSA/MCSE core exams and upgrade exams for the Windows Server 2003 track include the following:

➤ 70-290—Managing and Maintaining a Microsoft Windows Server 2003 Environment

➤ 70-291—Implementing, Managing, and Maintaining a Microsoft Windows Server 2003 Network Infrastructure

➤ 70-292—Managing and Maintaining a Microsoft Windows Server 2003 Environment for an MCSA Certified on Windows 2000

➤ 70-293—Planning and Maintaining a Microsoft Windows Server 2003 Network Infrastructure

➤ 70-294—Planning, Implementing, and Maintaining a Microsoft Windows Server 2003 Active Directory Infrastructure

➤ 70-296—Planning, Implementing, and Maintaining a Microsoft Windows Server 2003 Environment for an MCSE Certified on Windows 2000

New Exam Question Formats

Microsoft is introducing several new question types in addition to the more traditional types of questions that are still widely used on all Microsoft exams. These new, innovative question types have been highly researched and tested by Microsoft before they were chosen to be included in many of the newer exams for the MCSA/MCSE on the Windows 2000 track and for the MCSA/MCSE on the Windows Server 2003 track. These new question types are as follows:

➤ Hot area questions

➤ Active screen questions

➤ New drag-and-drop–type questions

➤ Simulation questions

Hot Area Question Types

Hot area questions ask you to indicate the correct answer by selecting one or more elements within a graphic. For example, you might be asked to select multiple objects within a list, as shown in Figure 1.8.

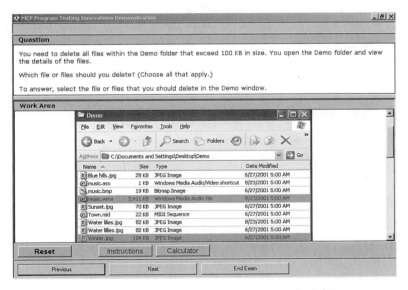

Figure 1.8   Selecting objects within a list box to answer a hot area question.

Active Screen Question Types

Active screen questions ask you to configure a dialog box by modifying one or more elements. These types of questions offer a realistic interface in which you must properly configure various settings, just as you would within the actual software product. For example, you might be asked to select the proper option within a drop-down list box, as shown in Figure 1.9.

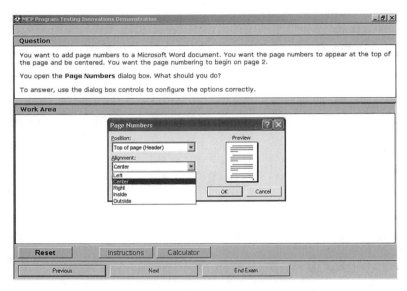

Figure 1.9 Configuring an option from a dialog box's drop-down list box to answer an active screen question.

New Drag-and-Drop Question Types

New drag-and-drop questions ask you to drag source elements to their appropriate corresponding targets within a work area. These types of questions test your knowledge of specific concepts and their definitions or descriptions. For example, you might be asked to match a description of a computer program to the actual software application, as shown in Figure 1.10.

Simulation Question Types

Simulation questions ask you to indicate the correct answer by performing specific tasks, such as configuring and installing network adapters or drivers, configuring and controlling access to files, or troubleshooting hardware devices. Many of the tasks that systems administrators and systems engineers perform can be presented more accurately in simulations than in most traditional exam question types (see Figure 1.11).

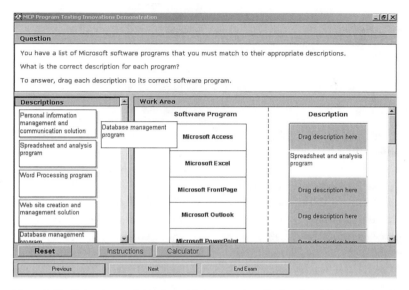

Figure 1.10 Using drag and drop to match the correct application description to each software program.

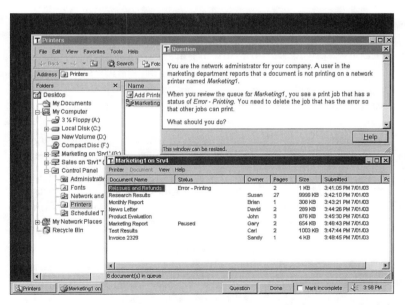

Figure 1.11 Answering a simulation question about how to troubleshoot a network printing problem.

Microsoft's Testing Formats

Currently, Microsoft uses four different testing formats:

➤ Fixed length

➤ Adaptive

➤ Short form

➤ Case study

Other Microsoft exams employ advanced testing capabilities that might not be immediately apparent. Although the questions that appear are primarily multiple-choice, the logic that drives them is more complex than that in older Microsoft tests, which use a fixed sequence of questions, called a *fixed-length test*. Some questions employ a sophisticated user interface, which Microsoft calls a *simulation*, to test your knowledge of the software and systems under consideration in a more-or-less "live" environment that behaves just like the real thing. You should review the Microsoft Training and Certification Web pages at `http://www.microsoft.com/traincert` for more information.

For some exams, Microsoft has turned to a well-known technique called *adaptive testing* to establish a test-taker's level of knowledge and product competence. Adaptive exams look the same as fixed-length exams, but they discover the level of difficulty at which an individual test-taker can correctly answer questions. Test-takers with differing levels of knowledge or ability therefore see different sets of questions; individuals with high levels of knowledge or ability are presented with a smaller set of more difficult questions, whereas individuals with lower levels of knowledge are presented with a larger set of easier questions. Two individuals might answer the same percentage of questions correctly, but the test-taker with a higher knowledge or ability level will score higher because his or her questions are worth more. Also, the lower-level test-taker will probably answer more questions than his or her more-knowledgeable colleague. This explains why adaptive tests use ranges of values to define the number of questions and the amount of time it takes to complete the test.

Adaptive tests work by evaluating the test-taker's most recent answer. A correct answer leads to a more difficult question, and the test software's estimate of the test-taker's knowledge and ability level is raised. An incorrect answer leads to a less difficult question, and the test software's estimate of the test-taker's knowledge and ability level is lowered. This process continues until the test targets the test-taker's true ability level. The exam ends when the test-taker's level of accuracy meets a statistically acceptable value (in other words, when his or her performance demonstrates an acceptable level of knowledge and ability) or when the maximum number of items has been presented (in which case the test-taker is almost certain to fail).

Microsoft has also introduced a short-form test for its most popular tests. This test delivers 25 to 30 questions to its takers, giving them exactly 60 minutes to complete the exam. This type of exam is similar to a fixed-length test in that it allows readers to jump ahead or return to earlier questions and to cycle through the questions until the test is done. Microsoft does not use adaptive logic in short-form tests, but it claims that statistical analysis of the question pool is such that the 25 to 30 questions delivered during a short-form exam conclusively measure a test-taker's knowledge of the subject matter in much the same way as an adaptive test. You can think of the short-form test as a kind of "greatest hits exam" (that is, it covers the most important questions) version of an adaptive exam on the same topic.

NOTE   Microsoft certification exams may use either the adaptive-question format or the more traditional fixed-length question format. Historically, Microsoft tests have been primarily fixed-length format; however, the company seems to be moving in the direction of publishing more adaptive-question format exams.

Because you won't know which form the Microsoft exam might take, you should be prepared for an adaptive exam instead of a fixed-length or a short-form exam. The penalties for answering incorrectly are built in to the test itself on an adaptive exam, whereas the layout remains the same for a fixed-length or short-form test, no matter how many questions you answer incorrectly.

TIP   The biggest difference between adaptive tests and fixed-length or short-form tests is that you can mark and revisit questions on fixed-length and short-form tests after you've read them. On an adaptive test, you must answer the question when it is presented and you cannot return to that question later.

Strategies for Different Testing Formats

Before you choose a test-taking strategy, you must determine what type of test it is—fixed-length, short form, adaptive, or case study:

➤ Fixed-length tests consist of 50 to 70 questions with a check box for each question. You can mark these questions for review so that you can revisit one or more of the more challenging questions after you finish the rest of the exam (provided that your exam time has not yet expired).

➤ Short-form tests have 25 to 30 questions with a check box for each question. You can mark these questions for review so that you can revisit one or more of the more challenging questions after you finish the rest of the exam (provided that your exam time has not yet expired).

➤ Adaptive tests are identified in the introductory material of the test. Questions have no check boxes and can be viewed and answered only once. You cannot mark these questions for review at the end of the exam.

➤ Case-study tests consist of a tabbed window that allows you to navigate easily through the sections of the case.

 You'll be able to tell for sure whether you are taking an adaptive, fixed-length, or short-form test by the first question. Fixed-length and short-form tests include a check box that allows you to mark the question for later review. Adaptive test questions include no such check box and can be viewed and answered only once.

Case-Study Exam Strategy

As mentioned earlier, the case-study approach appears in Microsoft's design exams. These exams consist of a set of case studies that you must analyze so that you can answer related questions. Such exams include one or more case studies (tabbed topic areas), each of which is followed by 4 to 10 questions. The question types for design exams and for the four core Windows 2003 exams are multiple-choice, build-list-and-reorder, create-a-tree, drag-and-connect, and select-and-place. Depending on the test topic, some exams are totally case based, whereas others are not.

Most test-takers find that the case-study type of test used for the design exams (including Exams 70-229, 70-297, and 70-298) is the most difficult to master. When it comes to studying for a case-study test, your best bet is to approach each case study as a standalone test. The biggest challenge you're likely to encounter with this type of test is that you might feel that you won't have enough time to get through all the cases that are presented.

Each case study provides a lot of material that you need to read and study before you can effectively answer the questions that follow. The trick to taking a case-study exam is to first scan the case study to get the highlights. You should make sure you read the overview section of the case so that you understand the context of the problem at hand. Then, you should quickly move on to scanning the questions.

As you are scanning the questions, you should make mental notes to yourself so that you'll remember which sections of the case study you should focus on. Some case studies might provide a fair amount of extra information that you don't really need to answer the questions. The goal with this scanning approach is to avoid having to study and analyze material that is not completely relevant.

When studying a case, read the tabbed information carefully. It is important to answer every question. You will be able to toggle back and forth from case to questions and from question to question within a case testlet. However, after you leave the case and move on, you might not be able to return to it. We suggest that you take notes while reading useful information to help you when you tackle the test questions. It's hard to go wrong with this strategy when taking any kind of Microsoft certification test.

The Fixed-Length and Short-Form Exam Strategy

One tactic that has worked well for many test takers is to answer each question as well as you can before time expires on the exam. Some questions you will undoubtedly feel better equipped to answer correctly than others; however, you should still select an answer to each question as you proceed through the exam. You should click the Mark for Review check box for any question that you are unsure of. In this way, at least you have answered all the questions in case you run out of time. Unanswered questions are automatically scored as incorrect; answers that are guessed at have at least some chance of being scored as correct. If time permits, once you answer all questions, you can revisit each question that you have marked for review. This strategy also allows you to possibly gain some insight to questions that you are unsure of by picking up some clues from the other questions on the exam.

Some people prefer to read over the exam completely before answering the trickier questions; sometimes, information supplied in later questions sheds more light on earlier questions. At other times, information you read in later questions might jog your memory about facts, figures, or behavior that helps you answer earlier questions. Either way, you could come out ahead if you answer only those questions on the first pass that you're absolutely confident about. However, be careful not to run out of time if you choose this strategy!

Fortunately, the Microsoft exam software for fixed-length and short-form tests makes the multiple-visit approach easy to implement. At the top-left corner of each question is a check box that permits you to mark that question for a later visit.

Here are some question-handling strategies that apply to fixed-length and short-form tests. Use them if you have the chance:

➤ When returning to a question after your initial read-through, read every word again; otherwise, your mind can miss important details. Sometimes, revisiting a question after turning your attention elsewhere lets you see something you missed, but the strong tendency is to see what you've seen before. Avoid that tendency at all costs.

➤ If you return to a question more than twice, articulate to yourself what you don't understand about the question, why answers don't appear to make sense, or what appears to be missing. If you chew on the subject awhile, your subconscious might provide the missing details, or you might notice a "trick" that points to the right answer.

As you work your way through the exam, another counter that Microsoft provides will come in handy—the number of questions completed and questions outstanding. For fixed-length and short-form tests, it's wise to budget your time by making sure that you've completed one-quarter of the questions one-quarter of the way through the exam period and three-quarters of the questions three-quarters of the way through.

If you're not finished when only five minutes remain, use that time to guess your way through any remaining questions. Remember, guessing is potentially more valuable than not answering. Blank answers are always wrong, but a guess might turn out to be right. If you don't have a clue about any of the remaining questions, pick answers at random or choose all As, Bs, and so on. Questions left unanswered are counted as answered incorrectly, so a guess is better than nothing at all.

 At the very end of your exam period, you're better off guessing than leaving questions unanswered.

The Adaptive Exam Strategy

If there's one principle that applies to taking an adaptive test, it could be summed up as "Get it right the first time." You cannot elect to skip a question and move on to the next one when taking an adaptive test because the testing software uses your answer to the current question to select the question it presents next. You also cannot return to a question after you've moved on because the software gives you only one chance to answer the question. You can, however, take notes, and sometimes information supplied in earlier questions sheds more light on later questions.

Also, when you answer a question correctly, you are presented with a more difficult question next, to help the software gauge your level of skill and ability. When you answer a question incorrectly, you are presented with a less difficult question, and the software lowers its current estimate of your skill and ability. This process continues until the program settles into a reasonably accurate estimate of what you know and can do, and it takes you, on average, through somewhere between 15 and 30 questions to complete the test.

The good news is that if you know your stuff, you are likely to finish most adaptive tests in 30 minutes or so. The bad news is that you must really, really know your stuff to do your best on an adaptive test. That's because some questions are so convoluted, complex, or hard to follow that you're bound to miss one or two, at a minimum, even if you do know your stuff. So the more you know, the better you'll do, especially on an adaptive test, even accounting for the occasionally weird or unfathomable questions that appear on these exams.

 Because you can't always tell in advance if a test is a fixed-length, short-form, or adaptive exam, you should prepare for the exam as if it were adaptive. That way, you will be prepared to pass no matter what kind of test you take. But if you do take a fixed-length or short-form test, you need to remember the tips from the preceding sections. These tips should help you perform even better on a fixed-length or short-form exam than on an adaptive test.

If you encounter a question on an adaptive test that you can't answer, you must guess an answer immediately. Because of how the software works, however, you might suffer for your guess on the next question if you guess right because you get a more difficult question next!

Question-Handling Strategies

For those questions that have only one right answer, usually two or three of the answers will be obviously incorrect and two of the answers will be plausible. Unless the answer leaps out at you (if it does, reread the question to look for a trick; sometimes those are the ones you're most likely to get wrong), begin the process of answering by eliminating those answers that are most obviously wrong.

You can usually immediately eliminate at least one answer out of the possible choices for a question because it matches one of these conditions:

➤ The answer does not apply to the situation.

➤ The answer describes a nonexistent issue, an invalid option, or an imaginary state.

After you eliminate all answers that are obviously wrong, you can apply your retained knowledge to eliminate further answers. You should look for items that sound correct but refer to actions, commands, or features that are not present or not available in the situation that the question describes.

If you're still faced with a blind guess among two or more potentially correct answers, reread the question. Picture how each of the possible remaining answers would alter the situation. Be especially sensitive to terminology; sometimes the choice of words ("remove" instead of "disable") can make the difference between a right answer and a wrong one.

You should guess at an answer only after you've exhausted your ability to eliminate answers and you are still unclear about which of the remaining possibilities is correct. An unanswered question offers you no points, but guessing gives you at least some chance of getting a question right; just don't be too hasty when making a blind guess.

Numerous questions assume that the default behavior of a particular utility is in effect. If you know the defaults and understand what they mean, this knowledge will help you cut through many of the trickier questions. Simple "final" actions might be critical as well. If you must restart a utility before proposed changes take effect, a correct answer might require this step as well.

Mastering the Inner Game

In the final analysis, knowledge breeds confidence, and confidence breeds success. If you study the materials in this book carefully and review all the practice questions at the end of each chapter, you should become aware of the areas where you need additional learning and study.

After you've worked your way through the book, take the practice exams in the back of the book. Taking these tests provides a reality check and helps you identify areas to study further. Make sure you follow up and review materials related to the questions you miss on the practice exams before scheduling a real exam. Don't schedule your exam appointment until after you've thoroughly studied the material and you feel comfortable with the whole scope of the practice exams. You should score 80% or better on the practice exams before proceeding to the real thing. (Otherwise, obtain some additional practice tests so you can keep trying until you hit this magic number.)

> If you take a practice exam and don't get at least 70% to 80% of the questions correct, keep practicing. Microsoft provides links to practice-exam providers and also self-assessment exams at **http://www.microsoft.com/traincert/mcpexams/prepare/**.

Armed with the information in this book and with the determination to augment your knowledge, you should be able to pass the certification exam. However, you need to work at it, or you'll spend the exam fee more than once before you finally pass. If you prepare seriously, you should do well.

The next section covers other sources that you can use to prepare for Microsoft certification exams.

Additional Resources

A good source of information about Microsoft certification exams comes from Microsoft itself. Because its products and technologies—and the exams that go with them—change frequently, the best place to go for exam-related information is online.

If you haven't already visited the Microsoft Training and Certification Web site, you should do so right now. Microsoft's Training and Certification home page resides at `http://www.microsoft.com/traincert` (see Figure 1.12).

Coping with Change on the Web

Sooner or later, all the information we've shared with you about the Microsoft Certified Professional pages and the other Web-based resources mentioned throughout the rest of this book will go stale or be replaced by newer information. In some cases, the URLs you find here might lead you to their replacements; in other cases, the URLs will go nowhere, leaving you with the dreaded "404 File not found" error message. When that happens, don't give up.

There's always a way to find what you want on the Web if you're willing to invest some time and energy. Most large or complex Web sites—and Microsoft's qualify on both counts—offer search engines. All of Microsoft's Web pages have a Search button at the top edge of the page. As long as you can get to Microsoft's site (it should stay at **http://www.microsoft.com** for a long time), you can use the Search button to find what you need.

The more focused you can make a search request, the more likely the results will include information you can use. For example, you can search for the string

`"training and certification"`

to produce a lot of data about the subject in general, but if you're looking for the preparation guide for Exam 70-290, Managing and Maintaining a Microsoft Windows Server 2003 Environment, you'll be more likely to get there quickly if you use a search string similar to the following:

`"Exam 70-290" AND "preparation guide"`

Likewise, if you want to find the Training and Certification downloads, you should try a search string such as this:

`"training and certification" AND "download page"`

Finally, you should feel free to use general search tools—such as **http://www.google.com**, **http://www.altavista.com**, and **http://www.excite.com**—to look for related information. Although Microsoft offers great information about its certification exams online, there are plenty of third-party sources of information and assistance that need not follow Microsoft's party line. Therefore, if you can't find something where the book says it lives, you should intensify your search.

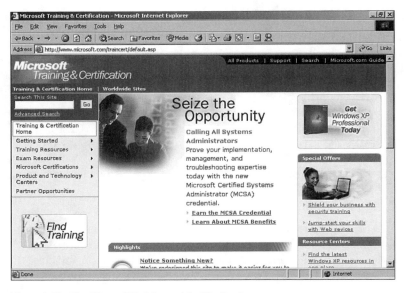

Figure 1.12 The Microsoft Training and Certification home page.

Managing Hardware Devices and Drivers

. . . .

Terms you'll need to understand:

✓ Device Manager
✓ Driver signing
✓ Driver roll back
✓ Add Hardware Wizard
✓ Hardware requirements for Windows Server 2003
✓ Plug and Play versus non-Plug and Play devices
✓ Network adapter or network interface card (NIC)
✓ Universal Serial Bus (USB) devices
✓ FireWire or IEEE (Institute of Electrical and Electronics Engineers) 1394 devices

Techniques you'll need to master:

✓ Installing, configuring, and troubleshooting hardware devices and drivers
✓ Updating drivers and system files
✓ Rolling back drivers to a previous version
✓ Managing and troubleshooting driver signing

The term "computer hardware" includes any physical device that is connected to a computer that is controlled by the computer's processors. It includes equipment connected to the computer at the time that it is manufactured as well as equipment that you add later. Modems, disk drives, CD-ROM drives, printers, network cards, keyboards, display adapter cards, and USB cameras are all examples of devices. Each device attached to a system must also have a corresponding software driver, which allows the device to interface (communicate) with the computer's operating system. Administering and troubleshooting hardware devices and their associated drivers is vital to maintaining server uptime. Administering, diagnosing, and resolving hardware-related issues is the focus of this chapter.

Windows Server 2003 Hardware Requirements and Installation Issues

Windows Server 2003 comes in several different versions to solve business problems for organizations large, medium, and small; these various editions cover a wide range of computing scenarios. The Windows Server 2003 family of products is designed to scale up (the ability to run on one large machine with plenty of RAM and a lot of storage) as well as scale out (to accommodate server farms with many servers working together). In addition to a monitor, display adapter, keyboard, pointing device, CD-ROM drive, and network card, there are standard minimum hardware requirements for the entire Windows Server 2003 product line (see Table 2.1). The following list discusses the various editions of Windows Server 2003:

➤ *Windows Server 2003, Web Edition*—A scaled down version from the Standard Edition to be used as a dedicated Web and FTP server. The maximum amount of RAM supported is 2GB for this version. This edition cannot be promoted to a domain controller, but it can be a member server. IIS is installed by default.

➤ *Windows Server 2003, Standard Edition*—This version supports remote storage, removable storage, shared fax services, services for Macintosh, Remote Installation Services (RIS), Terminal Services, and promotion to domain controller status, among many other features. This edition supports up to 4GB of RAM and is targeted for small to medium organizations.

➤ *Windows Server 2003, Enterprise Edition*—This version is touted as a high-volume, industrial-strength solution for medium to large organizations. It supports all of the features from the Standard Edition plus it also supports up to 8 CPUs, up to 8-way clustering, and up to a maximum of 32GB of RAM.

➤ *Windows Server 2003, Datacenter Edition*—This version is designed to replace mini-computers such as IBM AS/400s and other UNIX-based equipment for mission-critical applications. It supports all of the features in the Enterprise Edition and it supports up to 32 CPUs, but it does not support Internet Connection Sharing (ICS) or Internet Connection Firewall (ICF) services. This edition is the high-end, cream-of-the-crop variety that supports up to 64GB of RAM. You can only purchase it as a turnkey solution from original equipment manufacturers (OEMs) such as Dell, HP, and IBM.

➤ *Windows Server 2003, 64-Bit Enterprise Edition*—This version represents Microsoft's initial foray into the 64-bit computing arena. It can support up to 64GB of RAM. It supports all of the features in the 32-bit Enterprise Edition, but it installs only on Intel Itanium- and Itanium-2-based computers. Support for AMD Opteron and AMD Athlon 64-bit processors is forthcoming.

➤ *Windows Server 2003, 64-Bit Datacenter Edition*—This version also represents Microsoft's initial foray into the 64-bit computing arena. It can support up to 512GB of RAM! It supports all of the features in the 32-bit Datacenter Edition and it supports up to 64 CPUs, but it too installs only on Intel Itanium- and Itanium-2-based computers. Support for AMD Opteron and AMD Athlon 64-bit processors is forthcoming.

Table 2.1 Windows Server 2003 Minimum Hardware Requirements				
Edition	RAM	Storage	CPUs	Clustering
Web	128MB	1.5GB	1-2	No
Standard	128MB	1.5GB	1-4	No
Enterprise	128MB	1.5GB	1-8	Yes, up to 8 nodes
Datacenter	512MB	1.5GB	8-32	Yes, up to 8 nodes
Enterprise 64-bit	128MB	2.0GB	1-8	Yes, up to 8 nodes
Datacenter 64-bit	512MB	2.0GB	8-64	Yes, up to 8 nodes

For the 32-bit editions, Windows Server 2003 requires a computer with one or more Pentium-class compatible processors from vendors such as Intel and AMD. A Pentium III-compatible class of computer or better is recommended. For the two 64-bit editions, Windows Server 2003 installs and runs only on 64-bit Intel Itanium-based computers. You cannot install these editions on 32-bit-based computers.

Supported Upgrades

The ideal scenario when moving to a new server platform is to perform a fresh installation. However, if you need to perform an upgrade installation of Windows Server 2003 over a previous version of a Microsoft server product, you can accomplish this task from the following Microsoft server operating systems:

➤ Windows NT Server 4.0 with Service Pack 5 (SP5) or higher

➤ Windows NT Server 4.0, Enterprise Edition with SP5 or higher

➤ Windows NT Server 4.0, Terminal Server Edition with SP5 or higher

➤ Windows 2000 Server

➤ Windows 2000 Advanced Server

 You must install Windows Server 2003, Web Edition as a fresh software installation. You cannot upgrade it from any previous Microsoft operating system. Once installed, Windows Server 2003, Web Edition cannot be upgraded to any other edition of Windows Server 2003.

Servers running Windows NT Server 3.51 must first upgrade to Windows NT Server 4.0 before you can upgrade them to Windows Server 2003. Computers running Windows 2000 Server can be upgraded to either Windows Server 2003, Standard Edition, or Windows Server 2003, Enterprise Edition. However, computers running Windows 2000 Advanced Server can be upgraded only to Windows Server 2003, Enterprise Edition. Computers running Windows Server 2000 Datacenter Server cannot be upgraded to Windows Server 2003, Datacenter Edition because the Datacenter Edition is offered only as an integrated hardware/software solution through authorized OEMs and the Microsoft Windows Datacenter Program.

NOTE You cannot upgrade computers running desktop operating systems such as Windows NT Workstation 4.0, Windows 2000 Professional, or Windows XP Professional to any Windows Server 2003 edition.

Microsoft Product Activation

Microsoft introduced the concept of product activation with the Windows XP desktop operating system in an attempt to reduce software piracy. Product activation is mandatory in retail and OEM releases of the Windows Server 2003 product family. After you install a retail or OEM version of a Windows Server 2003 product, you have 60 days from the date of the installation to activate the product. You can activate the system via the Internet or by phone. If you do not activate the server before the 60-day grace period expires, no user or administrator will be able to log onto the system from the console, over the network, or through Remote Desktop (Terminal Server) sessions. Administrators can log onto the system in Safe Mode to access any data on the server after the grace period expires. The 64-bit editions and copies of Windows Server 2003 media purchased through Microsoft Volume Licensing channels are not subject to product activation; these releases ship on the CD as already activated.

Managing Hardware Devices and Drivers

Windows Server 2003 offers full support for Plug and Play (PnP) devices and offers limited support for non-Plug and Play devices. Be sure to always consult the latest Windows Server 2003 Hardware Compatibility List (HCL) before installing a new device to verify that the device is supported. You can access the online version of the HCL at http://www.microsoft.com/hwdq/hcl/search.asp. Of course, even if it's on the HCL, it's not a bad idea to test a device yourself to be sure that it will work with Windows Server 2003 and the existing hardware that you will be connecting it to.

For a device to work properly with Windows Server 2003, you must install software (a device driver) on the computer. Each hardware device has its own unique device driver, which the device manufacturer typically supplies. However, many device drivers are included with Windows Server 2003, and these drivers often work even better with Windows Server 2003 than the manufacturers' own drivers. Look for Microsoft to recommend using its own drivers for a given device rather than those of the manufacturer, because Microsoft understands the inner workings of the operating system better than anyone else.

Because Windows Server 2003 manages your computer's resources and configuration based on PnP standards, you can install most PnP hardware devices without restarting your computer. Windows Server 2003 automatically identifies (enumerates) the new hardware and installs the drivers it needs. Windows Server 2003 fully supports computers with Basic Input/Output System (BIOS) versions that are compliant with the Advanced Configuration and Power Interface (ACPI) specification. Windows Server 2003 also supports computers with certain BIOS versions that are compliant with the older Advanced Power Management (APM) specification. Just remember that ACPI-compliant computers and hardware devices usually make your Windows Server 2003 hardware setup experiences more enjoyable.

Windows Server 2003 prompts you for a reason why you are shutting down or restarting the server every time you attempt to reboot or power down the system and records this information in the system log. You can review each system shutdown or restart in the system log in the Event Viewer under Event ID 1074. For testing environments, or if your organization decides it does not want to track unplanned server reboots, there is a way to disable the Shutdown Event Tracker. Click Start, Run; type **gpedit.msc**; and click OK. For the Local Computer Policy, navigate to the Computer Configuration, Administrative Templates, System node. Double-click the Display Shutdown Event Tracker setting and select Disabled. Click OK to save the setting and exit from the Group Policy Object Editor. Now you won't be pestered about why you are restarting the system every time that you simply need to install a hotfix or update the server.

Installing, Configuring, and Managing Hardware

You might need to configure devices on Windows Server 2003 machines using the Add Hardware Wizard in the Control Panel or by clicking the Add Hardware Wizard button from the Hardware tab on the System Properties window. Keep in mind that in most cases, you need to be logged on to the local computer as a member of the Administrators group to add, configure, and remove devices. Many devices completely configure themselves without any administrator intervention at all; other devices require some administrative effort.

Installing PnP Devices and Non-PnP Devices

Connect the device to the appropriate port or slot on your computer according to the device manufacturer's instructions. You might need to start or restart your computer, but this step happens much less often than it did with previous versions of Windows. Plan for necessary downtime on production servers. If you are prompted to restart your computer, go ahead and do so when it is appropriate for the users' environment. For PnP devices, Windows Server 2003 should detect the device and then immediately start the Found New Hardware Wizard. If a new device does not immediately install, you might need to use a special setup driver disk, CD-ROM, or DVD from the manufacturer that ships with the device. If you are still unable to install the device, or if you are installing a non-PnP device, perform the following manual installation steps:

1. Click the Add Hardware icon in the Control Panel.

2. Click Next and then click Yes, I Have Already Connected the Hardware. Click Next again.

3. Scroll down the Installed Hardware list to the very bottom, select Add a New Hardware Device, and click Next.

4. Select one of the following options:

   ➤ *Search for and Install the Hardware Automatically (Recommended)*—Do this step if you want Windows Server 2003 to try to detect the new device that you want to install.

   ➤ *Install the Hardware That I Manually Select from a List (Advanced)*— Do this step if you know the type and model of the device you are installing and you want to select it from a list of devices.

5. Click Next, and then follow the instructions on your screen.

6. You might be prompted to restart your computer, depending on the type of device you just installed.

Troubleshooting Installed Devices with the Add Hardware Wizard

Sometimes, an installed hardware device is not automatically recognized by the Windows Server 2003 PnP enumeration. If an installed device fails to be discovered or fails to function, you should troubleshoot the device by performing the following steps:

1. Click the Add Hardware icon in the Control Panel.

2. Click Next and then click Yes, I Have Already Connected the Hardware. Click Next again.

3. Select the installed hardware device that you are having trouble with and click Next, as shown in Figure 2.1.

4. Follow the subsequent instructions on your screen. Click Finish to launch the Hardware Update Wizard or to go through a hardware troubleshooter from the Windows Server 2003 Help and Support Center, depending on the device in question, to try to resolve the problem. Otherwise, click Cancel to exit the Add Hardware Wizard.

Figure 2.1 Troubleshooting hardware devices with the Add Hardware Wizard.

Troubleshooting Hardware with Device Manager

The Windows Server 2003 Device Manager is quite similar to the Device Manager in Windows XP and Windows 2000. The Device Manager window displays all the hardware devices connected to the computer. You can view the devices by type or by connection, or you can view the resources that the devices use or how the resources are connected to each device by selecting the appropriate option from the View menu (see Figure 2.2). Device Manager gives administrators the power to update device drivers, enable or disable devices, uninstall devices, scan for hardware changes, roll back drivers, and even work with resource settings for devices, all in one centralized interface.

To run Device Manager, follow these steps:

1. Right-click My Computer from the Windows desktop or from the Start menu and select Properties. Alternatively, you can double-click the System icon from the Control Panel.

2. From the System properties window, click the Hardware tab and then click the Device Manager button.

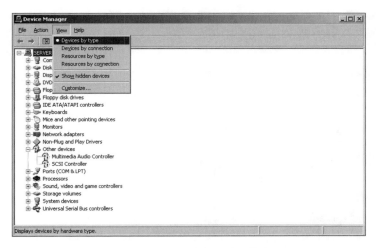

Figure 2.2   The display options from the View menu in Device Manager.

When you view devices by type, Device Manager categorizes devices into logical groups such as computer, disk drives, display adapter, and so on. To work with an individual device, click the plus sign to expand the appropriate category and then right-click the device itself and select Properties to display its properties sheet. Devices that are not set up or functioning properly have their categories automatically expanded, and each problem device is shown with a yellow question mark or an exclamation point to denote a problem with the device. To enable or disable a device from its properties sheet, click the Device Usage drop-down list box and select either Use This Device (Enable) or Do Not Use This Device (Disable), as shown in Figure 2.3.

To install or reinstall a driver for a device, perform the following steps:

1. Open Device Manager and expand the device category that you want to work with.

2. Right-click the device for which you want to install or reinstall drivers.

3. Click the Reinstall Driver button from the General tab and follow the onscreen instructions. You might need the CD-ROM or disk containing the device drivers from the manufacturer.

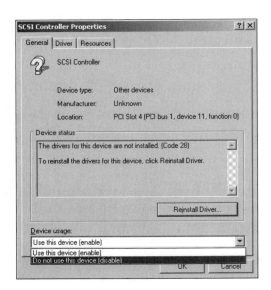

Figure 2.3 The properties sheet for a device from Device Manager.

Managing Device Drivers and System Updates

Keeping drivers and system files updated ensures that your operating system performs at its peak level. Microsoft recommends using Microsoft digitally signed drivers whenever possible. Microsoft has thoroughly tested Microsoft digitally signed drivers for compatibility with Windows Server 2003, so these drivers are much more stable than unsigned drivers. The driver.cab cabinet file is stored in the \I386 folder on the Windows Server 2003 CD-ROM, and this file contains all the drivers that Windows Server 2003 works with at the time that the operating system is released to manufacturing. This cabinet file is copied to the %systemroot%\Driver Cache\i386 folder when Windows Server 2003 is installed. Whenever a driver is updated, Windows Server 2003 looks in the driver.cab file first. The location of driver.cab is stored in a Registry key, and you can change it if you use the Registry Editor (regedit.exe) and navigate to HKLM\Software\Microsoft\Windows\CurrentVersion\Setup\DriverCachePath.

Automatically Updating Operating System Files

Windows Server 2003 supports automatic updates for critical operating system files. In Windows Server 2003, you must be logged on as a member of the Administrators group to install updated components or to change Automatic Updates settings. If the computer is a member of a Windows Active Directory domain, Group Policy settings might further restrict your ability to modify these settings and install updated components. To turn on, turn off, or modify Windows Server 2003 Automatic Updates notification settings, follow these steps:

1. Log on to the computer as the administrator or as a member of the Administrators group.

2. Right-click My Computer from the Start menu or the Windows desktop and select Properties.

3. Click the Automatic Updates tab.

4. To enable automatic updates, be sure that the Keep My Computer Up to Date check box is marked; it is the default setting. To disable automatic updates, clear this check box.

5. When automatic updates are enabled, select from one of three available notification Settings, as shown in Figure 2.4:

   ➤ Notify Me Before Downloading Any Updates and Notify Me Again Before Installing Them on My Computer.

   ➤ Download the Updates Automatically and Notify Me When They are Ready to be Installed. (This option is the default selection.)

   ➤ Automatically Download the Updates, and Install Them on the Schedule That I Specify. (You must then choose the day and time when you want the updates downloaded and installed.)

6. Click OK to accept the new settings.

After the successful installation of certain updated components, Windows Server 2003 might prompt you to restart the computer. As a best practice, you should always restart the machine immediately as instructed. Failure to follow these instructions can result in an unstable or nonfunctioning server. Because you must restart the server after an update, you should install updates only during nonproduction hours. In addition, you should consider turning off the Automatic Updates feature so that you can first manually install all updates on nonproduction servers in a test environment. As a general rule, only after you have thoroughly tested an update, should you install it on a production server.

Windows Server 2003 reminds you about downloading or installing automatic updates by placing an auto update icon in the notification area of the system tray (located in the right corner of the taskbar). If you choose not to install one or more updates that you downloaded to your PC, Windows Server 2003 deletes those update files from your computer. If you later decide that you want to install any of the updates that you previously declined, click the Declined Updates button on the Automatic Updates tab. If any of the previously declined updates still apply to your system, Windows Server 2003 displays them the next time that the system notifies you of newly available updates.

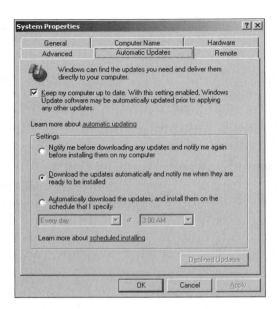

Figure 2.4 You can configure automatic updates via the Automatic Updates tab of the System Properties window.

Manually Updating Device Drivers

Automatic updates might be convenient for desktop computers, but when it comes to servers, it's a good idea to be more vigilant and protective. One bad driver can severely cripple or completely disable an important server. Be sure to test all updated drivers and other critical system files on test machines in a nonproduction environment before you deploy them. To update drivers on individual components, such as network cards or SCSI disk controllers, perform the following steps:

1. Open Device Manager and expand the device category where the device that you want to update is located.

2. Perform one of these two steps:

   ➤ Right-click the device that you want to update, select Update Driver from the right-click menu, and follow the onscreen instructions.

   ➤ Right-click the device that you want to update and select Properties from the right-click menu. Click the Driver tab, click the Update Driver button, and follow the onscreen instructions.

You can use the Driver Verifier utility to troubleshoot and isolate driver problems. It is not enabled by default. To use it, you must enable it by running the Driver Verifier Manager part of **verifier.exe** by executing it from the GUI first or by changing a Registry setting and then restarting the computer. When you run the Driver Verifier tool (**verifier.exe**) from the command line, it offers several options for troubleshooting drivers. For example, if you run the command **verifier /all**, it verifies all the drivers installed on the system. See the Microsoft Knowledge Base article 244617 for more information.

Updating Drivers and System Files with Windows Update

Windows Update is a Microsoft database of important operating-system files such as drivers, patches, help files, and other components stored on public Microsoft Web servers that you can download to keep your Windows Server 2003 installation up to date. From the Windows Update Web site, you can scan the server for outdated system files, drivers, and help files and automatically replace them with the most recent versions. However, once again, before you get too carried away with the quick convenience of updating a server from a Web page on the Internet, remember that you should be much more careful with servers than with ordinary desktop machines.

Only operating-system files are included in Windows Update. Other server applications, such as Exchange Server or SQL Server, must be manually updated with security hotfixes and service packs to keep those server-side applications current. Always test each update on a nonproduction server to ensure the integrity of your network. To update your system files using Windows Update, follow these steps:

1. Use the server's Web browser to navigate to the Windows Update Web site at `http://windowsupdate.microsoft.com/`.

2. Click Yes if you are prompted about whether to allow ActiveX or other components from Microsoft Corporation to be downloaded to your system.

3. Click Scan for Updates.

4. Follow the onscreen instructions to review and install all or some of the applicable updates to the local server.

 You must be logged on as a member of the Administrators group to complete the installation of various Windows Update components or procedures. If the server is a member of an Active Directory domain, Group Policy settings might prevent you from updating any system files or drivers.

Introducing Software Update Services

The Software Update Services (SUS) feature is related to the Windows Update service in that both features enable administrators to download the latest updated components directly from Microsoft via the Internet. However, Windows Update is designed to manually update one computer at a time. SUS is designed for network administrators to download patches to a central server, test the updates, mark approved updates for deployment, and then schedule and deploy those updates automatically to both servers and workstations over the network. SUS is discussed in detail in Chapter 6, "Monitoring, Optimizing, and Troubleshooting Server Performance."

Using Driver Roll Back

Driver roll back was first introduced as a new feature in Windows XP. If you encounter problems with a hardware device after you install an updated driver for it, you can easily revert back to the previously installed software driver for that device by using the Roll Back Driver option within Device Manager. Follow these steps to roll back a driver for a specific device:

1. Open Device Manager and expand the device category where the device driver that you want to roll back is located.

2. Right-click the device and select Properties.

3. Click the Driver tab.

4. Click the Roll Back Driver button.

Managing and Troubleshooting Device Conflicts

You configure, diagnose, and modify settings for hardware devices using the Device Manager. Each resource—for example, a memory address range, interrupt request (IRQ), input/output (I/O) port, Direct Memory Access (DMA) channel, and so on—that is assigned to each device must be unique or the device won't function properly. For PnP devices, Windows Server 2003 attempts to ensure automatically that these resources are configured properly. If a device has a resource conflict or is not working properly, you see a yellow circle with an exclamation point inside it next to the device's name. If a device has been improperly installed or if it's been disabled, you see a red X next to the device name in Device Manager.

If you're having trouble with a particular device, sometimes it's helpful to simply uninstall the device's driver, reboot the computer, and then attempt to reinstall the driver. Because PnP devices automatically invoke the installation procedure from Windows Server 2003, you might want to disable a particular device rather than uninstall its driver if you do not want the operating system to attempt to install it each time that the server restarts.

Occasionally, two devices require the same resources, but keep in mind that this does not always result in a device conflict—especially if the devices are PnP-compliant. If a conflict arises, you can manually change the resource settings to be sure that each setting is unique. Sometimes, two or more devices can share resources, such as interrupts on Peripheral Connection Interface (PCI) devices, depending on the drivers and the computer. For example, you might see Windows Server 2003 share IRQ 9 or 10 among multiple PCI devices, such as USB host controllers, SCSI adapters, and audio controllers. In many instances, you cannot change resource settings for PnP devices because no other settings are available.

When you install a non-PnP device, the resource settings for the device are not automatically configured. Depending on the type of device you are installing, you might have to manually configure these settings. The appropriate range of settings should appear in the user's manual that ships with your device. To change resource settings for a device, follow these steps:

1. Open Device Manager and expand the device category where the device is located.

2. Right-click the device for which you want to adjust its resource settings and select Properties.

3. Click the Resources tab and clear the Use Automatic Settings check box (if available). If the Use Automatic Settings check box is dim (unavailable), you cannot change the resource settings for this device.

4. Choose one of the following courses of action:

   ➤ Click the Settings Based on drop-down list box to select from the predefined list of settings.

   ➤ Click a Resource Type item shown in the Resource Settings list box and then click the Change Setting button to individually modify the resource's setting. Change the setting and click OK. Repeat this action for each resource setting that you want to change.

5. Click OK for the device's properties sheet to return to the Device Manager window.

Generally, you should not change resource settings manually, because when you do so, the settings become fixed and Windows Server 2003 then has less flexibility when allocating resources to other devices. If too many resources become fixed, Windows Server 2003 might not be able to install new PnP devices. In addition, if you manually change resource settings to incompatible values, the device might no longer function or it might function improperly.

Uninstalling and Reinstalling Device Drivers

If you need to uninstall a driver for a particular device, simply open Device Manager and locate the device that you want to uninstall. Right-click the device name and select Uninstall. Click OK in the Confirm Device Removal dialog box. The driver for an installed device does not get deleted from the system. When the computer restarts, Windows Server 2003 attempts to reinstall the PnP device unless you designate the device as disabled from its properties sheet in Device Manager. If you need to reinstall a driver for a non-PnP device, perform the following steps:

1. Right-click My Computer and select Properties.

2. Click the Hardware tab and click the Add Hardware Wizard button to launch the wizard and then click Next.

3. Click Yes, I Have Already Connected the Hardware and then click Next.

4. Select the device that you want to reinstall from the Installed Hardware list box and click Next.

5. Follow the instructions that the wizard displays to finish the reinstallation process.

Managing and Troubleshooting Driver Signing

Microsoft touts digital signatures for device drivers as a method for improving the overall quality of software drivers. Better quality device drivers, in turn, help reduce support costs for vendors and help lower the total cost of ownership (TCO) for customers. Windows Server 2003 uses the same type of driver-signing process as Windows XP and Windows 2000 to make sure that drivers have been certified to work correctly with the Windows Driver Model (WDM) in Windows Server 2003. Depending on the Driver Signing Options configured for each specific Windows Server 2003 computer, you might be allowed to install nondigitally signed drivers without any warning, you might be warned but still permitted to proceed with installing nondigitally signed drivers (see Figure 2.5), or you might be completely prevented from installing drivers that do not have digital signatures.

If your server is experiencing a device-driver problem, it might be because you are using a driver that was not correctly (or specifically) written for Windows Server 2003. To identify such drivers, you can use the Signature Verification tool. This utility, sigverif.exe, helps you quickly identify unsigned drivers. Feel free to take advantage of this tool whether a device is not currently working or if you simply want to make sure that all drivers in use are properly signed. To use this digital-signature verification tool, perform the following steps:

1. Click Start, Run; type sigverif.exe; and click OK to launch the program.

2. Click the Advanced button.

3. Select the option Look for Other Files That Are Not Digitally Signed.

4. Mark the Include Subfolders check box.

5. Click the Logging tab to make any changes for the log file and then click OK. Note the log file name: sigverif.txt.

6. Click Start to run the signature-verification process.

7. After the process finishes, the Signature Verification Results windows will appear. Review the list of unsigned drivers and click Close to exit. You can review the results again later by double-clicking the sigverif.txt log file located by default in the %systemroot% folder (for example, C:\Windows).

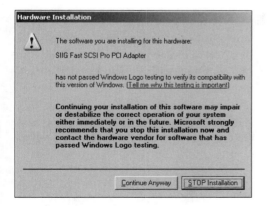

Figure 2.5   A Hardware Installation warning message box about installing an unsigned device driver.

Setting Driver Signing Options via System Properties

Windows Server 2003 offers administrators some control over whether users can install signed drivers, unsigned drivers, or both, for a chosen device. Signed drivers are software device drivers that have been tested by Microsoft for compatibility with Windows Server 2003 (or other versions of Windows). Microsoft issues a catalog (`*.cat`) file that contains a digital signature for each device driver that successfully passes its compatibility test. Manufacturers then distribute the associated catalog file as part of each device driver's set of installation files. Unsigned drivers are drivers that either have not been tested or drivers that are actually not compatible with specific versions of Windows: These drivers do not include catalog files as part of their set of installation files.

To change the system's driver-signing options, right-click My Computer, select Properties, click the Hardware tab, and click the Driver Signing button. Select one of the following actions for the operating system to take (as shown in Figure 2.6) when you attempt to install an unsigned device driver:

➤ *Ignore*—This option bypasses driver-signing checks, allowing the user to proceed with the driver installation even if a driver is not signed.

➤ *Warn*—This option issues a dialog box warning if an unsigned driver is encountered during a device driver installation. It gives the user the option of continuing with the installation or terminating the device driver's setup. This setting is the default.

➤ *Block*—This option is the most restrictive of the three settings. To prevent the installation of any unsigned device drivers, you should select this option.

When you are logged onto the server as the administrator or a member of the Administrators group, the Administrator Option for driver signing is also available. If you mark the Make This Action the System Default check box, the driver-signing setting that you have chosen will become the default setting for all other users who log onto this server.

NOTE

Nonadministrator users can make the driver-signing policy for a given system more stringent than the current default setting; however, they cannot make the driver-signing policy more liberal.

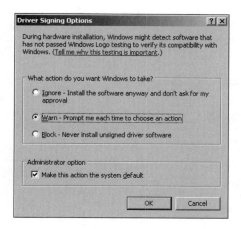

Figure 2.6 The Driver Signing Options dialog box for unsigned device driver installation behavior.

Setting Driver Signing Options via Policy Settings

Instead of modifying the driver-signing options from the GUI, you can manipulate Windows Server 2003 driver-signing options using either a Local Policy setting or a Group Policy Object (GPO) setting. Both the Local Policy setting and the Group Policy Object setting appear in the Local Policies, Security Options container named Devices: Unsigned Driver Installation Behavior. The three options for the unsigned driver behavior policy are the same as the options in the System Properties window shown earlier in Figure 2.6; they are just worded differently, as shown in Figures 2.7 and 2.8. To configure driver-signing options using Local Policy for a standalone server or a member server, follow these steps:

1. Click Start, (All) Programs, Administrative Tools, Local Security Policy.

2. Expand the Local Policies node and select the Security Options subnode.

3. Double-click the Devices: Unsigned Driver Installation Behavior policy, select one of the following options, and click OK:

   ➤ *Silently Succeed*—Selecting this setting ignores whether a driver is signed or not, allowing the user to proceed with the driver installation.

   ➤ *Warn but Allow Installation*—Selecting this setting issues a dialog box warning if an unsigned driver is encountered during a device installation. It gives the user the option of continuing with the installation or terminating the device's setup.

> *Do Not Allow Installation*—This option is the most restrictive of the three settings. To prevent the installation of any unsigned device drivers, you should select this option.

4. Exit from the Local Security Settings console.

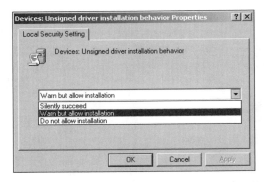

Figure 2.7 The Local Policy setting for Devices: Unsigned Driver Installation Behavior.

Of course, because GPOs are applied via the LDSO (local, domain, site, organizational unit) methodology, Local Policy settings can be overridden by Group Policy settings within an Active Directory environment. Configuring the Group Policy for Devices: Unsigned Driver Installation Behavior is quite similar to working with the Local Policy setting; however, you must use the Group Policy Object Editor Microsoft Management Console (MMC) snap-in instead of the Local Security Settings MMC snap-in. To configure driver-signing options using Group Policy, follow these steps:

1. Log on to an Active Directory domain controller as the administrator or as a member of the Administrators group.

2. Click Start, (All) Programs, Administrative Tools, Domain Security Policy to affect all member computers within the domain, or click Start, All Programs, Administrative Tools, Domain Controller Security Policy to affect only domain controllers within the domain.

3. For either the Default Domain Security Settings console or the Default Domain Controller Security Settings console, expand the Local Policies node and select the Security Options subnode.

4. Double-click the Devices: Unsigned Driver Installation Behavior policy, select one of the following options, and click OK:

> *Silently Succeed*—Selecting this setting ignores whether a driver is signed or not, allowing the user to proceed with the driver installation.

➤ *Warn but Allow Installation*—Selecting this setting issues a dialog box warning if an unsigned driver is encountered during a device installation. It gives the user the option of continuing with the installation or terminating the device's setup.

➤ *Do Not Allow Installation*—This option is the most restrictive of the three settings. To prevent the installation of any unsigned device drivers, you should select this option.

5. Exit from the security settings console.

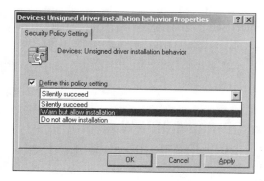

Figure 2.8 The Group Policy Object setting for Devices: Unsigned Driver Installation Behavior under Active Directory.

Supporting CD and DVD Devices

Windows Server 2003 supports a variety of CD read-only memory (CD-ROM), CD recordable (CD-R), CD rewritable (CD-RW), DVD read-only memory (DVD-ROM), DVD recordable (DVD-R and DVD+R), DVD rewritable (DVD-RW and DVD+RW), and DVD random access memory (DVD-RAM) drives and disc formats. Check with the most recent HCL or your hardware vendor to see whether your CD or DVD device will work with Windows Server 2003.

If the CD or DVD device is PnP-compliant, you can rely on Windows Server 2003 to detect the device and install the appropriate drivers as well as allocate system resources for the device. If you are using a CD or DVD drive that is not PnP-compliant, use the Add Hardware applet in the Control Panel to install the drivers and assign resources for the device.

The Windows Server 2003 Compact Disc File System (CDFS) reads CDs that are formatted according to the ISO 9660 standard. Windows Server 2003 also supports the Joliet standard, which is an extension to the ISO 9660 standard. Joliet supports Unicode characters and supports a folder hierarchy extending deeper than eight levels of subfolders. Windows Server 2003 also offers integrated support for writing data directly onto CD-R and CD-RW media without requiring any third-party CD-burning software.

A DVD drive needs either a hardware or software decoder to play movies on your Windows Server 2003 computer, even if you want to use the built-in Windows Media Player as the preferred playback device. Of course, the computer also requires a Windows Server 2003-compatible sound card and video display card with their respective drivers to play multimedia DVD titles. Your DVD decoder must be Windows Server 2003-compliant to play movies under Windows Server 2003 if you upgrade from a previous Windows Server version. You do not need a decoder for reading data DVDs. Windows Server 2003 supports the Universal Disk Format (UDF) file system on DVDs (and CDs) for read-only access to data. However, in general, servers should not be used for playing any types of movies or video clips to entertain the IT staff.

Writing Files and Folders to CD-R and CD-RW Media

Under Windows Server 2003, the ability to write to CD-R and CD-RW media is disabled by default. You must first enable the IMAPI CD-Burning COM Service before you can burn any CDs. To turn on this service, click Start, Run; type in services.msc; and click OK. Double-click the IMAPI CD-Burning COM Service and change the startup type to Automatic. Click Start to run the service without having to reboot the server. If you set the startup type to Automatic, the computer will be ready to create CDs every time that it restarts. To write to CD-R and CD-RW media under Windows Server 2003 without third-party software, follow these steps:

1. Right-click individual files (and folders), or right-click selected groups of files (and folders) and select Send to CD-R (or CD-RW) Drive. Repeat this step for all files and folders that you want to write to the CD. You can also copy and paste or drag and drop files and folders onto the CD-R/CD-RW drive letter in My Computer.

2. Open the CD-R/CD-RW drive in My Computer or the Windows Explorer to review all of the files and folders that have been placed there for creating the CD.

3. Click Write These Files to CD from the left task pane, or click the File menu and select Write These Files to CD.

4. In the CD Writing Wizard dialog box that appears, type in a name for this new CD. Be sure that there is a blank CD-R or CD-RW disc in the drive and click Next. The data will be written to the CD.

5. Click Finish when the wizard finishes writing the data to the CD.

When you are selecting files and folders for CD burning by either copying them into the CD-R/CD-RW drive or by using the Send to right-click menu option, they are temporarily stored in a CD burning staging area. This staging area is a hidden folder located, by default, in `%systemdrive%\Documents and Settings\`*`username`*`\Local Settings\Application Data\Microsoft\CD Burning`. The environment variable `%systemdrive%` represents the drive letter where the operating system is installed, for example C:, if Windows Server 2003 is installed in `C:\Windows`. Windows Server 2003 does not natively support writing data to DVD-R, DVD-RW, DVD+R, or DVD+RW media. However, some third-party utilities do support writing to DVD-based media from Windows Server 2003. Of course, Windows Server 2003 can read DVD-based media. Windows Server 2003 does support DVD-RAM drives and discs and uses the FAT32 file system for read and write operations on DVD-RAM media.

Configuring CD-R/CD-RW Device Settings

You can configure settings for desktop CD recording by right-clicking the CD-R/CD-RW drive letter in My Computer and selecting Properties. From its properties sheet, you can click the Recording tab to modify the drive's CD-burning characteristics as shown in Figure 2.9. From the Recording tab, you can enable or disable CD recording on the drive, and you change the drive letter where temporary files are stored before CDs are burned (the staging area). You can also select the writing speed for CD burning and you can specify whether the CD media should be ejected after each CD has been burned.

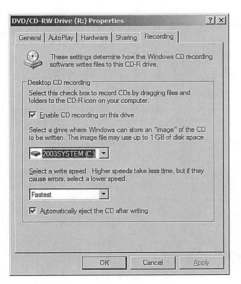

Figure 2.9   The Recording tab of the properties sheet for a CD-R/CD-RW drive.

Installing, Configuring, and Troubleshooting USB Devices

Windows Server 2003 offers built-in support for many USB devices. Because all USB devices fully support PnP, USB peripherals can be easily connected to (and disconnected from) Windows Server 2003 computers that have USB ports by using standard USB cables and connectors. Windows Server 2003 and Windows XP Professional with Service Pack 1 (SP1) provide support for the USB 2.0 specification and are fully backward compatible with the USB 1.1 standard. In theory, USB devices can be safely connected and disconnected while the computer is running. Windows Server 2003 detects USB devices when they are plugged into the computer and attempts to install the proper device driver for each detected USB device. If Windows Server 2003 cannot locate an appropriate device driver, it prompts you to insert a driver disk or CD-ROM from the manufacturer of the device.

Working with USB Controllers and Hubs

To support USB, a computer needs either a USB host controller built into the motherboard or a USB controller adapter card installed. The USB host controller directs all USB traffic and also serves as a hub that USB devices connect to. You can connect additional (external) USB hubs to connect multiple USB devices to the host controller, which is also known as the root hub. Hubs are either self-powered or bus-powered. Some devices, such as mice and keyboards, can function fine when plugged into bus-powered USB hubs. Other devices, such as external hard drives, printers, and scanners, might require more power than bus-powered hubs can provide. You should connect these kinds of USB devices to self-powered hubs. USB supports up to a maximum of 127 devices connected to one USB host controller (root hub) with no more than seven tiers (seven layers of USB hubs daisy-chained together). You can use no more than five external hubs in one physical chain of hubs. Each device can be no more than 5 meters away from the port of the hub that it is connected to.

 NOTE USB devices that install and function properly under Windows 98, Windows Me, Windows 2000, or Windows XP are not guaranteed to work under Windows Server 2003. Be sure to check for upgraded drivers before you upgrade a computer to Windows Server 2003. Verify that USB peripherals are on the Windows Server 2003 HCL, or check with the USB device vendor regarding compatibility with Windows Server 2003.

Viewing Power Allocations for USB Hubs

USB devices must share electrical power. The USB root hub is allocated a certain amount of power that any USB hubs and USB devices connected to it must share. As you add USB devices, less power is available to each connected device. To view power allocations for USB hubs, perform the following steps:

1. Open Device Manager.

2. Expand the entry for Universal Serial Bus Controllers.

3. Right-click USB Root Hub and then click Properties.

4. Click the Power tab to view the power consumed by each device in the Attached Devices list.

As mentioned previously, hubs for USB devices are either self-powered or bus-powered. Self-powered hubs (hubs plugged into an electrical outlet) provide maximum power to the device, whereas bus-powered hubs (hubs plugged only into another USB port) provide minimum power. You should plug devices that require a lot of power, such as cameras and hard drives, into self-powered hubs.

In Device Manager, the Universal Serial Bus Controllers node appears only if you have a USB port installed on the computer. The Power tab appears only for USB hubs.

Troubleshooting USB Devices

Sometimes, when you install a USB device on a computer, the computer might start functioning poorly or the system might even freeze entirely. The first step to take in such a scenario is to power off the computer, wait about 60 seconds, and then power it back on. You might even need to completely disconnect the power for some newer devices that are power-management aware. If that doesn't help, try one or more of the following steps:

➤ Follow the manufacturer's installation instructions, which might require that you run a setup program before connecting the USB device to the computer.

➤ Connect the device to a different computer to verify that it is not defective.

➤ Plug the device directly into a USB root hub on the back of the computer instead of plugging it into a USB hub that is daisy-chained off the root hub.

➤ Look at the Windows Server 2003 event log for USB-related error messages.

➤ Check Device Manager to verify that all USB devices on the Universal Serial Bus Controllers tree are operating correctly.

➤ Check whether one or more USB devices are drawing more power (more than 500 milliamps) than the bus or hub can provide. Use a separate power adapter for high power consumption devices (if available) or use a self-powered USB hub for such devices.

➤ Replace the USB cables.

➤ Make sure that no more than five hubs are connected in one continuous chain.

Working with NICs

Most, if not all, NICs on the market today are PnP PCI devices that Windows Server 2003 installs automatically. If necessary, you can attempt to install non-PnP network adapters, or PnP NICs that don't get detected automatically, by using the Add New Hardware applet in the Control Panel. You can access the Network Connections applet from the Control Panel or by clicking Start, Settings, Network Connections if you use the classic Start menu. The options that are available from the Advanced menu of the Network Connections window follow:

➤ *Operator-Assisted Dialing*—You can enable or disable this feature for dial-up connections.

➤ *Remote Access Preferences*—You configure location information for dial-up connections with this option for settings such as country/region, area code/city code, carrier code, outside line access code, and tone or pulse dialing. You also can configure Autodial, Callback, and Diagnostics settings from this option.

➤ *Network Identification*—This option displays the Computer Name tab from the System Properties window where you can change the server's NetBIOS name and join the server to a domain or a workgroup.

➤ *Bridge Connections*—You can join together multiple network connections to form a network bridge by first selecting the connections in the Network Connections window and then clicking this option.

➤ *Advanced Settings*—You can make changes to the binding order of protocols, bind and unbind protocols to network adapters, and modify the network provider order by selecting this option.

➤ *Optional Networking Components*—You can install or remove Windows
  Server 2003 additional networking components such as Management
  and Monitoring Tools, Networking Services, and Other Network File
  and Print Services (such as support for Macintosh and UNIX computers) by selecting this option.

Configuring Networking Connections and Protocols

Each network adapter has its own separate icon in the Network Connections
folder. Right-click a network adapter icon (network connection) to access its
properties. In the properties dialog box, you can install protocols, change
addresses, or perform any other configuration changes for the connection.
The properties window for each network connection has three tabs: General,
Authentication, and Advanced. The General tab displays the network adapter
(NIC) for the connection along with the networking components for the connection. (Client for Microsoft Networks, File and Printer Sharing for
Microsoft Networks, and Internet Protocol are the defaults.) You can also
install, configure, and uninstall networking components from the General tab.

The Authentication tab is where you can enable or disable IEEE 802.1x
authentication, which is enabled by default. You can select the Extensible
Authentication Protocol (EAP) to be used on the system from the EAP Type
drop-down list box: MD5-Challenge, Protected EAP (PEAP), or Smart
Card or Other Certificate (default). The Advanced tab is where you can turn
on or off the Internet Connection Firewall (ICF) feature and the Internet
Connection Sharing (ICS) feature. When you mark the check box for ICF,
you can click the Settings button to configure advanced settings for ICF, as
shown in Figure 2.10. The Services tab for ICF allows you to select which
services (or ports) should be open for passing data through an Internet connection.

TCP/IP is the default protocol installed by Windows Server 2003, and it
cannot be uninstalled. The properties window for Internet Protocol
(TCP/IP) now sports a new tab that was not present under Windows 2000
Server—Alternate Configuration. By using the Alternate Configuration tab,
you can set up alternate IP settings that will be used if no Dynamic Host
Configuration Protocol (DHCP) server is available. By clicking the
Advanced button from the Internet Protocol (TCP/IP) Properties window,
you can add default gateway IP addresses and metrics, configure DNS settings, configure WINS settings, and set up TCP/IP filtering, among other
things.

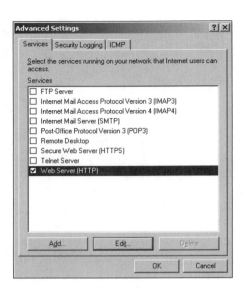

Figure 2.10   The Advanced Settings dialog box for configuring which ports to open for ICF.

Wireless Networking Support

Windows Server 2003 and Windows XP both include support for the IEEE standard 802.11 for wireless networks. The Wireless Configuration service is installed and enabled at startup by default. This service is responsible for handling the automatic configuration of wireless network adapters. Wireless network support under Windows Server 2003 includes a new roaming feature that enables the operating system to detect a move to a new wireless access point and forces re-authentication to verify appropriate network access at a new location. By default, wireless network support under Windows Server 2003 uses the zero client configuration feature to automatically configure and use IEEE 802.1x authentication on the wireless network. (It includes the different "flavors" of wireless networking—802.11a, 802.11b, 802.11g, and so on.) You can configure wireless networking settings by opening the Network Connections applet from the Control Panel, right-clicking the wireless connection you want to modify, and selecting Properties. From the wireless connection's properties dialog box, you can enable or disable the automatic wireless configuration, set up or disable IEEE 802.1x authentication, and specify a connection to a wireless network with or without a Wired Equivalent Privacy (WEP) Network Key, as shown in Figure 2.11.

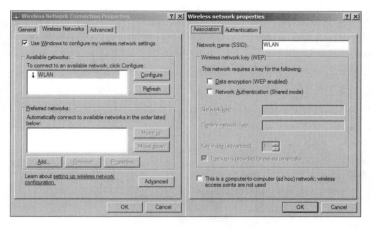

Figure 2.11   Wireless Network Connection properties windows.

Working with Video Display Adapters and Settings

When Windows Server 2003 is installed, your system's BIOS selects the primary video display adapter based on PCI slot order. You can install and configure any additional video adapters you want to use with your system by using the Display applet or the Add Hardware applet in the Control Panel. Video problems often occur for one of three reasons:

➤ An incorrect video device driver is installed.

➤ The display settings for the video adapter are configured incorrectly.

➤ The graphics hardware acceleration setting is set too high.

If you select an incorrect video driver or if you configure a video driver's settings incorrectly, your Windows Server 2003 system can become unusable or even display the dreaded blue screen of death (BSOD). Fortunately, Windows Server 2003 offers several ways to restore the previous (functional) video display settings. When you restart the computer, press the F8 key as Windows Server 2003 is restarting, which enables you to select one of the following options (see Figure 2.12) from the Windows Advanced Options menu:

➤ *Safe Mode*—Enables you to manually update, remove, or even roll back the problem video driver.

➤ *Enable VGA Mode*—Enables you to boot the system using standard VGA 640x480 resolution with just 16 colors. You can then correct any incorrect video settings. Unlike in Safe Mode, all other device drivers are loaded.

➤ *Last Known Good Configuration (Your Most Recent Settings That Worked)*— Enables you to revert the system's Registry and device-driver configurations back to how they were the last time that a user started the computer and logged on successfully.

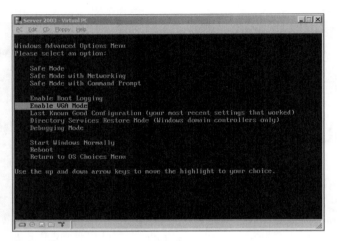

Figure 2.12   The Windows Advanced Options startup menu.

Configuring Multiple-Monitor Support

Windows Server 2003 continues to support multiple-monitor functionality that increases your work productivity by expanding the size of your desktop. Multiple displays still must use PCI or Accelerated Graphics Port (AGP) devices to work properly with Windows Server 2003. PCI or AGP video adapters that are built into the motherboard are also supported under the multiple-monitor feature.

You can connect up to 10 individual monitors to create a server desktop large enough to hold numerous programs, management consoles, and other windows.

You can easily work on more than one task at a time by moving items from one monitor to another or by stretching them across numerous monitors. You can work with the Computer Management console on one monitor while moving users and groups into organizational units (OUs) in the Active Directory Users and Computers MMC snap-in on another. You can also open multiple pages of a single, long document and drag them across several monitors to easily view the layout of text and graphics. You can stretch an Excel workbook across two monitors so that you can view numerous columns without scrolling.

Arranging Multiple Monitors

One monitor serves as the primary display. It is the monitor on which you see the Logon dialog box when you start your computer. Most application programs, system windows, and dialog boxes display themselves on the primary monitor when you initially open them. However, you can rearrange program windows, the Windows Explorer window, dialog boxes, and the like, and you can place them on the monitor of your choice. You can even set different resolutions and different color depths for each monitor. You can also connect multiple monitors to individual graphics adapters or to a single adapter that supports multiple outputs; computers with these types of video display adapters can take full advantage of the DualView feature of multiple-monitor support. To arrange multiple monitors, perform the following steps:

1. Open the Display applet in the Control Panel.

2. Click the Settings tab.

3. Click and drag each monitor icon to the position that represents the physical arrangement of the monitors on your desk. Click either OK or Apply to view the changes. You can also click the Identify button to briefly flash the monitor number on each monitor's screen as assigned by Windows Server 2003.

The positions of the monitor icons determine how you move windows and other objects from one monitor to another. For example, if you are using two monitors and you want to move objects from one monitor to another monitor by dragging them left or right, place the monitor icons side by side, as shown in Figure 2.13. To move objects between monitors by dragging them up and down, place the monitor icons one above the other. The icon positions do not have to correspond to the physical positions of the monitors. You can place the icons one above the other even though your monitors might be situated side by side. In most situations, however, your best move is to make sure that the monitor icons match the physical positions of your monitors.

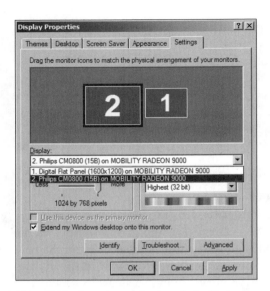

Figure 2.13 Arranging monitor icons in the Display Properties dialog box for the multiple monitor feature.

Troubleshooting the Multiple Monitor Feature

The default refresh frequency setting is typically 60Hz, although your monitors might support a higher setting. A higher refresh frequency might reduce flicker on your screens, but choosing a setting that is too high for your monitor can make your display unusable and might even damage your hardware. If the refresh frequency is set to anything higher than 60Hz and one or more of the monitor displays goes black when you start Windows Server 2003, restart the system in Safe Mode. Change the refresh frequency for all monitors to 60Hz. If you are using unattended installation for servers, you might need to double-check this setting in your unattended installation script file, commonly called unattend.txt, to ensure that it is configured for 60Hz.

Managing Tape Backup Devices

Windows Server 2003 provides you with a high degree of flexibility and control for tape backup devices. You can back up or restore from tape devices, enable or disable specific tapes in your library, insert and eject media, and mount and dismount media. Tape devices are not the only media that the Backup Utility program supports. You can back up to network shares, to local hard drives, or to removable media such as Zip disks, Jaz disks, USB hard drives, and IEEE 1394 (FireWire) hard drives. Backing up to tape is still very popular, however, despite some of its drawbacks.

The Windows Server 2003 Backup Utility does not support backing up directly to CD-R, CD-RW, DVD-R, DVD-RW, DVD+R, or DVD+RW media. You can copy files directly to a CD-R or a CD-RW disc, or you can copy a backup file that was created by the Backup Utility to a CD-R or CD-RW disc. During a restore, the Windows Server 2003 Backup Utility can read directly from CD-R or CD-RW media to perform the restore procedure. Unfortunately, if the backed-up data to be restored exceeds the capacity of a single CD, both the backup and restore procedures become very labor-intensive and not very automated.

If the tape device is PnP-compliant, you can rely on Windows Server 2003 to detect the device and install the appropriate drivers as well as allocate system resources for the device. If you are using a tape device that is not PnP-compliant, use the Add Hardware applet in the Control Panel to install the drivers and assign resources for the device. Use Device Manager to enable, disable, or adjust the settings for any tape device.

Upgrading a System from Uniprocessor to Multiprocessor

Windows Server 2003 supports up to two processors (CPUs) for the Web edition, and it supports more than two processors on the Standard, Enterprise, and Datacenter editions. When more than one processor is present in the computer at the time that the operating system is installed, Windows Server 2003 installs either the ACPI Multiprocessor Hardware Abstraction Layer (HAL) or the MPS Multiprocessor HAL. These HALs allow the operating system to support symmetric multiprocessing (SMP), which spreads different processing tasks among the installed CPUs. However, if Windows Server 2003 is installed with just one CPU present (a uniprocessor system) and you later want to add one or more additional processors (to create a multiprocessor system), you must use the Hardware Update Wizard to install a new HAL, which enables support for multiple processors. To install support for multiple CPUs, perform the following steps:

1. Right-click My Computer and then select Properties.

2. Click the Hardware tab and then click the Device Manager button.

3. Expand the Computer node and note the type of support you currently have.

4. Right-click the icon for the current type of PC that is installed and select Update Driver to launch the Hardware Update Wizard.

5. Select the option Install from a List or Specific Location (Advanced) and click Next.

6. Click the option Don't Search. I Will Choose the Driver to Install and click Next.

7. Select the appropriate type of computer from the Model list box, or click the Have Disk button if you have a disk or CD from the manufacturer, and then click Next.

8. Click Finish to exit from the wizard. You must restart the computer for the change to take effect.

Changing a server's HAL is never a trivial matter. You should take great care whenever attempting to install a HAL. If you upgrade the BIOS from supporting APM to ACPI, you need to reinstall Windows Server 2003 so that the operating system will properly support that type of upgrade.

Supported Multiprocessor HAL Updates

Windows Server 2003 only supports a few very specific HAL updates because of the fact that the installation of an incorrect HAL can render the operating system unusable. For a server with the MPS Multiprocessor HAL installed, you can update the system to either of the following two HAL options:

➤ Standard PC HAL

➤ MPS Multiprocessor HAL (this is a reinstallation option)

For a server with the ACPI Multiprocessor HAL installed, you can update the system to any one of the following three HAL options:

➤ MPS Multiprocessor HAL

➤ ACPI PC HAL

➤ ACPI Multiprocessor HAL (this is a reinstallation option)

You cannot switch to the MPS Uniprocessor HAL or the ACPI Uniprocessor HAL if the computer already has a Multiprocessor HAL installed. To install a Uniprocessor HAL for Multiprocessor HAL systems, you must reinstall Windows Server 2003.

Managing Hardware Profiles

A *hardware profile* stores configuration settings for a collection of devices and services. Windows Server 2003 can store different hardware profiles so that you can meet different needs for various device and service settings depending on the circumstances. One example is a server that might have one or more external hard drives or tape backup drives connected, and perhaps those devices interfere with the server when it's in production; you can disable those devices during production hours. You select hardware profiles when the server boots. Hardware profiles can store alternate network settings and various hardware configuration options that you can select each time the system restarts.

You can enable and disable devices for a specific hardware profile through their properties dialog boxes in Device Manager. You manage enabling and disabling of services in each hardware profile by using the Services MMC snap-in, as shown in Figure 2.14. You create and manage hardware profiles using the System applet in the Control Panel, or by right-clicking My Computer and choosing Properties. Once inside the System applet, click the Hardware tab and click the Hardware Profiles button to open the Hardware Profiles dialog box, shown in Figure 2.15. At installation, Windows Server 2003 creates a single hardware profile called Profile 1 (Current), which you can rename later. You are only prompted to select a hardware profile at system startup when two or more hardware profiles are stored on your machine. You can create and store as many hardware profiles on your machine as you like. You select the desired hardware profile at Windows Server 2003 startup to specify which device and service configuration settings you need for the current session.

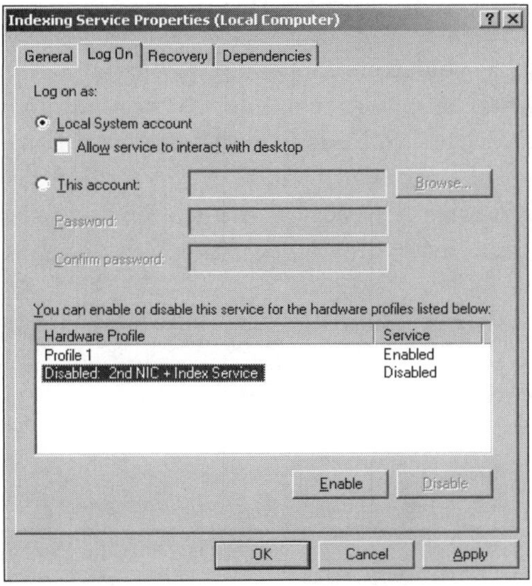

Figure 2.14 Disabling the indexing service for a specific hardware profile.

To configure a hardware profile, copy the default profile and rename it appropriately. Restart the computer and select the profile you want to configure, if you are configuring hardware devices. From Device Manager, in the properties dialog box for any device, you can specify whether that device is enabled or disabled for the current profile. To configure services, you can specify which hardware profile a particular service is enabled or disabled for; the computer does not need to be restarted with a specific hardware profile when you configure services.

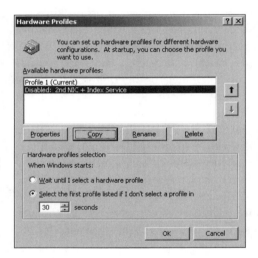

Figure 2.15   Working with the Hardware Profiles dialog box.

If Windows Server 2003 detects that your computer is a portable (laptop or notebook), it tries to determine whether your system is docked or undocked; it then selects the appropriate hardware profile for the current conditions. When more than one hardware profile is present, Windows Server 2003 displays the Hardware Profile/Configuration Recovery menu each time the computer restarts, as shown in Figure 2.16.

Do not confuse hardware profiles with user profiles: The two are not related! Hardware profiles deal with devices and services settings for the entire computer; user profiles deal with user configuration settings for individual users.

Figure 2.16   The Hardware Profile/Configuration Recovery menu.

Managing Card Services

Card services play an important role in Windows Server 2003 for security purposes due to the compact size and tamper-resistant qualities of today's high-tech card-like devices. Support for card services includes PC Cards as peripheral devices and smart-card technology for logon authentication. The operating system supports both the PC Card (formerly known as PCMCIA) standard as well as the CardBus (PC Card 32) standard. The many benefits of these devices include their convenient size, low power requirements, and support for the PnP standard. The CardBus specification is a combination of the PC Card 16 standard and the Peripheral Component Interconnect (PCI) standard. This combination provides 32-bit performance and the PCI bus in a compact, portable package. You can find several types of PC Cards that are often used in mobile computers: network adapter cards, hard drive cards, modem cards, wireless network cards, and so on.

Smart Cards

Support for smart card technology is fully integrated into Windows Server 2003. Smart cards play an important role in Windows Server 2003's Public Key Infrastructure (PKI) security architecture for logon authentication and other security-related services. Smart cards are credit card–size devices that have integrated circuits built into them. These electronic cards securely store both public and private encryption keys and also perform cryptographic functions such as digital-signature and key-exchange operations.

Windows Server 2003 and Windows XP support only PnP-compliant smart card reader devices. Smart card readers connect to standard PC interfaces such as serial (RS-232) ports, PS/2 ports, USB ports, and PC Card slots. To install a smart card reader, use the Add Hardware applet in the Control Panel. Smart card configurations typically use the Extensible Authentication Protocol-Transport Level Security (EAP-TLS) authentication protocol. When you use a smart card to log on to a Windows Server 2003 computer, or to log on to a Windows XP Professional computer, at least one Cryptographic Service Provider (CSP) service must be installed and running on the system. CSPs enable other application programs to have access to the cryptographic services of a smart card, such as digital signature, key generation, and key exchange.

Before a user can log on to a system with a smart card, the user must be enrolled for a smart card certificate by an administrator who has the proper security privileges to enroll other users. This enrollment process creates a certificate and a public encryption key for the user. The user also needs to create or to be assigned a personal identification number (PIN) code, which he or she must use in conjunction with the smart card when logging on to a smart card–enabled computer.

Exam Prep Questions

Question 1

> Tim is a network administrator for his company. One of the company's servers has just been upgraded to Windows Server 2003 from Windows 2000 Server. Unfortunately, one of the internal SCSI adapters cannot be installed because the operating system cannot find a suitable driver for it. Each time the system restarts, the PnP feature attempts to install the SCSI adapter without any success. Which is the easiest and fastest way to avoid having Windows Server 2003 try to install the device until the manufacturer publishes a driver that is compatible with Windows Server 2003?
>
> ○ A. Uninstall the SCSI adapter in Device Manager.
>
> ○ B. Physically remove the SCSI adapter from the server.
>
> ○ C. In Device Manager, right-click the SCSI adapter and Select Disable.
>
> ○ D. Create a new hardware profile, restart the server using the new hardware profile, and disable the SCSI adapter for the new hardware profile.

Answer C is correct because it offers the easiest and fastest way to stop Windows Server 2003 from repeatedly attempting to install a driver for the SCSI device. Answer A is incorrect because it would only result in having the operating system redetect the device each time it restarts and then it would continue to try to install the device. Answer B is incorrect because you would have to take the server out of production to power it down and physically remove the SCSI adapter. Answer D is incorrect because it is easier to simply disable the device until a suitable driver becomes available instead of creating a new hardware profile and having to restart the computer under that profile to disable the SCSI adapter.

Question 2

> Which of the following unsigned driver options are available under Windows Server 2003 from the graphical user interface? (Choose three.)
>
> ❑ A. Install for administrators only
>
> ❑ B. Ignore
>
> ❑ C. Prompt
>
> ❑ D. Block
>
> ❑ E. Warn
>
> ❑ F. PnP drivers only

Answers B, D, and E are correct. Answers A, C, and F are incorrect because Windows Server 2003 offers only three options for unsigned driver installation behavior from the System Properties window—Ignore, Warn, or Block.

Question 3

On which types of media does Windows Server 2003 support the Universal Disk Format (UDF)? (Choose two.)

- ❏ A. Hard disks
- ❏ B. Floppy disks
- ❏ C. CD-ROMs
- ❏ D. DVDs
- ❏ E. Zip disks

Answers C and D are correct because Windows Server 2003 supports UDF on DVD, CD-R, and CD-RW media for read-only access. Answers A, B, and E are incorrect because UDF is not supported on hard disks, floppy disks, or Zip disks.

Question 4

Brendan is a network administrator who is responsible for deploying 1,000 new Windows XP Professional desktop computers within an Active Directory domain in a Windows Server 2003 network environment. What is the easiest, most dynamic, and most effective way for him to ensure that all the new desktop computers do not allow any unsigned device drivers to be installed?

- ○ A. Set the Unsigned Driver Options to Block in the System Properties window for a model computer. Then, image that model machine using the Sysprep tool and a third-party disk cloning software utility, such as Ghost, and copy the image to each of the 1,000 new workstations.
- ○ B. Use a GPO for the Default Domain Policy, or create a GPO for an OU where all the workstations will be placed. In the GPO, go to the Computer Policy, Security Settings, Local Policies, Security Options node. Set the Devices: Unsigned Driver Installation Behavior policy to Do Not Allow Installation. Mark the No Override check box for the GPO.
- ○ C. Keep the default installation setting for Unsigned Driver Options under Windows XP Professional because it is Block—Never Install Unsigned Driver Software.
- ○ D. As a local computer policy, set the Devices: Unsigned Driver Installation Behavior policy to Do Not Allow Installation for a model computer. Then, image that model machine using the Sysprep tool and a third-party disk cloning software utility, such as Ghost, and copy the image to each of the 1,000 new workstations.

Answer B is correct because using a GPO setting for the domain or for the OU in which the workstations are placed is the fastest and easiest way to implement an unsigned driver signing policy. A GPO setting is also the most flexible because you can change it at any time, and the change will be propagated to all the workstations simultaneously. Answer A is incorrect because setting a local configuration and imaging it out is only a static solution and the local configuration can be overridden by a GPO setting. Answer C is incorrect because the default setting for Unsigned Driver Options is not Block, it is Warn—Prompt Me Each Time to Choose an Action. Answer D is incorrect because disk cloning solutions create static configurations rather than configurations that you can easily change later on a mass scale, such as GPO settings.

Question 5

If you have a USB device that requires more than 450 milliamps of electrical power, which courses of action would be appropriate to take as a server administrator for Windows Server 2003? (Choose three.)

❑ A. Disconnect all other USB devices from the server and only connect that one device.

❑ B. Use a separate power adapter for the USB device and connect it along with any other USB devices to the USB root hub or into a daisy-chained hub.

❑ C. Connect the USB device into a self-powered USB hub.

❑ D. You cannot use a USB device that requires more than 450 milliamps of power under Windows Server 2003.

❑ E. Purchase and install an adapter for the USB device that allows it to be plugged into an IEEE 1394 (FireWire) port so that the device has access to more power.

❑ F. Purchase and install an adapter for the USB device that allows it to be plugged into a high-speed bidirectional parallel port so that the device has access to more power.

Answers A, B, and C are correct. Windows Server 2003 provides up to 500 milliamps of power for any and all connected USB devices; each USB device must share this power allocation with all the other connected USB devices. If only one device is connected, it can use all the allocated power. If the device supports its own separate power adapter, it can get the extra power it needs from the power adapter. If you connect the device to a USB powered hub, the powered hub can provide the additional power. Answer D is incorrect because there is no 450 milliamp limitation for connecting USB devices under Windows Server 2003. Answer E is incorrect because you cannot plug a USB device into an IEEE 1394 port to gain more power for the USB device. Answer F is incorrect because you cannot plug a USB device into a high-speed bidirectional parallel port to gain more power for the USB device.

Question 6

Mike is a network administrator for XYZ Corporation. Mike is responsible for managing a Windows Server 2003 computer that currently has several USB devices connected to several different USB hubs that are all plugged into the root USB hub on the back of the server. Management tells Mike to purchase and install a USB scanner on the server. Mike buys the scanner, connects it to a 12-foot USB cable, and plugs the cable into one of the daisy-chained hubs. The server does not detect the new USB scanner. Even when Mike attempts to use the Add Hardware Wizard, the server cannot detect the device. What is the most likely cause of this problem?

○ A. The 12-foot long USB cable exceeds the supported length for USB cabling.

○ B. The scanner is not PnP-compliant because it also has a SCSI interface connection.

○ C. USB scanners can only be connected to USB root hubs to function properly.

○ D. The USB hub that the scanner is connected to happens to be the sixth hub in a daisy-chained row of hubs.

Answer D is correct. Windows Server 2003 only supports daisy-chained USB hubs up to five levels deep in one continuous chain. Answer A is incorrect because USB cables that are 12 feet in length are supported. Answer B is incorrect because, by definition, all USB-compatible devices are PnP-compliant. Answer C is incorrect because USB scanners do not need to be connected to USB root hubs to function properly; however, they usually require their own separate power adapters.

Question 7

Under Windows Server 2003, where can you change the network binding order of protocols in addition to unbinding protocols to network adapters?

○ A. From the Network Connections window, click the Advanced menu and then select Advanced Settings.

○ B. From the Network Connections window, click the Advanced menu and then select Optional Networking Components.

○ C. In Device Manager, right-click Network Adapters and then click Properties.

○ D. In Device Manager, right-click a network adapter name, select Properties, and click the Advanced tab.

Answer A is correct. You can change network protocol binding order and you can bind and unbind protocols to network adapters from the Advanced Settings dialog box off the Advanced menu in the Network Connections window. Answer B is incorrect because the protocol binding options do not appear under Optional Networking Components. Answers C and D are incorrect because you cannot change protocol bindings from Device Manager.

Question 8

How can you set up a new hardware profile for disabling a network interface card on a Windows Server 2003 computer? (Choose two.)

❑ A. Copy an existing profile from the Hardware Profiles dialog box and name it **NIC Disabled** by clicking the Hardware Profiles button on the System Properties window.

❑ B. Create a new hardware profile by copying the **LocalService** folder in the **%systemdrive%\Documents and Settings** folder and name it **NIC Disabled**.

❑ C. In Device Manager, right-click the device and select Properties. Click the Log on tab, select the Hardware Profile NIC Disabled, and click Disable.

❑ D. Restart the system under the new profile named NIC Disabled option. Open Device Manager, right-click the network interface card that you want to disable and select Disable.

❑ E. Create a new user account named **NIC Disabled** and log on using that user account each time that you want the computer to start up with the NIC disabled.

Answers A and D are correct. You create hardware profiles by either renaming an existing profile or copying an existing profile from the Hardware Profiles dialog box. You must first create a hardware profile and then start the server under that profile to enable or disable devices for that profile. Answer B is incorrect because you cannot create hardware profiles from the `%systemdrive%\Documents and Settings` folder. Answer C is incorrect because devices do not have a Log on tab for their properties windows; you configure services for hardware profiles in this manner. Answer E is incorrect because you cannot implement a hardware profile by creating any type of user account, nor by logging onto the computer under a particular user account.

Question 9

Which of the following types of removable media can Windows Server 2003 write to without requiring any third-party software? (Choose three.)

- ❑ A. Zip disks
- ❑ B. CD-R discs
- ❑ C. CD-RW discs
- ❑ D. DVD+R discs
- ❑ E. DVD-RW discs
- ❑ F. DVD-R discs
- ❑ G. DVD+RW discs

Answers A, B, and C are correct because Windows Server 2003 does support reading and writing to Zip disks, CD-R, and CD-RW media. Answers D, E, F, and G are incorrect because Windows Server 2003 does not support writing to DVD media without third-party software. However, it can read from DVD media.

Question 10

If you add a second processor to a Windows Server 2003, Web Edition computer after the operating system has already been installed, what procedure must you follow for Windows Server 2003 to take advantage of that second processor?

- ○ A. Reinstall the operating system.
- ○ B. The Web Edition does not support more than one processor.
- ○ C. Upgrade the HAL driver from Uniprocessor to Multiprocessor in Device Manager.
- ○ D. Upgrade the HAL driver from Uniprocessor to DualProcessor in Device Manager.

Answer C is correct. All editions of Windows Server 2003 support at least up to two processors: you use Device Manager to right-click the computer type (HAL) and select Update Driver from the right-click menu to launch the Hardware Update Wizard. Answer A is incorrect because you do not need to reinstall the operating system to add support for a second processor. Answer B is incorrect because all editions support at least two processors. Answer D is incorrect because Windows Server 2003 allows you switch from a Uniprocessor HAL to a Multiprocessor HAL, but you cannot switch from a Multiprocessor HAL to a Uniprocessor HAL.

Need to Know More?

 Boswell, William. *Inside Microsoft Windows Server 2003*. Boston, Massachusetts: Addison-Wesley Professional, 2003.

 Scales, Lee, and John Michell. *MCSA/MCSE 70-290 Training Guide: Managing and Maintaining a Windows Server 2003 Environment*. Indianapolis, Indiana: Que Publishing, 2003.

 Stanek, William R. *Microsoft Windows Server 2003 Administrator's Pocket Consultant*. Redmond, Washington: Microsoft Press, 2003.

 Search the Microsoft Product Support Services Knowledge Base on the Internet: http://support.microsoft.com. Find technical information using keywords from this chapter such as driver signing, Plug and Play, Universal Serial Bus, IEEE 1394, and Device Manager.

Managing Server Storage

Terms you'll need to understand:

✓ Basic versus dynamic disks
✓ Partitions and volumes
✓ Simple, spanned, and striped volumes
✓ Mirrored and RAID-5 volumes
✓ **Diskpart.exe** utility

Techniques you'll need to master:

✓ Using the Disk Management console
✓ Using Disk Defragmenter
✓ Configuring and troubleshooting RAID-5 volumes
✓ Configuring and troubleshooting mirrored volumes
✓ Using **diskpart.exe** to manage disk drives and volumes from the command line

Managing server storage is vital for serving the needs of network users and safeguarding their data. If you are familiar with managing hard disks and volumes under Windows 2000, you should feel quite at home working with disk storage administration in Windows Server 2003. You can manage disk storage under Windows Server 2003 using the Disk Management console in both the Server and Professional editions of Windows 2000. For administrators who are more accustomed to working with Windows NT 4.0 Server, Windows Server 2003 will introduce you to some new concepts that appeared in Windows 2000, such as basic and dynamic disk storage. Even so, the Disk Management Microsoft Management Console (MMC) snap-in does share a resemblance to the old Disk Administrator utility of Windows NT 4.0. This chapter focuses on managing data storage in a Windows Server 2003 environment.

Disk Storage Management

Windows Server 2003 supports two types of hard disk designations: basic and dynamic. Microsoft introduced these two concepts with Windows 2000 Server. All disks begin as basic disks until a server administrator converts them to dynamic status, one physical disk at a time. The biggest advantage that dynamic disks have when compared to basic disks is that you can create software-based fault-tolerant volumes via the operating system from the volumes stored on dynamic disks; you cannot create fault-tolerant disk sets (volumes) from partitions stored on basic disks. Fault-tolerant volumes under Windows Server 2003 are mirrored volumes and Redundant Array of Independent Disks level 5 (RAID-5) volumes only. Of course, you can always implement a hardware RAID solution using a RAID controller and the disks can retain their basic status, or they can be converted to dynamic status under Windows Server 2003.

Basic Disks

A basic disk under Windows Server 2003 is essentially the same as the disk configuration under earlier versions of Windows: It is a physical disk with primary and extended partitions. Prior to Windows 2000, Microsoft did not call disks *basic* because that was the only type of disk available. There were no dynamic disks. As long as you use the File Allocation Table (FAT or FAT32) file system, Windows XP Professional and Home editions, Windows 2000, Windows NT, Windows 9x, and the MS-DOS operating systems can access basic disks. You can create up to three primary partitions and one extended partition on a basic disk or four primary partitions. You can create a single extended partition with logical drives on a basic disk. You can also extend a basic partition, but only by using the diskpart.exe command-line tool, which is covered in a note in the section "Partitions and Logical Drives on Basic Disks." Extending a disk "attaches" a second hard disk to an existing hard disk volume while the operating system makes the extra hard disk appear to be part of the original volume, increasing the volume's total size. In other words, you gain more disk storage while maintaining the same drive volume letter.

Basic disks store their configuration information in the Partition Table, which is stored on the first sector of each hard disk. The configuration of a basic disk consists of the partition information on the disk. Fault-tolerant disk sets inherited from Windows NT 4 Server are based on these simple partitions, but they extend the configuration with some extra partition relationship information, which is stored on the first track of the disk. Windows NT 4 Server fault-tolerant disk sets use basic disks.

Under Windows NT 4.0, basic disks can contain spanned volumes (called *volume sets* in Windows NT 4), mirrored volumes (called *mirror sets* in Windows NT 4), striped volumes (called *stripe sets* in Windows NT 4), and RAID-5 volumes (called *stripe sets with parity* in Windows NT 4) that were created using Windows NT 4 or earlier. The section "Basic Partitions" later in this chapter covers these kinds of hard disk configurations. Under Windows Server 2003, Windows XP, and Windows 2000, basic disks cannot contain any of the just mentioned disk configurations; such disk configurations are reserved for dynamic disks. For Windows 2000 and later operating systems, basic disks can store only "partitions"; dynamic disks can store only "volumes."

Mirrored and RAID-5 volumes are fault-tolerant volumes that are only available under the Windows 2000 Server or the Windows Server 2003 family of server operating systems. You cannot create these types of volumes on basic or dynamic disks using a desktop operating system such as Windows XP Professional or Windows 2000 Professional. Fault-tolerant volumes are designed to withstand a single disk failure within a set of disks and to continue functioning until the failed disk is replaced. A mirror set (called a *mirrored volume* in Windows Server 2003) duplicates data to a second physical disk; a stripe set with parity (called a *RAID-5 volume* in Windows Server 2003) writes data across several disks (between 3 and 32 physical disks) and stores parity information across all the drives to be able to retrieve data in the event of a single failed disk. RAID-5 volumes cannot recover data if more than one drive in the set fails at the same time.

Dynamic Disks

A Windows Server 2003 dynamic disk is a physical disk configuration that does not use partitions or logical drives, and the Master Boot Record (MBR) is not used. Instead, the basic partition table is modified and any partition table entries from the MBR are added as part of the Logical Disk Manager (LDR) database that stores dynamic disk information at the end of each dynamic disk. Dynamic disks can be divided into as many as 2,000 separate volumes, but you should limit the number of volumes to 32 for each dynamic disk. Dynamic disks do not have the same limitations as basic disks. For example, you can extend a dynamic disk "on-the-fly" without requiring a reboot. Dynamic disks are associated with disk groups, which are disks that are managed as a collection. This managed collection of disks helps organize dynamic disks. All dynamic disks in a computer are members of the same disk group. Each disk in a disk group stores replicas of the same configuration data. This configuration data is stored in the 1MB LDR region at the end of each dynamic disk.

Dynamic disks support five types of volumes: simple, spanned, mirrored, striped, and RAID-5. (The section "Dynamic Volumes" later in this chapter covers these volumes in detail.) You can extend a volume on a dynamic disk. Dynamic disks can contain a virtually unlimited number of volumes, so you are not restricted to four volumes per disk as you are with basic disks. Regardless of the type of file system, only computers running Windows XP Professional, Windows 2000 Professional or Server, or Windows Server 2003 can directly access dynamic volumes on hard disks that are physically connected to the computer. However, computers running other operating systems can access dynamic volumes remotely when they connect to shared folders over the network.

Dynamic disks are not supported under Windows XP Home edition.

Managing Basic Disks and Dynamic Disks

When you install Windows Server 2003, the system automatically configures the existing hard disks as basic disks, unless they have been configured as dynamic from a previous installation. Windows Server 2003 does not support dynamic disks on mobile PCs (laptops or notebooks). If you're using an older desktop machine that is not Advanced Configuration and Power Interface (ACPI)-compliant, the Convert to Dynamic Disk option (covered in the section "Converting Basic Disks to Dynamic Disks" later in this chapter) is not available. Dynamic disks have some additional limitations. You can install Windows Server 2003 on a dynamic volume that you converted from a basic disk, but you cannot extend either the system or the boot volume on a dynamic disk. Any troubleshooting tools that cannot read the dynamic disk management database work only on basic disks.

Dynamic disks are only supported on computers that use the Small Computer System Interface (SCSI), Fibre Channel, Serial Storage Architecture (SSA), Integrated Drive Electronics (IDE), Enhanced IDE (EIDE), Ultra Direct Memory Access (DMA), or Advanced Technology Attachment (ATA) interfaces. Portable computers, removable disks, and disks connected via Universal Serial Bus (USB) or FireWire (IEEE 1394) interfaces are not supported for dynamic storage. Dynamic disks are also not supported on hard drives with a sector size of less than 512 bytes. Cluster disks—groups of several disks that serve to function as a single disk—are not supported either.

Basic and dynamic disks are nothing more than Windows Server 2003's way of looking at a hard disk configuration. If you're migrating to Windows Server 2003 from Windows NT 4, the dynamic disk concept might seem odd in the beginning, but once you understand the differences, working with dynamic disks is not complicated. You can format partitions with the FAT16, FAT32, or New Technology File System (NTFS) on a basic or a dynamic disk. However, you can only format a dynamic volume as NTFS from the Disk Management console because NTFS is the most stable, secure, and feature-rich file system for Windows Server 2003. You must use Windows Server 2003 Explorer to format a dynamic volume as FAT or FAT32. Table 3.1 compares the terms used with basic and dynamic disks.

Table 3.1 Terms Used with Basic and Dynamic Disks	
Basic Disks	**Dynamic Disks**
Active partition	Active volume
Extended partition	(Not applicable)
Logical drive	Simple volume
Mirror set	Mirrored volume (servers only)
Primary partition	Simple volume
Stripe set	Striped volume
Stripe set with parity	RAID-5 volume (servers only)
System and boot partitions	System and boot volumes
Volume set	Spanned volume

Windows Server does not support formatting partitions or volumes larger than 32GB as FAT32. Partitions or volumes larger than 32GB that have been upgraded from previous operating systems can be mounted and used under Windows Server 2003. Partitions or volumes larger than 32GB that have been created by third-party utilities can also be mounted and used under Windows Server 2003.

When you install a fresh copy of Windows Server 2003 or when you perform an upgrade installation from Windows NT 4.0 Server with SP5, the computer system defaults to basic disk storage. One or more of the disk drives could already be configured as dynamic if you upgraded from Windows 2000 Server (or if you import a "foreign disk" from a Windows 2000 Server or from another Windows Server 2003 computer). A disk is considered "foreign" when you move it from one computer to another computer, until you select the import option for it in the Disk Management console. Dynamic disks are proprietary to Windows Server 2003, Windows 2000, and Windows XP Professional. On desktop operating systems, such as Windows 2000 Professional and Windows XP Professional, dynamic disks provide support for advanced disk configurations, such as disk striping and disk spanning. On Windows Server 2003 and Windows 2000 Server computers, dynamic disks provide support for fault-tolerant configurations, such as disk mirroring and disk striping with parity (also known as RAID-5).

Converting Basic Disks to Dynamic Disks

From the graphical user interface (GUI), you use the Windows Server 2003 Disk Management console (an MMC snap-in) to upgrade a basic disk to a dynamic disk. To access Disk Management, click Start, Administrative Tools, Computer Management or right-click the My Computer icon on the Start menu and click Manage. If you are using the Classic Start menu, click Start, Administrative Tools, Computer Management or simply right-click the My Computer icon on the desktop and select Manage. You'll find Disk Management by expanding the Storage folder. You must be a member of the local Administrators group or the Backup Operators group, or else the proper authority must be delegated to you if you are working within an Active Directory environment to make any changes to the computer's disk-management configuration.

For the conversion to succeed, any disks to be converted must contain at least 1MB of unallocated space. Disk Management automatically reserves this space when creating partitions or volumes on a disk, but disks with partitions or volumes created by other operating systems might not have this space available. (This space can exist even if it is not visible in Disk Management.) Windows Server 2003 requires this minimal amount of disk space to store the dynamic database, which is maintained by the operating system that created it. Before you convert any disks, close any programs that are running on those disks. After you convert a disk to dynamic, remember that you can have only one operating system that is bootable on each dynamic disk!

NOTE Many third-party disk partitioning utilities do not automatically leave the necessary 1MB of space at the end of a disk for converting a basic disk to dynamic. If you use tools such as Partition Magic, you need to manually allocate the required 1MB of disk space with these tools.

To convert a basic disk to a dynamic disk from the Disk Management console, perform the following steps:

1. Open the Disk Management console.

2. Right-click the basic disk you that want to convert to a dynamic disk and then click Convert to Dynamic Disk (see Figure 3.1).

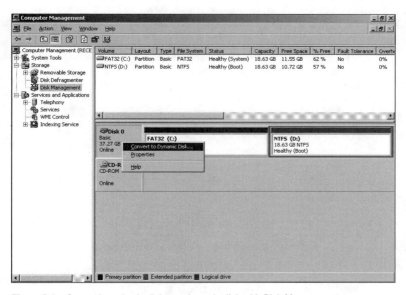

Figure 3.1   Converting a basic disk to a dynamic disk with Disk Management.

When you upgrade an empty basic disk to a dynamic disk, you do not need to reboot. However, if you convert a basic disk that already has partitions on it, or if the basic disk contains the system or boot partitions, you must restart your computer for the change to take effect. The good news is that you do not need to select a special command such as Commit Changes Now (as with Windows NT 4.0) before restarting your computer or closing the Disk Management tool.

If you use a basic disk for storing volume shadow copies of files using the Volume Shadow Copy service (VSS), you must take special measures to avoid losing shadow-copy data if you convert the disk to a dynamic disk. For a nonboot volume that stores shadow copy data for a different volume, you first need to dismount the volume where the original files are stored. After you take that volume offline, you should convert the basic disk containing the shadow-copy volume to a dynamic disk. Immediately following the conversion, you must bring the volume that holds the original files back online within 20 minutes or you will lose the existing shadow-copy data for that volume. If the shadow-copy volume is also the boot volume, you can convert the disk to dynamic without having to take the original volume offline to avoid losing shadow-copy data.

 You can mount and dismount volumes from the command line with the **mountvol.exe** command. On basic disks, if you type **mountvol** *x:* **/p**, where *x:* represents the volume's drive letter, you can dismount a volume and take it offline. Unfortunately, the **/p** parameter is not supported on dynamic disks. The command **mountvol** *x:* **/l** displays the specified drive letter's volume ID. By using the syntax **mountvol** *x:* *volume_ID*, you can assign a drive letter to the volume and remount it to bring it back online. For example, the command **mountvol S: \\?\Volume{55e769f0-40d5-11d4-b223-806d6172696f}** would assign drive letter S: to the volume ID specified. You can also use Disk Management to mount and dismount volumes from the GUI. You can mount and dismount volumes by right-clicking a volume and selecting Change Drive Letter and Paths. By removing the drive letter and any other paths (mount points) for the volume, you take the volume offline.

To convert a basic disk to a dynamic disk from the Windows Server 2003 command line, perform these steps:

1. Open a command prompt window, type `diskpart`, and press Enter.

2. Type `commands` or `help` to view a list of available commands.

3. Type `select disk 0` to select the first hard disk (`select disk 1` to select the second hard disk, and so on) and press Enter.

4. Type `convert dynamic` and press Enter (see Figure 3.2).

5. Type `exit` to quit the `diskpart.exe` tool and then restart the computer to have the new configuration take effect.

 In addition to the **diskpart** command, Windows Server 2003 administrators can take advantage of another command-line tool for managing FAT, FAT32, and NTFS file systems—**fsutil.exe**. With **fsutil**, Windows Server 2003 administrators can perform tasks such as managing disk quotas, managing mount points, and several other advanced disk-related tasks. Type **fsutil** at a command prompt to view a list of supported commands.

When you convert a basic disk to a dynamic disk, any existing partitions on the basic disk become simple volumes on the dynamic disk. Any existing mirror sets, stripe sets, stripe sets with parity, or volume sets become mirrored volumes, striped volumes, dynamic RAID-5 volumes, or spanned volumes, respectively. Once you convert a basic disk to a dynamic disk, you cannot change the volumes back to partitions. Instead, you must first delete all dynamic volumes on the disk, right-click the disk in Disk Management, and then select the Convert to Basic Disk option.

Figure 3.2 Using the **diskpart.exe** command-line tool to convert a basic disk to a dynamic disk.

 Converting to a dynamic disk is a one-way process. Yes, you can convert a dynamic disk back to a basic disk, but you'll lose all your data. Obviously, this loss is a major consideration! If you find yourself needing to do it, first back up your data and then you can delete all the volumes on the disk, convert the disk to basic, and restore your data.

Because the conversion process from basic to dynamic is per physical disk, a disk will have all dynamic volumes or all basic partitions. Remember, you do not need to restart your computer when you upgrade from an empty basic to a dynamic disk from the Disk Management console. However, you do have to restart your computer if you use the diskpart.exe command-line tool for the conversion; if you convert a disk containing the system volume, boot volume, or a volume with an active paging file; or if the disk contains any existing volumes or partitions.

 When you upgrade or convert a basic disk to a dynamic disk, at least 1MB of free space must be available for the dynamic disk database. Under normal circumstances, this requirement should not be a problem.

Converting Dynamic Disks Back to Basic Disks

You must remove all volumes (and therefore all data) from a dynamic disk before you can change it back to a basic disk. After you convert a dynamic disk back to a basic disk, you can only create partitions and logical drives on that disk. After being converted from a basic disk, a dynamic disk can no longer contain partitions or logical drives, nor can any operating systems other than Windows Server 2003, Windows 2000, or Windows XP Professional access it. To revert a dynamic disk to a basic disk, perform the following steps:

1. Back up the data on the dynamic disk.

2. Open Disk Management.

3. Delete all the volumes on the disk.

4. Right-click the dynamic disk that you want to change back to a basic disk and then click Convert to Basic Disk.

5. Restore the data to the newly converted basic disk.

Moving Disks to Another Computer

To move disks to another computer, perform the following steps:

1. Before you disconnect the disks, use Disk Management on the source computer and make sure the status of all volumes on each of the disks is healthy. For any volumes that are not healthy, repair the volumes before you move the disks.

2. If the disks are dynamic, right-click each disk and select Remove Disk.

3. Power off the computer, remove the physical disks, and then install the physical disks on the target computer.

4. When you restart the target computer, the Found New Hardware dialog box should appear. If not, click Start, Control Panel, Add Hardware to launch the Add Hardware Wizard. Use the wizard to properly install the disks on the computer.

5. Open Disk Management on the target computer.

6. Click Action, Rescan Disks from the menu bar.

7. For any disks that are labeled Foreign, right-click on them, click Import Foreign Disks, and then follow the instructions provided by the Disk Management console.

You can move dynamic disks only to Windows Server 2003, Windows 2000, or Windows XP Professional computers.

Reactivating a Missing or Offline Disk

A dynamic disk can become "missing" or "offline" when it is somehow damaged, it suddenly loses power, or it has its data cable disconnected while still powered on. Unfortunately, you can reactivate only dynamic disks—not basic disks.

To reactivate a missing or offline dynamic disk, perform the following steps:

1. Launch the Disk Management console.

2. Right-click the disk marked Missing or Offline and then select the Reactivate Disk option.

3. After the disk is reactivated, the disk should be labeled as "online."

4. Exit from the Disk Management MMC.

Basic Partitions

Basic disks include partitions and logical drives, as well as special partition sets created using Windows NT 4.0 or earlier operating systems. Before Windows 2000, basic disks contained all partition types: primary partitions, extended partitions with logical drives, volume sets, stripe sets, mirror sets, and stripe sets with parity (also known as RAID-5 sets). For Windows Server 2003, Windows 2000, and Windows XP Professional, these volumes can be created only on dynamic disks and they have been renamed to simple volumes, spanned volumes, striped volumes, mirrored volumes, and RAID-5 volumes. Under Windows Server 2003, you can create basic partitions on basic disks only. In addition, you can create fault-tolerant volumes (mirrored volumes and RAID-5 volumes) only on dynamic disks under the Windows 2000 Server or the Windows Server 2003 operating systems. See the upcoming section "Dynamic Volumes" to find out how to migrate data from striped sets or volume sets that are stored on a basic disk under Windows NT 4.0 Workstation or Windows 2000 Professional.

 Only Microsoft server operating systems support fault-tolerant features such as mirrored volumes and RAID-5 volumes. Windows Server 2003 and Windows 2000 Server operating systems require fault-tolerant volumes to be stored on dynamic disks. Desktop (client-side) operating systems, such as Windows XP Professional and Windows 2000 Professional, do not support any type of fault-tolerant volumes, even though they do support dynamic disks.

Partitions and Logical Drives on Basic Disks

You can create primary partitions, extended partitions, and logical drives only on basic disks. You should create basic disks rather than dynamic disks if your computer also runs a down-level Microsoft operating system, such as Windows NT 4.0 Server. You must be a member of the local Administrators group or the Backup Operators group, or else the proper authority must be delegated to you (if you are working within an Active Directory environment) to create, modify, or delete basic volumes.

Partitions and logical drives can reside only on basic disks. You can create up to four primary partitions on a basic disk or up to three primary partitions and one extended partition. You can use the free space in an extended partition to create multiple logical drives.

 You can extend a basic partition, but it must be formatted as NTFS, it must be adjacent to contiguous unallocated space on the same physical disk, and it can be extended only onto unallocated space that resides on the same physical disk. With these requirements met, you can only perform the extension using the **diskpart.exe** command-line utility.

 On a local computer set up in a dual-boot configuration, you should create basic partitions on basic disks. In this way, the computer can run earlier versions of Microsoft operating systems (prior to Windows 2000), and those earlier versions will be able to access those basic partitions (drive letters). For example, if a computer dual boots between Windows Server 2003 and Windows NT 4.0 Server, the Windows NT 4.0 Server operating system would not be able to access any data stored on a dynamic disk on the same computer.

Creating or Deleting a Partition or Logical Drive

To create or delete a partition or logical drive, you can use the `diskpart.exe` command-line tool or use the GUI and perform the following steps:

1. Open the Disk Management console.

2. Perform one of the following options:

   ➤ Right-click an unallocated region of a basic disk and click New Partition.

   ➤ Right-click an area of free space within an extended partition and click New Logical Drive.

   ➤ Right-click a partition or logical drive and select Delete Partition to remove that partition or logical drive. Click Yes to confirm the deletion.

3. When you choose to create a new partition or logical drive, the New Partition Wizard appears. Click Next to continue.

4. Click Primary Partition, Extended Partition, or Logical Drive and answer the prompts regarding disk space allocation and so on as requested by the wizard to finish the process.

You must first create an extended partition before you can create a new logical drive, if no extended partition exists already. If you choose to delete a partition, all data on the deleted partition or logical drive is lost. You cannot recover deleted partitions or logical drives. You cannot delete the system partition, boot partition, or any partition that contains an active paging file. The operating system uses one or more paging files on disk as virtual memory that can be swapped into and out of the computer's physical random access memory (RAM) as the system's load and volume of data dictate.

 Windows Server 2003 requires that you delete all logical drives and any other partitions that have not been assigned a drive letter within an extended partition before you delete the extended partition itself.

Dynamic Volumes

What were called sets (such as mirror sets and stripe sets) under previous operating systems are now called volumes (such as mirrored volumes and striped volumes) in Windows Server 2003, Windows 2000, and Windows XP. Dynamic volumes are the only type of volume that you can create on dynamic disks. With dynamic disks, you are no longer limited to four volumes per disk (as you are with basic disks). You can install Windows Server 2003 onto a dynamic volume; however, these volumes must contain the partition table (which means that these volumes must have been converted from basic to dynamic under Windows Server 2003, Windows XP Professional, or Windows 2000). You cannot install Windows Server 2003 onto dynamic volumes that you created directly from unallocated space. Only computers running Windows XP Professional, the Windows 2000 family of operating systems, or the Windows Server 2003 family of products can access dynamic volumes. The five types of dynamic volumes are simple, spanned, mirrored, striped, and RAID-5. Windows Server 2003 supports all five dynamic volume types. Windows XP Professional and Windows 2000 Professional support only simple, spanned, and striped dynamic volumes. You must be a member of the local Administrators group or the Backup Operators group, or you must have the proper permissions delegated to you (if you are working within an Active Directory environment) to create, modify, or delete dynamic volumes.

 When you create dynamic volumes on dynamic disks using the Disk Management console, you only have the option of formatting new dynamic volumes with the NTFS file system. However, you can use the **format.exe** command at a command prompt window to format a dynamic volume using the FAT or FAT32 file system. For example, you can create a new dynamic volume using Disk Management; do not format the drive, and be sure to assign a drive letter to it. Then, at a command prompt, type **format x: /fs:fat32**, where *x* represents the drive letter and **fat32** represents the file system that you want to format on the volume. You can alternatively specify **fat** or **ntfs** as the file system when you use the **format** command.

Simple Volumes

A simple volume consists of disk space on a single physical disk. It can consist of a single area on a disk or multiple areas on the same disk that are linked together. To create a simple volume, perform the following steps:

1. Open Disk Management.

2. Right-click the unallocated space on the dynamic disk where you want to create the simple volume and then click New Volume.

3. Using the New Volume Wizard, click Next, click Simple, and then follow the instructions and answer the questions asked by the wizard.

Here are some guidelines about simple volumes:

➤ You can create simple volumes on dynamic disks only.

➤ Simple volumes are not fault tolerant.

➤ Simple volumes cannot contain partitions or logical drives.

➤ Neither MS-DOS nor Windows operating systems other than Windows Server 2003, Windows XP Professional, and Windows 2000 can access simple volumes.

Spanned Volumes

A spanned volume consists of disk space from more than one physical disk. You can add more space to a spanned volume by extending it at any time. To create a spanned volume, perform the following steps:

1. Open Disk Management.

2. Right-click the unallocated space on one of the dynamic disks where you want to create the spanned volume and then click New Volume.

3. Using the New Volume Wizard, click Next, click Spanned, and then follow the instructions and answer the questions asked by the wizard.

Here are some guidelines about spanned volumes:

➤ You can create spanned volumes on dynamic disks only.

➤ You need at least two dynamic disks to create a spanned volume.

➤ You can extend a spanned volume onto a maximum of 32 dynamic disks.

➤ Spanned volumes cannot be mirrored or striped.

➤ Spanned volumes are not fault tolerant.

Extending Simple or Spanned Volumes

Simple volumes are the most basic volumes on dynamic disks. If you extend a simple volume to another dynamic disk, it automatically becomes a spanned volume. You can extend a simple volume to make it a spanned volume, and you can also further extend a spanned volume to add disk storage capacity to the volume. To extend a simple or a spanned volume, perform the following steps:

1. Open Disk Management.

2. Right-click the simple or spanned volume you want to extend, click Extend Volume, and then follow the instructions and answer the questions asked by the Extend Volume Wizard.

You should be aware of the many rules about extending a simple or a spanned volume:

➤ You can extend a volume only if it contains no file system or if it is formatted using NTFS. You cannot extend volumes formatted using FAT or FAT32.

➤ After a volume is extended onto multiple disks (spanned), you cannot mirror the volume, nor can you make it into a striped volume or a RAID-5 volume.

➤ You cannot extend boot volumes, system volumes, striped volumes, mirrored volumes, and RAID-5 volumes.

➤ After a spanned volume is extended, no portion of it can be deleted without the entire spanned volume being deleted.

➤ You can extend a simple or a spanned volume only if the volume was created as a dynamic volume under Windows Server 2003. You cannot extend a simple or spanned volume that was originally converted from basic to dynamic under Windows 2000 or Windows XP Professional.

➤ You can extend simple and spanned volumes on dynamic disks onto a maximum of 32 dynamic disks.

➤ Spanned volumes write data only to subsequent disks as each disk volume fills up. Therefore, a spanned volume writes data to physical disk 0 until it fills up, then it writes to physical disk 1 until its available space is full, then it writes to physical disk 2, and so on. However, if just one disk fails as part of the spanned volume—*all of the data contained on that spanned volume is lost.*

Which One Is the Boot Partition or Volume?

The boot partition is a partition on a basic disk that contains the Windows Server 2003 operating system files; the default location is **C:\Windows**. The boot volume is the same as the boot partition, but the term *volume* is used when it is located on a dynamic disk.

The system partition is a partition on a basic disk that stores the files necessary for the operating system to load when the computer is starting up, such as the **ntldr** file, **ntdetect.com**, and **boot.ini**. The system volume is the same as the system partition, but the term *volume* is used when it is located on a dynamic disk. The system partition or volume is often the same as the boot partition or volume, but of course, this setup is not required and many times the operating system files are stored in an entirely different partition or volume. Just remember:

➤ *Boot*—The drive letter where the \Windows (**%windir%**) folder is located.

➤ *System*—The drive letter where the computer's boot-up files are located, usually the C: drive.

Seems backward, doesn't it?

Striped Volumes

A striped volume stores data in stripes on two or more physical disks. Data in a striped volume is allocated alternately and evenly (in stripes) to the disks contained within the striped volume. Striped volumes can substantially improve the speed of access to the data on disk. Striped volumes are often referred to as RAID-0; this configuration tends to enhance performance, but it is not fault tolerant. To create a striped volume, perform the following steps:

1. Open Disk Management.

2. Right-click unallocated space on one of the dynamic disks where you want to create the striped volume and select New Volume from the menu that appears.

3. Using the New Volume Wizard, click Next, select the Striped option, and follow the instructions and answer the questions asked by the wizard.

Here are some guidelines about striped volumes:

➤ You need at least two physical dynamic disks to create a striped volume.

➤ You can create a striped volume onto a maximum of 32 disks.

➤ Striped volumes are not fault tolerant.

➤ For increased volume capacity, select disks that contain similar amounts of available disk space. A striped volume's capacity is limited to the space available on the disk with the smallest amount of available space.

➤ Whenever possible, use disks that are the same model and from the same manufacturer.

➤ Striped volumes cannot be extended or mirrored. If you need to make a striped volume larger by adding another disk, you first have to delete the volume and then re-create it.

Mirrored Volumes and RAID-5 Volumes

You can create mirrored volumes and RAID-5 volumes only on dynamic disks running on Windows Server 2003 or Windows 2000 Server computers. Both mirrored volumes and RAID-5 volumes are considered fault tolerant because these configurations can handle a single disk failure and still function normally. Mirrored volumes and RAID-5 volumes both require that an equal amount of disk space be available on each disk that will be a part of these volumes. A mirrored volume must use two physical disks—no more and no fewer than two physical hard disk drives. A RAID-5 volume must use at least three physical hard disks up to a maximum of 32 physical disks.

Many network administrators and consultants agree that hardware-based fault-tolerant solutions are more robust and reliable than software-based fault-tolerant configurations. By installing one or more RAID controller adapter cards into a server, you can set up several different types of hardware fault tolerance, such as mirroring, RAID-5, RAID 10 (mirrored volumes that are part of a striped array set), and RAID 0+1 (striped volumes that are part of a mirrored set). When you use hardware RAID, you can retain basic disks or you can convert disks to dynamic; hardware RAID is hidden to Windows Server 2003. Of course, it's less expensive to implement a software solution, such as setting up mirrored volumes or RAID-5 volumes using the Disk Management console in Windows Server 2003, but often the performance, reliability, and flexibility of hardware-based RAID far outweighs its extra cost.

Working with Mirrored Volumes

A mirrored volume uses volumes stored on two separate physical disks to "mirror" (write) the data onto both disks simultaneously and redundantly. This configuration is also referred to as RAID-1. If one of the disks in the mirrored configuration fails, Windows Server 2003 writes an event into the system log of the Event Viewer. The system functions normally (unless the second disk fails) until the failed disk is replaced and then the volume can be mirrored again. Mirrored volumes cost you 50% of your available storage space because of the built-in redundancy. If you mirror two 70GB disks, you are left with just 70GB of space rather than 140GB.

You can make mirrored volumes more robust by installing a separate hard disk controller for each disk; technically, this is known as disk duplexing. Disk duplexing is better than disk mirroring because you alleviate the single point of failure by having one controller for each disk. Under Windows Server 2003, disk duplexing is still referred to as disk mirroring. You can create mirrored volumes only by using dynamic disks. To create a new empty mirrored volume from unallocated space, perform the following steps:

1. Open Disk Management.

2. Right-click an area of unallocated space on a dynamic disk and select New Volume.

3. Click Next for the New Volume Wizard welcome window.

4. Click Mirrored as the volume type option and click Next.

5. Select one of the available dynamic disks and click Add (see Figure 3.3).

6. Enter the amount of storage space to be used (in MB) for this mirrored volume, up to the maximum available space on the first disk that you selected, and then click Next.

7. Assign the new volume a drive letter, mount the volume in an empty NTFS folder, or choose not to assign the volume a drive letter or path and click Next.

8. Choose whether to format the new mirrored volume. If you choose to format the new volume, specify the following settings:

➤ File system (NTFS is the only option for dynamic volumes under the Disk Management console).

➤ Allocation unit size.

➤ Volume label.

➤ Mark the check box to Perform a Quick Format (if desired).

➤ Mark the check box to Enable File and Folder Compression (if desired).

9. Click Next to continue.

10. Click Finish to complete the New Volume Wizard.

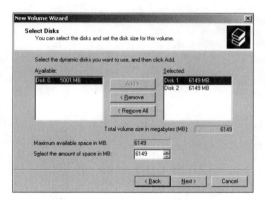

Figure 3.3   Use the Select Disks dialog box to create a mirrored volume with the New Volume Wizard.

To create a mirrored volume from a boot or system volume, or to create a mirrored volume from an existing volume that already contains data, perform the following steps:

1. Open Disk Management.

2. Right-click an existing dynamic volume and select Add Mirror.

3. Select one of the available dynamic disks on which to create the redundant volume and click Add Mirror (see Figure 3.4).

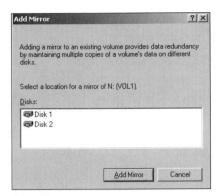

Figure 3.4 Use the Add Mirror dialog box to create a mirrored volume from an existing dynamic volume.

 When you add a mirrored volume to the boot volume, Windows Server 2003 automatically adds an entry to the computer's **boot.ini** file (located on the system volume or partition) as an additional startup option that displays each time the server reboots. Unless your primary mirror disk is the system volume, this option allows you to boot to the secondary disk in the mirror without using a boot disk if the primary disk in the mirror fails. The additional startup option displays like this: **Boot Mirror X: - secondary plex**, where **X:** represents the secondary mirror drive letter.

You should be aware of some important issues and guidelines before you attempt to mirror system or boot volumes:

➤ When you mirror volumes stored on ATA disks, you must change the jumper switch on the nonfailed drive to the master position (upon restart) if the master disk on the primary IDE channel fails, until you replace the failed disk.

➤ Microsoft does not recommend mirroring the system volume using one ATA disk and one SCSI disk because the system can encounter startup problems if one of the drives fails.

➤ If you plan to use separate SCSI controllers for each SCSI disk that you will mirror, you should use identical controllers from the same manufacturer.

➤ For a mirrored system volume, be sure to run a test to simulate a disk failure and attempt to start the system from the remaining mirrored volume. Perform this test regularly as part of your backup routine *before* a real failure occurs.

If you mirror the system or boot volume of a Windows Server 2003 computer, be sure to create a system boot disk in case the computer does not boot normally after one disk fails as part of the mirrored volume. You can make a system boot disk by formatting a blank disk under Windows Server 2003 and copying the following Windows Server 2003 startup files onto the disk: **ntldr**, **ntdetect.com**, **boot.ini**, and **ntbootdd.sys**, if it exists. Edit the **boot.ini** file so that the ARC path points to the correct **partition()** number for the nonfailed boot volume hard disk. See Microsoft Knowledge Base article Q325879 for more information.

You can stop mirroring a volume by either breaking the mirror or by removing the mirror. When you break a mirrored volume, each volume that makes up the mirror becomes an independent simple volume and they are no longer fault tolerant. When you remove a mirrored volume, the removed mirrored volume becomes unallocated space on its disk, whereas the remaining mirrored volume becomes a simple volume that is no longer fault tolerant. All data that was stored on the removed mirrored volume is erased. To break a mirrored volume, perform the following steps:

1. Open Disk Management.

2. Right-click one of the mirrored volumes that you want to break and select Break Mirrored Volume (see Figure 3.5).

3. Click Yes in the Break Mirrored Volume message box (see Figure 3.6).

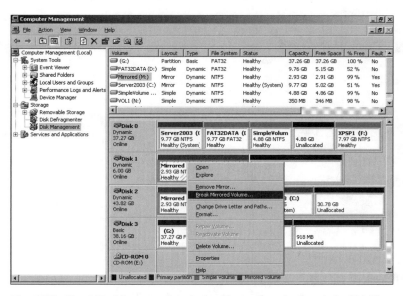

Figure 3.5 The right-click menu options for breaking a mirrored volume in the Disk Management console.

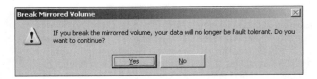

Figure 3.6 The Break Mirrored Volume message box.

If you want to completely destroy one of the mirrored volumes and leave just one of the volumes intact, you need to perform a removal procedure instead of simply breaking the mirrored volumes. To remove a mirrored volume, do the following:

1. Open Disk Management.

2. Right-click a mirrored volume and then select Remove Mirror.

3. At the Remove Mirror dialog box, select the disk from which you want to completely erase the mirrored volume and turn the volume into unallocated space. The remaining volume will stay with all of its data intact as a simple volume (see Figure 3.7).

4. Click the Remove Mirror button.

5. Click Yes to confirm the removal action in the Disk Management message box that appears.

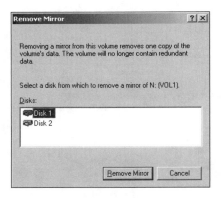

Figure 3.7 The Remove Mirror dialog box.

Working with RAID-5 Volumes

Windows Server 2003 supports disk striping with parity (RAID-5) volumes with the Disk Management console and through the `diskpart.exe` command-line utility. You need a minimum of three physical disks to create a RAID-5 volume. You are limited to a maximum of 32 physical disks in creating a

RAID-5 volume under Windows Server 2003. In creating a fault-tolerant volume using a RAID-5 configuration, you effectively lose an amount of storage equivalent to the capacity of one of the disks due to parity information that gets stored across all the disks (disk striping with parity). For example, if you use three 70GB disks, your RAID-5 volume will be able to store up to approximately 140GB of data. The remaining 70GB is used for storing the important parity data across all three disks in case of a failure—a 33% loss of available storage capacity. However, as you add disks to a RAID-5 volume, the percentage of lost storage space diminishes. For example, if you use five 70GB disks, you would again lose 70GB of available storage capacity, but that accounts only for a 20% overall loss in capacity (70GB divided by 350GB total available disk space equals .20 or 20%). In the event that one disk within the RAID-5 volume fails, the remaining disks can re-create the data stored on the failed disk as soon as a new disk is installed to replace the failed disk. To create a RAID-5 volume using Disk Management, perform the following steps:

1. Open Disk Management. Be sure that the computer has three or more dynamic disks—each with unallocated space.

2. Right-click an area of unallocated space on one of the dynamic disks that you want to use for the RAID-5 volume and select New Volume.

3. Click Next for the Welcome to the New Volume Wizard window.

4. Select the RAID-5 option button and click Next.

5. Select each available disk that you want to use as part of the RAID-5 volume from within the Available list box and click Add for each one (see Figure 3.8). You must select at least three disks and no more than 32 disks.

6. Select any disks that you do not want to use as part of the RAID-5 volume within the Selected list box and click Remove to remove any disks that you do not want to include as a part of the RAID-5 volume.

7. Enter the storage capacity that you want for the RAID-5 volume in the Select the Amount of Space in MB spin box and click Next to continue.

8. Choose to assign the volume a drive letter, mount the volume in an empty NTFS folder, or choose to not assign a drive letter or path to the new RAID-5 volume and click Next.

9. Choose whether to format the new RAID-5 volume. If you choose to format the new volume, specify the following settings:

> File system (NTFS is the only option for dynamic volumes under the Disk Management console).

> Allocation unit size.

> Volume label.

> Mark the check box to Perform a Quick Format (if desired).

> Mark the check box to Enable File and Folder Compression (if desired).

10. Click Next to continue.

11. Click Finish to complete the New Volume Wizard.

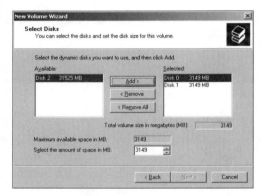

Figure 3.8 The Select Disks dialog box of the New Volume Wizard for a RAID-5 volume.

NOTE

Mirrored and RAID-5 volumes are available only on computers that are running Windows Server 2003 or Windows 2000 Server. Windows XP Professional and Windows 2000 Professional computers can use basic and dynamic disks, but they cannot host software-based fault-tolerant disk configurations such as mirrored volumes and striped sets with parity (RAID-5) volumes. You can, however, use a computer running Windows XP Professional (or Windows 2000 Professional) to create mirrored and RAID-5 volumes on a remote computer running the Windows Server 2003 or the Windows 2000 Server network operating system. The Disk Management MMC snap-in can administer both local and remote disk storage.

If one disk within a RAID-5 volume is intermittently failing, you can attempt to reactivate it by right-clicking the disk and selecting Reactivate Disk. If one disk within a RAID-5 volume appears to be permanently failed, you can replace that failed disk with another dynamic disk attached to the computer or you can install a new disk. To regenerate the RAID-5 volume, right-click the RAID-5 volume on the failed disk and select Repair Volume. The replacement disk must contain at least as much unallocated space as that used by the failed disk for the RAID-5 volume.

Troubleshooting Issues on Basic and Dynamic Disks

You should use basic disks and dynamic disks appropriately. In certain instances, you cannot use basic disks and partitions; in other situations, you cannot use dynamic disks and volumes. Understanding when and where you can use these two kinds of storage is key to implementing robust server storage policies and procedures. Knowing how to structure basic and dynamic storage allows you to plan properly for upgrading existing servers and for installing new ones.

Installing Windows Server 2003 on a Dynamic Disk

If you create a dynamic volume from unallocated space on a dynamic disk under Windows 2000, Windows XP, or Windows Server 2003, you cannot install a copy of Windows Server 2003 on that volume. This setup limitation occurs because the Windows Server 2003 setup program recognizes only dynamic volumes that contain partition tables. Partition tables appear in basic volumes and in dynamic volumes only when they have been converted from basic to dynamic. If you create a new dynamic volume on a dynamic disk, that new dynamic volume does not contain a partition table.

Extending a Volume on a Dynamic Disk

If you convert a basic volume to a dynamic volume (by converting the basic disk to a dynamic disk), you can install Windows Server 2003 on that volume, but you cannot extend the volume. The limitation on extending volumes occurs because the boot volume, which contains the Windows Server 2003 system files, cannot be part of a spanned volume. If you extend a simple volume that contains a partition table (that is, a volume that was converted from basic to dynamic), Windows Server 2003 Setup recognizes the spanned volume but cannot install to it, because the boot volume cannot be part of a spanned volume.

You can extend volumes that you create after you convert a basic disk to a dynamic disk. You can extend volumes and make changes to the disk configuration without rebooting your computer (in most cases). If you want to take advantage of these features in Windows Server 2003, you must convert a disk from basic to dynamic status. Use dynamic disks if your computer runs only Windows Server 2003 and you want to create more than four volumes per disk or if you want to extend, stripe, or span volumes onto one or more dynamic disks.

Upgrading from Windows NT 4 Server with Basic Disks

If you need to upgrade a computer running Windows NT 4 Server that has hard drives configured as volume sets, striped sets, mirror sets, or striped sets with parity, you must first back up all the data stored on each particular set. Windows Server 2003 does not support volume sets, stripe sets, mirror sets, or stripe sets with parity on basic disks. These four types of special storage sets are supported only by dynamic disks under Windows Server 2003.

To migrate data on volume sets, stripe sets, mirror sets, or stripe sets with parity from Windows NT 4 Server to Windows Server 2003, perform the following steps:

1. Under Windows NT 4 Server, back up the data.

2. Delete the special storage sets.

3. Upgrade the operating system to Windows Server 2003 Professional.

4. Convert the appropriate hard disks from basic to dynamic disks.

5. Create the appropriate dynamic volumes.

6. Restore the backed-up data.

If you upgrade a computer to Windows Server 2003 from Windows NT 4 Server without backing up the data stored on mirror sets or stripe sets with parity on basic disks, the operating system will not mount those volumes. However, if you install the Windows Server 2003 support tools on the installation CD-ROM in the **\support\tools** folder, you can utilize the **ftonline.exe** command-line tool. **Ftonline** will mount fault-tolerant volume sets stored on basic disks. **Ftonline** is designed to be a temporary measure, and it allows you to access the data stored on fault-tolerant volumes in read-only mode so that you can copy the data onto dynamic fault-tolerant volumes.

Diagnosing Hard Disk Problems

Physical disk problems do occur because disks are mechanical devices. Both the Add Hardware Wizard and Device Manager can assist you in troubleshooting physical disk problems and disk device driver problems. To diagnose disk or disk device driver problems, perform the following steps:

1. Right-click My Computer from the Start menu or from the Windows desktop and click Properties.

2. In the System Properties dialog box, click the Hardware tab and then click the Add Hardware Wizard button.

3. Click Next for the welcome window and then the wizard will search for new hardware devices that you have connected to the computer.

4. Click Yes, I Have Already Connected the Hardware and then click Next.

5. Select the hardware device that you want to diagnose and fix from the Installed Hardware list box and click Next.

6. The wizard will inform you of the device's current status. Click Finish to launch the Help and Support Center's troubleshooter window to assist you with diagnosing the problem, or click Cancel to exit the wizard.

Another way to troubleshoot hardware problems is with Device Manager. Right-click My Computer from the Start menu or from the Windows desktop and select Properties. In the System Properties dialog box, click the Hardware tab and then click the Device Manager button. Expand the hardware category that you need to troubleshoot. Right-click the device that you want to inquire about and select Properties to display the device's properties sheet, as shown in Figure 3.9. All the pertinent information about the device is available from this window, including its device status as determined by the operating system. Hard disks display four tabs on their properties sheets: General, Policies, Volumes, and Driver. The General tab shows device status and other basic information. The Policies tab displays options for enabling and disabling write caching (for ATA and SCSI disks only) and for optimizing for either quick removal or performance (for USB and FireWire disks only), as shown in Figure 3.10.

Detecting and Repairing Disk Errors

In Windows Server 2003, you can use the Error-Checking tool to check for file system errors and bad sectors on the computer's hard disks. It's a good idea to periodically run this utility as a proactive step in monitoring a server's hard disks and for repairing any minor issues before they turn into big problems. To run the Error-Checking tool, perform the following steps:

1. Open My Computer, right-click the local disk that you want to check, and select Properties.

2. Click the Tools tab.

3. Under Error-Checking, click the Check Now button.

4. Under Check Disk Options, mark both the Automatically Fix File System Errors check box and the Scan for and Attempt Recovery of Bad Sectors check box.

5. Click the Start button to begin the error-checking process. After the process finishes, a message box will notify you of any errors.

Figure 3.9 Using Device Manger to troubleshoot hardware problems.

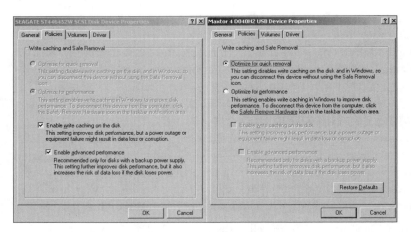

Figure 3.10 Using disk device policies for specifying different options for removable and nonremovable drives.

All files must be closed for the Error-Checking utility to run. The volume (drive letter) is not available to run any other tasks while this process is running. If the volume is currently in use, a message asks whether you want to reschedule the disk checking for the next time you restart the system. The next time you restart the computer, the Error-Checking tool runs. If your volume is formatted as NTFS, Windows Server 2003 automatically logs all file transactions, replaces bad clusters, and stores copies of key information for all files on the NTFS volume.

Removable Storage Support

Windows Server 2003 provides removable storage services for applications and network administrators that enhance the sharing and management of removable media hardware such as backup tape drives, optical discs, and automated (robotic) media pool libraries. Removable storage and media support in Windows Server 2003 precludes the need for third-party software developers to write custom application programs to support each different type of removable media device. In addition, removable storage services allow organizations to leverage their investment in expensive removable storage equipment by having multiple removable storage applications share these devices.

Windows Server 2003 Removable Storage implements a set of Application Programming Interfaces (APIs) that enable third-party software solutions to catalog all removable media, such as DVDs, tapes, and optical discs. Both offline (shelved) and online (housed in a library) media can be cataloged. Removable Storage organizes media using media pools. These media pools control access to the removable media, categorize the media according to each type of use, and permit applications to share the media. Removable Storage tracks the application programs that share the removable media. Removable Storage is logically structured into five basic components: media units, media libraries, media pools, work queue items, and operator requests. You manage Removable Storage from the MMC snap-in named, strangely enough, Removable Storage. The Removable Storage snap-in is also available as part of the default Computer Management console.

The Disk Defragmenter Tool

The Disk Defragmenter utility rearranges files, programs, and unused space on your server's hard disks, allowing programs to run faster and data files to open more quickly. Putting the pieces of files and programs in a more contiguous arrangement on disk reduces the time the operating system needs to access requested items. To run Disk Defragmenter, perform the following steps:

1. Click Start, All Programs, Accessories, System Tools and click Disk Defragmenter. Alternatively, you can right-click a drive letter in My Computer, select Properties, click the Tools tab, and click Defragment Now. You can also run the Disk Defragmenter from the Computer Management console.

2. Select which disks you want to defragment and any additional options you want to set.

3. Click the Analyze button to determine whether the disks could benefit from a defragmenting procedure. The Disk Defragmenter will display a message box informing you of its findings, as shown in Figure 3.11.

4. Click View Report to see the details for the level of fragmentation on the disk, as shown in Figure 3.12.

5. Click the Defragment button to start the defragmentation process on the disk that you have selected.

6. After the defragmentation procedure is complete, a message box pops up to alert you. Click View Report to read the details about the improved level of fragmentation on the disk, or click Close to return to the Disk Defragmenter console and you can then exit the program or you can select another disk to analyze or defragment.

Figure 3.11   The Disk Defragmenter's message box after performing an analysis of a disk.

Windows Server 2003 ships with a command-line version of the disk defragmenter—**defrag.exe**. You can run this program within a batch file or inside of a Windows script, which in turn can be scheduled to run automatically using the Scheduled Tasks folder.

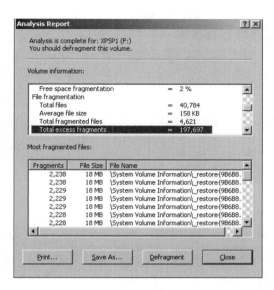

Figure 3.12   The Disk Defragmenter's Analysis Report dialog box.

On NTFS volumes, Windows Server 2003 reserves a portion of the free space for a system file called the Master File Table (MFT). The MFT is where Windows stores all the information it needs to retrieve files from the volume. Windows stores part of the MFT at the beginning of the volume and Windows reserves the MFT for exclusive use, so the Disk Defragmenter cannot and does not move files to the beginning of volumes.

The Chkdsk and ChkNTFS Command-Line Tools

The chkdsk.exe command-line utility runs diagnostic tests on the file system for a drive letter and generates a report. It also corrects file-system errors when you use the /f option. If the computer is powered down suddenly due to a loss of power, Windows Server 2003 marks each drive volume as "dirty" by setting the dirty bit on each drive volume. When the system restarts, chkdsk.exe automatically runs for each drive volume marked as dirty. For system and boot partitions and volumes, you can specify for chkdsk.exe to run during the next restart by typing the command chkntfs /c at a command prompt. Extensive help information is available for both chkdsk.exe and chkntfs.exe utilities by simply typing chkdsk /? or chkntfs /? at any command-prompt window.

Exam Prep Questions

Question 1

Which of the following hard disk configurations is the boot volume under Windows Server 2003? (Choose two.)

- ❑ A. The C: drive (a dynamic disk) that contains the boot files such as **ntldr**, **ntdetect.com**, and **boot.ini**, whereas the **\Windows** folder is located on a different drive letter
- ❑ B. The E: drive (a basic disk) where the **\Windows** folder is located
- ❑ C. The F: drive (a dynamic disk) where the **\Windows** folder is located
- ❑ D. The C: drive (a dynamic disk) where the boot files such as **ntldr**, **ntdetect.com**, and **boot.ini** are stored and where the **\Windows** folder is also located
- ❑ E. The G: drive where the Windows Server 2003 CD-ROM is located

Answers C and D are correct because the boot volume is a dynamic disk that contains the Windows files (the \Windows folder by default). The system volume is a dynamic disk that stores the boot files such as ntldr, ntdetect.com, and boot.ini. The system volume and the boot volume can be one and the same. Answer A is incorrect because the \Windows folder is located on a different drive letter; this answer would be the system volume, not the boot volume. Answer B is incorrect because the boot volume is stored on a dynamic disk; the boot partition is stored on a basic disk. Answer E is incorrect because a CD-ROM drive is never considered a boot or system volume or partition.

Question 2

Which of the following types of hard disks can you convert from basic disks to dynamic disks under Windows Server 2003? (Choose five.)

- ❑ A. EIDE (ATA) hard disks
- ❑ B. SCSI hard disks
- ❑ C. USB hard disks
- ❑ D. IEEE 1394 (FireWire) hard disks
- ❑ E. Fibre Channel disks
- ❑ F. Ultra DMA disks
- ❑ G. Solid-state keychain (flash) disks

Answers A, B, E, F, and G are correct because these types of hard disks are compatible with Windows Server 2003 dynamic disks. Answers C and D are incorrect because Windows Server 2003 dynamic disks are not supported on USB Version 1.1 or 2.0 hard disks nor are dynamic disks supported on IEEE 1394 disks.

Question 3

Which of the following types of fault-tolerant (RAID) configurations (without using a RAID controller or third-party software) can you set up using either Disk Management or the **diskpart.exe** command-line tool under Windows Server 2003? (Choose three.)

❑ A. RAID 0

❑ B. RAID 2

❑ C. RAID 5

❑ D. RAID 1

❑ E. RAID 0+1

❑ F. RAID 10

Answers A, C, and D are correct because Windows Server 2003 supports disk striping (RAID 0), disk striping with parity (RAID 5), and disk mirroring (RAID 1). Answer B is incorrect because Windows Server 2003 does not natively support hammering code error-correcting code (ECC) disk configurations (RAID 2). Answer E is incorrect because Windows Server 2003 does not natively support striped volumes that are part of a mirrored set (RAID 0+1). Answer F is incorrect because Windows Server 2003 does not natively support mirrored volumes that are part of a striped array set (RAID 10).

Question 4

How can an administrator create and format a new 33GB dynamic volume as FAT32 under Windows Server 2003?

○ A. Use the Disk Management console and the New Volume Wizard to create a new 33GB volume on an existing dynamic disk, and have the wizard format it as FAT32.

○ B. Use the Disk Management console and the New Volume Wizard to create a new 33GB volume on an existing dynamic disk. Use the **format.exe** tool at a command prompt to format the volume as FAT32.

○ C. At a command prompt, use the **diskpart.exe** tool to create a new 33GB volume on a dynamic disk and use the **format.exe** tool to format the volume as FAT32.

> ○ D. Use the Disk Management console and the New Partition Wizard to
> create a new 33GB partition on an existing basic disk. Use the
> **format.exe** tool at a command prompt to format the volume as FAT32.
>
> ○ E. You cannot format a 33GB volume or partition as FAT32 under
> Windows Server 2003 using Disk Management or the **format.exe**
> command-line tool.

Answer E is correct because Windows Server does not support formatting partitions or volumes larger than 32GB as FAT32. Answers A, B, C, and D are all incorrect because Windows Server 2003 only supports formatting partitions or volumes larger than 32GB as NTFS. Partitions or volumes larger than 32GB that have been upgraded from previous operating systems can be mounted and used under Windows Server 2003. Partitions or volumes larger than 32GB that have been created by third-party utilities can also be mounted and used under Windows Server 2003.

Question 5

> On which of the following hard-disk configurations can you install a fresh copy
> of Windows Server 2003? (Choose two.)
>
> ❑ A. On a basic partition
>
> ❑ B. On a dynamic volume that was created from unallocated space
>
> ❑ C. On a dynamic volume that was upgraded from a basic volume
>
> ❑ D. On a basic volume that is part of a removable disk
>
> ❑ E. On a dynamic disk that already has Windows XP Professional installed
> on it

Answers A and C are correct. You can install a fresh copy of Windows Server 2003 onto a basic partition and onto a dynamic volume if the volume was originally a basic partition that was upgraded to dynamic because Windows Server 2003 can only be installed on a disk that contains a partition table. Answer B is incorrect because a dynamic volume that is created from unallocated space does not contain a partition table. Answer D is incorrect because Windows Server 2003 Setup does not support installation onto removable media such as USB disks or IEEE 1394 (FireWire) disks. Answer E is incorrect because you can install only one operating system per dynamic disk.

Question 6

How many primary partitions without an extended partition can reside on a basic disk under Windows Server 2003?

○ A. Three

○ B. Four

○ C. One

○ D. Unlimited

Answer B is correct. You can create up to four primary partitions on a basic disk without an extended partition. Answer A is incorrect because you are limited to three primary partitions only if there is an extended partition on the disk. Answer C is incorrect because you can have more than one primary partition on a basic disk. Answer D is incorrect because you are limited to a maximum of four primary partitions on a basic disk.

Question 7

Which of the following statements are true about basic disks under Windows Server 2003? (Choose two.)

❑ A. Basic disks are not supported under Windows Server 2003.

❑ B. Basic disks that were configured as one disk striping with parity set under Windows NT Server 4.0 are mounted automatically after the server is upgraded to Windows Server 2003.

❑ C. Basic disks can only be formatted as FAT or FAT32.

❑ D. You cannot convert dynamic disks back to basic disks without deleting all data and volumes on the disks first.

❑ E. IEEE 1394 disks can only be basic disks.

Answers D and E are correct. To convert dynamic disks back to basic disks, you must remove all volumes on the disk, which means that all data must be removed as well. IEEE 1394 (or FireWire) disks cannot be converted to dynamic; therefore they can only be basic disks. Answer A is incorrect because basic disks are supported under Windows Server 2003. Answer B is incorrect because basic disk sets that were created under previous versions of Microsoft server products are not mounted by the operating system; you must use the `ftonline.exe` tool on the setup CD-ROM. Answer C is incorrect because basic disks (and dynamic disks) can be formatted as FAT, FAT32, or NTFS.

Question 8

> How can you extend a basic partition under Windows Server 2003? (Choose three.)
>
> ❑ A. You must extend the basic partition onto unallocated space on the same physical disk.
>
> ❑ B. The basic partition must be formatted as FAT or FAT32.
>
> ❑ C. You cannot extend a basic partition; you can only extend a simple volume that resides on a dynamic disk. The simple volume becomes a spanned volume.
>
> ❑ D. The basic partition must be formatted as NTFS.
>
> ❑ E. The basic partition must be located physically adjacent to the unallocated space onto which you will extend the volume.
>
> ❑ F. You can only use the Disk Management console to extend the basic partition.

Answers A, D, and E are correct. You can extend a basic partition formatted as NTFS onto adjacent, unallocated space on the same physical disk. Answer B is incorrect because the basic partition must be formatted as NTFS, not FAT or FAT32. Answer C is incorrect because you can extend a basic partition if certain requirements are met. Answer F is incorrect because you can only use the `diskpart.exe` command-line tool to extend a basic partition.

Question 9

> How can you schedule regular disk-defragmentation procedures under Windows Server 2003?
>
> ○ A. Install a third-party product.
>
> ○ B. Use the Disk Defragmenter console.
>
> ○ C. Use the **defrag.exe** command-line tool.
>
> ○ D. You cannot schedule disk defragmentation.

Answer C is correct because you can put the `defrag.exe` command into a batch file or script and then you can schedule that batch file or script using the Scheduled Tasks folder. Answer A is incorrect because you do not need to purchase and install a third-party product to schedule disk defragmentation. Answer B is incorrect because you cannot natively schedule disk-defragmentation events using the Disk Defragmenter console. Answer D is incorrect because you can schedule disk defragmentation under Windows Server 2003.

Question 10

Which of the following hardware-storage configurations is considered a best practice if you are going to set up RAID 1 fault tolerance using only software settings that are available natively under Windows Server 2003?

- ○ A. Install one RAID controller.
- ○ B. Install one fibre channel controller.
- ○ C. Install two SCSI controllers—one for each physical disk.
- ○ D. Install three SCSI controllers—one for each physical disk.

Answer C is correct. RAID 1 is the referred to as disk mirroring, which uses only two physical disks. A best practice is to connect each disk to a separate controller to eliminate a single point of failure—which is known as disk duplexing. Answer A is incorrect because a RAID controller is used for configuring hardware-based RAID, not software-based RAID. Answer B is incorrect because installing just one controller for two physical disks creates a single point of failure; it does not matter which type of controller is used: EIDE, SCSI, or Fibre Channel. Answer D is incorrect because RAID 1 (disk mirroring) can only use two physical disks. Installing three controllers for three separate disks might bode well for using RAID-5 under Windows Server 2003, but you cannot use three disks for disk mirroring.

Need to Know More?

 Boswell, William. *Inside Microsoft Windows Server 2003*. Boston, Massachusetts: Addison-Wesley Professional, 2003.

 Scales, Lee, and John Michell. *MCSA/MCSE 70-290 Training Guide: Managing and Maintaining a Windows Server 2003 Environment*. Indianapolis, Indiana: Que Publishing, 2003.

 Stanek, William R. *Microsoft Windows Server 2003 Administrator's Pocket Consultant*. Redmond, Washington: Microsoft Press, 2003.

 Search the Microsoft Product Support Services Knowledge Base on the Internet: http://support.microsoft.com. Find technical information using keywords from this chapter such as dynamic disks, RAID-5, mirrored volumes, spanned volumes, diskpart.exe, boot volume, NTFS, and FAT32.

4

Administering Users, Groups, and Computers in Active Directory

. . . .

Terms you'll need to understand:

✓ Domains
✓ User accounts
✓ Computer accounts
✓ Security groups
✓ Distribution groups
✓ Global groups
✓ Universal groups

✓ Domain local groups
✓ Globally unique identifiers (GUIDs)
✓ Organizational units (OUs)
✓ Domain and forest functional levels
✓ Active Directory Users and Computers (ADUC) console

Techniques you'll need to master:

✓ Adding and removing computer accounts
✓ Prestaging computer accounts
✓ Adding, modifying, and removing groups
✓ Understanding group scopes
✓ Importing user accounts
✓ Adding, modifying, and removing user accounts

✓ Using command-line tools for modifying Active Directory objects
✓ Troubleshooting user account problems
✓ How to create roaming and mandatory user profiles

Microsoft introduced Active Directory with the debut of Windows 2000 Server in February 2000. Active Directory provides a directory service for Microsoft-based networks in the same way that Novell Directory Services (NDS) provides a directory service for NetWare environments. For Windows Server 2003, Microsoft enhanced and refined Active Directory by making the directory service more flexible, more scalable, and more manageable than its Windows 2000 predecessor. Active Directory is a vital element in Windows Server 2003 and its many benefits can offer a compelling reason to upgrade, especially if you are coming from a Windows NT Server environment.

Understanding how to manage users, groups, and computers within Active Directory is critical for a successful deployment and reliable day-to-day operations of a Windows Server 2003 Active Directory-based network. In this chapter, we introduce you to Active Directory for Windows Server 2003. You'll discover how to add, remove, and manage computer accounts in Active Directory. You'll also find out how to set up and manage both user accounts and groups. You'll learn how to work with local, roaming, and mandatory user profiles. Of course, network administration doesn't always go smoothly, so you'll also learn about how to troubleshoot computer accounts, user accounts, and user authentication problems in Windows Server 2003 and Active Directory.

Introduction to Active Directory

The many improvements to Active Directory encompass some of the major feature enhancements of Windows Server 2003. Active Directory is a replicated and distributed database that stores computer-related information such as usernames, passwords, phone numbers, addresses, email addresses, group names, and computer names, to name a few. Active Directory is called a directory service because it provides users and computers with the ability to look up information in a similar way that you look up information using a telephone book directory.

Special servers called domain controllers (DCs) are designated to store a copy of the Active Directory database, and these DCs are responsible for synchronizing the Active Directory database with all of the other DCs that share the database. Server computers as well as workstation computers that are members of an Active Directory domain perform several Active Directory queries (or lookups) in their day-to-day operations. For example, Active Directory domain-member computers need to know where nearby DCs are for authentication purposes.

Active Directory is based on open, Internet-related standards, such as the Transmission Control Protocol/Internet Protocol (TCP/IP), the Domain Name System (DNS), the Kerberos authentication protocol, and the Lightweight Directory Access Protocol (LDAP), among many others. In fact, you cannot install Active Directory without TCP/IP and DNS installed and functioning within the network environment. You must name Active Directory domains using a full DNS name such as `examcram2.informit.com`.

Domains, Domain Trees, and Domain Forests

A Windows Server 2003 computer (or a Windows 2000 Server computer) becomes a DC when an administrator runs the Active Directory Installation Wizard. You can run the wizard by clicking Start, Run; typing `dcpromo.exe`; and clicking OK. This process promotes a server to a DC. The wizard makes several changes to the server computer to prepare it to become a DC. One of the major changes is the creation of the Active Directory database file itself. This file is named `ntds.dit`, and it must reside on a hard disk that is formatted as NTFS. The default location for the `ntds.dit` file is the `%systemroot%\ntds` folder (for example, `c:\windows\ntds`).

The very first Windows Server 2003 (or Windows 2000 Server) DC that you promote creates the *root domain*. For example, if you promote a DC and name the domain `examcram2.net`, this domain becomes the root domain within the new Active Directory forest. The basic logical components of Active Directory are as follows:

➤ *Domain*—One or more DC servers and a group of users and computers that share the same Active Directory database for authentication and can share common server resources.

➤ *Domain Tree*—One or more Active Directory domains that share a common hierarchical DNS namespace (parent-child-grandchild and so on). For example, `examcram2.net` could be the parent domain, `northamerica.examcram2.net` could be the child domain, `us.northamerica.examcram2.net` could be the grandchild domain, and so on.

➤ *Domain Forest*—One or more Active Directory domain trees (each tree has its own DNS namespace) that share the same Active Directory database. An Active Directory forest is a logical container for one or more related domains.

No Primary or Backup Domain Controllers

Windows NT Server 3.5x and Windows NT Server 4.0 used the concept of one primary DC (PDC) and backup DCs (BDCs), where only one of the DCs could act as the PDC at any one time. The PDC stores the read/write copy of the security accounts manager (SAM) database, whereas each BDC stores a read-only copy of the SAM database. Instead, Active Directory uses a technique called multimaster replication to distribute copies of the Active Directory database to all other DCs that share the same Active Directory namespace. This replication technology means that administrators can make additions, changes, or deletions to the Active Directory database from any DC, and those modifications get synchronized with all of the other DCs within an Active Directory forest. Active Directory assigns the role of PDC Emulator to the first DC to come online in an Active Directory forest. The DC that has the PDC Emulator role can communicate between Active Directory and down-level PDCs and BDCs running on Windows NT Server 3.5x and Windows NT Server 4.0 Server.

Organizational Units

To improve network administration, Microsoft created organizational units (OUs) to provide for logical groupings of users, groups, computers, and other objects within a single domain. You can delegate administrative authority over each OU to other administrators for distributing network-management chores. The delegated authority can be limited in scope, if necessary, so that you can grant junior administrators just specific administrative powers—not complete administrator-level authority. In addition, you can apply specific group policy object (GPO) settings at the OU level, allowing users and computers to be managed differently according to the OU in which they are placed.

The Active Directory Schema

The Active Directory database has a default design for the type of data that it stores. For example, Active Directory stores usernames, passwords, and email addresses for each user in the domain; therefore, the database's design must allow for storing this type of information. The Active Directory database structure is referred to as its schema. The two components that make up the schema are attributes and classes. You can extend the Active Directory schema to include other types of information that Active Directory does not store by default. However, for each new element that you add to the schema, that element becomes a permanent part of the schema; added classes and attributes can be disabled, but they can never be removed.

For instance, an application such as Microsoft Exchange Server 2003 can extend the schema by adding new fields and new data types to Active Directory so that the domain can store Exchange Server data. The extended schema allows one or more servers within the domain to operate as Exchange Server computers. In this way, an application such as Microsoft Exchange Server can leverage Active Directory for accessing user information, storing data, and replicating data across an entire network.

Active Directory Naming Conventions

Because Active Directory is based on the Lightweight Directory Access Protocol (LDAP), you can reference each object within Active Directory using different types of LDAP naming conventions. Distinguished names (DNs) and relative distinguished names (RDNs) are two of the naming conventions that Active Directory uses for its objects. DNs and RDNs use specific naming components to define the location of the objects that they are identifying. DN and RDN components (or attributes) are the following:

➤ *CN*—Common name

➤ *OU*—Organizational unit name

➤ *DC*—Domain component name

Active Directory creates an RDN in addition to a canonical name (CN) for each object based upon the available information when the object is created. Every Active Directory object can also be identified by a DN, which is derived from the RDN of the object plus all of its higher-level (parent) container objects. Active Directory uses the following types of names:

➤ The LDAP DN must be unique throughout the forest. For example, the DN of a computer named station01 located in the Sales OU, which is part of the domain named amazon.com, would be CN=station01,OU=sales,DC=amazon,DC=com.

➤ The LDAP RDN uniquely identifies the object within its parent container. For example, the LDAP RDN of a computer named station01 is CN=station01. The RDNs of objects must be unique within the same OU.

➤ The CN identifies an object as does its DN; however, it uses a different syntax and it reverses the sequence of the name. For example, if the LDAP DN of a computer is CN=station01,OU=sales,DC=amazon,DC=com, the CN of the same computer is amazon.com/sales/station01.

➤ Security principal names are Active Directory objects, such as users, groups, and computers, that are authenticated by an Active Directory domain. These Security principals are assigned security IDs (SIDs) that uniquely identify these objects during authentication. Users and computers need a SID to log on to an Active Directory domain. You can assign users, computers, and groups security permissions for accessing domain resources. An administrator needs to provide a name that is unique throughout the entire domain for each security principal object when the object is created. Globally unique identifiers (GUIDs) are also used to uniquely identify objects, such as computers, within Active Directory.

Windows Server 2003 Active Directory Functional Levels

Windows 2000 Active Directory domains offer two modes of functionality—mixed mode (the default) and native mode (enhanced). If you switch a Windows 2000 Active Directory domain to native mode, legacy Windows NT BDCs can no longer be members of the domain. As a bonus, universal security groups become available when you switch to Active Directory native mode under Windows 2000. *The switch to native mode is a one-time, non-reversible option.* Active Directory under Windows Server 2003 introduces two additional functional levels for domains while offering three new functional levels that operate at the forest level.

Windows Server 2003 Domain Functional Levels

Active Directory under Windows Server 2003 supports four levels of domain functionality. These different levels help ensure backward compatibility with previous versions of Windows and legacy Windows NT Server 4.0 domains. The four domain functional levels for Active Directory are the following (see Figure 4.1):

➤ *Windows 2000 Mixed*—This domain functional level is the most basic. This level supports Windows NT, Windows 2000, and Windows Server 2003 DCs.

➤ *Windows 2000 Native*—This level supports Windows 2000 DCs and Windows Server 2003 DCs only. Windows 2000 DCs in native mode move to Windows 2000 native functional level when upgraded to Windows Server 2003.

➤ *Windows Server 2003 Interim*—This level *applies only to Windows NT Server 4.0 DCs that have been upgraded to Windows Server 2003*. This level functions in much the same way as the Windows 2000 mixed level; however, it does not support Windows 2000 Server DCs.

➤ *Windows Server 2003*—This level is the highest, and it supports Windows Server 2003 DCs exclusively.

 As you switch a domain to an advanced domain functional level, remember that it is a one-time option that cannot be reversed. You can only upgrade (raise) functional levels; you can never downgrade (lower) to previous levels.

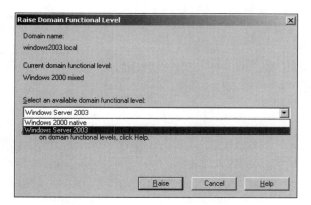

Figure 4.1 Raising the domain functional level on a Windows Server 2003 DC.

Windows Server 2003 Forest Functional Levels

New features in Active Directory require Active Directory forests to have their own set of functional levels similar to domains. New support for domain renaming and restructuring, schema class and attribute deactivation, and cross-forest trusts, as well as others, necessitate a higher forest functional level than the basic default setting. The three forest functional levels are

➤ *Windows 2000*—This forest functional level is the most basic. This level supports Windows NT 4.0, Windows 2000, and Windows Server 2003 DCs.

➤ *Windows Server 2003 Interim*—This level supports Windows NT 4.0 and Windows Server 2003 DCs only. It does not support Windows 2000 DCs.

➤ *Windows Server 2003*—This forest functional level is the highest, and it supports Windows Server 2003 DCs exclusively.

Before you can raise the forest functional level of a forest to Windows Server 2003, all DCs within the entire forest must be running the Windows Server 2003 operating system. All domains within the forest must also be operating at either the Windows 2000 native or the Windows Server 2003 domain functional level. Any DCs operating at the Windows 2000 native level will be automatically raised to the Windows Server 2003 domain functional level at the time that the forest functional level is raised to Windows Server 2003.

Administering Computer Accounts in Active Directory

Computers, such as workstations and member servers, must be authenticated to access Active Directory resources under Windows Server 2003, just as they must be authenticated under Active Directory in Windows 2000 Server. To become a participant in an Active Directory domain, Windows NT, Windows 2000, Windows XP, and other Windows Server 2003 computers must formally join a domain by establishing a computer account within the domain. Windows 95 and Windows 98 (Windows 9x) computers cannot formally join a domain; however, users can log onto a Windows Server 2003 Active Directory domain and access resources as if it were a Windows NT 4.0 domain under both the Windows 2000 mixed and the Windows 2000 native domain functional levels.

The Active Directory Client for Windows 9x and Windows NT 4.0

The Windows 2000 mixed domain functional level supports the NTLM (NT LAN Manager) authentication protocol that is used by Windows NT BDCs to authenticate users and computers. The older LM (LAN Manager) authentication protocol and the NTLM protocol are responsible for authenticating Windows 9x- and Windows NT-based computers. Windows 2000 mixed also supports the newer Kerberos authentication protocol that is used by the Windows 2000 native and the Windows Server 2003 domain functional levels. In addition to Kerberos, the Windows 2000 native and the Windows Server 2003 functional levels support the newer NTLM version 2 (NTLM v2) authentication protocol. Windows 9x computers do not natively support NTLM v2, nor do Windows NT 4.0 computers unless they have Service Pack 4 (SP4) or higher installed. Windows 9x computers and Windows NT 4.0 computers can natively log onto a Windows Server 2003 Active Directory domain in the following circumstances:

➤ The Windows Server 2003 domain is set at Windows 2000 mixed and either a PDC emulator or a Windows NT 4.0 BDC is available.

➤ The Windows Server 2003 domain is set at Windows 2003 interim and either a PDC emulator or a Windows NT 4.0 BDC is available.

> When Windows 9x computers log onto a Windows NT 4.0 domain, they can only access Active Directory resources via one-way trust relationships that have been set up by network administrators with Windows Server 2003 Active Directory domains.

To add support for Windows 9x and Windows NT 4.0 computers to access Active Directory resources, you can install the Active Directory client software so that these legacy clients can access resources stored in Windows Server 2003 domains. The Active Directory client software (`dsclient.exe`) for Windows 9x computers is located on the Windows 2000 Server CD-ROM (it's *not* on the Windows Server 2003 CD-ROM) in the `Clients\Win9x` folder. The Windows NT 4.0 version of the Active Directory client is available from Microsoft's Web site at `http://www.microsoft.com/windows2000/server/evaluation/news/bulletins/adextension.asp`.

Creating Computer Accounts

You can create computer accounts in one of four ways:

➤ Log onto each (Windows NT 4.0, Windows 2000, Windows XP, or Windows Server 2003) computer and join it to the domain.

➤ Prestage the computer accounts on a DC using the Active Directory Users and Computers (ADUC) MMC snap-in.

➤ Prestage the computer accounts on a DC using the `dsadd.exe` command-line utility.

➤ Prestage the computer accounts on a DC using some other scripted or command-line utility.

For computers running Windows NT, Windows 2000, Windows XP, and Windows Server 2003, you create accounts for those computers when you join them to the Windows Server 2003 Active Directory domain, provided that computer accounts for those computers have not been prestaged. For example, on a Windows 2000 (Professional or Server) system, you join the computer to a domain by following these steps:

1. Double-click the System icon in the Control Panel.

2. Click the Network Identification tab from the System Properties window.

3. Click the Properties button.

4. Click the Domain option button, type in the name of the Active Directory domain that you want to join, and click OK.

5. Type in the name and password for a user account in the domain that has administrative-level permission to join computers to this domain and click OK (see Figure 4.2).

6. Click OK for the Welcome message box that confirms you have successfully joined the computer to the domain.

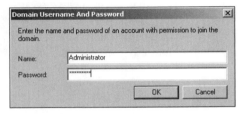

Figure 4.2   Joining a Windows 2000 computer to a Windows Server 2003 Active Directory domain.

Troubleshooting Joining a Computer to a Domain

If you have difficulty joining the domain, be sure to check the computer for any physical network connectivity problems. If you verify that the physical network connection is functioning properly, use the TCP/IP `ping` command at a command prompt window to test the connectivity to a domain controller by pinging the DC's IP address. For example, you can type `ping 192.168.0.10` at a command prompt if the DC's IP address is 192.168.0.10. If that works, attempt to ping the DC by its fully qualified domain name (FQDN)—for example, `ping dc1.windows2003.local`.

Using the FQDN for the DC should uncover a DNS name resolution problem, if one exists. If you simply try to ping the server's NetBIOS or host name by typing `ping DC1`, the name could be resolved by a NetBIOS broadcast, making you think that DNS name resolution is not a problem. If pinging the FQDN does not work, you might very well have a DNS name-resolution problem. You should check the computer's DNS server settings as well as the network's DNS setup. Perhaps the computer is not registered with an appropriate DNS server on your network. If you verify that the computer's DNS server settings are pointed to the appropriate DNS server(s), you can remedy a DNS registration issue on Windows 2000/XP/2003 computers by performing these steps:

1. Open a command prompt window.

2. Type `ipconfig /flushdns` and press Enter.

3. Type `ipconfig /registerdns` and press Enter.

4. Restart the computer to ensure that these changes take effect.

Prestaging Computer Accounts from the GUI

You can use the ADUC console to view, add, modify, and delete computer accounts, user accounts, and groups from the Windows GUI. On a Windows Server 2003 DC computer, click Start, Administrative Tools, Active Directory Users and Computers to launch the ADUC console. You can also click Start, Run; type `dsa.msc`; and click OK to run the ADUC console. By creating a computer account in Active Directory before the computer joins the domain, you can determine exactly where in the directory the computer account will be placed. The default location for computers joined to a domain without prestaging is the Computers container. In addition, prestaging computer accounts gives administrators more control over Remote Installation Services (RIS) installations. You can specify that only prestaged computer accounts can be installed via RIS.

 You can install the Windows Server 2003 Administration Tools Pack on a Windows XP Professional computer with SP1 or higher or on a Windows Server 2003 member server so that you can manage Active Directory without physically logging onto a DC. You can download the Windows Server 2003 Administration Tools Pack from Microsoft's Web site at **http://microsoft.com/downloads/details.aspx?familyid= c16ae515-c8f4-47ef-a1e4-a8dcbacff8e3&displaylang=en**.

For a new Active Directory domain, the default containers are Built-in, Computers, Domain Controllers, Foreign Security Principals, and Users. If you click the ADUC's View menu and select Advanced Features, you can view the advanced containers that are hidden by default. The advanced containers are LostAndFound, NTDS Quotas, Program Data, and System. To create a new computer account in ADUC, follow these steps:

1. Open the ADUC MMC snap-in (console).

2. Right-click the container or OU into which you want to place the computer account, select New, and then click Computer.

3. Type in the computer name.

4. Type in the pre-Windows 2000 computer name, if different from the computer name.

5. To change the user or group that has permission to join computers to the domain, click the Change button. The default group is the Domain Admins group: Any member of this group has authority to join computer accounts to the domain.

6. If this computer account is a Windows NT computer, mark the Assign This Computer Account as a Pre-Windows 2000 Computer check box.

7. If this computer account is for a Windows NT BDC computer, mark the Assign This Computer Account as a Backup Domain Controller check box (see Figure 4.3).

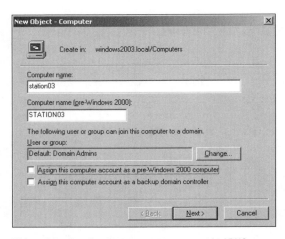

Figure 4.3 Creating a new computer account in ADUC.

8. Click Next.

9. If you are prestaging the computer account for later installation via RIS, mark the This Is a Managed Computer check box and type in the computer's unique ID (GUID/UUID), referred to as its globally unique identifier or its universally unique identifier. This extra security measure prevents unauthorized RIS client installations because only computers with matching GUIDs are allowed to be installed via RIS when you follow this procedure. You can find the GUID or UUID in the computer's BIOS or by using a third-party software utility (see Figure 4.4).

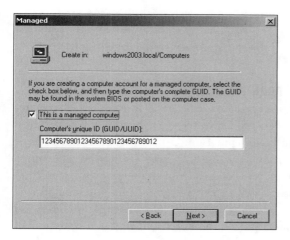

Figure 4.4   Specifying a computer's GUID for prestaging a computer account.

10. Click Next.

11. Select an option for specifying the type of RIS server support for this computer account:

   ➤ Any Available Remote Installation Server

   ➤ The Following Remote Installation Server

12. To specify a particular RIS server, select The Following Remote Installation Server option and type in the fully qualified DNS hostname, or click the Search button to locate the server (see Figure 4.5).

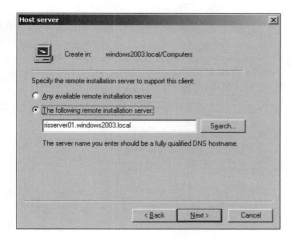

Figure 4.5   Specifying the RIS server for prestaging a computer account.

13. Click Next.

14. Click Finish for the New Object-Computer summary window.

Prestaging Computer Accounts from the Command Line

Windows Server 2003 offers several new command-line tools for working with Active Directory. For a detailed list of these commands and their functions, see the section "Using Command-Line Utilities for Active Directory Objects" later in this chapter. You can use the dsadd.exe tool to add Active Directory objects such as computer accounts from any Windows Server 2003 command prompt. With dsadd.exe, you can add one computer account at a time from the command line, or you can redirect standard input for dsadd.exe and use a text file that contains the computer account that you want added. For parameters with embedded spaces, such as names of OUs, surround the DN with quotes. The following two examples in Table 4.1 and in Figure 4.6 demonstrate some of the possibilities and their associated syntax for adding computer accounts via the command line.

Table 4.1   Examples of the dsadd.exe Command

dsadd Commmand	**dsadd** Results
dsadd computer cn=station77,cn= Computers,dc=windows2003,dc=local	Adds a computer account named **station77** to Active Directory in the **Computers** container for the domain named **windows2003.local**.
dsadd computer "cn=station88,ou= west coast,dc=windows2003,dc=local"	Adds a computer account named **station88** to Active Directory in the West Coast OU for the domain named **windows2003.local**.

Computer account NetBIOS names cannot be longer than 15 characters; computer account DNS names can be up to 63 characters in length. A fully qualified domain name (FQDN) for a computer account can be up to 255 characters in length, such as **server01.sales.northamerica.microsoft.com**.

Figure 4.6   Adding computer accounts using the **dsadd.exe** command.

Managing and Troubleshooting Computer Accounts

You can manage problems with computer accounts from the ADUC console. To modify the properties of a computer account, right-click the computer name listed in the ADUC console and select Properties. From the properties sheet, you can make several changes to the account such as trusting the computer for delegation, viewing which operating system the computer is running, adding or removing group memberships, and modifying security permissions and dial-in permissions (see Figure 4.7), among other options.

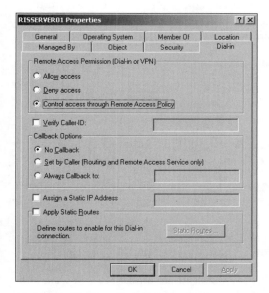

Figure 4.7   Working with dial-in properties for a computer account.

Administering and Troubleshooting Computer Accounts

You can easily move one or several computer accounts from one container to another container under Windows Server 2003. The ADUC console now supports both cut-and-paste and drag-and-drop functionality. You can select one or more computer accounts, right-click the accounts, and select Cut from the right-click menu. Alternatively, you can click and drag one or more selected computer accounts and drop the accounts into a different container. As a third option, you can select one or more computer accounts, right-click the accounts, and select Move. When the Move dialog box appears, select the Active Directory container where you want the accounts moved and click OK.

In addition to working with the properties sheet for each computer account, you have several administrative tasks available to you when you right-click a computer account, including the following:

➤ *Name Mappings*—This option maps X.509 security certificates and Kerberos names for the computer account.

➤ *Disable Account*—This option prevents any users from logging onto the domain from the computer account. After you select this option, it toggles to read *Enable Account*, which you can later use for re-enabling the computer account.

➤ *Reset Account*—This option changes the computer account password that is used to authenticate the computer on the domain. If you reset a computer account, you must rejoin the computer to the domain.

➤ *Move*—This option allows you to relocate the computer account to a different container or OU.

➤ *Manage*—This option launches the Computer Management console for remotely administering the selected computer.

➤ *All Tasks, Resultant Set of Policy (Planning)*—This option lets you view simulated policy settings for a selected computer or a selected user.

➤ *All Tasks, Resultant Set of Policy (Logging)*—This option lets you view policy settings for a specific computer on the network.

Windows 2000, Windows XP Professional, and Windows Server 2003 computers that are members of an Active Directory domain communicate with a DC using what's known as a secure channel. The secure channel's password is stored with the computer account on the domain controller. For Windows 2000, Windows XP, and Windows Server 2003 computers, the system-generated computer account password is automatically changed every 30 days by default. If, for some reason, the password stored on the domain member computer cannot be validated against the password stored on the DC, the Netlogon service generates one or both of the following errors on the domain member computer:

The session setup from the computer DOMAINMEMBER failed to authenticate. The name of the account referenced in the security database is DOMAINMEMBER$. The following error occurred: Access is denied.

NETLOGON Event ID 3210:

Failed to authenticate with \\DOMAINDC, a Windows NT domain controller for domain DOMAIN.

Either one or both of these errors indicate that you need to reset the computer account.

Managing Groups in Active Directory

Windows Server 2003 groups play an important role in allowing administrators to grant or deny access to files, folders, printers, and other resources for entire groups of users (or computers) at once instead of individually for every user. Applying security permissions to groups of users instead of to individual users greatly eases the administrative burden of managing control over data and other resources. In a non-Active Directory environment, Windows Server 2003 only provides support for local groups. Local groups are created, deleted, and maintained in the Local Users and Groups node of the Computer Management console for nondomain member computers. Local groups are sometimes referred to as machine groups because they apply specifically to the computer that they reside on. Windows Server 2003 supports two types of Active Directory groups:

➤ *Security*—These groups contain security descriptors that determine access permissions on resources for users who are group members. You can also use security groups as email distribution lists.

➤ *Distribution*—These groups do not contain security descriptors, and you cannot use them to determine access permissions. Distribution groups are used as email distribution lists only.

 You can change the type of a group from security to distribution or from distribution to security at any time, provided that the domain is set at the Windows 2000 native or the Windows Server 2003 domain functional level. You cannot change group types under the Windows 2000 mixed domain functional level.

Understanding Group Scopes

Groups must take on a specific role, or scope, regarding how they can be used and where they are valid within Active Directory. Each group is assigned one of the following scopes:

➤ *Domain local*—A group assigned as domain local can only specify permissions on resources within a single domain.

➤ *Built-in local*—These groups are created automatically whenever an Active Directory domain is created, and they have the same scope as domain local groups. You cannot create nor delete built-in local groups, but you can modify their members and their membership within other groups.

➤ *Global*—A global group can contain users, groups, and computers from its own domain as members. Global groups are available under any domain functional level.

➤ *Universal*—A universal group can contain users, groups, and computers from any domain in its forest. These groups are available only when the domain functional level is set at Windows 2000 native or Windows Server 2003. The membership list of universal groups is maintained by global catalog (GC) servers, unlike global groups and domain local groups. Certain DCs must be assigned as GCs so that applications and computers can locate resources within the Active Directory database. When a member is added to or removed from a universal group, global catalog servers must track the change, and each change must be replicated to all the global catalog servers in the forest. The increased overhead and network replication traffic for universal groups is why Microsoft recommends that you use them conservatively.

Limiting Group Membership Based on a Group's Scope

Computer accounts, user accounts, and other groups can become members of Windows Server 2003 groups. However, not all computer accounts, user accounts, and groups can join all types of groups; the ability to join a group depends upon the group's scope. In turn, a group's scope is affected by the current domain functional level. Table 4.2 summarizes the types of computer and user accounts (accounts) as well as the types of groups that can become members of a group based on the current scope of the group and the current domain functional level.

Table 4.2 Group Members Allowed Based on Group Scope			
Domain Functional Level	**Domain Local Groups Can Contain**	**Global Groups Can Contain**	**Universal Groups Can Contain**
Windows 2000 mixed	Accounts and global groups from any domain.	Accounts from the same domain only.	Not available.
Windows 2000 native or Windows Server 2003	Domain local groups from the same domain only. Accounts and global and universal groups from any domain.	Accounts and other global groups from the same domain only.	Accounts from any domain and all global and universal groups from any domain.

For nondomain member computers, the only available groups are called local groups. You can create local groups only on each local computer, and they can only contain local users, not domain user accounts. You can assign permissions only to local groups for the local computer where they reside. You create local users and local groups in the Local Users and Groups node of the Computer Management console. Domain member servers can still create local users and groups using Computer Management; however, you cannot use those users and groups as part of any Active Directory domain. Local users and groups are unavailable for DCs.

Changing a Group's Scope

Administrators can change the scope of domain local groups, global groups, and universal groups. Built-in groups cannot have their scopes changed, and domain local groups cannot be changed to global groups. In addition, global groups cannot be changed to domain local groups. However, you can change all three Active Directory group scopes according to the following guidelines:

➤ *Domain local groups*—You can change these groups to universal groups when the domain functional level is set to Windows 2000 native or higher. No member group of a domain local group may have domain local scope for the scope to change to universal. Domain local groups may be nested inside one another in native or Windows Server 2003 domain functional levels.

➤ *Global groups*—You can also change these groups to universal groups when the domain functional level is set to Windows 2000 native or higher. No member group of a global group may have global scope for the scope to change to universal. Global groups may be nested inside one another in native or Windows Server 2003 domain functional levels.

➤ *Universal groups*—You can change these groups to either domain local groups or global groups. Security universal groups are only available when the domain functional level is set to Windows 2000 native or higher. Distribution universal groups are available under any domain functional level. No member group of a universal group may have global scope for the scope to change to global. Universal groups may be nested inside one another in the Windows 2000 native or the Windows Server 2003 domain functional levels.

Maintaining Groups and Group Membership

You manage Active Directory groups from the ADUC console. Default groups are stored within the Built-in container and within the Users container. To change a group's name, you must right-click the group name listed within the ADUC and select Rename. After you change the name, the Rename Group dialog box appears, allowing you to change the pre-Windows 2000 group name as well. Click OK for the Rename Group dialog box when you are done. When you double-click a group, you can view the group's name, the group's pre-Windows 2000 name, the group type, and the group scope from the General tab of the group's Properties window, as shown in Figure 4.8. From the group's properties window, you can

➤ Rename the group.

➤ Type in a description and an email address.

➤ Change the group scope and group type.

➤ Add and remove members.

➤ Add or remove the group as a member of another group.

➤ Specify Managed By information.

➤ View the canonical name of the group along with its object class, the date it was created, the date it was modified, and its Update Sequence Numbers (USNs) from the Object tab.

➤ View, add, or remove security permissions.

Figure 4.8 Working with a group's properties window.

Special Identity Groups

In addition to the Built-in groups, Windows Server 2003 supports special identity (SI) built-in groups that the operating system uses internally. No user can change the membership of these groups; membership is situational and the membership of these groups is determined by what activities users are involved in on the server and on the network. Group scopes do not apply to special identity groups. However, you can apply user rights and assign security permissions to SI groups for specific resources. Special identity groups include the following:

➤ *Anonymous Logon*—This SI group encompasses users and services that access computer resources without supplying an account name, a password, or a domain name. This group is not a member of the everyone group by default.

➤ *Authenticated Users*—This SI group encompasses all users whose logons have been authenticated. This is a more secure group to assign permissions to than the everyone group.

➤ *Batch*—This SI group reflects all accounts that are logged on as part of a batch process that is executing.

➤ *Creator Owner*—This SI group represents the creator and the owner of objects such as files, folders, and print jobs.

➤ *Dial-up*—This SI group contains all users who are currently accessing the computer using a dial-up connection.

➤ *Everyone*—This SI group encompasses all current users who are logged on over the network.

➤ *Interactive*—This SI group contains users who are currently physically logged on to the local computer (console) and accessing local resources. It includes users logged on via remote desktop connections (terminal services).

➤ *Network*—This SI group encompasses all current network users who are accessing resources remotely (as opposed to a user who is logged on locally accessing local resources).

➤ *Service*—This SI group identifies any accounts that are currently logged onto the computer as a service that is running.

➤ *System*—This SI group refers to the operating system itself.

➤ *Terminal Server User*—This SI group refers to any user accessing the system via terminal services as a remote desktop client.

Creating New Groups Using ADUC

You can create new groups from the ADUC console. Members of the account operators group, domain admins group, and the enterprise admins group can create domain local, global, and universal groups from the ADUC console under Windows Server 2003 Active Directory. Other users who are not members of those groups can be delegated the authority to create groups. The ability to create universal groups requires that the domain be set at either the Windows 2000 native or the Windows Server 2003 domain functional level. Group nesting becomes available under these levels as well. To create a new group under any domain functional level, perform these steps:

1. Right-click the container or OU where you want to place the new group and select New, Group.

2. At the New Object—Group dialog box, type in the Group Name and the pre-Windows 2000 Group Name (if different).

3. Select the group scope: domain local, global, or universal (if available).

4. Select the group type: security or distribution.

5. Click OK to create the new group.

Creating New Groups Using the Command Prompt

The same requirements for creating new groups using the ADUC apply for using the dsadd.exe command. The only required parameter is that you must specify the new group's DN. If you do not specify any optional parameters, by default, the group is created as a security group with global scope. For example, typing dsadd group "cn=staff,ou=east coast,dc=windows2003,dc=local" creates a new global security group named staff within the OU named east coast for the domain named windows2003.local. Use quotation marks if any of the parameters have spaces, such as the OU name of "east coast". Type dsadd group /? at any command prompt for help with the syntax and parameters for adding a group via the command line. To create a distribution group named sales managers with universal scope in the Users container, follow these steps:

1. Open a command prompt.

2. Type dsadd group "cn=sales managers,cn=users,dc=windows2003,dc=local" -secgrp no -scope u.

3. The `dsadd group` command should process the command and then display `"dsadd succeeded:CN=SALE MANAGERS,CN=USERS,DC=WINDOWS2003,DC=LOCAL"`.

> Group names may not be longer than 63 characters in Windows Server 2003 Active Directory.

Using Command-Line Utilities for Active Directory Objects

Microsoft added several useful command-line tools for managing Active Directory and Active Directory objects. In this chapter, you've already learned how to use the `dsadd` command for adding new computers and groups, but `dsadd` can do more than just add computers and groups. You can use these new command-line utilities for Active Directory both locally and remotely, provided that you possess the necessary security permissions for the task that you are trying to complete. The following list details the commands that are available and discusses how you can use them:

➤ *DSADD.exe*—This command adds a single computer, contact, group, OU, user, or quota specification to Active Directory. For help with the specific parameters and syntax for each type of object, type `dsadd ObjectType /?` at a command prompt. For example, `dsadd user /?` displays the available parameters (options) and syntax for adding a user to Active Directory.

➤ *DSGET.exe*—This command displays the properties for computers, contacts, groups, OUs, partitions, quotas, servers (DCs), sites, subnets, and users in Active Directory. For help with the specific parameters and syntax for each type of object, type `dsget ObjectType /?` at a command prompt. For example, `dsget server /?` displays the available parameters (options) and syntax for viewing the properties of a specific domain controller.

➤ *DSMOD.exe*—This command modifies the properties of a single computer, contact, group, OU, partition, quota, server, or user. For help with the specific parameters and syntax for each type of object, type `dsmod ObjectType /?` at a command prompt. For example, `dsmod group /?` displays the available parameters (options) and syntax for changing the properties of a specific group, including the ability to change the group type and group scope and adding or removing users.

➤ *DSMOVE.exe*—This command moves or renames a single object within Active Directory. For help with the specific parameters and syntax for this command, type dsmove /? at a command prompt.

➤ *DSQUERY.exe*—This command allows you to perform a search to locate computers, contacts, groups, OUs, partitions, quotas, servers (DCs), sites, subnets, or users within Active Directory. You can specify search criteria for finding Active Directory objects. The dsquery * command can find any type of Active Directory object. For help with the specific parameters and syntax for each type of object, type dsquery *ObjectType* /? at a command prompt. For example, dsquery computer /? displays the available parameters (options) and syntax for finding computers in Active Directory.

➤ *DSRM.exe*—This command removes (deletes) objects within Active Directory. For help with the specific parameters and syntax for this command, type dsrm /? at a command prompt.

➤ *CSVDE.exe*—This command exports data from Active Directory and imports data into Active Directory using the comma-separated values (CSV) file format. Programs such as Microsoft Excel and Microsoft Exchange Server administration utilities can read and write to CSV files. This tool is Microsoft's preferred method for automating the creation of user accounts in Active Directory using a bulk importing procedure. For help with the specific parameters and syntax for this command, type csvde (with no parameters) at a command prompt.

➤ *LDIFDE.exe*—This command exports data from Active Directory and imports data into Active Directory using the LDAP Data Interchange Format (LDIF) file format. The LDIF files use the .ldf extension and you can view and edit them using any simple text editor such as Notepad. For help with the specific parameters and syntax for this command, type ldifde (with no parameters) at a command prompt. This tool is not Microsoft's preferred method for automating the creation of user accounts in Active Directory using a bulk importing procedure.

Although it's been around for a long time, the **net** command can still prove useful. To view a list of all the available **net** command options, type **net** and press Enter at a command prompt. To get help on usage, type **net** *command_name* **/?** and press Enter. For example, you can view a list of user accounts for the domain by typing **net user** and pressing Enter.

Managing Users in Active Directory

Users are the only reason why computers and networks exist in the first place. You can manage users in two distinct ways under Windows Server 2003 Active Directory—from the GUI or from the command line. The ADUC console provides the graphical method to manage users, whereas command-line tools such as dsadd, dsmod, and dsmove provide the means for adding, changing, and moving users within the directory service. Which method you use for managing users is strictly a preference on your part as the network administrator, or it could be a companywide decision on the part of the IT department that establishes policies for IT administration. The Windows GUI is relatively straightforward, but the command-line tools lend themselves to batch files for a more automated approach.

Adding New Users

Creating new users in Active Directory is a fairly simple process. You need to assign both a display name and a user logon name for each user. The display name consists of the first name, initials, and last name of the user, by default. The display name appears in the ADUC console. The display name cannot contain more than 64 characters. The user logon name is used for logging onto the Active Directory domain. The rules for user logon names are as follows:

➤ They must be unique within each domain.

➤ They can contain up to 256 characters.

➤ You must assign a pre-Windows 2000 User Logon name to each user account. By default, the first 20 characters of the logon name are used, but you can assign a different name.

➤ User logon names cannot contain the following special characters:

"/ \ [ ] ; | = , + * ? < >

➤ Spaces embedded in user logon names are allowed but not recommended.

NOTE You can use either the user logon name or the pre-Windows 2000 user logon name to log onto an Active Directory domain, regardless of the domain functional level in effect.

Creating New User Objects from the GUI

The initial information required to create a user is minimal. Active Directory can store a vast amount of user information, but you must enter most of those details after a user is created. To create a new user from the ADUC console, follow these steps:

1. Open the ADUC console.

2. Right-click the container or OU where you want to place the new user and select New, User.

3. Type in the first name, initials, and last name of the user.

4. Change the full name, if desired.

5. Type in the user logon name. The user logon name combined with the @*domain.name* drop-down list box compose the user principal name (UPN) that you can use to log on to Active Directory from Windows 2000, Windows XP, and Windows Server 2003 computers.

6. If desired, you can change the pre-Windows 2000 user logon name or else leave it at the default.

7. Click Next to continue.

8. Type in a password for the user in both the Password box and the Confirm Password box. The password must conform to the domain's password policy requirements or else you will receive an error message, as shown in Figure 4.9.

9. To keep the assigned password for the user, clear the User Must Change Password at Next Logon check box.

10. If desired, mark the User Cannot Change Password, Password Never Expires, and Account Is Disabled check boxes.

11. Click Next to review a summary of how the new user will be created. Click Back to make any changes.

12. Click Finish to create the user.

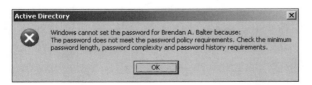

Figure 4.9 Viewing an error message for a password that does not meet Active Directory's password-policy requirements.

Creating New User Objects from the Command Line

Using the new dsadd command, you can also create users from any command prompt or batch file under Windows Server 2003. The dsadd user command offers many options. To get detailed information on the syntax and available parameters, type dsadd user /? at a command prompt. In the following step-by-step example, let's create a new user with a display name (CN) of Bill Gates. The user's first name (-FN) is William, his middle initial (-MI) is H, and his last name (-LN) is Gates. The user's user logon name (-UPN) is bgates, his pre-Windows 2000 user logon name (-SAMID) is bgates, and his password (-PWD) is 111-MS$$$, and we will create him within the East Coast OU for the Active Directory domain windows2003.local. To create a new user with this minimal amount of detail from the command line, follow these steps:

1. Open a command prompt window.

2. At the command prompt, type the following all on one line and then press Enter (if the length of the command is too long for the command prompt window, it will automatically wrap around to the next line):

   ```
   DSADD USER "CN=Bill Gates,OU=EAST COAST,DC=WINDOWS2003,DC=LOCAL"
   -UPN bgates@WINDOWS2003.LOCAL -SAMID bgates -FN William -MI H -LN Gates
   -PWD 111-MS$$$
   ```

3. The dsadd user command should process the command and then display "dsadd succeeded:CN=Bill Gates,OU=EAST COAST,DC=WINDOWS2003, DC=LOCAL".

To import many users into Active Directory at one time, use the **csvde** command-line tool. CSVDE reads and writes using the CSV file format. To import new users from a file named **newusers.csv**, type **csvde –i –f newusers.csv** and press Enter. For help with command-line options and syntax, type **csvde** (with no parameters) and press Enter.

Managing User Password Policies

Computer security has become a focal point the world over due to the tremendous amount of computer viruses and the huge rise in computer hacking incidents. To respond to these security threats, Microsoft pledged to make its new products "secure by design and secure by default." To this end, Active Directory under Windows Server 2003, by default, does not permit blank passwords nor passwords that do not meet its built-in minimum complexity requirements. To view or change these built-in default password settings, perform the following steps:

1. On a DC, click Start, Administrative Tools, Domain Security Policy.

2. From the Default Domain Security Settings console (as shown in Figure 4.10), you can view and edit policy settings for the domain.

3. Expand the Account Policies node and click the Password Policy sub-node to view the settings that are currently in effect for the entire domain. The default settings are

   ➤ *Enforce Password History*—24 passwords remembered

   ➤ *Maximum Password Age*—42 days

   ➤ *Minimum Password Age*—1 day

   ➤ *Minimum Password Length*—7 characters

   ➤ *Passwords Must Meet Complexity Requirements*—Enabled

   ➤ *Store Passwords Using Reversible Encryption*—Disabled

4. Double-click each setting that you want to change to modify the setting and click OK.

5. Exit from the Default Domain Security Settings console.

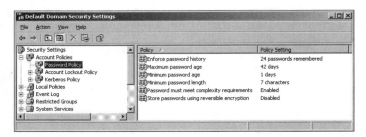

Figure 4.10   Working with default password policy settings for an Active Directory domain.

The Password Must Meet Complexity Requirements setting, when enabled, enforces the following rules for all passwords:

➤ Passwords cannot contain all or part of the user's account name.

➤ Passwords must contain at least six characters.

➤ Passwords must contain at least three of the following four different types of characters:

   ➤ Numerals 0 through 9.

   ➤ English lowercase letters a through z.

➤ English uppercase letters A through Z.

➤ Nonalphanumeric characters such as %, $, #, !, +, and &.

Passwords that meet these standards are considered strong passwords by Microsoft. Microsoft (and other security experts) recommend that you maintain an overall policy of strong passwords as a best practice. The maximum character length for passwords under Windows Server 2003 is 127; however, Windows 9x computers can only support up to 14-character passwords. A password is considered *weak* if it is blank, if it contains the user's name or company name, if it contains a complete word that appears in a dictionary, or if any of these examples with numbers incremented on the beginning or end of the word. For example, the password *computer* is a weak password, as are the passwords *sunshine1* or *1password*.

To reset a user's password from the ADUC console, right-click the user's name and select Reset Password. Read the warning dialog box explaining the implications of changing the password, and then click Proceed. In the Set Password dialog, type the new password in both the New Password box and the Confirm Password box. Mark the User Must Change Password at Next Logon check box to enable this setting. Click OK to change the password.

Modifying and Deleting Users

Active Directory can store a lot of information for each user, as you can see in Figure 4.11. You can double-click a user's name in the ADUC console to view a user's properties sheet. From the properties sheet, you add, change, or delete information for the user. By default, Active Directory can store users' phone numbers, addresses, email addresses, logon information, group memberships, remote control settings, terminal services settings, user dial-in settings, and Active Directory security permission settings, among many other options. By extending the Active Directory schema, Active Directory can store more information, such as Microsoft Exchange Server email settings.

Modifying User Accounts from the ADUC

When you right-click a user name in the ADUC console, you have several options available to you (see Figure 4.12). With the Copy option, you can copy the user's settings to create a new user with the same settings (a user template). You can add the user to an existing group. You can view, add, edit, or remove X.509 certificates and trusted non-Windows Kerberos realms by selecting the Name Mappings option. You can disable or enable a user account and reset the user's password. You can also move the user account to a different container, open the home page for the user (if specified), and send an email message to the selected user. You can run the Resultant Set of Policy

(RSoP) Wizard in planning mode by selecting All Tasks, Resultant Set of Policy (Planning). You can run the RSoP Wizard in logging mode by selecting All Tasks, Resultant Set of Policy (Logging).

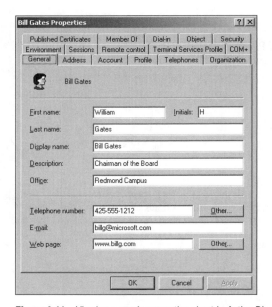

Figure 4.11 Viewing a user's properties sheet in Active Directory.

You can move a user by using the Cut option from the right-click menu, instead of using the Move option and instead of dragging a user account to a different container or OU and dropping it into the other container. You can easily delete a user account by right-clicking it and selecting Delete or by selecting the user account in the ADUC console and then pressing the Delete key on the keyboard. You can rename a user by right-clicking the user account and selecting Rename or by selecting the user account and pressing the F2 key on the keyboard.

Modifying User Accounts from the Command Line

You can use the dsmod user command to change user properties from the command prompt. The dsmod user command has several different options. For assistance with using the command, type dsmod user /? at a command prompt. As an example, let's change the last name to Fences, the description to Executive, and the office to Los Angeles for a user account named Bill Gates. This user is located in the East Coast OU in the Active Directory domain windows2003.local. To modify an existing user account from the command line, follow these steps:

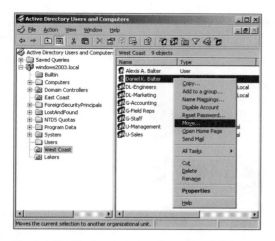

Figure 4.12 Viewing the options from right-clicking a user in the ADUC console.

1. Open a command prompt window.

2. At the command prompt, type the following all on one line and then press Enter (if the length of the command is too long for the command prompt window, it will automatically wrap around to the next line):

   ```
   DSMOD USER "CN=Bill Gates,OU=EAST COAST,DC=WINDOWS2003,DC=LOCAL" -LN
   Fences -DESC Executive -OFFICE "Los Angeles"
   ```

3. The dsmod user command should process the command and then display

   ```
   dsmod succeeded:CN=Bill Gates,OU=EAST COAST,DC=WINDOWS2003,DC=LOCAL.
   ```

To delete a user account from the command line, use the dsrm command. Following the previous example, typing dsrm "CN=Bill Gates,OU=EAST COAST,DC=WINDOWS2003,DC=LOCAL" and pressing Enter will prompt you to confirm that you want to remove the user account from the directory. Type Y to confirm the deletion or type N to cancel the operation. After you confirm the deletion, the user account is removed. The dsrm command then displays dsrm succeeded:CN=Bill Gates,OU=EAST COAST,DC=WINDOWS2003,DC=LOCAL.

To find out which domain groups that a user is a member of, as well as view other pertinent information about a user, type net user *user_logon_name* and press the Enter key, as shown in Figure 4.13.

Figure 4.13 Using the **net user** command to find domain groups in which a user is member.

Troubleshooting User Account Problems

A user cannot log on to the domain if his or her user account is either disabled or locked out. An administrator can temporarily or permanently disable a user account by right-clicking the account in the ADUC console and selecting Disable, as shown in Figure 4.14. When you select the Disable option, a message box appears confirming that the user account is now disabled and the user account icon displays with a red X over it. Disabling an account is a good practice for users who take a temporary leave of absence to prevent possible unauthorized access from people who might know those users' logon names and passwords. To re-enable a user account, simply right-click the user account name in the ADUC and select the Enable option.

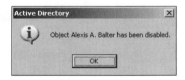

Figure 4.14 Disabling a user account in the ADUC console.

Locked-Out User Accounts

If a user attempts to log onto the domain but forgets his or her logon name or password, by default, Windows Server 2003 Active Directory permits an *unlimited* number of logon attempts! The policy settings for the Account Lockout Policy for the domain are configurable from the Default Domain Security Settings console, in the Account Policies, Account Lockout Policy subnode. When you change the default Account Lockout Duration policy setting, you are prompted to configure or accept default settings for the other two domain account lockout policies, as you can see in Figure 4.15. The three domain lockout policies and their available settings are as follows:

➤ *Account Lockout Duration*—This policy defines how long locked-out accounts remain locked out. The default setting is none (or undefined) because you must enable the Account Lockout Threshold policy for this policy to be in effect. The available range is from 0 minutes through 99,999 minutes.

➤ *Account Lockout Threshold*—This policy defines the number of failed logon attempts allowed before the user account is locked out. The default setting is 0, which means that the account lockout feature is disabled. The available range is from 0 attempts through 999 attempts.

➤ *Reset Account Lockout Counter After*—This policy defines the number of minutes that must elapse after one or more failed logon attempts (for each user) before the failed logon attempt counter gets reset to 0 bad logon attempts. The default setting is none (or undefined) because you must enable the Account Lockout Threshold policy for this policy to be in effect. The available range is from 1 minute through 99,999 minutes. This policy setting must be less than or equal to the Account Lockout Duration setting.

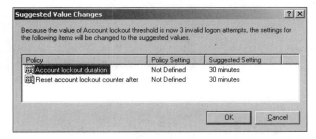

Figure 4.15 Managing user account lockout settings from the Default Domain Security Settings console.

Once a user account is locked out, it cannot be used for logging the user onto the domain until the account lockout is reset by an administrator or until the lockout duration has expired (see Figure 4.16). By default, the Administrator account *cannot* be locked out; if the Account Lockout Threshold is exceeded for the Administrator account, the Account Is Locked Out check box becomes checked on the Administrator account's properties sheet. However, the Administrator can still log on successfully with the proper username and password from any computer or DC in the domain. For all other user accounts other than the Administrator account, an administrator must clear the Account Is Locked Out check box in the user account's properties sheet or the Account Lockout Duration time must expire before a locked-out user can log on again.

Figure 4.16   Viewing the Logon Message box for a user attempting to log onto the domain with a locked-out account.

Troubleshooting User Authentication Problems

By default, Windows Server 2003, Windows XP, Windows 2000, and Windows NT computers all provide the ability for domain user accounts to log on to the computer even if the network connection is down or if there is no DC available to authenticate the user's logon. The user must have logged onto that computer and been authenticated by a DC previously, and the number of users that can log on in such circumstances is limited to 10 by default. Logging on in this manner is referred to as using cached credentials. These cached credentials are stored on the domain-member computer. You can limit or disable the cached-credentials feature by modifying an entry in the Windows Registry for each domain member computer or by configuring a group policy setting for the domain.

Changing Cached Credential Settings Through the Registry

For Windows Server 2003, Windows XP, and Windows 2000 domain-member computers, you can edit the Registry to modify the `cachedlogonscount` value. Remember, however, making any changes to the Windows Registry can render a computer unstable or completely unusable: Always take great care and be sure to have good data backups before editing the Registry. To change the number of cached-credential accounts stored on a computer, follow these steps:

1. On a domain-member computer running Windows Server 2003, Windows XP, or Windows 2000, click Start, Run; type `regedit`; and click OK to run the Windows Registry editor.

2. Starting at the `HKEY_LOCAL_MACHINE` node, expand the Registry keys and subkeys and navigate to `SOFTWARE\Microsoft\Windows NT\CurrentVersion\Winlogon`.

3. Double-click the `cachedlogonscount` value name to display the Edit String dialog box, as shown in Figure 4.17.

4. Type in a new value data number to reflect how many cached accounts you want the computer to store (0 disables the use of cached credentials on the computer).

5. Click OK to save your new settings and exit from the Registry editor.

6. Restart the computer to ensure that the new settings take effect.

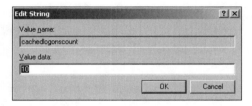

Figure 4.17   Modifying the **cachedlogonscount** entry in the Windows Registry.

Changing Cached Credential Settings Through Group Policy

An easier, more efficient, and immensely more manageable method of dealing with the number of available stored cached logon credentials is through a group policy setting. By defining a domainwide policy, you can effectively manage all domain-member computers with just one configuration setting. To change the number of cached-credential accounts stored on each domain-member computer, follow these steps:

1. On a DC, open the Default Domain Security Settings console.

2. Expand the Local Policies node and select the Security Options subnode.

3. Double-click the policy named Interactive Logon: Number of Previous Logons to Cache (in Case Domain Controller Is Not Available) as shown in Figure 4.18.

4. Mark the Define This Policy Setting check box.

5. Type the number of previous logons to store in the Cache: spinner box; the minimum number is 0 (disables cached credentials) and the maximum number is 50.

6. Click OK and exit from the Default Domain Security Settings console.

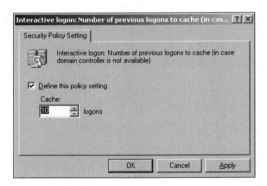

Figure 4.18   Defining a Group Policy setting for Interactive Logon: Number of Previous Logons to Cache.

Managing User Profiles

A user profile is the group of settings that together compose the look and feel of the user's desktop environment. A profile is a combination of folders, data, shortcuts, application settings, and personal data. For example, users can configure their computers with the screen savers they prefer along with their favorite desktop wallpaper. These settings are independent of other users' settings for a specific local computer. When users log on to their computers for the very first time, a new profile is created for those users from the profile named default user.

When user DanB logs on to a Windows Server 2003, Windows XP, Windows 2000, or Windows NT computer for the very first time, a profile is created just for DanB from that computer's default user profile. This type of profile is known as a *local profile*, and it is stored on the computer on which it was created. If DanB logs on to a different computer, his local profile does not follow him to the other computer. However, you can have a user's profile follow the user around the network, if you so choose. This type of profile is called a *roaming user profile*. These profiles are stored on a network server. A local copy of the roaming profile also appears on the client computer.

 You can customize a computer's default user profile by logging on as a new user (for example, JoeNew) and customizing the user settings such as the desktop wallpaper, the Windows color scheme, the folder options, and so on. When you log off as that new user (JoeNew), the user settings that you have configured are saved to the new user's profile. You should then restart the computer and log on as the administrator. If you copy the entire contents of JoeNew's profile folder into the default user folder, you customize the default user profile to match all the settings of that user, JoeNew.

Managing Local User Profiles

User profiles under Windows Server 2003 and Windows XP employ a similar folder structure as introduced under Windows 2000. This structure is different from the one used with Windows NT 4.0. One of the folders within a user's profile is called Local Settings. The Local Settings folder is local to the computer it resides on and it does not roam from workstation to workstation. Also, a folder called My Documents appears within each profile. This folder is the location where users' files are saved to disk by default. The My Documents folder does have the capability to follow users around the network (roam) as they log on to different workstations.

Local profiles stored on Windows Server 2003, Windows XP, and Windows 2000 computers appear in a different location from those local profiles stored on Windows NT 4.0 computers, perhaps. If you perform a clean install of Windows Server 2003, Windows XP Professional, or Windows 2000, user profiles are stored in the root of the system drive partition (or volume). The default location for user profiles is `%system`**`drive`**`%\Documents and Settings\`*`user_logon_name`* (for example, `C:\Documents and Settings\DanB`). If, however, you upgrade a Windows NT Workstation 4.0 computer to Windows XP Professional or to Windows 2000 Professional, the local profile appears in the same location as it was originally: `%systemroot%\Profiles\`*`user_logon_name`*, as in `C:\Winnt\Profiles\DanB`. The same holds true for Windows NT Server 4.0 computers that are upgraded to either Windows Server 2003 or Windows 2000 Server.

Working with User Logon Scripts

When a user logs on to a Windows NT domain or to a Windows Active Directory domain from a Windows Server 2003, Windows XP Professional,

Windows 2000, or Windows NT computer, a *logon script* can execute and a *home folder* can be assigned to the user. Logon scripts are often used to map network drives or to execute several commands from a batch file or some other script file. Using a GPO setting, you can assign a logon script to users within a site, domain, or OU by following these steps:

1. Open the Active Directory Sites and Services (ADSS) console to assign a logon script to a site, or open the Active Directory Users and Computers (ADUC) console to assign a logon script to a domain or an OU. If you have installed the Group Policy Management Console (GPMC), which you can download from Microsoft, open the GPMC.

2. For the ADSS or the ADUC, right-click the site, domain, or OU for which you want to assign a logon script and select Properties. Click the Group Policy tab.

3. For the GPMC, select the site, domain, or OU for which you want to assign a logon script, right-click an existing GPO and select Edit, or right-click the domain or OU and select Create and Link a GPO Here and then right-click the new GPO and select Edit. For the ADSS or the ADUC, click the New button to create a GPO and then click Edit, or select an existing GPO and click Edit.

4. From the Group Policy Object Editor, go to the User Configuration node and expand the Windows Settings subnode.

5. Select the Scripts (Logon/Logoff) object and then double-click the Logon option in the right-hand details pane.

6. From the Logon Properties window, click the Add button. Type in the logon script's name or click Browse to locate it (see Figure 4.19). The script needs to reside within the `Logon` subfolder from the Active Directory–designated folder tree that starts from the shared folder `SysVol\<domain.name>\Policies\<GUID folder>\User\Scripts\Logon` (see Figure 4.20).

7. Click OK for the Add a Script dialog box after you enter the script's name in the Script Name box.

8. Click OK to close the Logon Properties dialog box.

9. Close the Group Policy Object Editor window.

10. Close the GPMC or click Close for the Properties dialog box for the site, domain, or OU that you are working with, and then you can close the ADSS or the ADUC.

Figure 4.19 Adding a logon script file to a GPO.

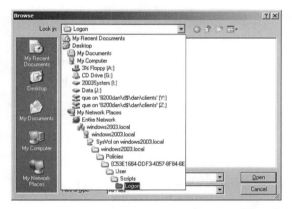

Figure 4.20 Viewing the default location of logon script files for a GPO.

You can also choose to be "old school" and use the Netlogon share to store logon scripts. This method is particularly useful if you have to support legacy operating systems such as Windows 9x and Windows NT 4.0. To configure a logon script for a user without using group policy, perform the following steps on a Windows 2000 Server or on a Windows Server 2003 Active Directory DC:

1. Place the logon script file in the `%SystemRoot%\sysvol\`*domain.name*`\scripts` folder (the default location for logon scripts for Windows servers acting as DCs). An example is `C:\Windows\Sysvol\Sysvol\Windows2003.local\` `scripts`.

2. Open the ADUC console.

3. Right-click the name of the user account and select Properties.

4. Click the Profile tab and type the name of the logon script in the Logon Script box.

5. Click OK to save the setting.

Working With Users' Home Folders

A *home folder* is a central location on a network server where users can store their files. All users can have their own home folders to store data. This way, if a workstation fails, a user doesn't lose all his or her data. Home folders also provide one central location in which users can back up all their data. To create a home folder, perform the following steps on a Windows 2000 Server or on a Windows Server 2003 DC:

1. Create a shared folder on a network server to designate it for storing users' home folders.

2. Open the ADUC console.

3. Right-click the name of the user account and select Properties.

4. Click the Profile tab and then click the Connect option button.

5. Click the drop-down list box and choose an available drive letter.

6. Type in the Uniform Naming Convention (UNC) path to the user's home folder (for example, \\server1\homedir\danb).

7. Click OK to save the setting.

NOTE   Microsoft suggests that users store their data in the My Documents folder instead of using home folders. Fortunately, you can enable a group policy setting under Active Directory to redirect My Documents from the local computer to a network file server. The group policy also activates offline caching of My Documents to the user's local computer.

Managing Roaming User Profiles and Mandatory User Profiles

If you have users who move from computer to computer, you can configure their profiles to move with them. A roaming profile is stored on a network server so that the profile is accessible regardless of which computer a user logs on to anywhere within the domain. You can place user profiles on a server in two ways. One way is to copy (upload) user profiles that are stored locally on client computers to a server that you have designated for storing roaming user profiles. A second method involves creating and customizing a user profile on a client computer that you use as a companywide standard. You can then manually copy it to the server that stores the roaming profiles.

 Roaming user profiles behave differently in Windows Server 2003, Windows XP, and Windows 2000 than in Windows NT 4.0. When a user logs on to a computer for the first time, the roaming profile is copied to the client computer. From that point forward, whenever a user logs on to a computer, the locally cached copy of the profile is compared to the roaming user profile stored on a server. If the local profile and the roaming profile are the same, the local copy is used. Windows Server 2003, Windows XP, and Windows 2000 computers copy only files that have changed, not the entire profile, as was the case in Windows NT 4.0.

You can convert a local profile into a roaming profile without first copying a local user profile to a shared folder on a network server. You simply need to specify the location of the roaming profile in the properties sheet of a user's account in Active Directory. Once a roaming profile is established, you can convert the roaming profile back into a local profile. Use the following steps to configure a roaming profile and copy it from a Windows XP Professional computer to a Windows Server 2003 computer:

1. Create a shared folder on a server for the profiles, such as `C:\Users\Profiles`. For Windows Server 2003 computers, be sure to change the default share permissions for the folder to at least Everyone:*Change* instead of the default share permissions of Everyone:*Read*.

2. On a Windows XP Professional computer, right-click My Computer and select Properties to view the System Properties dialog box.

3. Click the Advanced tab.

4. From the User Profiles section, click the Settings button.

5. Select the user's profile you want to use as a roaming profile and select Copy to. Then, type in the UNC path to the shared folder that was created and append the name of the profile for this user, as in `\\DC1\profiles\DBalter` (see Figure 4.21).

6. In the ADUC console, open the properties sheet for the user account, click the Profile tab, and type in the UNC path to the shared roaming profile folder on the server in the Profile Path box.

7. The first time that the roaming user successfully logs on and then subsequently logs off from a Windows XP computer, the user's profile is uploaded to the profile server and stored. The second, and subsequent,

times that the user logs on to the domain, the roaming profile is compared with the local profile and the most recent profile is used.

8. To change the user profile's type, revisit the User Profiles dialog box from the System Properties window and click the Change Type button, as shown in Figure 4.22.

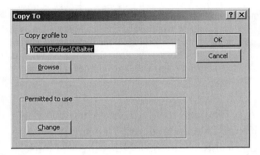

Figure 4.21   Copying a local user profile to a shared folder on a server to make it a roaming user profile.

 NOTE   You might not always be able to copy a local user profile to another local user profile folder or to a shared folder on a server. Once a user has logged onto the computer, his or her local user profile gets loaded into memory, and often, the computer's RAM keeps that profile locked, even after the user logs off. If you reboot the computer and log on as a different user with administrative permissions, you should have no trouble copying any of the local user profiles, except for the profile that you're currently logged on as!

Figure 4.22   Changing a roaming user profile back to a local user profile.

Managing Mandatory User Profiles

You can protect both local and roaming profiles from being permanently changed by users if you simply rename the ntuser.dat file to ntuser.man. By renaming this file, you have effectively made the user profile read-only, meaning that the operating system does not save any changes made to the profile when the user logs off. Microsoft recommends this method for creating mandatory user profiles. ntuser.dat appears in the root of a profile folder and is hidden by default. This file is responsible for the user portion of the Registry and contains all the user settings, such as the Windows desktop background color, the location of the taskbar, and many other desktop settings. Obviously, in addition to renaming this file, you should apply appropriate NTFS security permissions on this file and on the entire user profile folder so that users cannot simply rename the file back to `ntuser.dat`.

If the server where user profiles are stored is not available when a user logs on, the operating system defaults to using an existing local profile for the user. If the user has no local profile on that computer, it creates a local profile for the user from the local default profile. If you want to strictly enforce a policy that states that no user can log on without a roaming profile, you can append the extension of `.man` to the roaming user profile folder's name. For example, if JoeUser's roaming profile is stored on server1 in the `profiles` share, you can rename the `JoeUser` profile folder to `JoeUser.man`, in addition to renaming `ntuser.dat` to `ntuser.man`. In this case, the operating system does not allow the user to log on unless the roaming profile is available.

If you enable user profiles on Windows 9x computers, the file that stores the user settings is named **user.dat** instead of **ntuser.dat**. You can rename **user.dat** to **user.man** to make the user profile mandatory (read-only).

Exam Prep Questions

Question 1

> How can you support users on Windows 9x and Windows NT 4.0 computers for logging onto Windows Server 2003 Active Directory domains that have been raised to the Windows 2000 native or the Windows Server 2003 domain functional levels? (Choose the best answer.)
>
> ○ A. Upgrade those computers to Windows 2000 or Windows XP Professional.
>
> ○ B. Install the Active Directory client software.
>
> ○ C. Make sure that the Windows Server 2003 Active Directory forest remains at the Windows 2000 forest functional level.
>
> ○ D. Disable the NTLM v2 authentication protocol on all DCs.

Answer B is correct because when you install the Active Directory client software on Windows 9x and Windows NT 4.0 computers, those computers will perform Active Directory searches and have access to Active Directory resources. Answer A is incorrect because upgrading the operating system on workstation computers is a significant task in terms of labor and expenses; installing the Active Directory client software is less time-consuming and much less expensive. Answer C is incorrect because the forest functional level can remain at Windows 2000 while you raise the domain functional level to Windows 2000 native or Windows Server 2003. Answer D is incorrect because disabling the NTLM v2 authentication protocol means only that Kerberos is used exclusively; this procedure does not enable Windows 9x- or Windows NT 4.0-based computers to access Active Directory resources.

Question 2

> Which of the following methods can you use to create computer accounts in Active Directory under Windows Server 2003? (Choose three.)
>
> ❏ A. Log onto a domain from a Windows 98 computer.
>
> ❏ B. Join a domain from a Windows NT 4.0 computer.
>
> ❏ C. Prestage a computer account from the ADUC console.
>
> ❏ D. Prestage a computer account using the **dsget computer** command.
>
> ❏ E. Prestage a computer account using the **dsadd computer** command.
>
> ❏ F. Join a domain from a Windows 95 computer with the Active Directory client software installed.

Answers B, C, and E are correct. You can create a computer account when you join a computer to a domain from a Windows NT 4.0, Windows 2000, Windows XP, or Windows Server 2003 computer. You can prestage a computer account by using either the ADUC console or by using the dsadd computer command from a command prompt. Answer A is incorrect because logging onto a domain from a Windows 98 computer does not create a computer account in Active Directory. Answer D is incorrect because the dsget computer command displays properties of computers in the directory. Answer F is incorrect because you cannot join a Windows 95 computer to a domain, even with the Active Directory client software installed.

Question 3

Which of the following groups are not part of an Active Directory domain? (Choose two.)

- ❑ A. Local groups
- ❑ B. Domain local groups
- ❑ C. Global groups
- ❑ D. Built-in groups
- ❑ E. Universal groups
- ❑ F. Domain global groups

Answers A and F are correct. Local groups are also sometimes referred to as machine groups: they apply on the computer where they are located. Domain global groups do not exist in Active Directory. Answers B, C, D, and E are incorrect because these groups do all exist within an Active Directory domain.

Question 4

For which of the following domain functional levels can administrators nest groups within other groups and change the scope of groups. (Choose two.)

- ❑ A. Windows 2000 native
- ❑ B. Windows 2000 mixed
- ❑ C. Windows Server 2003
- ❑ D. Windows Server 2003 interim
- ❑ E. Windows Server 2003 mixed

Answers A and C are correct. Administrators can nest groups and change the scope of groups for the Windows 2000 native and Windows Server 2003 domain functional levels. Answer B is incorrect because administrators cannot nest groups nor change the scope of groups under the Windows 2000 mixed domain functional level. Answer D is incorrect because administrators cannot nest groups nor change the scope of groups under the Windows Server 2003 interim domain functional level. Answer E is incorrect because the Windows Server 2003 mixed level does not exist.

Question 5

> Which of the following groups can be members of a universal group for a domain set at the Windows Server 2003 domain functional level? (Choose three.)
>
> ❏ A. Domain local groups
> ❏ B. Other universal groups from the same domain only
> ❏ C. Global groups from the same domain only
> ❏ D. Global groups from any domain
> ❏ E. Universal groups from any domain
> ❏ F. User accounts from the same domain only
> ❏ G. Computer accounts from any domain

Answers D, E, and G are correct. Universal groups can contain other universal groups and global groups from any domain. Universal groups can also have computer accounts (and user accounts) from any domain as members. Answer A is incorrect because universal groups cannot have domain local groups as members. Answer B is incorrect because universal groups from any domain can be members of a universal group. Answer C is incorrect because univeral groups can contain global groups from any domain. Answer F is incorrect because universal groups can contain user and computer accounts from any domain.

Question 6

> What is Microsoft's recommended method for creating a mandatory user profile?
>
> ○ A. Rename the user profile folder with the **.dat** extension.
> ○ B. Set the NTFS folder permissions to read-only for the user profile folder.
> ○ C. Within the user profile folder, rename the file **ntuser.dat** to **ntuser.man**.
> ○ D. Create a roaming user profile and leave the network share permissions for the shared network folder at Everyone:Read.

Answer C is correct. Renaming the `ntuser.dat` file, stored within each user profile folder, to `ntuser.man` makes the user profile mandatory, whether it is a local or roaming profile. Answer A is incorrect because renaming the user profile folder with the `.dat` extension does not make the profile mandatory. Answer B is incorrect because Microsoft does not recommend this method for creating mandatory user profiles. Answer D is incorrect because Microsoft does not recommend this method either for creating mandatory user profiles.

Question 7

How can you perform a bulk import of users into Active Directory to create many user accounts at one time?

- ○ A. Use the **dsadd.exe** command.
- ○ B. Use the ADUC console.
- ○ C. Use the **net user** command.
- ○ D. Use the **csvde.exe** command.
- ○ E. Use the **dsmod.exe** command.

Answers D is correct. You can use the `csvde.exe` command from a command prompt to import many users into Active Directory from `.csv` files. Answer A is incorrect because the `dsadd.exe` only creates a single user at time. Answer B is incorrect because the ADUC console can only create one user at a time. Answer C is incorrect because the `net user` command can only create one user at a time.

Question 8

Which of the following default built-in groups are considered special identities? (Choose two.)

- ❏ A. Administrators
- ❏ B. Guests
- ❏ C. Remote Desktop Users
- ❏ D. Terminal Server User
- ❏ E. Dial-up
- ❏ F. TelnetClients

Answers D and E are correct. Terminal Server User and Dial-up are both special identity groups that refer to how a user is accessing the computer, and membership in each special identity group only lasts as long as the user continues to access the computer in that manner. Answer A is incorrect because the Administrators group is a built-in group, but it is not a special identity. Answer B is incorrect because the Guests group is a built-in group, but it is not a special identity. Answer F is incorrect because the TelnetClients group is a built-in group, but it is not a special identity.

Question 9

Which of the following command-line commands can you use to rename an object within Active Directory?

○ A. **dsadd**

○ B. **dsquery**

○ C. **dsmove**

○ D. **dsrm**

○ E. **dsget**

○ F. **net user**

Answer C is correct. You can use the dsmove command to move and rename objects in Active Directory. Answer A is incorrect because you cannot rename any Active Directory object with the dsadd command; you use it for adding users. Answer B is incorrect because you cannot rename any Active Directory object with the dsquery command; you use it for performing search operations. Answer D is incorrect because you cannot rename any Active Directory object with the dsrm command; you use it for removing objects. Answer E is incorrect because you cannot rename any Active Directory object with the dsget command; you use it for displaying an object's properties. Answer F is incorrect because you cannot rename any Active Directory object with the net user command; you use it for adding users and for viewing user information.

Question 10

Which of the following user passwords is acceptable based on the default settings in Active Directory for a user with the logon name of Dan?

○ A. dan$456

○ B. zM!993

○ C. 33#abcd

○ D. ttrrr789021

Answer C is correct. The default settings for user passwords in an Active Directory domain include the following:

➤ The minimum password length is seven characters.

➤ Passwords must meet complexity requirements; they must contain at least three of the following types of characters: numerals 0 through 9, lowercase letters a to z, uppercase letters A to Z, and special nonalphanumeric characters such as %, $, #, !, and so on.

Answer A is incorrect because even though it contains at least seven characters, it also contains the user's logon name. Answer B is incorrect because it contains all the necessary characters but is not seven or more characters in length. Answer D is incorrect because even though it is more than seven characters in length, it only contains lowercase letters and numerals.

Need to Know More?

Minasi, Mark, et al. *Mastering Windows Server 2003*. Alameda, California: Sybex Inc., 2003.

Scales, Lee, and John Michell. *MCSA/MCSE 70-290 Training Guide: Managing and Maintaining a Windows Server 2003 Environment*. Indianapolis, Indiana: Que Publishing, 2003.

Stanek, William R. *Microsoft Windows Server 2003 Administrator's Pocket Consultant*. Redmond, Washington: Microsoft Press, 2003.

Search the Microsoft Product Support Services Knowledge Base on the Internet: http://support.microsoft.com. You can also search through Microsoft TechNet on the Internet: http://www.microsoft. com/technet. Find technical information using keywords from this chapter, such as computer accounts, user accounts, global groups, domain functional levels, active directory, universal groups, dsadd, and dsmod.

Managing Network Resources and Terminal Services

You must manage network resources effectively to meet the changing needs of networked computer users. Setting up shared resources and controlling access to those shared resources are two of the most important jobs that network administrators face. Fortunately, Windows Server 2003 comes well equipped with the tools that administrators require to maintain a secure network infrastructure. Share permissions, NTFS file system permissions, offline files, data encryption, and shadow copy backups provide IT staff members with the ability to share and lock down resources as well as keep them safe for retrieval if necessary. Terminal services and remote desktop connections offer remote administrators and remote users unprecedented access to server resources from a distance. In this chapter, you will discover the benefits, the possible drawbacks, and the many nuances of administering these network services.

Working with Shared Network Folders

You need to set up shared network folders if you want users on remote computers to be able to access files stored on Windows Servers (or files stored on Windows desktop computers). For users who need access to shared data over the network, you can use standard shared folders. For users who need access to shared data over the Internet or over an intranet using a Web browser, you can use Web folders. To use Web folders, you must first install Internet Information Services (IIS) 6.0 on a Windows Server 2003 computer; IIS 6.0 is not installed by default. You install IIS 6.0 with the Add or Remove Programs applet in the Control Panel. Only members of the Administrators group or the Server Operators group have the necessary permissions to create, manage, and remove shared folders under Windows Server 2003.

Creating Shared Folders from Windows Explorer

Sharing folders under Windows Server 2003 is similar to setting up shared folders under Windows XP and Windows 2000. Shared folders are often referred to simply as "shares." From the GUI, you can use the Windows Explorer (or My Computer) to right-click any available folder that you want to share with remote users over the network. To create a shared folder on a Windows Server 2003 computer, follow these steps:

1. Open My Computer or Windows Explorer.

2. Right-click the folder that you want to share and select Sharing and Security.

3. From the Sharing tab, click the Share This Folder button.

4. Type the new shared folder's name in the Share Name box.

5. Optionally, type in a description in the Description box.

6. In the User Limit section, either accept the default setting of Maximum Allowed, or click Allow This Number of Users and type in the number in the spinner box, as shown in Figure 5.1.

7. Click OK to create the shared folder with default share permissions.

 Under Windows Server 2003, the default share permissions are now Everyone: Allow Read as opposed to Everyone: Allow Full Control, which was the case for Windows NT and Windows 2000. Windows XP Professional was Microsoft's first operating system to employ this new default security setting.

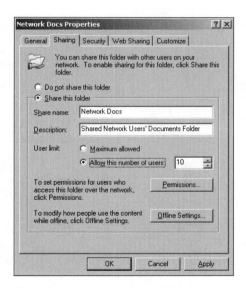

Figure 5.1 Creating a new shared folder.

 If you'd like to create multiple shares with different share names that all point to the same physical folder, maybe even with different access permissions on each share, click the New Share button that appears at the bottom of the Sharing tab for an existing shared folder.

Removing Share Names and Shared Folders

To remove a share when you have multiple shares for the same physical folder, select the share from the Share Name drop-down list box and click the Remove Share button at the bottom of the dialog box. To stop sharing the folder entirely, click the Do Not Share This Folder option button at the top of the dialog box; this action removes all shares from the network browse list, and the folder will no longer be accessible by remote users as a network shared folder.

Creating Shared Web Folders

If you installed IIS 6.0 (now known as Application Server), with the World Wide Web Service component, you can create shared Web folders. Web folders are accessible from remote computers using a Web browser, or you can access them from a program that supports the Web Distributed Authoring and Versioning (WebDAV) protocol, such as Microsoft Word. WebDAV allows users to connect to shared folders through Hypertext Transport Protocol (HTTP) using TCP port 80. This is the same HTTP that you use when browsing Web sites over the Internet.

To connect to a Web folder, a user must possess the appropriate permissions for the folder. By typing the URL for the folder in the Open dialog box for a program such as Microsoft Word, you can access the shared Web folder via HTTP instead of accessing it using the usual Server Message Block (SMB) protocol. From the Open dialog box, you can type the URL for the Web folder that you want to access in the File Name box and press the Enter key to connect to the shared Web folder (see Figure 5.2). You must enable directory browsing for the Web folder for users to view the contents of the folder. To set up and configure a shared Web folder, perform the following steps:

1. Open My Computer or Windows Explorer.

2. Right-click the folder that you want to share and select Sharing and Security.

3. From the Web Sharing tab, select the Web site that will host this shared Web folder from the Share On drop-down list box.

4. Click the Share This Folder option button; the Edit Alias dialog box will appear immediately, as shown in Figure 5.3.

5. Type in the Alias (share name) for this Web folder (or accept the default). Remote users can only access the Web folder by using its alias name.

6. In the Access Permissions section, mark the check box for each permission that you want to assign to this Web folder as it applies to remote users. The default permission, Read, is automatically checked. Select from Write, Script Source Access, and Directory Browsing. To use the

Web folders interface, you must select Read, Write, and Directory Browsing access permissions for each Web folder.

7. In the Application Permissions section, click the option button for which level you want to grant: None, Scripts, or Execute (Includes Scripts). The default is Scripts.

8. Click OK to save the settings for the Web folder's properties.

9. Click OK to exit from the Properties dialog box and create the Web folder.

To add more than one alias, click the Add button from the Web Sharing tab of a folder's properties dialog box. To modify an alias's settings, select the alias you want to modify and click the Edit Properties button. Finally, to delete an alias for a Web folder, select the alias and click the Remove button. To remove the shared Web folder entirely, click the Do Not Share This Folder radio button. Click OK for the folder's properties dialog box when you finish.

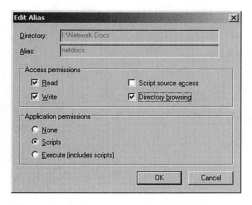

Figure 5.2   Setting up a new shared Web folder.

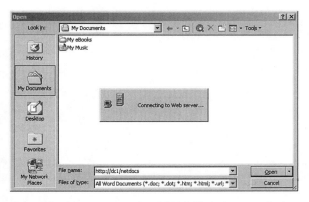

Figure 5.3   Connecting to a shared Web folder using an application such as Microsoft Word, which supports WebDAV.

Creating Shared Folders from the Command Line

Windows Server 2003 supports an unprecedented degree of command-line functionality compared to previous Windows versions. However, the net series of commands has been around for a number of years, as has the net share command. Using the net share command, you can easily create new shared folders from the command prompt. For help with the syntax and options for the net share command, type net share / ? and press the Enter key at any command prompt. To create a shared folder, type net share name_of_share=driveletter:\path and press Enter. For example, to create a shared folder named companypayroll for the folder c:\Payroll, at a command prompt type net share companypayroll=c:\payroll. To remove the share, type net share companypayroll /delete.

Working with the Shared Folders Snap-In

Another way to work with shared folders is with the Shared Folders Microsoft Management Console (MMC) snap-in. This snap-in is available as a node within the Computer Management console, or you can add it individually from a custom console shell. The Shared Folders snap-in provides a central location for managing all shared folders on a server. To add the fsmgmt.msc file to an MMC shell, follow these steps:

1. Click Start, Run; type mmc; and click OK to open a blank console.

2. At the blank console window, click File, Add/Remove Snap-In.

3. Click the Add button.

4. Select the Shared Folders snap-in from the Available Standalone Snap-Ins list and click Add.

5. Be sure that the Local Computer is selected (if you will be creating shared folders for the local computer), or select Another Computer and click Browse to locate it.

6. Click Finish.

7. Click Close for the Add Standalone Snap-In dialog box and click OK for the Add/Remove Snap-In dialog box. The Shared Folders node appears within the MMC window, as shown in Figure 5.4.

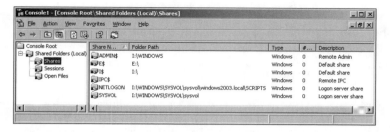

Figure 5.4 Viewing shared folders from the Shared Folders MMC snap-in.

Creating Shares from the Shared Folders Snap-In

Microsoft added more functionality to the Shared Folders snap-in for Windows Server 2003. You now use a new wizard to create shares from the Shared Folders snap-in. The Share a Folder wizard gives you the ability to customize both share permissions and NTFS folder permissions (if the folder resides on an NTFS drive). To create a new share from the Shared Folders snap-in, follow these steps:

1. Open the Shared Folders node.

2. Right-click the Shares subnode, select New Share, and click Next.

3. Type the drive letter and path for the folder you want to share in the Folder Path box, or click Browse to locate the folder.

4. Click Next.

5. Type an optional description in the Description box.

6. Click the Change button to select an Offline Setting, if you do not want to accept the default—Selected Files and Programs Available Offline. The section "Working with Shared Folder Offline Settings" later in this chapter covers offline settings.

7. Click Next.

8. From the Specify Permissions for the Share dialog box, select one of the following folder access security options, as shown in Figure 5.5:

   ➤ All Users Have Read-Only Access.

   ➤ Administrators Have Full Access; Other Users Have Read-Only Access.

   ➤ Administrators Have Full Access; Other Users Have Read and Write Access.

   ➤ Use Custom Share and Folder Permissions.

9. If you select the Use Custom Share and Folder Permissions option, click the Customize button to set both share permissions and security (NTFS) file-system permissions on the folder.

10. Click Finish to create the new share.

 Remember that share permissions are quite different from (NTFS) file-system security permissions! Share permissions only affect remote users when they access shared folders over the network. NTFS file-system permissions, on the other hand, are more granular than share permissions, and file-system permissions apply to both folders and files. Share permissions apply only to shared folders; you cannot apply them to individual files. File-system permissions also apply to both local users and remote network users; users cannot circumvent file-system permissions by logging on to the local computer where the shared folder resides! Users who log on using Remote Desktop Connections to a Terminal Server are treated as local users. The section "Working with Share Permissions" later in this chapter covers share permissions. The section "NTFS File and Folder Permissions" later in this chapter covers file-system permissions.

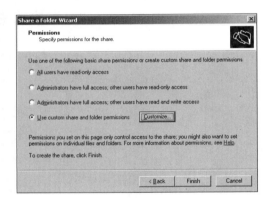

Figure 5.5 Specifying folder permissions for a share with the Share a Folder Wizard.

You can publish shares in Active Directory from the Shared Folders snap-in but not from Windows Explorer or My Computer windows. Publishing shares in Active Directory makes it easier for users to locate those shares, and users can search for published shares using different criteria, such as keywords. The Publish tab of a shared folders properties sheet allows you to add a description, the name of an owner, and specific keywords for searches to each share (see Figure 5.6). To publish a share in Active Directory, follow these steps:

1. Open the Computer Management console, expand the Shared Folders node and click the Shares subnode.

2. Right-click the shared folder that you want to publish and select Properties.

3. From the properties sheet, click the Publish tab.

4. Mark the Publish This Share in Active Directory check box.

5. As an option, type a description in the Description box.

6. As an option, type the name of an owner for the share in the Owner box.

7. As an option, click the Edit button to type in appropriate keywords to aid users in searching for this share. Click OK for the Edit Keywords dialog box when you are done.

8. Click OK to save the publish settings for the share.

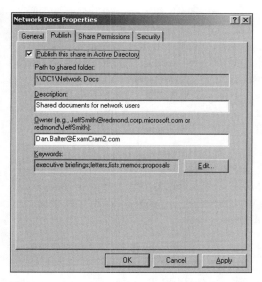

Figure 5.6   Publishing a share from the Shared Folders snap-in.

Working with Hidden and Administrative Shares

Windows Server 2003, along with Windows XP, Windows 2000, and Windows NT, automatically creates specific shared folders by default each and every time you start the computer. These default shares are often referred to as *hidden* or *administrative* shares because a dollar sign ($) is appended to their share names, which prevents the shared folder from appearing on the network browse list; users cannot easily discover that these shares exist.

Microsoft Windows networking does not allow hidden shares to appear when someone rummages through My Network Places, for example. The NETLOGON, SYSVOL, and Microsoft UAM volume shares are not hidden; these administrative shares are visible to all users. The default hidden or administrative shares include the following:

- ➤ *CS$, DS$, ES$, and so on*—These shares get created for the root of each available drive letter on the local computer.

- ➤ *ADMINS$*—This share exposes the `%systemroot%` folder to the network (for example, `C:\Windows`).

- ➤ *FAX$*—This share supports shared network faxing.

- ➤ *IPC$*—This share is used for interprocess communications (IPCs). IPCs support communications between objects on different computers over a network by manipulating the low-level details of network transport protocols. IPCs enable the use of distributed application programs that combine multiple processes working together to accomplish a single task. The `IPC$` share is on every Windows-based server; it enables you to authenticate using a different set of user credentials to a remote server. For example, if I'm logged on to computer1 as Domain1\DanB, I can use the `net use` command to log on to server1 as the administrator with the command `net use \\server1\share1\ /user:domain1\administrator`.

- ➤ *Microsoft UAM volume*—This share is not hidden. This share does not exist unless you install at least one optional Macintosh service. It is used by the File Services for Macintosh service and by the Print Services for Macintosh service for providing Macintosh computers with access to Windows Server 2003 file and print services.

- ➤ *NETLOGON*—This share is not hidden. The Net Logon service uses it for processing logon scripts. This share is used for backward compatibility with Windows NT 4.0 and Windows 9x computers that do not have the Active Directory client software installed.

- ➤ *PRINT$*—This share holds the printer drivers for the printers installed on the local machine. When a remote computer connects to a printer over the network, it downloads the appropriate printer driver.

- ➤ *SYSVOL*—This share is not hidden. It stores Active Directory objects and data, such as group policy objects or user login scripts.

Although you can temporarily disable the default hidden shares or administrative shares, you cannot delete them without modifying the Registry (which is not recommended) because they get re-created each time the computer restarts. You can connect to a hidden share but only if you provide a user account with administrative privileges along with the appropriate password for that user account. Administrators can create their own custom hidden shares simply by adding a dollar sign to the share name of any shared folder. Administrators can view all the hidden shares that exist on a Windows Server 2003 computer from the Shared Folders MMC snap-in. When you create your own hidden shares, any user can connect to them provided that the user knows the exact uniform naming convention (UNC) path and that the user possesses the necessary permissions for accessing that shared folder.

Working with Shared Folder Offline Settings

Offline access to files by network users is enabled by default for each share that you create under Windows Server 2003. However, you can specify the offline-files setting for each share from its properties sheet. To configure offline settings, follow these steps:

1. Right-click a folder that is already shared in Windows Explorer, My Computer, or the Shared Folders snap-in and select Properties.

2. If you're using the Shared Folders snap-in, click the Offline Settings button from the General tab. If you're using Windows Explorer or My Computer, click the Offline Settings button from the Sharing tab.

3. Select one of the available options for offline files, as shown in Figure 5.7:

   ➤ *Only the Files and Programs That Users Specify Will Be Available Offline*—This default setting is also known as *manual caching*.

   ➤ *All Files and Programs That Users Open from the Share Will Be Automatically Available Offline*—This setting is known as *automatic caching*. This feature automatically caches offline all data files that users open. When you enable this setting, you can mark the Optimized for Performance check box to automatically cache program files on each local computer to reduce network traffic for network-based applications.

   ➤ *Files or Programs from the Share Will Not Be Available Offline*—This setting disables offline files for the share.

4. Click OK for the Offline Settings dialog box and then click OK for the share's properties sheet to save the settings.

You can also configure offline settings from the command line using the **net share** command. Type **net share /?** and press Enter at a command prompt to view the proper syntax and available options for this command. The **/cache:*setting_name*** is an optional parameter for this utility. You can type **net share** *name_of_shared_folder* **/cache:manual** for manual caching, **net share** *name_of_shared_folder* **/cache: programs** for automatic caching of network programs and data files, **net share** *name_of_shared_folder* **/cache:documents** for automatic caching of data files only, or **net share** *name_of_shared_folder* **/cache:none** to turn off offline files for the share.

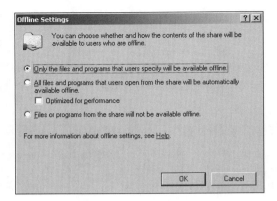

Figure 5.7 Configuring a share's offline settings.

Restricting Offline Files Usage with Group Policy

You can choose from several different group-policy settings to limit or disable the use of offline files. By default, the Offline Files feature is enabled on Windows 2000 Professional and Windows XP Professional computers, but this feature is disabled on Windows 2000 Server and Windows Server 2003 computers. You can change the default behavior for offline files using group policy for an entire site, domain, or organizational unit (OU).

Just after Windows Server 2003 was publicly released, Microsoft officially released the Group Policy Management Console (GPMC). The GPMC provides administrators with a much improved way to manage group policy object (GPO) settings across the enterprise. To download the GPMC, go to **http://www.microsoft.com/downloads**, select Windows Server 2003 from the Product/Technology drop-down list box, and search for the keyword "GPMC." After you download the **GPMC.msi** file, double-click the file to install it on your computer. After you install it, the Group Policy Management icon appears in the Administrative Tools folder off the Start menu. The GPMC runs only on Windows Server 2003 and Windows XP Professional with SP1. However, you can manage Windows 2000 Server DCs as long as those DCs have Windows 2000 SP2 or later installed.

Many settings are available from the GPMC or from the GPO Editor under `Computer Configuration\Administrative Templates\Network\Offline Files`. For example, to enable or disable offline files, double-click the Allow or Disallow Use of the Offline Files Feature policy to specify a setting in the GPO Editor, as shown in Figure 5.8. Several other GPO settings are available under `User Configuration\Administrative Templates\Network\Offline Files`. Just remember that any conflicting GPO settings are always overridden by the GPO setting in the Computer Configuration container.

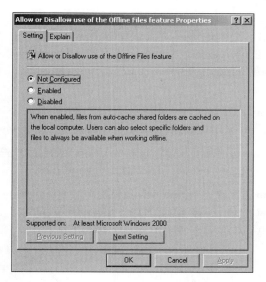

Figure 5.8   Configuring a GPO setting for offline files.

 NOTE   For a Windows Server 2003 computer, when used as a workstation, the Offline Files feature is not available if the server has Terminal Services installed. This holds true whether you are working directly from the console of the Terminal Server or through a Terminal Services (Remote Desktop Connection) session. However, Windows XP and Windows 2000 computers can still connect to any Terminal Server and make the files stored on that server available offline from their local workstations. In addition, you can use offline files to manually cache files over the network when you connect to any Windows computer that uses the SMB protocol, whether it's running Windows 9x, Windows 2000, Windows XP, or Windows Server 2003. Unfortunately, Novell NetWare servers do not use SMB, so you cannot use offlines files for files stored on NetWare servers.

Working with Share Permissions

When you create a new share under Windows Server 2003 and Windows XP Professional, the default share permissions are Everyone: Allow Read. Share permissions determine the level of access to files and folders stored within the share only for remote users accessing the share over the network; local users accessing local files are not affected by share permissions. For the highest level of security, use NTFS (file system) permissions in addition to share permissions to ensure that local users accessing the files are also subject to any restrictions. You must create a share to allow network access, but you should rely more heavily on the NTFS settings because NTFS permissions apply to both local and network users and NTFS security provides a wider array of permission levels.

Share permissions offer only three levels of security access: Read, Change, or Full Control, as shown in Figure 5.9. Each permission level can be allowed (Allow check box marked), implicitly denied (Allow check box cleared), or explicitly denied (Deny check box marked). The share permissions and their levels of access follow:

➤ *Read*—This default permission lets users view folder names and file-names, view data within files, and execute application program files.

➤ *Change*—This permission allows all Read permissions and lets users add folders and files, change data within files, and delete folders and files.

➤ *Full Control*—This permission grants the same privileges as the Change permission for share permission purposes. (For NTFS file-system per-mission purposes, Full Control provides more extensive permissions than Change.)

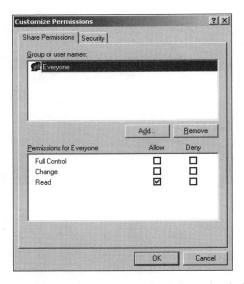

Figure 5.9 Configuring share permissions using the Share a Folder Wizard.

Setting Share Permissions

Customizing share permissions is optional when creating a shared folder; the Everyone: Allow Read permission automatically applies to all new shares. You can change the default share permissions for a new share or for an exist-ing share. To modify share permissions, follow these steps:

1. Right-click the shared folder in Windows Explorer or My Computer and select Sharing and Security.

2. Click the Permissions button.

3. Select a user or group name that is listed.

4. Mark the appropriate Allow or Deny check box for the permission that you want to configure: Read, Change, or Full Control.

5. Click the Add button to add a user or group to the list.

6. Select the user or group that you added and mark the appropriate Allow or Deny check box for the permission that you want to configure: Read, Change, or Full Control.

7. To remove a user or group that is listed, select it and click the Remove button.

8. Click OK for the Share Permissions dialog box and then click OK for the folder's properties sheet to save the settings.

Windows Server 2003 File Systems

Windows Server 2003 supports three file systems for disk storage access: the File Allocation Table 16-bit (FAT or FAT16), the File Allocation Table 32-bit (FAT32), and the native Windows Server 2003 NTFS file system. The FAT file system originated from the legacy MS-DOS character-based operating system. Microsoft improved on the FAT file system with Windows 95 OEM Service Release 2 (OSR2)—extending it to a 32-bit version for supporting larger hard disks and for speeding up disk access. However, neither FAT nor FAT32 supports file-system permissions, and they are not nearly as robust for storing and securing both programs and data as the NTFS file system. NTFS is the preferred file system for all Windows Server 2003 disk partitions and volumes whether they reside on basic or dynamic disks.

The FAT and FAT32 File Systems

Windows Server 2003 has full FAT and FAT32 file-system support with the following restrictions:

➤ Pre-existing FAT32 partitions up to 2TB are supported in Windows Server 2003.

➤ By design, Windows Server 2003 allows you to format new FAT32 volumes of only 32GB or smaller.

> FAT volumes are limited to a maximum size of 4GB and can support a maximum file size of 2GB.

> FAT32 volumes can support a maximum file size of 4GB.

> You can install Windows Server 2003 onto FAT, FAT32, or NTFS partitions or volumes. Keep in mind that you have no local security for Windows Server 2003 unless you place the operating system on an NTFS partition.

The NTFS File System

Windows Server 2003 inherits the Windows XP and Windows 2000 NTFS version 5 file system. NTFS is Windows Server 2003's native file system. This version of NTFS includes capabilities such as support for very granular file and folder permissions, support for disk quotas, support for data privacy using the Encrypting File System (EFS), and a number of other useful features. When you install Windows Server 2003 onto an NTFS partition (or volume), part of the setup process is to apply default security settings to the system files and folders located on the boot partition (or volume)—essentially the %systemdrive%\Windows and %systemdrive%\Program Files folders.

 When you install Windows Server 2003, any pre-existing NTFS volumes from previous versions of Windows are automatically upgraded to NTFS version 5. You do not have the option to choose NTFS version 5 during the installation. The existing volumes are simply converted to NTFS version 5 whether you want them to be converted or not. Computers running Windows NT 4.0 with SP4, SP5, or SP6 installed can read and write to NTFS version 5 drive volumes.

Converting from FAT or FAT32 to NTFS

Let's say that you want to convert drive E to NTFS, from either FAT or FAT32; this change is easy to do. From any command prompt, type convert e: /fs:ntfs. If the FAT or FAT32 drive is the boot partition (or volume), the conversion takes place when the computer gets restarted because many of the operating-system files are locked. This command is a one-way procedure that is not reversible. You can type convert.exe /? to view all the command's options. You can use the /x option to force the target drive volume to dismount before the conversion to NTFS. You can use the /NoSecurity option to specify that the files and folders stored on the newly converted NTFS drive volume be accessible to all users.

You cannot convert an NTFS partition (or volume) to a FAT or FAT32 partition (or volume). Unfortunately, a simple conversion using the convert.exe command-line utility is not possible. Your only course of action to return the partition (or volume) to FAT again is to use the Disk Management console to reformat the drive to FAT or FAT32. If you want to keep the data, you must first back up all the data on the drive. You can then restore the backed-up data to your newly formatted partition (or volume) after you finish the reformat.

NTFS Disk Quotas

NTFS disk quotas track and control disk usage on a per-user, per-drive letter (partition or volume) basis. You can apply disk quotas only to NTFS-formatted drive letters under Windows Server 2003, Windows XP Professional, and Windows 2000. Quotas are tracked for each drive letter, even if the drive letters reside on the same physical disk. The per-user feature of quotas enables you to track every user's disk space usage regardless of which folder the user stores files in. Disk quotas do not use compression to measure disk-space usage, so users cannot obtain or use more space simply by compressing their own data. To enable disk quotas, open Windows Explorer or My Computer, right-click a drive letter and select properties, click the Quota tab, and configure the options as shown in Figure 5.10.

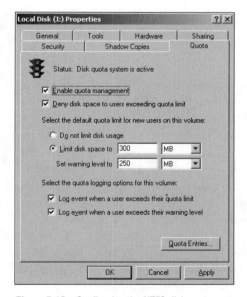

Figure 5.10 Configuring the NTFS disk quota system.

After you turn on the disk quota system, you can establish individual disk-quota limits for each user by clicking the Quota Entries button at the bottom of the Quota tab. By default, only members of the Administrators group can view and change quota entries and settings. In addition, all members of the Administrators group inherit unlimited disk quotas by default. NTFS disk quotas are based on file ownership; operating system accounts are not immune to disk quotas. System accounts such as the local system are also susceptible to running out of disk space due to disk quotas having been set. From the Quota Entries window (see Figure 5.11), you can change an existing quota entry for a user by double-clicking the quota entry. To set up a new quota entry for a user, click the Quota menu and select the New Quota Entry option. When a user no longer stores data on a volume, you should delete the user's disk-quota entries. The catch is that you can only delete the user's quota entries after you remove all the files that the user owns or after another user takes ownership of the files.

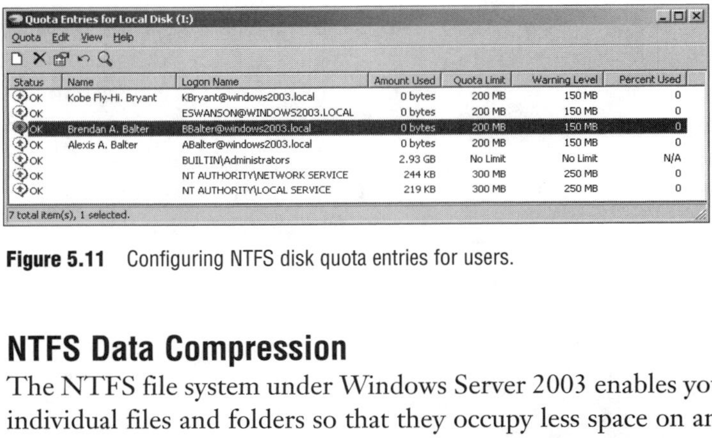

Figure 5.11 Configuring NTFS disk quota entries for users.

NTFS Data Compression

The NTFS file system under Windows Server 2003 enables you to compress individual files and folders so that they occupy less space on an NTFS drive volume. Any Windows- or MS-DOS–based program can read and write to NTFS compressed files without having to decompress them first. The compressed files decompress when opened and recompress when closed. The Windows Server 2003 NTFS file system handles this entire process transparently to the user. Setting the compression state (compressed or uncompressed) on a file or folder is as simple as setting a file or folder attribute. Compressed folders and files are displayed in blue in My Computer and the Windows Explorer. You can turn off this default color distinction in My Computer or Windows Explorer by clicking Tools, Folder Options, View and marking the box next to Show Encrypted or Compressed NTFS Files in Color. To compress or uncompress a file or folder, follow these steps:

1. Open Windows Explorer or My Computer.

2. Right-click the file or folder that you'd like to compress or uncompress and select Properties.

3. On the General tab, click the Advanced button.

4. From the Advanced Attributes dialog box, mark (or clear) the Compress Contents to Save Disk Space check box to compress (or uncompress) the file or folder that you selected (see Figure 5.12).

5. Click OK for the Advanced Attributes dialog box and then click OK for the properties window.

Figure 5.12   Configuring NTFS file and folder compression from the Advanced Attributes dialog box.

Instead of compressing individual files or folders, you can choose to compress an entire NTFS drive volume. To compress an entire NTFS volume, right-click an NTFS drive volume in My Computer or Windows Explorer, select Properties, and mark the check box labeled Compress Drive to Save Disk Space. Click OK to close the drive volume's Properties window. For command-line junkies, you can use the compact.exe tool to compress and uncompress folders and files. If a lot of files are compressed on a server and many users access those files, the compression and decompression operations can degrade server performance. Compressed files that are moved to FAT or FAT32 drive volumes become uncompressed. Compressed files that are moved or copied to uncompressed folders stored on NTFS drive volumes become uncompressed. Compressed files that are moved or copied to compressed folders stored on NTFS drive volumes remain compressed. Finally, uncompressed files that are moved or copied to compressed folders become compressed.

NTFS Data Encryption

The NTFS file system for Windows Server 2003 also supports data encryption. Just as with NTFS data compression, you set data encryption as an advanced attribute for a file or folder. With NTFS data encryption, Microsoft provided a secure method for keeping confidential documents private. Microsoft designed the Encrypting File System (EFS) to ensure the confidentiality of sensitive data. EFS employs public key/private key cryptography. EFS works only with the NTFS 5 file system under Windows Server 2003, Windows XP, and Windows 2000. EFS encryption and decryption is transparent to users. You can either compress or encrypt files and folders, but you can't use both compression and encryption on the same file or folder.

Folders that are encrypted using EFS set the encryption attribute on files that are moved or copied into them; those files automatically become encrypted once they reside in that folder. Files that are encrypted using EFS remain encrypted even if you move or rename them. Encrypted files that you back up or copy also retain their encryption attributes as long as they reside on NTFS-formatted drive volumes. EFS leaves no file remnants behind because it modifies an encrypted file, nor does it leave any traces of decrypted data from encrypted files in temporary files or in the Windows Server 2003 paging file. You can encrypt and decrypt files and folders from the graphical user interface (GUI) by using Windows Explorer and My Computer, as well as from the command line by using the `cipher.exe` tool. Encrypted folders and files appear in green in My Computer and Windows Explorer. You can turn off this default color distinction by clicking Tools, Folder Options, View in My Computer or Windows Explorer. To encrypt a file or folder from the GUI, follow these steps:

1. Open Windows Explorer or My Computer.

2. Right-click the file or folder that you'd like to encrypt or unencrypt and select Properties.

3. On the General tab, click the Advanced button.

4. From the Advanced Attributes dialog box, mark (or clear) the Encrypt Contents to Secure Data check box to encrypt (or unencrypt) the file or folder that you selected. Click OK to close the Advance Attributes dialog box and then click OK for the properties sheet to apply this setting. (When you encrypt a folder, you are prompted to select between applying this setting to the folder only and applying it to the folder, subfolders, and files.)

5. To share access to an encrypted file, click the Details button from the Advanced Attributes dialog box. *You cannot share access to encrypted folders.*

6. From the Encryption Details dialog box, click the Add button to add more users' EFS certificates to the encrypted file to share access with those users, as shown in Figure 5.13.

7. From the Select User dialog box, click the user whose EFS certificate you want to add for shared access to the encrypted file and click OK. You see only certificates for users who have encrypted a folder or file previously.

8. Click OK for the Encryption Details dialog box.

9. Finally, click OK for the Advanced Attributes dialog box and then click OK for the properties window.

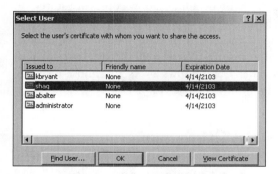

Figure 5.13   Adding users for shared access to an EFS-encrypted file.

After a file has the encryption attribute, only the user who originally encrypted the file, a user who has been granted shared access to the encrypted file, or the designated Data Recovery Agent (DRA) who was the DRA at the time the file was encrypted may access it. DRAs are users who are designated as recovery agents for encrypted files. Only these users have the ability to decrypt any encrypted file regardless of who has encrypted it. DRAs do not need to be granted shared access to encrypted files; they have access by default. Any other users who attempt to access an encrypted file receive an Access Is Denied message. However, a user with the necessary NTFS access permissions can still move encrypted files within the same drive volume or delete them entirely; therefore, the enforcement of proper NTFS permissions remains extremely important for encrypted files. The default DRAs are as follows:

➤ The local administrator user account on Windows 2000 nondomain member (standalone) computers. Standalone Windows XP and standalone Windows Server 2003 computers have no DRAs by default.

➤ The domain administrator user account on Windows Server 2003 or Windows 2000 Server domain controllers and for Windows Server 2003, Windows XP, and Windows 2000 domain member computers.

Shadow Copies of Shared Folders

Windows Server 2003 introduces a new feature called shadow copies of shared folders. Shadow copies, when configured, automatically create backup copies of the data stored in shared folders on specific drive volumes at scheduled times. The drive volumes must be formatted as NTFS. Shadow copies are set up per individual drive volume, and the copies are created at scheduled times by the new Volume Shadow Copy service (VSS) in conjunction with the Task Scheduler service. By default, shadow copies are stored on the same drive volume of the shared folders being backed up. Shadow copies allow users to retrieve previous versions of files and folders on their own, without requiring IT personnel to restore files or folders from backup. This feature reduces IT staffing overhead and allows users to almost instantly restore deleted or damaged data files by themselves.

Setting Up Shadow Copies

Best practice dictates that you should place the shadow copies on a separate physical disk, if possible, as an extra fault-tolerant measure. At least 100MB of free space must be available on a drive volume where shadow copies are to be stored. Obviously, you might need more disk space depending on the size of the data in the shared folders that are being shadowed. To set up shadow copies for a drive volume, follow these steps on a Windows Server 2003 computer:

1. From My Computer or Windows Explorer, right-click an NTFS drive volume, select Properties, and click the Shadow Copies tab. Alternatively, from the Computer Management console, right-click the Shared Folders node and select All Tasks, Configure Shadow Copies.

2. From the Shadow Copies tab, select the drive volume that you want to shadow and then click the Settings button.

3. From the Settings dialog box, click the Located on This Volume drop-down list box to select the drive volume where the shadow copies for this drive volume will be stored (see Figure 5.14). You can select the same volume or a different NTFS drive volume.

4. Select a maximum size by clicking either the No Limit option, or click the Use Limit option and type the storage restriction in the spinner box.

5. Click the Schedule button to specify how often you want to create shadow copies for this drive volume.

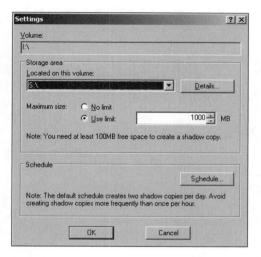

Figure 5.14 Configuring drive volume storage options from the Settings dialog box for shadow copies of shared folders.

6. From the Schedule tab, you have two daily scheduled shadow copies set up by default: 7:00 a.m. and 12:00 Noon, Monday through Friday of each week (see Figure 5.15).

➤ To accept the defaults, make no changes.

➤ To set up an additional scheduled shadow copy, click the New button.

➤ To remove an existing scheduled shadow copy, select the schedule from the drop-down list box and click the Delete button.

➤ To modify an existing scheduled shadow copy, select the schedule from the drop-down list box and make the appropriate changes to the Scheduled Task drop-down list box, the Start Time spinner box, and the Schedule Task section.

7. Click OK to save your settings for the shadow copies scheduling.

8. Click OK to save your settings for the Settings dialog box and return to the Shadow Copies tab. Shadow copies for the drive volume are now enabled, as shown in Figure 5.16.

➤ You can manually create additional shadow copies by clicking the Create Now button.

➤ You can delete previous shadows copies by selecting one of the date and time stamps in the Shadow Copies of Selected Volume list box and clicking the Delete Now button.

➤ To disable shadow copies for a volume, select the volume and click the Disable button.

9. Click OK to close the properties window for the Shadow Copies tab.

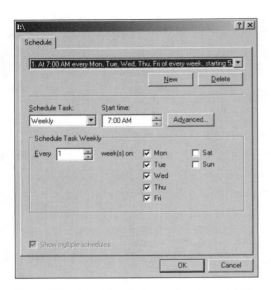

Figure 5.15 Scheduling shadow copies of shared folders.

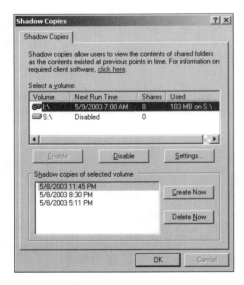

Figure 5.16 Setting up and managing shadow copies of shared folders.

Accessing Shadow Copies

For users to be able to access shadow copies of shared folders from their workstations, administrators must install client software on those computers. You find this software on a Windows Server 2003 computer in the `%systemroot%\system32\clients\twclient` folder. For the x86 platform (Intel-compatible 32-bit CPUs), double-click the `twcli32.msi` file to install the Previous Versions Client program. After you install the Previous Versions software, when a user selects a data file that has one or more shadow copies available, the View Previous Versions option will appear in the File and Folder task pane in Windows Explorer and My Computer. A Previous Versions tab is also available when a user views the properties sheet for a data file that has one or more shadow copies, as shown in Figure 5.17.

You can only install the Previous Versions Client software on Windows XP or later operating systems. You must install the Previous Versions Client to retrieve shadow-copy versions of files. Computers running Windows 2000 SP3 and Windows 98 are also supported for retrieving previous versions of folders and files from a shared network folder stored on a Windows Server 2003 computer where shadow copies have been set up. You must download and install the Shadow Copy Client software at **http://www.microsoft.com/windowsserver2003/downloads/shadowcopyclient.mspx**. Windows 2000 SP3 computers and Windows 98 computers must have the Shadow Copy Client software installed on the Windows Server 2003 computer where the shadow copies are stored as well as have this software installed on the workstations.

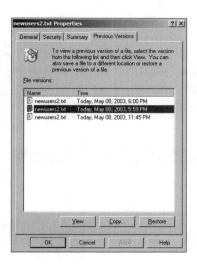

Figure 5.17　Viewing previous versions (shadow copies) of a file from its properties sheet.

NTFS File and Folder Permissions

You can assign NTFS security permissions to both users and groups and apply them to various resources such as folders, files, printers, and other objects. NTFS permissions are access control list (ACL) settings and access control entries (ACEs). The ACL details who (which users or groups) is granted access to a file or a folder. ACEs detail the specific permission settings (read, write, and so on) for each user or group on each specific file or folder. NTFS permissions for Windows Server 2003 can become complex and granular if you use advanced (also known as "special") permissions. Basic permissions are simpler; they enable you to allow or deny access to resources based on six fundamental levels: Read, Read & Execute, List Folder Contents (applies to folders only), Write, Modify, and Full Control. Advanced (special) permissions enable you to fine-tune permission settings for allowing or denying such activities as reading or writing extended object attributes.

Working with Basic NTFS Permissions

Basic NTFS permissions actually consist of predefined advanced NTFS permissions, and you apply them per user and per group. Individual file permissions differ slightly from the permissions that apply to folders. Table 5.1 highlights the basic permissions available for files, whereas Table 5.2 outlines the basic permissions available for folders. In many instances, basic permissions are sufficient for granting or denying fundamental privileges to both users and groups. Best practice dictates that you always assign permissions to groups of users rather than to individual users. It's much easier to manage permissions assigned to groups than having to set and maintain different permissions for each user.

Table 5.1 Basic NTFS Security Permissions for Files	
Permission Name	Levels of Access
Read	View and list files and folders; view attributes, extended attributes, and permissions of files.
Read & Execute	Run program files; view and list files; view attributes, extended attributes, and permissions of files.
Write	Write data to files; delete file contents; create new files; append data to files; set attributes and extended attributes.

Table 5.1 Basic NTFS Security Permissions for Files *(continued)*	
Permission Name	**Levels of Access**
Modify	View and list files; view the contents of files; write data to files; delete files and file contents; view and set attributes and extended attributes.
Full Control	View and list files; view the contents of files; write data to files; delete files and file contents; view and set attributes and extended attributes; change permissions for files; take ownership of files.

Table 5.2 Basic NTFS Security Permissions for Folders	
Permission Name	**Levels of Access**
Read	View and list folders and files; view attributes, extended attributes, and permissions of folders.
Read & Execute	Run program files; view and list folders and files; view attributes, extended attributes, and permissions of folders and files.
List Folder Contents	View and list folders and files; run program files.
Write	Add files to a folder.
Modify	View and list folders and files; view the contents of files; write data to files; add folders and files; delete folders, files, and file contents; view and set attributes and extended attributes.
Full Control	View and list folders and files; view the contents of files; write data to files; add folders and files; delete folders, files, and file contents; view and set attributes and extended attributes; change permissions for folders and files; take ownership of folders and files.

NOTE

The List Folder Contents permission is inherited by folders, but not by files, and it appears only when you view folder permissions and drive volume permissions. Read & Execute is inherited by both files and folders and is always present when you view file or folder permissions. By default, NTFS security permissions are inherited from an object's parent. An administrator can manually override the default inheritance and explicitly configure permission settings.

When you create a new NTFS drive volume, Windows Server 2003 automatically assigns default basic NTFS permission settings for five default users and groups. Advanced NTFS permissions are also assigned by the operating system; they are covered in the section "Working with Advanced NTFS Permissions" later in this chapter. The five default groups and their associated default basic permissions follow (see Figure 5.18):

> *Administrators*—Allow Full Control.

> *Creator Owner*—No basic permissions set for the root of the drive volume; all check boxes are cleared.

> *Everyone*—No basic permissions set for the root of the drive volume; all check boxes are cleared.

> *System*—Allow Full Control.

> *Users*—Allow Read, Allow Read & Execute, and Allow List Folder Contents.

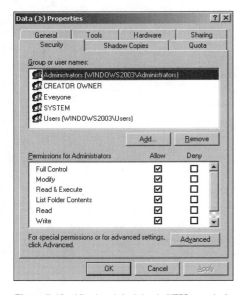

Figure 5.18 Viewing default basic NTFS permissions for a new drive volume.

Understanding Inherited Permissions

Each object's NTFS security permissions are automatically inherited from the object's parent container. A file's NTFS permissions are inherited from the folder the file is located in. A subfolder's NTFS permissions are inherited from the folder that the subfolder is located in. Folders stored in the root of a drive volume inherit their NTFS permissions from the drive volume's permissions, which are set by default. Inheritance is the default behavior for NTFS permissions; if you remove inherited permissions, explicit permissions take their place. When you view the Security tab for an object's properties sheet, if the Allow and Deny check boxes for NTFS basic permissions are shaded and not changeable, the file or folder has inherited the permissions from the parent folder.

By clicking the Advanced button at the bottom of the Security tab, you can work with the Advanced Security settings dialog box. From the Advanced Security Settings dialog box, you can clear the Allow Inheritable Permissions from the Parent to Propagate to This Object and All Child Objects. Include These with Entries Explicitly Defined Here check box. By clearing this check box, you can choose to copy the existing inherited permissions and turn them into explicit permissions, or you can remove them entirely and manually establish new explicit permissions. As soon you clear the check box, the Security message box appears, and you must choose one of the following options (see Figure 5.19):

➤ Copy the existing inherited permissions.

➤ Remove the existing inherited permissions.

➤ Cancel the action and leave the inherited permissions intact.

NTFS security permissions are cumulative. Users obtain permissions by having them assigned directly to their user accounts, in addition to obtaining permissions via group memberships. Users retain all permissions as they are assigned. If a user named Brendan has been granted the Allow Read permission for a folder named Contracts, and if Brendan is also a member of the Managers group, which was assigned the Allow Write permission for the same folder, Brendan has both the Allow Read and Allow Write permissions for the Contracts folder. Assigned permissions continue to accumulate; however, Deny entries always override Allow entries for the same permission type (Read, Write, Modify, and so on).

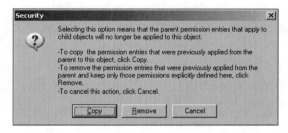

Figure 5.19 Choosing to copy or remove NTFS inherited permissions and apply only explicit permissions.

Assigning Basic NTFS Permissions to Users and Groups

Keep in mind that NTFS security permissions apply to all users whether they are local or remote; share permissions apply only to remote users accessing files and folders over the network. However, share permissions can have a major impact on access control to files and folders. If you apply both share permissions and NTFS permissions to a shared folder, the most restrictive permissions apply! This rule is why it is considered a best practice to set either restrictive share permissions or restrictive NTFS permissions, but not both. Microsoft recommends that you use NTFS permissions instead of share permissions. Of course, you must first share a folder before users can access it over the network; you must assign appropriate share permissions to the users or groups who will access the share because the default share permission is Everyone: Read.

To change NTFS security permissions, you must be the owner of the file or folder whose permissions you want to modify, or the owner must grant you permission to make modifications to the object's security settings. Groups or users who are granted Full Control on a folder can delete files and subfolders within that folder regardless of the permissions protecting those files and subfolders. To view or assign basic NTFS permissions on a file or a folder for users and groups, follow these steps:

1. Open Windows Explorer or My Computer, right-click a file or folder stored on an NTFS drive volume, and select Properties.

2. Click the Security tab.

3. To add a user or group to the list of Group or User Names, click the Add button.

4. Type the user or group name in the Enter the Object Names to Select box.

5. To pick from a list of user and group names, click the Advanced button.

   ➤ From advanced Select Users, Computers, or Groups dialog box, verify that the settings for Object Types and Locations are correct; change these settings if necessary.

   ➤ Click the Find Now button to display the names in the Search Results list box, as shown in Figure 5.20.

   ➤ Select one or more names from the Search Results list box and click OK.

6. Click OK for the Select Users, Computers, or Groups dialog box.

7. To remove a user or group, select the name and click Remove.

8. To assign permissions to a user or group, select the name and mark the Allow or Deny check box for each permission that you want to assign.

9. Click OK to save your settings and close the properties window.

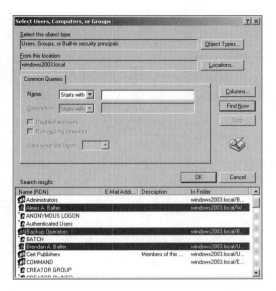

Figure 5.20 Choosing users and groups for assigning NTFS permissions from the advanced Select Users, Computers, or Groups dialog box.

Working with Advanced NTFS Permissions

NTFS advanced permissions are called *special* permissions. These special permissions are the building blocks for basic permissions. In Windows Server 2003, special permissions give administrators granular control over exactly what types of security access users can have over files and folders. Special permissions are somewhat hidden from view. They allow administrators to fine-tune ACE security settings. From the Security tab of a file or folder's properties sheet, click the Advanced button to view, add, modify, or remove special NTFS permissions.

When you click the Advanced button, you see the Advanced Security Settings dialog box, which shows each access control entry assigned to every user and group that has permissions on that resource (see Figure 5.21). To remove a permission entry, select the entry and click the Remove button. To view existing individual special permission entries, select one of the users or groups listed and then click the Edit button. When you click the Edit button, the Permission Entry dialog box appears, as shown in Figure 5.22. This dialog gives administrators a fine level of control over the access allowed to individual users and groups on specific resources. For example, this capability gives administrators granular control over the specific permissions users have to manipulate data and program files that are stored on NTFS drive volumes. From the Permission Entry dialog box, you can perform the following tasks for the specified user or group:

➤ Click the Change button to change the user or group listed in the Name box so that this permission entry applies to some other user or group.

➤ Click the Apply Onto drop-down list box to specify exactly where these special permissions should apply.

➤ Change the actual permission entries themselves by marking or clearing the Allow or Deny check box for each permission that you want to assign.

To add a user or a group to the Permission Entries list, click the Add button, select a user or group, and then follow the steps just outlined for editing permission entries. Table 5.3 lists the special NTFS permissions available under Windows Server 2003.

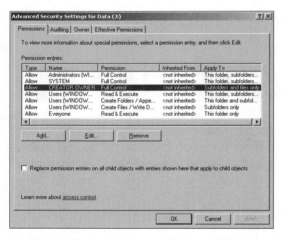

Figure 5.21   Viewing default special NTFS permissions for a new drive volume.

Table 5.3 Special NTFS Security Permissions for Files and Folders	
Permission Name	**Levels of Access**
Full Control	Assign the Allow check box entry for all basic and special NTFS security permissions, including the entries for Change Permissions and Take Ownership.

Table 5.3 Special NTFS Security Permissions for Files and Folders *(continued)*	
Permission Name	**Levels of Access**
Traverse Folder/Execute File	Move through folders to reach other files or folders, even if the user has no permissions for the folders being navigated through (applies to folders only). Traverse Folder takes effect only when the group or user is not granted the Bypass Traverse Checking user right in the Group Policy snap-in. The Execute File permission allows or denies running application program files.
List Folder/Read Data	View filenames and subfolder names within the folder and view data within files.
Read Attributes	View the attributes—such as read-only, hidden, and archive—for a file or folder.
Read Extended Attributes	View the extended attributes of a file or folder. Some extended attributes are defined by application programs and can vary by application.
Create Files/Write Data	Create files within a folder, make changes to a file, and overwrite the existing data.
Create Folders/Append Data	Create subfolders within a folder and make changes to the end of a file; does not include changing, deleting, or overwriting existing data.
Write Attributes	Change the attributes—such as read-only or hidden—for a file or folder.
Write Extended Attributes	Change the extended attributes of a file or folder. Some extended attributes are defined by application programs and can vary by application.
Delete Subfolders and Files	Delete subfolders and files, even if the Delete permission was not granted on the subfolder or file.
Delete	Delete files and folders. If you don't have the Delete permission on a file or folder, you can still delete it if you were granted the Delete Subfolders and Files permission on the parent folder.
Read Permissions	View the permissions that exist on a file or folder.
Change Permissions	Change permissions on files and folders, such as Full Control, Read, Write, and so on.
Take Ownership	Become the owner of a file or folder. The owner of a file or folder can always change permissions on it, even if other permissions were assigned to safeguard the file or folder.

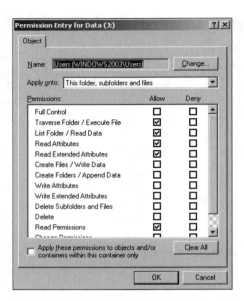

Figure 5.22 Viewing default special NTFS permission entries for a group.

Determining NTFS Effective Permissions

Before you assign additional permissions to users or groups for a file or a folder, you should be aware of each user or group's effective permissions based on the current settings. NTFS under Windows Server 2003 provides a way for users and administrators to view current effective permissions from the Advanced Security Settings dialog box for a file or folder. Local administrators logged into nondomain member computers cannot view NTFS effective permissions for domain users.

The Effective Permissions tab calculates effective permissions based on user permissions, permissions inherited due to group memberships, and permissions inherited from parent folders. It does not use share permissions to calculate effective permissions. To view effective permissions on a file or a folder for a user or group, follow these steps:

1. Open Windows Explorer or My Computer, right-click a file or folder stored on an NTFS drive volume, and select Properties.

2. Click the Security tab.

3. Click the Advanced button to display the Advanced Security Settings dialog box.

4. Click the Effective Permissions tab.

5. Click the Select button, type a user or group name for which you want to view effective permissions, and click OK. (Click the Advanced button and then click Find Now to select from a list of user and group names.)

6. View the effective permissions for the user or group that you selected, as shown in Figure 5.23.

7. Click OK to close the Advanced Security Settings dialog box and then click OK to close the properties sheet.

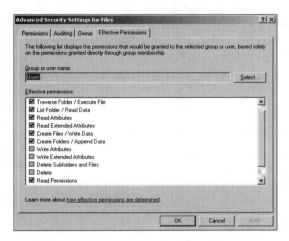

Figure 5.23 Viewing NTFS effective permissions for a user or a group from the Advanced Security Settings dialog box.

Understanding Ownership of Files and Folders

Under the NTFS file system in Windows Server 2003, every object, including files and folders, has an owner. The owner of an object has complete control over how permissions are assigned to that object and also over which users or groups can be assigned permissions on the object. The owner of an object retains the power to change permissions on an object at all times, even if the owner's permissions deny him or her access to the object; the role of owner overrides any Deny ACEs on the object. In general, the user who creates a file or folder becomes the owner of that object. However, if the system creates an object, the default owner is the Administrators group, which is the case for files and folders created during the installation of the operating system. One of the following can take ownership over an object:

➤ Users who have been assigned the Restore Files and Directories user right as a local policy or a group policy setting.

➤ A user or group who has been assigned the Allow Take Ownership permission for a specific object.

➤ Any member of the Administrators group because the Administrators group is granted the Take Ownership of Files or Other Objects user right by default.

Changing Ownership of Files and Folders

Windows Server 2003 sports a new feature for NTFS objects—the ability of an owner to transfer ownership of a file or folder to some other user or group. Under previous Windows versions, a user first had to be granted the Take Ownership permission for an object, and then that user could take ownership of it. Now, the owner of an object can assign ownership over that object to another user or group. Ownership over an object can transfer in any one of the following ways:

➤ A member of the Administrators group can take ownership of an object.

➤ The current owner of an object can assign the Allow Take Ownership permission to another user. The user who is assigned Allow Take Ownership permission must actually take ownership of the object to become the new owner.

➤ Any user who is granted the Restore Files and Directories user right can click the Other Users or Groups button at the bottom of the Owner tab for the Advanced Security Settings dialog box (from the object's properties sheet) to assign ownership to some other user or group (see Figure 5.24).

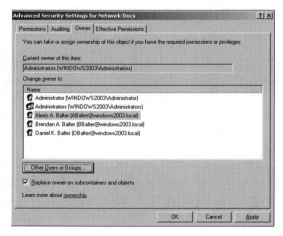

Figure 5.24 Changing ownership on a folder from the Owner tab of the Advanced Security Settings dialog box.

When you change the ownership of a folder, you can mark the Replace Owner on Subcontainers and Objects check box at the bottom of the Owner tab, as shown in Figure 5.24, to have the new owner take ownership over all files and subfolders stored within the folder. All child objects below the level of the current folder are affected by this setting.

Troubleshooting Access to Files and Shared Folders

When you manage a network environment where several different factors control access to files and folders, sometimes the user might not be able to access files that he needs. In these instances, it becomes the network administrator's job to diagnose and fix the problem. The major contributing factors for access control issues are

➤ Shared folder permissions

➤ NTFS file system permissions

➤ EFS-encrypted files

If you review these three major factors in the sequence listed, you should be able to solve most access-control issues. Obviously, share permissions do not apply to local users trying to access local folders and files. However, NTFS permissions and EFS encryption apply to both local and network users.

Checking Share Permissions

For remote users attempting access files over the network, always check the share permissions first. Remember that the most restrictive permissions take precedence between share permissions and NTFS permissions. Also, the default share permissions are Everyone: Allow Read for Windows Server 2003 and Windows XP Professional. If you quickly share a folder without changing the default share permissions, users will be limited to read-only access for all the files accessed through that share, regardless of the NTFS permissions set on the folders and files available through that share.

Checking NTFS Permissions

Share permissions have no effect on local file access by local users; local access includes users interactively logged on to a computer and users logged on to a computer via Terminal Services (Remote Desktop Connections).

After you verify the share permissions for a folder, check the NTFS file-system permissions. NTFS permissions apply to all users—whether they are local users or network users. Be sure to review all special NTFS permissions, not just the basic NTFS permissions. Right-click the folder or file in question, select Properties, and click the Security tab. Click the Advanced button to view and adjust the special NTFS permissions, if necessary. Also, from the Advanced Security Settings dialog box, click the Effective Permissions tab and check the effective permissions for each user and group that you are investigating. These measures should reveal why users can't access the folders or files that they need.

Checking for EFS Encryption

After you verify and make any necessary changes to the share permissions and NTFS permissions to allow users to access the files and folders that they need, be sure to check for EFS encryption if the access problem still persists. To check a file or folder for EFS encryption, right-click the object and select Properties. From the General tab, click the Advanced button to display the Advanced Attributes dialog box. If the Encrypt Contents to Secure Data check box is marked, the object is encrypted: Encryption limits access to the user who originally encrypted the file, any users who have been granted shared access to the encrypted file, and the designated DRA.

You can see which users (if any) were granted shared access to an encrypted file by clicking the Details button on the Advanced Attributes dialog box. If users are being denied access to a file even though they possess the proper share and NTFS permissions to the file, check for encryption and check whether the users were granted shared access to the encrypted file. If the file is encrypted and users who need to access the file do not have shared access, you need to add those users to the Users Who Can Transparently Access This File list box in the Encryption Details dialog box. The Encryption Details dialog box appears when you click the Details button from the Advanced Attributes dialog box.

 NOTE You can use the **cipher.exe** tool at a command prompt to encrypt files, unencrypt files, list files and folders that are encrypted, and perform many other EFS-related activities. Type **cipher.exe /?** and press Enter to display the syntax and options for this command.

Troubleshooting Terminal Services and Remote Desktop Connections

Microsoft introduced Terminal Services with the debut of Windows NT Server 4.0, Terminal Server Edition. Since that time, Microsoft has enhanced and improved Windows Terminal Services with each subsequent new operating system release—Windows 2000, Windows XP Professional, and now Windows Server 2003. Terminal Services uses the Remote Desktop Protocol (RDP) for sending and receiving keyboard and mouse input; for presenting video and audio output; and for redirecting printers, disk drives, and other devices between a Terminal Server and a Remote Desktop client computer. Windows Server 2003 implements RDP version 5.2, Windows XP Professional employs RDP 5.1, and Windows 2000 Server uses RDP 5.0. On the server side, the RDP services are called Terminal Services; on the client side, the RDP connections are called Remote Desktop Connections.

Remote Desktop Connection Client Settings

On Windows Server 2003 and on Windows XP Professional computers, the Remote Desktop Connection software program is installed by default. It is located on the Start menu under (All) Programs, Accessories, Communications, Remote Desktop Connection. From the Remote Desktop Connection dialog box, you can click the Options button to configure several different settings—General, Display, Local Resources, Programs, and Experience. On the General tab, a user can type in her username, password, and domain (see Figure 5.25) so that these security credentials can automatically pass through to the Terminal Server without the user typing them each time when logging on. Windows Server 2003 permits this logon credential passthrough by default; Windows 2000 Server does not permit this passthrough by default.

NOTE

The Remote Desktop Client software is available free of charge from Microsoft's Web site at **http://www.microsoft.com/windowsxp/pro/downloads/rdclientdl.asp**. You can install and run this program on Windows 95, Windows 98, Windows Me, Windows NT 4.0, and Windows 2000. This software is the same version found under Windows XP Service Pack 1. Microsoft also offers an RDP Client version for Macintosh OS X computers at **http://www.microsoft.com/mac/DOWNLOAD/ MISC/RDC.asp**.

Figure 5.25   Configuring the Remote Desktop Connection client to log onto a Terminal Server without prompting for a username and password.

Terminal Services Server Settings

Terminal Services Remote Desktop for Administration licensing mode is installed by default on all Windows Server 2003 computers. This default mode supports up to two concurrent RDP connections for remote administration purposes. One user can be working at the console of the server at the same time as two users connected to the server via RDP. If you want to set up the Terminal Server as an application server, you must purchase the appropriate licensing. Application Server mode licensing is covered in the section "Working with Terminal Server Licensing." Four basic MMC snap-ins are responsible for managing and maintaining Terminal Server users and their connections:

➤ *Active Directory Users and Computers (ADUC)* (dsa.msc)—This console allows you to configure a Terminal Services User Profile, logon permissions, Remote Control permissions, session settings, and TS startup and redirection settings for domain users.

➤ *Terminal Services Configuration* (tscc.msc)—This console allows you to configure server settings and global RDP settings.

➤ *Terminal Services Manager* (tsadmin.exe)—This tool allows you to view, connect, disconnect, log off, send messages, and remotely control RDP user sessions.

➤ *Terminal Server Licensing (licmgr.exe)*—This utility manages client licensing for RDP sessions. This type of licensing is only necessary when you configure the Terminal Server as an application server.

 Even though Terminal Services for Remote Administration mode is installed automatically, a Windows Server 2003 computer does not accept remote desktop connections by default. You must right-click My Computer, select Properties, click the Remote tab, and then mark the Allow Users to Connect Remotely to This Computer check box to enable remote desktop connections for the Administrators group. In addition, you must click the Select Remote Users button to grant access to nonadministrative users; all members of the Administrators group can connect to the computer via remote desktop by default after you turn on remote desktop connections.

Configuring User Accounts for Terminal Services

Use the ADUC console to set up and manage user accounts for Terminal Services (TS) within a domain environment. To work with user settings for Terminal Services, right-click a username and select Properties. Click the Terminal Services Profile tab, as shown in Figure 5.26. From this tab, you can set up a TS User Profile and a TS Home Folder and you can enable or disable permission for the user to log on to TS. The default setting is enable; the Allow Logon to Terminal Server check box is marked by default.

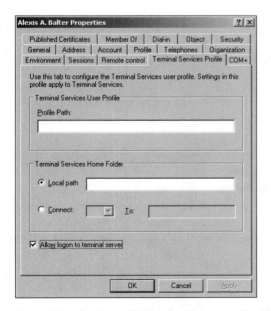

Figure 5.26 Configuring Terminal Services user-profile settings in the ADUC console.

The Remote Control tab allows you to specify TS remote control settings for each user (see Figure 5.27). The default settings turn on remote control; however, the TS user's permission is required by default to interact (or view) the user's TS session. You can clear the Enable Remote Control check box to turn off this feature, or you can clear the Require User's Permission check box to be able to interact with the user's TS session without his consent. The Remote Control tab and the Terminal Server Profile tab are two of the areas where administrators can configure individual user settings for domain user accounts.

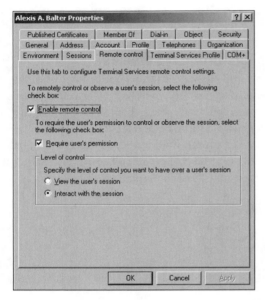

Figure 5.27 Configuring Terminal Services user remote-control settings in the ADUC console.

The Sessions tab lets you configure TS timeout periods and reconnection settings for each domain user. You can set timeout periods for disconnected sessions, active sessions, and idle sessions. You can specify to disconnect or end a session when a timeout period is reached. You can also stipulate that users can reconnect to a disconnected session from any computer or only from the client computer where the TS session originated. The Environment tab lets you designate an application program to run as soon as the user logs onto the Terminal Server. This tab also lets you specify user defaults for the redirection of local client devices within the TS session such as local disk drives, local printers, and maintaining the client's setting for its default printer.

Configuring Terminal Services Connections Settings

Click Start, (All) Programs, Administrative Tools, Terminal Services Configuration to launch this utility. From the Server Settings node, you can specify temporary folder settings and enable or disable Active Desktop for users, and you can restrict each TS user to just one session. (The default is to allow multiple sessions per user.) The setting Delete Temporary Folders on Exit provides extra security for any remnants of users' data, and it keeps .tmp files from multiplying on the server. The Use Temporary Folders Per Session forces all temporary files to be written to the %userprofile%\local settings\temp folder, which is more compatible for some applications than the default location, %userprofile%\local settings\temp*sessionID*.

The Active Desktop setting lets you display Active Desktop wallpaper and objects within remote desktop connection sessions. Unless you have unlimited bandwidth for your remote desktop connections, you probably want to disable this feature. The Restrict Each User to One Session setting does just that when you set it to "Yes." When you enable this feature, you eliminate the possibility that remote desktop users can inadvertently connect to the server multiple times and then disconnect each session. Users generally don't know which session to reconnect to; enabling this option eliminates this problem.

From the Connections node, you can double-click the RDP-Tcp connection icon in the details pane to view and configure several RDP settings. The RDP properties that you can configure are

➤ *General*—This tab lets you set the encryption level for data sent between Terminal Servers and their clients (see Figure 5.28). All levels use RSA RC4 standard encryption (see Table 5.4).

➤ *Logon Settings*—This tab lets you set specific logon information (username, domain, and password) for all users connecting to the server using RDP. This configuration works well for public kiosk computers. You can also specify that the server must always prompt Terminal Server users for a password. The defaults: Use client-provided logon information and do not always prompt for a password.

➤ *Sessions*—This tab allows you to override user settings for session limits and client reconnections.

➤ *Environment*—This tab lets you override user settings for a startup application program at logon time.

➤ *Remote Control*—This tab allows you to override user settings for remote-control options.

➤ *Client Settings*—This tab lets you override user settings for device redirection and maximum color depth.

➤ *Network Adapter*—This tab allows you to specify one individual network adapter or all network adapters for use with remote desktop connections. You can also limit the number of RDP connections from this dialog box.

➤ *Permissions*—This tab lets you set access permissions for users and groups for connecting via RDP.

Table 5.4   Terminal Services RDP Encryption Levels

TS Encryption Level	Description
Client Compatible (default)	Supports the highest level of encryption available on the client computer for encrypting data sent from client to server and from server to client.
Low	Supports 56-bit encryption *for data sent from the client to the server only*.
High	Supports the highest level of encryption available on the server computer for all data sent between client and server. Clients that do not support this level of encryption cannot connect to the server.
FIPS Compliant	Supports the Federal Information Processing Standard (FIPS) 140-1 validated encryption methods for all data sent between client and server.

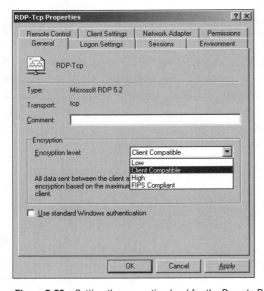

Figure 5.28   Setting the encryption level for the Remote Desktop Protocol.

Working with Terminal Services Manager

Click Start, (All) Programs, Administrative Tools, Terminal Services Manager to launch this RDP monitoring tool. From the Terminal Services Manager, you can view the users, sessions, and processes currently connected and running on each Terminal Server. As you can see in Figure 5.29, by right-clicking a user from the Users tab, you can connect to the current session, disconnect the user from the current session, send the user a message, remotely control the user's session, reset the session, view the current status of the session, and even log off the user from the current session. From the Sessions tab, you can view all the RDP sessions in progress. From the Processes tab, you can view all the processes that are currently active. If you right-click a process, you can select the End Process option to end that particular application or service.

The Connect option allows you to connect to the user's session, as long as you can provide that user's password. The user is kicked out of her session as you connect to it. If you are connecting to another session that you are already logged on to, or to your own disconnected session, no password is required. The Remote Control option allows you to "shadow" the user's session. Depending on the level of access permitted by the user's account settings, you can either view or interact with the session. By default, connecting via remote control requires the user's permission before you can connect. The Reset option lets you delete a session immediately and it can cause data loss: You should use this option only if the session appears to be malfunctioning or unresponsive. The Log Off option, on the other hand, more gracefully logs off the user; however, it can still result in data loss for the user if he is not aware that you are logging him off.

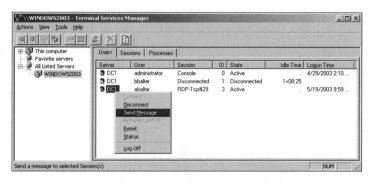

Figure 5.29 Monitoring user activity with the Terminal Services Manager tool.

Working with Terminal Server Licensing

Click Start, (All) Programs, Administrative Tools, Terminal Server Licensing to launch the RDP licensing-management utility. You need to install a Terminal Server License Server only for Terminal Servers configured in Application Server Mode. Under TS Application Server Mode, clients can connect to Terminal Servers using temporary TS licenses that get issued to each client for a maximum of 120 days from the first day of issuance. Owners of Windows XP Professional clients purchased prior to April 2003 can obtain Terminal Server 2003 Client Access Licenses through the Microsoft Terminal Server Activation Clearinghouse. All other clients, including Windows 9x, Windows NT 4.0, Windows 2000, and Windows XP clients purchased after April 2003, must have TS Client Access Licenses (TSCALs) purchased for each of them. Before the 120-day temporary license expires for the first client to connect to the Terminal Server, you must activate a license server and install TSCALs for each client that needs to connect to a Terminal Server.

Exam Prep Questions

Question 1

> Which of the following are default hidden shares under Windows Server 2003?
> (Choose three.)
>
> ❑ A. **SYSVOL**
> ❑ B. **ADMIN$**
> ❑ C. **CD$**
> ❑ D. **PRINTER$**
> ❑ E. **IPC$**
> ❑ F. **C$**

Answers B, E, and F are correct. Default hidden shares include ADMIN$, IPC$, and the root of each available drive letter, such as C$. Answer A is incorrect because although SYSVOL is a default administrative share, it is not hidden. Answer C is incorrect because there is no default share named CD$. Answer D is incorrect because there is no default share named PRINTER$, but there is a default hidden share named PRINT$.

Question 2

> What does the Shared Folders snap-in provide, in terms of setting permissions
> for a new share, that the Sharing tab of a folder's properties sheet does not
> offer?
>
> ○ A. Setting share permissions
> ○ B. Publishing the share in Active Directory
> ○ C. Specifying offline settings
> ○ D. Specifying both share permissions and NTFS permissions
> ○ E. Specifying Web Sharing access permissions

Answer D is correct. By clicking the Customize button from the permissions window, you can specify both share permissions and NTFS permissions when you create a new share using the Share a Folder Wizard from the Shared Folders snap-in. Answer A is incorrect because both methods allow you to set share permissions. Answer B is incorrect because publishing a share in Active Directory is not a permissions setting. Answer C is incorrect because both methods allow you to specify offline settings. Answer E is incorrect because you can only set Web Sharing access permissions from the Web Sharing tab of a folder's properties sheet.

Question 3

> Which of the following characteristics of shadow copies are true? (Choose three.)
>
> ❑ A. Previous versions of files stored as shadow copies are available under Windows 2000 Professional as long as you install the Previous Versions Client software.
>
> ❑ B. You must store shadow copies on NTFS drive volumes.
>
> ❑ C. You can only make shadow copies from files stored on NTFS drive volumes.
>
> ❑ D. Shadow copies are enabled by default on the **%systemdrive%** volume.
>
> ❑ E. You must store shadow copies on an NTFS drive volume other than the drive volume being shadowed.
>
> ❑ F. You can schedule shadow copies to occur automatically, and you can create them manually.

Answers B, C, and F are correct. You must store shadow copies on NTFS drive volumes, you can only make shadow copies from files stored on NTFS drive volumes, and you can schedule shadow copies to run automatically and create them manually. Answer A is incorrect because previous versions of files stored as shadow copies can only be retrieved under Windows XP and Windows Server 2003 with the Previous Versions Client software installed. Answer D is incorrect because shadow copies are not enabled by default for any drive volume. Answer E is incorrect because you can store shadow copies on any available NTFS drive volume, including the drive volume being shadowed.

Question 4

> When both share permissions and NTFS permissions exist on the same shared folder, how is access control to the shared folder affected for users trying to access the files stored in the shared folder over the network?
>
> ○ A. NTFS permissions take precedence.
>
> ○ B. Share permissions take precedence.
>
> ○ C. The most liberal permissions take precedence.
>
> ○ D. The most restrictive permissions take precedence.

Answer D is correct; the most restrictive permissions always override any other permissions, whether they are share permissions or NTFS permissions. Answer A is incorrect because NTFS permissions do not take precedence over share permissions unless they are the most restrictive. Answer B is incorrect because share permissions do not take precedence over NTFS permissions unless they are the most restrictive. Answer C is incorrect because the most restrictive permissions always override more liberal permissions.

Question 5

Which of the following characteristics apply to NTFS inherited permissions? (Choose three.)

❑ A.   Special permissions are inherited by default.

❑ B.   Basic permissions are inherited by default.

❑ C.   Explicit permissions are the same as inherited permissions.

❑ D.   NTFS permissions are inherited by default.

❑ E.   NTFS explicit permissions are not inherited by default.

❑ F.   You cannot set explicit permissions on files.

Answers A, B, and D are correct. Special permissions get inherited by child objects, basic permissions get inherited by child objects, and NTFS permissions (in general) all get inherited by default. Answer C is incorrect because explicit permissions are set by users; inherited permissions are set by parent containers. Answer E is incorrect because even explicit permissions set on parent containers (folders) are inherited by child objects (subfolders and files) by default. Answer F is incorrect because you can set explicit permissions on any object or container.

Question 6

The basic NTFS permission, Modify, when set on a folder, consists of which of the following special permissions? (Choose three.)

❑ A.   List Folder/Read Data

❑ B.   Create Files/Write Data

❑ C.   Change Permissions

❑ D.   Delete Subfolders and Files

❑ E.   Take Ownership

❑ F.   Write Extended Attributes

Answers A, B, and F are correct. When set on a folder, the Modify basic NTFS permission consists of the List Folder/Read Data, Create Files/Write Data, and Write Extended Attributes special permissions, among several others. Answer C is incorrect because the Change Permissions special permissions setting is not part of the Modify permission. Answer D is incorrect because the Delete Subfolders and Files special permission is not part of the Modify permission; however, the Delete special permission is included. Answer E is incorrect because the Take Ownership special permission is not part of the Modify permission.

Question 7

When you view NTFS effective permissions for a user or a group, which of the following permissions are displayed?

○ A. Basic permissions

○ B. Special permissions

○ C. Share permissions

○ D. Not inherited permissions

Answer B is correct; NTFS special permissions appear in the Effective Permissions dialog box. Answer A is incorrect because basic permissions do not appear in the Effective Permissions dialog box. Answer C is incorrect because share permissions do not appear in the Effective Permissions dialog box. Answer D is incorrect because both inherited and explicit NTFS permissions appear in the Effective Permissions dialog box.

Question 8

In which of the following ways can ownership of an NTFS file or folder change? (Choose three.)

❑ A. Any user who is a member of the Domain Users group can take ownership of any folder or file whether or not she has permissions to the folder or file.

❑ B. The current owner of a file or folder can assign the Take Ownership permission to another user for the file or folder; the other user must then take ownership of the object.

❑ C. A member of the Administrators group can assign ownership of a file or folder to another user.

❑ D. Any user who is granted the Restore Files and Directories user right can assign ownership of a file or folder to another user.

> ❑ E. Any member of the Backup Operators group can take ownership of any file or folder at any time.
>
> ❑ F. Any member of the Authenticated Users group can assign ownership of files or folders to another user at any time.

Answers B, C, and D are correct. A user who is the current owner of an object can assign the Take Ownership permission to another user, a member of the Administrators group can assign ownership, and any user who is assigned the Restore Files and Directories right can transfer ownership to another user. Answer A is incorrect because members of the Domain Users group cannot assign the Take Ownership permission to another user for an object. Answer E is incorrect because members of the Backup Operators group cannot take ownership of files or folders at any time. Answer F is incorrect because members of the Authenticated Users group cannot assign ownership of files to other users at any time.

Question 9

> Sue, a network administrator, just installed Windows Server 2003, Standard Edition, on a brand new 2.4GHz Pentium 4 computer. She installed the new operating system by accepting all the defaults. Sue knows that Terminal Services is installed by default. When Sue attempts to connect to the new server using the Remote Desktop Connection client on a Windows XP Professional computer, she is unable to log on to the server using Terminal Services. Why can't Sue log on to the Terminal Server?
>
> ○ A. The Windows XP computer requires Service Pack 1 (SP1).
>
> ○ B. Windows Server 2003 must be configured for Remote Administration mode.
>
> ○ C. The Allow Users to Connect Remotely to This Computer check box is cleared on the Remote tab of the System Properties window.
>
> ○ D. Sue must first set up a Terminal Services Licensing Server.

Answer C is correct. You must mark the Allow Users to Connect Remotely to This Computer check box on the Remote tab of the System Properties window to enable Terminal Services in Remote Administration mode. Answer A is incorrect because the Remote Desktop Connection client does not require Windows XP SP1. Answer B is incorrect because Windows Server 2003 installs Remote Administration mode for Terminal Services automatically. Answer D is incorrect because you do not need a Licensing Server for Terminal Services running in Remote Administration mode.

Question 10

> Where can you configure RDP encryption settings for a Terminal Server computer under Windows Server 2003?
>
> ○ A. In the Terminal Services Configuration utility
>
> ○ B. As a policy setting, under Local Security Settings, Windows Settings, Security Settings, Local Policies, Security Options, Terminal Server: Client Encryption Level
>
> ○ C. In the Terminal Services Manager tool
>
> ○ D. In the TS computer account's properties sheet in the ADUC console

Answer A is correct. On the General tab of the RDP-Tcp properties sheet, you can configure the RDP encryption level. Answer B is incorrect because there is no policy setting for Terminal Server: Client Encryption under the Security Options subnode. Answer C is incorrect because the Terminal Server Manager tool lets you work with current TS users, sessions, and processes. Answer D is incorrect because there is no provision for setting the RDP encryption level on a computer account's properties sheet.

Need to Know More?

Boswell, William. *Inside Windows Server 2003*. Boston, Massachusetts: Addison-Wesley, 2003.

Honeycutt, Jerry. *Introducing Microsoft Windows Server 2003*. Redmond, Washington: Microsoft Press, 2003.

Jones, Don, and Mark Rouse. *Microsoft Windows Server 2003 Delta Guide*. Indianapolis, Indiana: SAMS Publishing, 2003.

Search the Microsoft Product Support Services Knowledge Base on the Internet: http://support.microsoft.com. You can also search Microsoft TechNet on the Internet: http://www.microsoft.com/technet. Find technical information using keywords from this chapter, such as share permissions, NTFS permissions, offline files, shadow copies, Remote Desktop Connections, and Terminal Services.

Monitoring, Optimizing, and Troubleshooting Server Performance

Terms you'll need to understand:

- ✓ Event Viewer
- ✓ Task Manager
- ✓ System Monitor
- ✓ Performance logs and alerts
- ✓ Performance objects
- ✓ Performance counters
- ✓ Performance object instances
- ✓ Network print queues
- ✓ Enterprise licensing
- ✓ Software Update Services (SUS)

Techniques you'll need to master:

- ✓ Monitoring events with the Event Viewer
- ✓ Monitoring and managing applications, processes, and current system vital signs with Task Manager
- ✓ Using the Performance snap-in
- ✓ Viewing real-time server performance data with the System Monitor tool
- ✓ Recording logged server performance data with performance logs and alerts
- ✓ Choosing Microsoft licensing options: per server, per device or per user, and per processor
- ✓ Monitoring software licensing compliance
- ✓ Managing and troubleshooting network printing
- ✓ Monitoring and optimizing server performance
- ✓ Setting up Software Update Services (SUS)

Server performance can degrade over time as more users, more workstations, and more demands are placed on server resources. Windows Server 2003 offers administrators several built-in tools for monitoring, optimizing, and troubleshooting a server's performance. The Task Manager tool can tell us how the server's memory, network, and processor utilization are doing. The Event Viewer snap-in can show us both recent and past events that might be impacting the server's robustness. The System Monitor tool can diagram several vital aspects (or counters) of computer health in real time as well as create a historical log of these various system counters to establish a baseline of performance over a period of time.

You need the Licensing tool along with the Active Directory Sites and Services snap-in to properly set up, manage, and monitor software site licensing, which is also covered in this chapter. Network printing and network print queues need attention from time to time, so this chapter focuses on how to manage these important services. Finally, we look at the latest developments from Microsoft to help administrators more easily deploy hotfixes and other operating system updates using SUS—Software Update Services.

Monitoring and Analyzing System Events

Many different processes are constantly running on computers, especially on server systems. Operating system and third-party services run in the background, application programs run in the foreground for users on Terminal Server systems, and network applications, such as Microsoft SQL Server or Exchange Server, run in the background. Don't forget about other programs that run in the foreground that are executed by administrators performing routine management chores, such as the Active Directory Users and Computers console, Terminal Services Manager, and other utilities.

All the processes that run on a server communicate with the operating system, which in turn communicates with other subsystems and the computer's hardware devices. The messages that are sent back and forth between application programs and the operating system can generate different types of events. Windows Server 2003 records these events in log files. You can view the events stored in these log files by using the Event Viewer snap-in, `eventvwr.msc`. All the processes that run on a server are executing programming code that must be transferred into and out of the computer's memory. The programming code is executed by the computer's central processing unit

(CPU), often called the "processor," and the executing code resides within files that are stored on disk subsystems. The data that is manipulated by these processes is also stored on disk subsystems. The System Monitor node of the Performance snap-in can track processor utilization, memory utilization, and disk utilization, among several other items.

Working with the Event Viewer

You can launch the Event Viewer snap-in tool by clicking Start, (All) Programs, Administrative Tools, Event Viewer, or simply click Start, Run; type eventvwr.msc; and click OK. Events are recorded into log files by the Event Log service, which is configured to run at system startup by default. All Event Log files are stored in the %systemroot%\system32\config folder by default. Event log files are identified with the .evt filename extension. These log files are not text files; you cannot view them using a simple text editor such as Notepad. You can easily save the .evt files in various text-readable formats, which are covered later in this chapter. On Windows Server 2003 standalone computers and domain member servers, there are just three different event logs:

➤ *Application*—This log records events that are generated by application programs and network application services such as Microsoft SQL Server and Exchange Server. The name of this log file stored on disk is AppEvent.Evt.

➤ *Security*—This log records success and failure notifications for audited events. Administrators can configure various auditing settings through local or group policies; the results of those audited events get recorded in the security log. Only users who have been granted the user right called Manage Auditing and the Security Log may access the security log; members of the Administrators group retain this right by default. The name of this log file stored on disk is SecEvent.Evt.

➤ *System*—This log records events generated by the operating system and its subsystems, such as its device drivers and services. The name of this log file stored on disk is SysEvent.Evt.

For Windows Server 2003 computers that have been set up as domain controllers (DCs), the Active Directory Installation Wizard (DCPROMO.exe) adds three other event logs, as shown in Figure 6.1. These additional logs monitor vital parts of Active Directory, such as the directory service itself, the File Replication Service, and the DNS (Domain Name System) server (if the DNS Server service is installed on the DC). The three additional event logs for DCs are

➤ *Directory Service*—This log records events that are generated by the Active Directory service itself. The name of this log file stored on disk is NTDS.Evt.

➤ *DNS Server*—This log records DNS queries, DNS replies, and assorted other DNS-related activities. The name of this log file stored on disk is DnsEvent.Evt.

➤ *File Replication Service*—This log records activities related to the File Replication Service, including messages about replication problems between DCs. The name of this log file stored on disk is NtFrs.Evt.

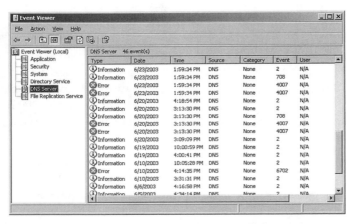

Figure 6.1 Looking at system events in the Event Viewer for a domain controller.

Viewing Event Logs

After you launch the Event Viewer, you can select the log you want to look at in the left pane; the events then appear in the right (details) pane, as you can see in Figure 6.1. When you double-click an event, its properties window appears, as shown in Figure 6.2. An event's properties window displays the details of the event, including the date, time, computer name, event ID, and a description of the event itself. The Event Viewer displays five types of events:

➤ *Error*—These events are recorded whenever significant problems occur, such as the loss of data or the loss of functionality. Unexpected system shutdowns and the failure of a service to start automatically at boot time are examples of events that are logged as errors.

➤ *Warning*—These events are recorded to indicate possible future problems. Low disk space for a drive volume is an example of an event that might get logged as a warning.

> *Information*—These events are recorded often. They indicate the successful operation of a program, a device driver, or a service. For example, Event ID 6005 indicates that "The Event Service was started"; this event usually occurs when the computer is started or restarted.

> *Failure Audit*—These events are recorded each time that any audited security event fails. For example, if a user attempts to log onto the computer without the proper username or password, a failure audit event is logged if the policy setting for Audit Account Logon Events is set to Success, Failure or if it's set only to Failure. You can configure Audit Policy settings at the local or group policy levels.

> *Success Audit*—These events are recorded each time that any audited security event succeeds. For example, if a user successfully logs onto the computer, a success audit event is logged if the policy setting for Audit Account Logon Events is set to Success, Failure or if it's set only to Success. You can configure Audit Policy settings at the local or group policy levels.

Figure 6.2   Viewing the event properties dialog.

Audit policy settings are available at the local, site, domain, DC, and organizational unit (OU) policy levels. You can use the Local Security Settings snap-in, the Default Domain Security Settings snap-in, the Default Domain Controller Security Settings snap-in, or the Group Policy Object Editor snap-in for a site or an OU to affect audit policy settings. From one of the snap-ins just mentioned, expand the Security Settings node, expand the Local Policies subnode, and select the Audit Policy subnode. Double-click the policy setting listed in the details pane to configure it, as shown in Figure 6.3.

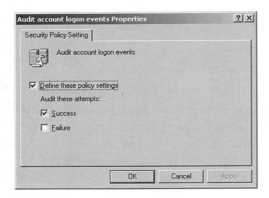

Figure 6.3 Configuring Audit Policy settings.

Archiving Event Logs, Setting Options, and Filtering Events

Event logs fill up over time. By default, the maximum log size for each event log is 16,384KB. By default, when the log reaches its maximum size, it overwrites events as needed. If you want to manually clear a log, right-click the log (in the left pane of the Event Viewer) and select Clear All Events. A message box asks whether you want to save the events contained in this log before you clear them. If you click Yes, the Save As dialog box prompts you to choose a location on disk, a filename for this log, and the file type to save this log as—Event Log (.evt), Text (tab delimited, *.txt), or CSV (comma delimited, *.csv).

You can open logs saved in the .evt file format within the Event Viewer. You can right-click a log in the Event Viewer, select Open Log File, and then specify the location and name of the file to open it. You can also right-click the Event Viewer root node and select Open Log File to open a log file without closing any of the existing logs. You can open logs saved in the .txt file format in any text editor or word-processing program. You can open logs saved in the .csv file format in applications such as Microsoft Excel or Notepad. However, the Event Viewer cannot itself open logs saved as .txt or .csv files.

If you right-click one of the Event logs in the left pane of the Event Viewer and select Properties, from the General tab, you can view and configure option settings for that specific Event Log, as shown in Figure 6.4. You can change the maximum log size, configure log overwrite settings, specify whether you're using a low-speed connection, clear the log, and restore all the default settings for the log from its properties sheet. The default setting for event logs is to overwrite events as necessary after reaching the maximum log size. Also from the log's properties sheet, you can click the Filter tab to filter and sort all the different events contained in the log (see Figure 6.5).

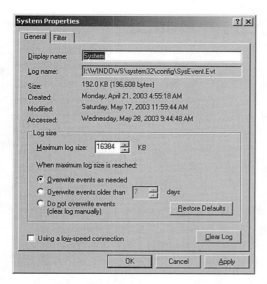

Figure 6.4   Configuring Event Log option settings for the System log.

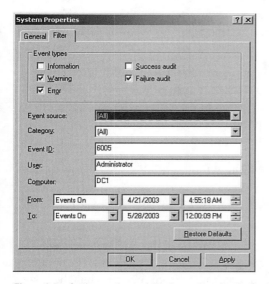

Figure 6.5   Setting sorting and filtering options for the System log.

 If you right-click a log, you can take advantage of a new feature of Windows Server 2003 called *new log view*. When you create a new log view, you can specify how the Event Viewer presents the log instead of always modifying the default display settings for the log. You can give this new log view a custom name, and you can manage it just like any other log. If you create a custom MMC snap-in, your customized settings for each new log view are maintained while the settings for the original log on which the new log view is based are left alone.

Working with the System Monitor

The System Monitor tool is available as a node within the Performance snap-in, `perfmon.msc`. The System monitor can display performance data about the local computer, or it can display performance data on one or more remote computers in real time. The System Monitor tool can also log a history of performance results over time for local or remote computers. To monitor system performance, you must specify performance *objects*, *counters*, and *instances* of those objects so that the System Monitor knows which areas of system performance to track and display. These performance specifiers are defined as follows:

➤ *Performance Objects*—These items are logical collections of performance metrics associated with a computer resource (CPU, disk, memory) or service that you can monitor. Processor, Memory, PhysicalDisk, and Paging File are all examples of performance objects.

➤ *Performance Object Instances*—These terms provide a method of identifying multiple performance objects of the same type. If a computer has more than one processor installed, its processor performance object displays multiple distinct instances of this object to monitor each individual processor separately.

➤ *Performance Counters*—These data items direct System Monitor about which areas of performance to track and display. Each performance object has several performance counters associated with it. Pages/sec, Available Bytes, and %Committed Bytes in Use are all examples of counters for the Memory performance object.

In Windows Server 2003, the System Monitor tool is preconfigured with three sets of performance objects, counters, and instances (object: counter:instance) by default each time that you launch the Performance snap-in, as shown in Figure 6.6:

➤ *Memory:Pages/sec*—This performance metric is the rate at which pages are read from or written to disk to resolve hard page faults. Hard page faults occur when a process requests a page from memory, but the system cannot find it and it must be retrieved from disk. This metric is a primary indicator of the kinds of faults that cause systemwide slowdowns. *This value should remain consistently between 0 and 20 but not consistently higher than 20.*

➤ *PhysicalDisk:Avg. Disk Queue Length:_Total*—This performance metric is the average number of both read and write requests that were queued (waiting) for the selected disk during the sample interval. *This value should remain consistently between 0 and 2 but not consistently higher than 2.*

➤ *Processor:% Processor Time:_Total*—This performance metric is the percentage of elapsed time that the processor spends to execute a non-idle thread. It is calculated by measuring the duration that the idle thread is active in the sample interval and subtracting that time from interval duration. (Each processor has an idle thread that consumes cycles when no other threads are ready to run.) This metric is the primary indicator of processor activity and displays the average percentage of busy time observed during the sample interval. It is calculated by monitoring the time that the service is inactive and subtracting that value from 100%. *This value should remain consistently below the 85% mark.*

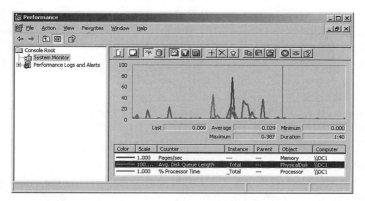

Figure 6.6 Watching the System Monitor in graph view with the default performance objects, counters, and instances.

The **diskperf.exe -y** command is no longer required under Windows Server 2003 to enable either LogicalDisk or PhysicalDisk objects and counters. All disk objects and counters are automatically enabled on demand for Windows Server 2003 and Windows XP computers.

Monitoring System Performance

You can monitor system performance in one of two ways—real-time monitoring and logged monitoring. Real-time monitoring measures the current performance of the server's processors, memory, physical disks, and network utilization, among other metrics. You can find out what type of usage load a server is currently experiencing by monitoring subsystems in real time. You use logged monitoring to analyze server performance over an extended period of time. By recording historical performance data into log files during "normal" usage periods, you can establish a baseline of performance data that you can use to compare against future performance data to help diagnose and alleviate performance bottlenecks that might occur.

Using System Monitoring in Real Time with Task Manager

You can use either the Task Manager tool or the System Monitor tool to measure system performance in real time. You can access the Task Manager in any one of three ways:

➤ Right-click the taskbar and select Task Manager.

➤ Press Ctrl+Shift+Esc on the keyboard.

➤ Press Ctrl+Alt+Del on the keyboard and select Task Manager.

The Task Manager utility under Windows Server 2003 displays five tabs—Applications, Processes, Performance, Networking, and Users, as shown in Figure 6.7. The Applications tab shows the application programs that are currently running in the foreground; background services do not appear on this page. The Processes tab displays the processes currently running on the computer; to view all processes from all users logged onto the computer, mark the Show Processes from All Users check box. The Performance tab shows current usage of the CPUs, the CPU Usage History charts, current Page File usage, Page File Usage History chart, and current memory usage statistics. The Networking tab is new for Windows Server 2003; it charts the current network adapters' network traffic utilization (see Figure 6.8). The Users tab lists the users who are currently logged onto the console or logged on via Remote Desktop connections (see Figure 6.9).

Task Manager offers you a quick glimpse at the following items:

➤ Applications currently in use

➤ Processes currently running

➤ Current processor usage

➤ Current paging file usage

➤ Overall current memory usage

➤ Current network utilization

➤ Currently logged-on users

For any other vital statistics on a system, or for more detailed and in-depth inquiries, you should use the System Monitor and the Performance Logs and Alerts tools.

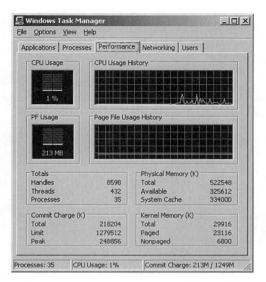

Figure 6.7   Monitoring system performance in real time with Task Manager.

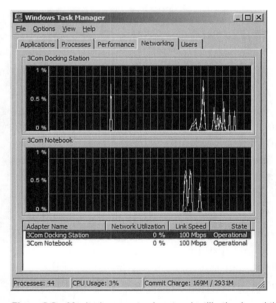

Figure 6.8   Monitoring a system's network utilization in real time with Task Manager.

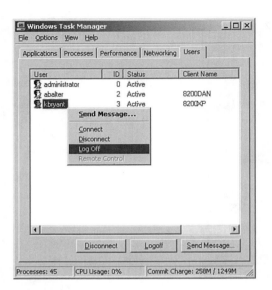

Figure 6.9 Viewing a system's currently logged-on users with Task Manager.

Using Real-Time Monitoring with System Monitor

You can configure the System Monitor tool to display its results in any of three different views—graph, histogram, or report. The graph view is the default, and it supports the most optional settings. The histogram view is a bar-chart configuration, as shown in Figure 6.10. The report view is simply a straightforward list of the performance objects, counters, and their associated instances in a report-like format (see Figure 6.11). Using the System Monitor, you can monitor the local computer or several remote computers over a network connection.

The default configuration is to monitor the local computer in real time. You can change the default settings to monitor one or more remote computers in real time. You can also choose to record the system performance of the local or remote computers to a log file using the Performance Logs and Alerts node of the Performance snap-in, which is covered in the section "Monitoring File and Print Services" later in this chapter. You can play back and view the results of those log files using the System Monitor tool.

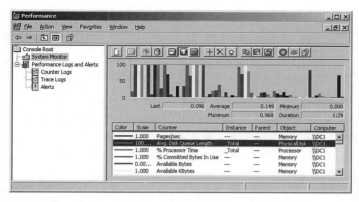

Figure 6.10   Watching the System Monitor in histogram view to track several performance objects and counters.

    To obtain the most accurate results when checking a computer's performance with System Monitor, you should monitor a computer remotely. System Monitor itself requires a certain amount of overhead to run. Therefore, when you run System Monitor on the same machine you are measuring, the performance data can be negatively affected and the results might be somewhat skewed.

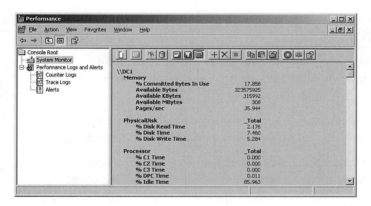

Figure 6.11   Watching the System Monitor in report view to track several performance objects and counters.

Adding and Removing Objects, Counters, and Instances

System Monitor offers you a variety of ways to add objects, counters, and instances to its list of monitored items; collectively, these items as referred to simply as *counters*. To add counters, you can click the plus sign (+) on the icon bar, you can press Ctrl+I on the keyboard, or you can right-click the right (details) pane in any view and select Add Counters. To both add and remove counters, you can right-click the details pane in any view, select Properties, and click the Data tab. To add counters to System Monitor, follow these steps:

1. Open the Performance snap-in and click the System Monitor node.

2. Click the plus sign (+) on the icon bar, press Ctrl+I on the keyboard, right-click the details pane and select Add Counters, or right-click the details pane and select Properties and use the Data tab.

3. From the Add Counters dialog box, select either the Use Local Computer Counters option or the Select Counters From Computer option; type in a computer name or select a remote computer.

4. Select the performance object that you want to monitor from the drop-down list box.

5. Click the All Counters option button or the Select Counters from List option button.

6. Select the counter that you want to monitor from the list of counters. Click the Explain button to view a definition of the specific counter that you have selected (see Figure 6.12).

7. Click the All Instances option button or the Select Instances from List option button.

8. Choose the instance of the object that you want to monitor. The _Total option monitors the sum of all the instances for that selected object:counter combination.

9. Click the Add button to add the selected object:counter:instance combination to System Monitor's list of performance items to monitor.

10. Repeat this process for each object:counter:instance combination that you want to add. Click Close when you are done adding counters.

To remove counters from System Monitor, you can select the counter that you want to remove at the bottom of the details pane and press the Del key on the keyboard. You can also remove counters another way by following these steps:

1. Right-click the details pane and select Properties.

2. Select the Data tab.

3. Select the counter (or several counters) that you want to delete from the Counters list box.

4. Press the Remove button.

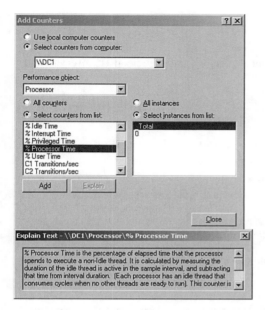

Figure 6.12 Adding performance counters to System Monitor with the Add Counters dialog box.

Using Logged Monitoring with Performance Logs and Alerts

The Performance Logs and Alerts tool in Windows Server 2003 is the other half of the Performance snap-in. Performance Logs and Alerts supports *logged monitoring* to log files larger than 1GB, up to the maximum supported file size for the file system on which the logs are stored. In addition, you can append performance data onto existing log files. Two new groups (installed by default) allow users to gather performance data for a computer *without* requiring that those users become members of the Administrators group:

➤ *Performance Log Users*—This is a local group on standalone and domain member servers and a domain local group on domain controllers. Members of this group have permission to *manage and schedule logged* performance counters, logs, and alerts on the local server or on servers within the domain, both interactively (locally) and remotely.

➤ *Performance Monitor Users*—This is a local group on standalone and domain member servers and a domain local group on domain controllers. Members of this group have permission to *monitor* performance counters, logs, and alerts on the local server or on servers within the domain, both interactively (locally) and remotely. Members of this group do not need to be members of the Administrators group or the Performance Log Users group to monitor performance.

The Performance Logs and Alerts tool offers administrators three major benefits:

➤ The ability to record system performance data at specified intervals over time using *counter logs*

➤ A method to record detailed system events after specific events occur using *trace logs*

➤ A configuration setting for being notified by the system when specific counters exceed certain preset thresholds using *alerts*

Counter logs enable you to collect data about a server's performance over time to establish a *baseline* of normal performance for a given computer system. You should collect baseline data during periods of regular activity, not during temporary periods of high or low server usage. Baselines can only be an effective barometer of average server performance under "normal" loads; recording performance data during peak usage times does not create an accurate baseline reading, nor does recording performance at times when the system is not being used. In some cases, it might be interesting to record the system without users on it to know the minimum level of activity the system generates on its own for replication traffic and so on. This no-user baseline gives the administrators another piece of information to use when considering system upgrades. You should create and use system performance baselines for future comparison purposes when you suspect that server performance has degraded over time or when you evaluate new purchases. By comparing baseline readings with current performance results, you can quickly determine whether there is truly a performance bottleneck or whether you might need additional hardware. Remember, if you change the server's hardware configuration, you need to re-establish a baseline for that system.

Configuring Counter Logs

Counter logs enable you to collect performance data on systems over periods of time to create performance baselines, chart and analyze performance trends, and diagnose performance bottlenecks. Once you configure one or more counter logs, you can schedule these logs to record data automatically at predetermined times. You can also start and stop counter logs manually if you want. You can choose from five different types of counter log storage formats—comma delimited (.csv) text files; tab delimited (.tsv) files; binary files (.blg); binary circular files (.blg) that overwrite themselves when they reach a maximum size; and SQL database files, which require a connection to a Microsoft SQL Server computer and access to an accompanying SQL database table. To set up a new counter log, follow these steps:

1. Launch the Performance console.

2. Expand the Performance Logs and Alerts node and select the Counter Logs subnode.

3. Right-click the Counter Logs subnode and select New Log Settings.

4. Type a name for this log in the Name box and click OK.

5. From the General tab of the properties dialog box that appears (see Figure 6.13), you can

   ➤ Click the Add Objects button to add objects with *all* their associated counters to the log.

   ➤ Click the Add Counters button to add individual counters and instances to the log.

   ➤ Select one or more objects or counters from the Counters list and click the Remove button to delete them.

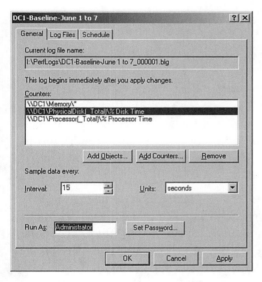

Figure 6.13 Adding objects and counters to a new counter log in Performance Logs and Alerts.

6. To change the sample interval, type a number or increment or decrement the interval using the up or down arrows on the Interval spinner box.

7. To change the sample interval time units, click the Units drop-down list box and select from Seconds, Minutes, Hours, or Days.

8. If you want to have the counter log record data under a specific user account's security context, type the user account name in the Run as box and then click the Set Password button to specify the proper password.

9. Click the Log Files tab to specify log-file options, as shown in Figure 6.14.

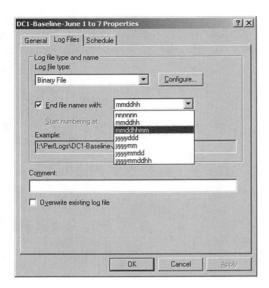

Figure 6.14 Specifying log-file formats for a new counter log.

10. Click the Log File Type drop-down list box to select the type of log storage format that you want for this log—binary file (default), text file (comma delimited), text file (tab delimited), binary circular file, or SQL database.

11. Click the Configure button to change the location of the log file, change the log filename, or establish a maximum log file size. If the Maximum Limit (default) option is selected, the logging will continue for this counter log until the log file uses all the available space on the disk where the log is located. Click OK for the Configure Log Files dialog box when finished.

12. Clear the End File Names with check box if you do not want the log file's name appended with a numeric sequence number or a date format.

13. If you leave the End File Names with check box marked, you can select from the nnnnnn setting or one or several date formats from the associated drop-down list box, such as mmddhh that uses the current month, day, and hour or mmddhhmm that uses the current month, day, hour, and minute.

14. Optionally, you can type a description in the Comment box.

15. Mark the Overwrite Existing Log File if you want to overwrite an existing file that has the same name.

16. Click the Schedule tab to specify start and stop times for logging to this counter log, as shown in Figure 6.15.

17. Click OK to create the new counter log.

Figure 6.15 Scheduling start and stop times for a counter log.

 You can create a counter log from an existing set of counters set up in the System Monitor tool by right-clicking anywhere in the details pane of System Monitor and selecting Save as. When the Save as dialog box appears, select a location on disk to save these settings, specify the Save as Type as a Web page (***.htm**, ***.html**) file, and click Save to save the settings file. Next, go to the Performance Logs and Alerts node, right-click the Counter Logs subnode, and select New Log Settings. Locate the settings file that you saved and click the Open button. Click OK for the message box that appears. Type a name for this new counter log in the Name box for the New Log Settings dialog box that pops up. Make any changes that you want to the new counter log's properties window that appears and click OK when you are done.

To manually start a counter log to record performance data, right-click the counter log name in the details pane of Performance Logs and Alerts and select Start. The icon for the counter log turns to green, indicating that logging is occurring. To manually stop a counter log from logging data, right-click the counter log name and select Stop. To modify a counter log's settings, right-click the log and select Properties.

To view the results of logging to a counter log, go to System Monitor and click the View Log Data icon from the icon bar or press Ctrl+L on the keyboard. Be sure that the Source tab is selected. Click the Log Files option button, if you are not using the SQL Database logging format. Next, click the Add button, locate the log file using the Select Log File dialog box, and click Open to select the file. If you are using the SQL database logging format, click the Database option button and select the SQL System DSN and Log Set from their respective drop-down list boxes. Click the Time Range button to adjust the period of time view for displaying the log file's results; use the slider bar to shorten or lengthen the time window. Lengthening the time window gives you more of an overall view of a performance trend; shortening the time window lets you zoom in to analyze the details of system performance for a specific period of time. Click OK for the System Monitor Properties dialog box, as shown in Figure 6.16.

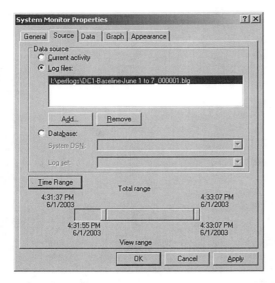

Figure 6.16   Setting the data source for a counter log to display its results in System Monitor.

 You can also create counter logs from the command line under Windows Server 2003 using the **logman.exe** tool. If you type **logman /?** at a command prompt, you can get help on the many "verbs," parameters, and options available with this tool. For example, the command line **logman create counter perf_log -c "\Processor(_Total)\% Processor Time"** creates a new counter log named **perf log** that uses the binary file format and uses the Processor object, the % Processor Time counter, and the _Total instance.

Configuring Alerts

Alerts send notifications whenever the predefined counter setting exceeds or falls beneath the specified alert threshold. When an alert is triggered based on its settings, it can perform several actions—create an entry in the application event log, send a network message to someone, initiate logging for a specific performance log, and run an application program. To create a new alert, follow these steps:

1. Launch the Performance console.

2. Expand the Performance Logs and Alerts node and select the Alerts subnode.

3. Right-click the Alerts subnode and select New Alert Settings.

4. Type a name for this Alert in the Name box and click OK.

5. From the General tab of the properties dialog box that appears (see Figure 6.17), click the Add button to add one or more counters to this alert.

Figure 6.17 Configuring threshold settings for an alert.

6. Select either Over or Under from the Alert When the Value Is dropdown list box.

7. Type the threshold value in the Limit box.

8. You can change the sample data interval and you can configure the alert to run under a specific user account, if you desire.

9. Click the Action tab to specify the actions that you want the alert to perform when the alert is triggered, as shown in Figure 6.18.

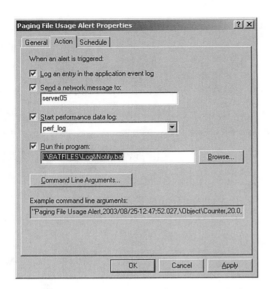

Figure 6.18   Configuring actions to be performed when an alert is triggered.

10. Click the Schedule tab to schedule when the alert should be operating.

11. Click OK to save the settings for the new alert.

To manually start an alert, right-click the alert name in the details pane of Performance Logs and Alerts and select Start. The icon for the alert turns to green, indicating that the alert is operating. To manually stop an alert from scanning the system, right-click the alert name and select Stop. To modify an alert's settings, right-click the alert and select Properties.

Monitoring File and Print Services

At a minimum, you should always monitor the four major performance areas that can have a significant impact on file and print server performance—processor utilization, memory utilization, disk utilization, and network utilization. These four major performance areas and the reasons for their impact on server performance are as follows:

➤ *Processor*—This is a key element in server performance. This element is measured in terms of percentages with 100% being full processor utilization. It is not good for a server to be fully utilized for prolonged periods.

The CPU Usage graph in Task Manager and the % Processor Time counter in the Performance snap-in measure processor utilization. Sustained usage of 85% or more can indicate a processor bottleneck.

➤ *Memory*—This resource is also a key element in server performance. A lack of sufficient physical memory in a server requires that more virtual memory is used. Virtual memory uses disk storage via the paging files to swap data and programs in and out of memory. Because disk is much slower than RAM (random access memory), insufficient RAM can cause a significant system slowdown. *Memory bottlenecks* occur when low memory conditions cause increased use of the paging file, and page faults occur when the system is unable to locate either data or programs in memory. Services and programs can become less responsive under these conditions. *Memory leaks* occur when programs allocate memory for their own use, but they never release that allocated memory back to the system's memory pool. Over time, memory leaks can lock up a server and make it stop functioning; rebooting the server temporarily fixes the problem. A server that is running low on memory can appear to have a disk problem due to excessive swapping of application code and data from physical memory to virtual memory (the paging file). This excessive swapping is known as *thrashing*.

➤ *Disk*—Disks can be a source of performance bottlenecking on a system if all three of the following conditions exist: the sustained disk activity greatly exceeds your established baseline, the persistent disk queues exceed two per disk, *and* there is not a high amount of paging occurring on the system. Disk fragmentation can slow down disk performance; you should have all the disks on a server regularly defragmented. If the % Disk Time performance counter averages greater than 50% on a regular basis, you might have a disk bottleneck. Replacing the disk subsystem with faster drives or replacing a software RAID configuration with a hardware RAID configuration can improve disk performance.

➤ *Network*—Network throughput can have a major impact on users as they request data from network servers. Network bandwidth includes how fast bytes are sent to and from a server and how fast data packages (packets, frames, segments, and datagrams) are transferred by a server. Network bottlenecks are often caused by too many requests for data on a particular server; too much data traffic on the network segment; or a physical network problem with a hub, switch, router, or other network device. The Network Utilization graph in Task Manager can assist you with troubleshooting a possible network bottleneck. This statistic should generally average below 30% utilization.

Monitoring General Server Workload with Task Manager

You can get a quick glimpse into a server's general health and well-being by using Task Manager. Press Ctrl+Alt+Del on the keyboard and select Task Manager or right-click a blank area on the taskbar and select Task Manager to display this tool. Click the Performance tab to view current CPU Usage; CPU Usage History; current PF (Page File) Usage; Page File Usage History; total Handles, Threads, and Processes; Physical Memory; Kernel Memory; and Commit Charge statistics (listed in kilobytes). Click the Networking tab to view current network utilization percentages for each installed network adapter.

Monitoring Disk Quotas with the Event Viewer

If you enable disk quotas for one or more drive volumes, you can monitor users who exceed their disk quota entry warning level and their disk quota limit threshold in Event Viewer. You must be sure to mark the check box Log Events When a User Exceeds Their Warning Level and the check box Log Events When a User Exceeds Their Quota Limit for these occurrences to be recorded in the System Event Log as a Category Disk, Event ID 36 logged entry. If you filter the log, it's easy to spot various kinds of warnings and errors such as this one. Figure 6.19 shows the Event Properties window for a user who hits his or her quota limit.

Troubleshooting Server Bottlenecks with System Monitor

You can usually discover performance bottlenecks on a server whenever one or more of the system's major elements, or subsystems, shows a decline in performance as compared to its historical baseline performance statistics. This discovery is why establishing and maintaining baseline performance data for each of the major server subsystems is so important! By default, performance for each counter is displayed in graph view in System Monitor. Each counter/instance combination is assigned a different color on the graph. As you select a counter/instance in the lower half of the window, its statistics also appear just below the graph. The following metrics appear below the graph:

Figure 6.19 Monitoring disk quota thresholds for users with the Event Viewer.

➤ *Last*—This metric shows the result for the current counter/instance as of the last recorded interval.

➤ *Average*—This metric shows the average result for the current counter/instance during the monitoring period.

➤ *Maximum*—This metric shows the maximum result for the current counter/instance during the monitoring period.

➤ *Minimum*—This metric shows the minimum result for the current counter/instance during the monitoring period.

➤ *Duration*—This metric shows the length of the current monitoring period.

By keeping baseline data on each server's processor (CPU), memory, disk, and network utilization, you can easily compare those baseline figures against current performance results. Use the Performance Logs and Alerts tool to log system baseline performance and then you can compare the baseline to current system performance by loading the logged data into System Monitor and displaying a second instance of the Performance snap-in to show current performance results. Figure 6.20 shows two instances of System Monitor: The top window is displaying current performance and the bottom window displays logged baseline data.

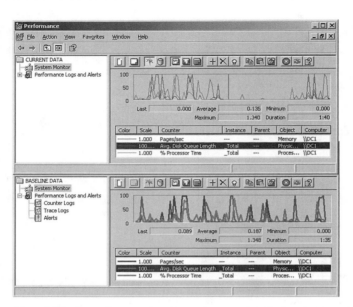

Figure 6.20 Comparing current system performance data (top) against logged baseline performance data (bottom).

Diagnosing and Resolving Performance Bottlenecks

In addition to monitoring and comparing current system performance metrics against baseline data, you can also keep tabs on several key areas of performance that might indicate the presence of performance problems. Tables 6.1, 6.2, 6.3, and 6.4 outline performance counters to monitor when checking for possible system bottlenecks. Each table lists general guidelines for performance counters that you should monitor, the threshold levels to check, and what remedial action that you can take to resolve the performance problem. Table 6.1 deals with processor bottlenecks, Table 6.2 deals with memory bottlenecks, Table 6.3 talks about disk bottlenecks, and Table 6.4 discusses network bottlenecks.

Table 6.1 Troubleshooting Processor Usage Bottlenecks		
Performance Object:Counter	**Unacceptable Threshold Level**	**Remedy**
Processor:% User Time Processor:% Processor Time Processor:% Privileged Time	Sustained usage higher than 85%.	Upgrade existing CPU to a faster CPU or install additional CPUs.

Table 6.1   Troubleshooting Processor Usage Bottlenecks *(continued)*

Performance Object:Counter	Unacceptable Threshold Level	Remedy
System:Processor Queue Length Server Work Queues: Queue Length	Sustained usage higher than 2.	Upgrade existing CPU to a faster CPU or install additional CPUs.
Processor:Interrupts/sec	Varies by processor; however, substantially higher values than the baseline can indicate a hardware problem with another device in the server, such as a faulty network adapter or a failing disk controller.	Locate and replace the hardware device that is generating the high number of interrupts.

Table 6.2   Troubleshooting Memory Usage Bottlenecks

Performance Object:Counter	Unacceptable Threshold Level	Remedy
Memory:Page Faults/sec	Consistent page fault rates higher than 5.	Identify the processes using disproportional amounts of RAM and install more memory.
Memory:Committed Bytes	Sustained value higher than 75% of total physical RAM installed.	Identify the processes using disproportional amounts of RAM and install more memory.
Memory:Available Bytes	Consistent value lower than 5% of total physical RAM installed.	Identify the processes using disproportional amounts of RAM and install more memory.
Memory:Pages/sec	Consistently higher than 20.	Identify the processes causing excessive paging and install more memory.
Memory:Nonpaged Bytes	Steady increases (compared to baseline) over time without an increased server load can indicate a memory leak.	Identify one or more programs that might have a memory leak, stop running the programs, or get updated versions.

Table 6.3 Troubleshooting Disk Usage Bottlenecks

Performance Object:Counter	Unacceptable Threshold Level	Remedy
PhysicalDisk:% Disk Time LogicalDisk:% Disk Time	Consistently higher than 50%.	First verify that excessive paging is not the cause of this problem; if not the result of excessive paging, replace the disk with a faster model.
PhysicalDisk:Current Disk Queue Length LogicalDisk:Current Disk Queue Length	Consistently higher than 2.	Replace the disk with a faster model.
PhysicalDisk:Avg. Disk Bytes/Transfer LogicalDisk:Avg. Disk Bytes/Transfer	Consistently lower than the server's baseline.	Replace the disk with a faster model.
PhysicalDisk:Disk Bytes/sec LogicalDisk:Disk Bytes/sec	Consistently lower than the server's baseline.	Replace the disk with a faster model.

Table 6.4 Troubleshooting Network Usage Bottlenecks

Performance Object:Counter	Unacceptable Threshold Level	Remedy
Server:Bytes Total/sec Network Interface:Bytes Total/sec	Sustained usage levels higher than the baseline averages for the server.	Replace the installed network adapters with faster models; install another network adapter; upgrade the physical network cabling, hubs, and switches.
Server:Bytes Received/sec	Sustained usage levels higher than 50% of the network adapter's bandwidth rating.	Replace the installed network adapters with faster models; upgrade the physical network cabling, hubs, and switches.
Network Interface:Bytes Sent/sec	Sustained usage levels lower than the baseline averages for the server.	Replace the installed network adapters with faster models; upgrade the physical network cabling, hubs, and switches.

Monitoring and Optimizing Application Server Performance

As discussed throughout this chapter, monitoring system performance is an important task for an administrator to perform on a regular basis. You can use System Monitor to display real-time data and to display the results of log files you created with the Performance Logs and Alerts tool. There are four major areas of server performance to monitor that will help identify and resolve performance slowdowns—processor, memory, disk, and network utilization. In this section, we show you how to set up the appropriate performance counters to make sure that a server is running smoothly.

Monitoring Processor Usage

One or more CPUs are the heart of any computer system. Processors on application servers tend to experience more activity than processors on file and printer servers; generally, more numbers are being crunched on an application server. You can monitor processor performance in any of the following ways:

➤ Run Task Manager and view real-time performance data from the Performance tab.

➤ Open the Performance snap-in and select System Monitor to view real-time data. Add performance counters for

  ➤ Processor:% Processor Time

  ➤ System:Processor Queue Length

  ➤ Server Work Queues:Queue Length

  ➤ Processor:Interrupts/sec

➤ Open the Performance snap-in and select Performance Logs and Alerts to collect logged data or establish baseline averages for the server. Add performance counters for

  ➤ Processor:% Processor Time

  ➤ System:Processor Queue Length

  ➤ Server Work Queues:Queue Length

  ➤ Processor:Interrupts/sec

Monitor these counters and watch for the threshold levels listed in Table 6.1 in the previous section "Diagnosing and Resolving Performance Bottlenecks."

Monitoring Memory Usage

Lack of adequate RAM is a common cause for poor server performance. Symptoms related to inadequate memory include excessive paging or a high rate of hard page faults. You can monitor memory performance in any of the following ways:

➤ Run Task Manager and view real-time performance data from the Performance tab.

➤ Open the Performance snap-in and select System Monitor to view real-time data. Add performance counters for

➤ Memory:Nonpaged Bytes

➤ Memory:Pages/sec

➤ Memory:Available Bytes

➤ Memory:Committed Bytes

➤ Memory:Page Faults/sec

➤ Open the Performance snap-in and select Performance Logs and Alerts to collect logged data or establish baseline averages for the server. Add performance counters for

➤ Memory:Nonpaged Bytes

➤ Memory:Pages/sec

➤ Memory:Available Bytes

➤ Memory:Committed Bytes

➤ Memory:Page Faults/sec

Monitor these counters and watch for the threshold levels listed in Table 6.2 in the previous section.

Monitoring Disk Usage

Disk storage can be a significant source of performance bottlenecking on a server due to the fact the disks are mechanical. Therefore, disk response times are generally much slower than the access times for nonmechanical components such as the processor, memory, or even network I/O. You can monitor PhysicalDisk counters, LogicalDisk counters, or both. PhysicalDisk counters measure individual hard disk drives. LogicalDisk counters measure logical partitions or volumes stored on physical disks. LogicalDisk counters help you isolate the source of bottlenecks to a particular logical drive volume so that you can more easily identify where disk access requests are coming from. You can monitor disk performance in the following ways:

➤ Open the Performance snap-in and select System Monitor to view real-time data. Add performance counters for

  ➤ PhysicalDisk:% Disk Time or LogicalDisk:% Disk Time

  ➤ PhysicalDisk:Current Disk Queue Length or LogicalDisk:Current Disk Queue Length

  ➤ PhysicalDisk:Avg. Disk Bytes/Transfer or LogicalDisk:Avg. Disk Bytes/Transfer

  ➤ PhysicalDisk:Disk Bytes/sec or LogicalDisk:Disk Bytes/sec

➤ Open the Performance snap-in and select Performance Logs and Alerts to collect logged data or establish baseline averages for the server. Add performance counters for

  ➤ PhysicalDisk:% Disk Time or LogicalDisk:% Disk Time

  ➤ PhysicalDisk:Current Disk Queue Length or LogicalDisk:Current Disk Queue Length

  ➤ PhysicalDisk:Avg. Disk Bytes/Transfer or LogicalDisk:Avg. Disk Bytes/Transfer

  ➤ PhysicalDisk:Disk Bytes/sec or LogicalDisk:Disk Bytes/sec

Monitor these counters and watch for the threshold levels listed in Table 6.3 in the previous section.

Monitoring Network Usage

Network usage bottlenecks can be difficult to troubleshoot because many factors can influence network bandwidth availability and because the larger networks become, the more complex they become. If you determine that network throughput is the source of your server's bottleneck, you can take some constructive measures such as the following:

➤ Add servers to distribute network traffic.

➤ Segment the network into smaller subnets and connect each subnet to a separate network card on the server.

➤ Remove network bindings from unneeded network cards.

➤ Install the latest networking equipment such as 100Mb or 1000Mb (Gigabit) switches, hubs, routers, and cabling.

You can monitor network performance in the following ways:

➤ Run Task Manager and view real-time performance data from the Networking tab. *In general, sustained network utilization should be lower than 30%.*

➤ Open the Performance snap-in and select System Monitor to view real-time data. Add performance counters for

➤ Server:Bytes Total/sec

➤ Network Interface:Bytes Total/sec

➤ Server:Bytes Received/sec

➤ Network Interface:Bytes Sent/sec

➤ Open the Performance snap-in and select Performance Logs and Alerts to collect logged data or establish baseline averages for the server. Add performance counters for

➤ Server:Bytes Total/sec

➤ Network Interface:Bytes Total/sec

➤ Server:Bytes Received/sec

➤ Network Interface:Bytes Sent/sec

Monitor these counters and watch for the threshold levels listed in Table 6.4 in the previous section.

Managing Software Site Licensing

Technically, Microsoft "licenses" each of its software products to individuals, companies, and organizations; it does not "sell" its software. When money is exchanged for Microsoft's (and many other software publishers') software products, ownership is not granted to the buyer. As the End User License

Agreement (EULA) states, the purchaser is buying a license to use the software in accordance with the terms of the EULA contract and copyright law. For Microsoft server products, the person or entity "buying" the software must purchase a license for each server product. Additionally, the licensed entity must purchase a separate Client Access License (CAL) for each user or device that will be connecting to the server software. If your organization is using Windows Terminal Services, each Terminal Server (Remote Desktop Connection) user or device must also have a Terminal Server Client Access License (TSCAL), or each user or device must qualify to use a built-in TSCAL, to connect to Windows Terminal Servers. Microsoft offers a total of five types of software licensing:

➤ *Full Packaged Product*—You can purchase full retail products in the box at stores such as Staples or Office Depot or from any one of a number of online resellers via the Internet. This low-volume purchase option is designed for consumers and small businesses that need fewer than five licenses. Media (CD-ROM, DVD-ROM) ships in each package.

➤ *Open Licensing*—This is the entry level volume-licensing program for corporate, academic, charity, and government customers that need at least five licenses per product or more. The Open, Select, and Enterprise licensing programs are more economical than purchasing retail packages. This program is designed for small- to medium-sized companies. You must purchase media separately for a nominal fee.

➤ *Select Licensing*—This volume licensing program is designed for corporate, academic, and government customers that need at least 250 licenses per product or more. This program is designed for medium, large, and multinational companies who want *decentralized* purchasing. You must purchase media separately for a nominal fee.

➤ *Enterprise Agreement Licensing*—This volume licensing program is designed for corporate customers that need at least 250 licenses per product or more. This program is designed for medium, large, and multinational companies who want *centralized* purchasing. You must purchase media separately for a nominal fee.

➤ *Enterprise Subscription Agreement Licensing*—This volume licensing program is also designed for corporate customers that need at least 250 licenses per product or more; however, this program provides companies with *nonperpetual licenses* for enterprise products, and these software products are licensed on a subscription basis.

Understanding Microsoft Licensing

Microsoft server licensing generally offers three licensing modes—per server, per device or per user, and per processor. Per-server licensing requires a CAL for each user or device that accesses a particular server. With this mode, CALs are associated with specific servers. If you choose the per-server option, you must purchase at least as many CALs for a given server as the maximum number of clients that might connect to that server any point in time. If you choose the per-device or per-user option, each CAL is associated with a specific user, computer, or device. Clients, therefore, are entitled to connect to *any* server on the network as long as each client (user or device) possesses a CAL for each type of server being accessed (for example, one CAL for Windows Server 2003, one CAL for SQL Server, one CAL for Exchange Server, and so on). Not all but selected server products offer per-processor licensing, such as SQL Server 2000. With per-processor licensing, CALs are not required. The server itself is licensed based on the number of processors installed in the server.

Microsoft permits organizations to make a one-time–only switch from per-server licensing to per-device or per-user licensing. Microsoft does not permit switching from per-device or per-user licensing to per-server licensing.

To keep track of software licensing for the different types of licensing options, Windows 2000 Server and Windows Server 2003 install the Licensing tool by default. You need to work directly with the proper licensing server if you want to manage software licenses for an entire site. To locate the software licensing server for a site, follow these steps:

1. Open the Active Directory Sites and Service snap-in and select the site that you want to work with.

2. Right-click the Licensing Site Settings object in the details pane and select Properties.

3. The licensing server for the site appears at the bottom of the window in the Licensing Computer section, as shown in Figure 6.21.

4. To change the licensing server for the site, click the Change button.

5. Click OK when you are finished.

The default licensing server for a site is the first DC installed in the site. However, a site license server does *not* have to be a DC. Microsoft recommends that a site license server and a DC should be located in the same site.

Figure 6.21   Locating the licensing server for an Active Directory site.

Using the Licensing Tools

Windows Server 2003 actually installs two licensing utilities by default. The Licensing icon in the Control Panel lets you configure licensing for the local server (see Figure 6.22). If you click Start, (All) Programs, Administrative Tools, Licensing, you launch the Enterprise Licensing tool for sites and domains (see Figure 6.23). To use either licensing tool, you must have the License Logging service running on the server that you are working on. By default, the License Logging service is *not* started automatically. You must be a member of the Administrators group for the local server or for the domain on which you want to manage licensing.

Figure 6.22   The Choose Licensing Mode utility for managing software licenses on the local server.

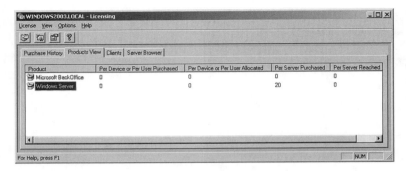

Figure 6.23   The Enterprise Licensing tool for managing software licenses for sites and domains.

Administering and Troubleshooting Network Print Queues

When a user sends a print job to a print device (printer) over the network, the print-server computer that hosts the printer first spools that print job to disk. The process of spooling the print job frees up the workstation computer so that it does not have to wait for the print job to complete before it can go on to a different task. The print jobs that have been spooled to disk wait in line (queue up) to be printed; this line is known as the *print queue*. Each printer has its own print queue. By default the print spooler folder is located in the `%systemroot%\system32\spool\printers` folder. For performance reasons or lack of available disk space reasons, you might need to move this folder to a different drive volume. To change the location of the print spooler folder as well as to configure several other print server settings, follow these steps:

1. Create an empty folder on the drive volume where you want to place the print spooler folder.

2. Click Start, Printers and Faxes or click Start, Settings, Printers and Faxes from the classic start menu.

3. From the Printers and Faxes window, click File, Server Properties to display the Print Server Properties window.

4. Click the Advanced tab.

5. Type the full local drive letter and path in the Spool Folder box, as shown in Figure 6.24. The new folder location must already exist.

6. Click OK to save the new settings.

7. Stop the Spooler service and then restart it for the change to take effect.

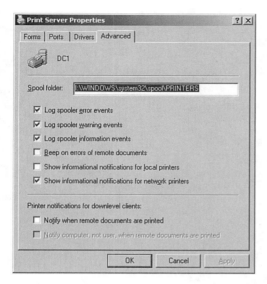

Figure 6.24   Changing the print spooler folder location and viewing other options on the Print Server Properties dialog box.

From the Advanced tab of the Print Server Properties dialog box, you can also specify whether the system should log error events, warning events, and information events in the Event Viewer for the print spooler service. If you want workstation computers running Windows NT, Windows 2000, or Windows XP to be notified when their documents are printed, be sure to mark the Notify When Remote Documents Are Printed check box. You can also work with forms from the Forms tab; you can add, delete, and configure ports from the Ports tab; and you can add, remove, reinstall, and view properties of printer drivers from the Drivers tab.

Setting Printer Priority and Availability Levels

You can establish different priority levels for different printers that are set up as a printer pool. You can also specify availability times for each printer if you want to limit the time period when a printer can be used. If you set up two or more printers using the same port, you can specify the priority for each printer from the Advanced tab of the printer's properties sheet (see Figure 6.25). You can specify a priority level for each printer between 1 and 99 (1 is the default). The highest priority number prints first; lower-priority numbers print after higher priorities. Print jobs sent by users to higher-priority logical printers will bypass other lower-priority print jobs that are waiting in the print queue. By scheduling printer availability, you can set up different logical printers in the Printers and Faxes folder that print to the same physical printer but at different times. In this way, you can offload the printing of long print jobs to nonpeak hours. Set printer availability on the Advanced tab of the properties sheet for each printer that you set up in the Printers and Faxes folder. The default availability is Always Available.

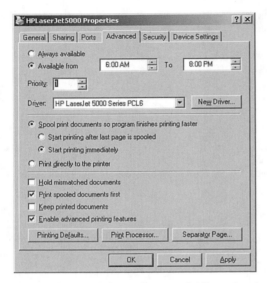

Figure 6.25 Specifying priority and availability settings from the Advanced tab of a printer's properties sheet.

 If you want to set up a printer pool among several of the same model printers using the same printer driver, click the Ports tab on the properties sheet for the printer that you will be using. Mark the Enable Printer Pooling check box and then select each port for each printer that you want to include as a part of the printer pool. Click OK when you are finished. Printing pooling enables you to set up one logical printer that actually connects to several identical print devices to greatly enhance printing output.

Working with Print Queues

To view and manage print jobs waiting to be printed in print queues, double-click a printer icon in the Printers and Faxes folder. From the printer's print management (queue) window, you can right-click a document name and choose to pause it, restart it, or view its properties sheet (see Figure 6.26). As an administrator, you have permission to modify each document's priority level and availability scheduling (see Figure 6.27).

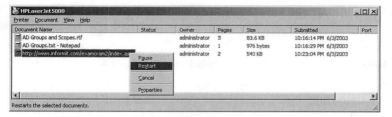

Figure 6.26 Managing print jobs from the print queue window.

From the Printer menu, you can pause printing for all the documents in the queue as well as cancel all documents in the queue. You can also set printing preferences for the printer, set up or modify sharing settings, use the printer offline, and work with the printer's properties sheet. From the Documents menu, you can perform the same actions as when you right-click a document—pause, restart, cancel, and properties. The Status column displays the current status for the documents; a printing problem for a document displays in this column. If there is a local or network connectivity issue when communicating with the printer, you see the message "Unable to connect" next to the printer's name in the title bar of the print queue window.

Figure 6.27 Working with the Document Properties window for a document waiting in the print queue.

Monitoring Print Queue Performance

You can monitor the performance of a print server's print queue by using the Performance snap-in. You can monitor real-time statistics using System Monitor and you can log performance over time using Performance Logs and Alerts. The performance object to specify is Print Queue. The object instances are the printers that are installed on the local print server computer along with the _Total instance. The available counters include Bytes Printed/sec, Job Errors, Jobs, Jobs Spooling, Not Ready Errors (since last restart), Out of Paper Errors (since last restart), Total Jobs Printed (since last restart), and Total Pages Printed (since last restart).

Managing Operating System Updates with SUS

Microsoft's SUS feature is an extension of the Windows Update Web site (http://windowsupdate.microsoft.com). Instead of requiring that each computer in an organization visit the Windows Update Web site individually, SUS is designed to have one computer install the server component to SUS, and then that designated computer can download the latest updates, network administrators can determine which updates are approved for deployment, and the Automatic Updates service on client computers can automatically download and install those approved updates. You can install the Automatic Updates client software as an .msi file on computers that do not already have this service. Computers running Windows 2000 Service Pack 3 (SP3), Windows XP SP1, and Windows Server 2003 already have the Automatic Updates software installed.

Updates to the various versions of the Windows operating are periodically published by Microsoft. Such updates include critical updates, recommended downloads, Windows tools, Internet and multimedia updates, and other related items. SUS allows you to control which updates get deployed to client computers and when to deploy each update. SUS also allows you to install multiple updates on computers simultaneously. Because SUS leverages Active Directory, you can easily specify which computers get updated and which do not through group policy. So now, you can create a GPO setting for deploying software patches almost as easily as you can create a GPO setting for deploying a new software application.

Installing SUS Server-Side Components

You can install the SUS version 1.0 with SP1 server-side components on a computer running Windows 2000 Server SP2 or higher or Windows Server 2003. The server computer should at least be a Pentium III-compatible machine running at 700Mhz or faster with a minimum of 512MB RAM, at least 6GB of available disk space on an NTFS drive volume, and IIS 5.0 or higher installed. Microsoft claims that such a configuration can support up to 15,000 client computers. Of course, the server computer requires an Internet connection and it needs Internet Explorer (IE) version 6.0 or later installed. To download SUS, go to `http://www.microsoft.com/windows2000/ windowsupdate/sus/default.asp` and you'll see the SUS Web page, shown in Figure 6.28.

Figure 6.28 Viewing the Microsoft SUS Web page.

After you download the self-extracting installation file, you can launch the installation and answer the prompts to complete the installation process. By default, SUS installs into an sus folder on a drive volume that is not the same as the %systemdrive% volume. To work with the SUS administration Web site, type `http://server_name/SUSAdmin` in Internet Explorer. At the SUS administration page, click the Set Options link in the left frame to configure the SUS server name, the synchronization setting, and the updates approval policy (see Figure 6.29).

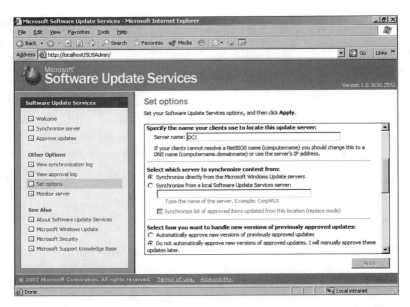

Figure 6.29 Configuring SUS option settings from the local SUS administration page.

Next, click the Synchronize Server link in the left frame and then click the Synchronization Schedule button to set up automatic downloads of Windows updates to the SUS server, as shown in Figure 6.30. Click OK to save your Schedule Synchronization settings. You can click the Synchronize Now button to manually synchronize your new SUS server with the Windows Update Web site for the first time. After you download the updates to the SUS server, you can click the Approve Updates link to designate which updates you will allow to be deployed automatically to the client computers. Close the SUS administration page when you are finished working with it.

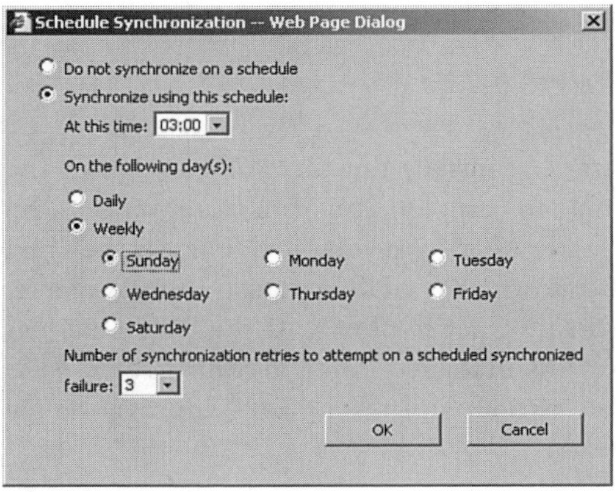

Figure 6.30 Scheduling Windows updates synchronization for the SUS server.

Setting Up SUS Automatic Updates for Client Computers

SUS is designed to update computers running Windows 2000, Windows XP, and Windows Server 2003 operating systems only. The most effective and efficient way to set up SUS automatic updates is through group policy. Two group policy settings are key to enabling SUS automatic updates on client computers—Configure Automatic Updates and Specify Intranet Microsoft Update Service Location. You can find both of these group policy settings by using the Group Policy Object Editor for a site, domain, or organizational unit (OU) under Computer Configuration\Administrative Templates\ Windows Components\Windows Update. Double-click the Configure Automatic Updates policy setting and select Enabled. For the Configure Automatic Updating drop-down list box (see Figure 6.31), choose one of the following options and then click OK to save the settings:

➤ 2-Notify for Download and Notify for Install

➤ 3-Auto Download and Notify for Install

➤ 4-Auto Download and Schedule the Install

    ➤ Select the Scheduled Install Day—0-Everyday, 1-Every Sunday, 2-Every Monday, 3-Every Tuesday, 4-Every Wednesday, 5-Every Thursday, 6-Every Friday, 7-Every Saturday—from the drop-down list box.

    ➤ Select the Schedule Install Time from the drop-down list box.

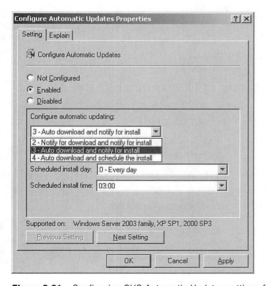

Figure 6.31   Configuring SUS Automatic Updates settings for client computers with group policy.

For the Specify Intranet Microsoft Update Service Location policy, double-click this policy setting and click Enabled. Type the appropriate DNS server name in the Set the Intranet Update Service for Detecting Updates box and in the Set the Intranet Statistics Server box, as shown in Figure 6.32. Click OK to save your settings and then close the Group Policy Editor when you are done. Now, client computers that are located in the appropriate container or OU where you applied the group policy settings should start receiving Windows updates via the SUS server.

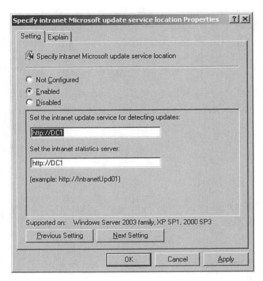

Figure 6.32   Using group policy to specify the SUS server name for updating client computers.

Backing Up the SUS Server

In case of server failure or other disaster, you should back up the SUS components on the server so that you could restore SUS to its previous operational state prior to the failure. You must back up the IIS metabase in addition to backing up other IIS components. You need to back up the `x:\inetpub\wwwroot` folder, the `x:\inetpub\msus` folder, (where `x`: is the appropriate drive letter), and the `%windir%\system32\inetsrv\metaback` folder using the Windows Backup Utility or third-party backup software. To restore SUS on a Windows Server 2003 computer after a failure, follow these steps:

1. Take the server offline by disconnecting it from the network.

2. Assign the same name to the computer as it had before the failure.

3. Be sure to install the same IIS components as were installed before the failure. The WWW service must be installed, at a minimum.

4. Install the latest service pack and security updates.

5. Install SUS into the same folder where it had been installed prior to the failure.

6. Restore the most recent backup for SUS from backup media.

7. Restore the IIS metabase. Open IIS Manager, right-click the server whose metabase you want to restore, point to All Tasks, and select Backup/Restore Configuration. Select the metabase backup that you want to restore and click the Restore button.

8. Open the SUS Administration (SUSAdmin) Web site and verify that the settings on the Set Options page are configured as they were before the failure. Confirm that the previously approved updates are still listed as approved on the Approve Updates page.

9. Put the server back online. (Connect it to the network.)

Exam Prep Questions

Question 1

Which of the following tools can you use to view real-time system performance data? (Choose two.)

- ❏ A. Performance Logs and Alerts
- ❏ B. Task Manager
- ❏ C. Event Viewer
- ❏ D. System Monitor
- ❏ E. **Services.msc**
- ❏ F. Licensing

Answers B and D are correct. You can monitor a computer system in real time under Windows Server 2003 using either the Task Manager tool or the System Monitor utility. Answer A is incorrect because Performance Logs and Alerts is not designed to display performance data in real time; its results are logged. Answer C is incorrect because the Event Viewer displays system event messages, not real-time performance data. Answers E and F are incorrect because neither the Services console (Services.msc) nor the Licensing applet offer real-time system performance monitoring.

Question 2

Which of the following event items is not one of the five default Event Viewer event types?

- ○ A. Information
- ○ B. Error
- ○ C. Caution
- ○ D. Failure Audit
- ○ E. Success Audit

Answer C is correct. Caution is not one of the default event types for the Event Viewer; Warning events are one of the five default event types. Answer A is incorrect because Information is a default event type. Answer B is incorrect because Error is a default event type. Answer D is incorrect because Failure Audit is a default event type. Answer E is incorrect because Success Audit is also a default event type.

Question 3

Which of the following items serve as performance metrics for specifying different computer resources to monitor? (Choose three.)

- ❑ A. Objects
- ❑ B. Counters
- ❑ C. Cycles
- ❑ D. Initiators
- ❑ E. _Totals
- ❑ F. Instances

Answers A, B, and F are correct. You use objects, counters, and instances of objects to measure system performance using System Monitor and Performance Logs and Alerts. Answer C is incorrect because cycles are not performance metrics. Answer D is incorrect because initiators are not performance metrics. Answer E is incorrect because _Totals are not performance metrics.

Question 4

Using the Performance Logs and Alerts tool, Jane, the network administrator, adds performance counters such as Memory:Pages/sec, PhysicalDisk:Avg. Disk Queue Length:_Total, and Processor:% Processor Time:_Total to a new counter log. She schedules this new counter log to start on Monday morning at 8:00 a.m. and she schedules the log to stop on Wednesday evening at 10:00 p.m. The company that Jane works for has a very seasonal business; computer usage is extremely high during this time of year due to increased marketing, sales, and accounting activities. Collecting this type of performance data can be referred to as

- ○ A. Establishing a baseline
- ○ B. Viewing real-time data
- ○ C. Logged performance monitoring
- ○ D. Collecting histogram data

Answer C is correct. The Performance Logs and Alerts tool collects performance data over time and records that data into log files. Answer A is incorrect because although you should use the Performance Logs and Alerts tool to create performance baseline data, you should not attempt to collect performance data as a baseline during peak usage times. Answer B is incorrect because you can only view real-time data using System Monitor or the Task Manager. Answer D is incorrect because both real-time data and logged performance data can be viewed as a histogram using the System Monitor tool; a histogram is a view, not a type of data.

Question 5

> On which of the following computer systems can you install Software Update Services (SUS) as a server? (Choose two.)
> ❑ A. Windows NT Workstation 4.0 with SP5
> ❑ B. Windows XP Professional with SP1
> ❑ C. Windows 2000 Server
> ❑ D. Windows 2000 Professional
> ❑ E. Windows 98 SE
> ❑ F. Windows Me

Answers B and C are correct. You can only set up SUS server-side components on Windows XP SP1, Windows 2000 Server, and Windows Server 2003. Answer A is incorrect because you cannot set up SUS as a server under Windows NT Workstation 4.0. Answer D is incorrect because you cannot set up SUS as a server under Windows 2000 Professional. Answer E and F are incorrect because you cannot set up SUS as a server under either Windows 98 SE or Windows Me.

Question 6

> Onto which of the following computer systems can you deploy Windows updates using SUS? (Choose three.)
> ❑ A. Windows NT Workstation 4.0 with SP5
> ❑ B. Windows XP Professional with SP1
> ❑ C. Windows 2000 Server
> ❑ D. Windows 2000 Professional
> ❑ E. Windows 98 SE
> ❑ F. Windows Me

Answers B, C, and D are correct. You can deploy Windows updates using SUS onto Windows XP, Windows 2000 Server, Windows 2000 Professional, and Windows Server 2003 computers. Answer A is incorrect because you cannot deploy updates using SUS to Windows NT Workstation 4.0 computers. Answer E and F are incorrect because you cannot deploy updates using SUS to either Windows 98 SE or Windows Me computers.

Question 7

Where do you change the location of the print spooler folder?

- ○ A. In the Registry by modifying the Spooler value data in HKEY_LOCAL_ MACHINE\SOFTWARE\Microsoft\Windows NT\CurrentVersion\ Windows.
- ○ B. By clicking Start, (All) Programs, Administrative Tools, Manage Your Server and selecting the Add a Printer Driver option.
- ○ C. By opening the Printers and Faxes window; clicking File, Print Server Properties; clicking the Advanced tab; and typing in the new spool folder location.
- ○ D. By going to the Control Panel, right-clicking the Printers and Faxes icon, and selecting Print Server Properties. Click the Advanced tab and type in the new spool folder location.

Answer C is correct. You can change the location of the print spooler folder from the Print Server Properties window. Answer A is incorrect because that Registry key and value name do not provide a way to change the location of the printer spool folder. Answer B is incorrect because you cannot change the location of the print spooler folder from the Add a Printer Driver Wizard. Answer D is incorrect because you cannot change the location of the print spooler folder by right-clicking the Printers and Faxes icon in the Control Panel.

Question 8

Which of the following licensing options is not permitted by Microsoft?

- ○ A. Per-processor licensing
- ○ B. Per-device or per-user licensing
- ○ C. Per-server licensing
- ○ D. Switching from per-device or per-user mode to per-server mode
- ○ E. Switching from per-server mode to per-device or per-user mode

Answer D is correct. You cannot switch from per-device or per-user licensing mode to per-server licensing mode. Answer A is incorrect because per-processor licensing is permitted. Answer B is incorrect because per-device or per-user licensing is allowed. Answer C is incorrect because per-server licensing is allowed. Answer E in incorrect because Microsoft does allow a one-time switch from per-server mode to per-device or per-user mode.

Question 9

How can you determine which computer is the site license server for a particular site as part of an Active Directory forest?

- ○ A. Use Active Directory Users and Computers.
- ○ B. Use Active Directory Domains and Trusts.
- ○ C. Use the Enterprise Licensing tool.
- ○ D. Use the License tool in the Control Panel.
- ○ E. Use Active Directory Sites and Services.

Answer E is correct. You use the Active Directory Sites and Services snap-in to determine the license server computer for a given site by double-clicking the Licensing Site Settings object. Answer A is incorrect because you cannot find this information using Active Directory Users and Computer. Answer B is incorrect because you cannot find this information using Active Directory Domains and Trusts. Answer C is incorrect because you cannot get this information from the Enterprise Licensing tool. Answer D is incorrect because you cannot discover this information from the License tool in the Control Panel.

Question 10

Which of the following print spooler events and notifications are logged or enabled by default? (Choose three.)

- ❑ A. Error events
- ❑ B. Warning events
- ❑ C. Notify when remote documents are printed
- ❑ D. Show informational notifications for local printers
- ❑ E. Beep on errors of remote documents
- ❑ F. Information events

Answers A, B, and F are correct. Error events, warning events, and information events are recorded in the Event Viewer System log by default. Answer C is incorrect because the Notify When Remote Documents Are Printed check box is not marked (enabled) by default. Answer D is incorrect because the Show Informational Notifications for Local Printers check box is not marked (enabled) by default. Answer E is incorrect because the Beep on Errors of Remote Documents check box is not marked (enabled) by default.

Need to Know More?

 Holme, Dan, and Orin Thomas. *MCSA/MCSE Self-Paced Training Kit (Exam 70-290): Managing and Maintaining a Microsoft Windows Server 2003 Environment.* Redmond, Washington: Microsoft Press, 2003.

 Microsoft Corporation. *Microsoft Windows Server 2003 Resource Kit.* Redmond, Washington: Microsoft Press, 2003.

 Morimoto, Rand, et. al. *Microsoft Windows Server 2003 Unleashed.* Indianapolis, Indiana: SAMS Publishing, 2003.

 Search the Microsoft Product Support Services Knowledge Base on the Internet: http://support.microsoft.com. You can also search Microsoft TechNet on the Internet: http://www.microsoft.com/technet. Find technical information using keywords from this chapter, such as system monitor, Performance Logs and Alerts, baselines, print queues, enterprise licensing, and Software Update Services.

 Review the SUS deployment white paper from Microsoft at http://www.microsoft.com/windows2000/windowsupdate/sus/default.asp.

Remote Server Administration and IIS Management

Terms you'll need to understand:

✓ The Run as command option
✓ Remote server management
✓ Remote Assistance
✓ Remote Desktops snap-in
✓ Remote Desktop Connections
✓ Terminal Services Remote Administration

✓ Internet Information Services (IIS)
✓ IIS 6.0 metabase
✓ World Wide Web service
✓ IIS 5.0 Isolation mode
✓ IIS 6.0 Worker Process Isolation mode

Techniques you'll need to master:

✓ Running programs and utilities as a different user
✓ Managing servers remotely
✓ Setting up and using Remote Assistance
✓ Configuring Terminal Services
✓ Setting up and using Remote Desktop connections
✓ Setting up Internet Information Services (IIS) 6.0

✓ Managing Web services
✓ Enabling IIS 5.0 Isolation mode
✓ Enabling IIS Direct Metabase Edit mode
✓ Backing up and restoring the IIS metabase
✓ Importing and exporting the IIS metabase
✓ Managing Web server security

Modern technology ushered in the Internet age, and lower-cost high-speed telecommunications services link us all together, more and more, into a "connected" world. Although true worldwide high-bandwidth connections are not yet available everywhere around the globe, high-speed, dedicated data networks are becoming commonplace in many countries. Network support technicians can sit at their desks in one city while remotely managing computers in other cities, near and far, thanks to relatively high-speed Internet virtual private network (VPN) connections and Windows support tools such as Remote Assistance and Terminal Services Remote Administration.

Several Windows management utilities have supported "single-seat administration" for years, such as the Event Viewer, the Performance console, and the Computer Management console. Remote administration is one of the major features of the Microsoft Management Console (MMC) shell. Most of the support tools that you can use locally can also be used remotely. Web sites, both for the public Internet and for internal use on companies' intranets, continue to play a larger and more important role in the mass dissemination of information. Managing those Web sites and maintaining their security under Internet Information Services (IIS) 6.0 and Windows Server 2003 is the other major focus of this chapter.

Taking Advantage of Server Administration Tools

To support both network security and network administration, IT support personnel should be granted sufficient network rights and permissions to accomplish their jobs, but they should not be given *carte blanche* to do anything that they want to network servers and other resources. These privileges should be sufficient but also very specifically allocated. For example, individuals in charge of data backups should have their user accounts placed in the Backup Operators group; these support technicians do not need to be members of the all-powerful Administrators group. Top-level network administrators should assign lower-level administrators to specific domain local groups that will provide them with sufficient permissions to do their jobs but nothing more. You can find the default built-in domain local security groups for an Active Directory domain in the Built-in container within the Active Directory Users and Computers (ADUC) console. These built-in groups and their associated permissions include the following:

➤ *Account Operators*—Members of this group can administer domain user and group accounts.

➤ *Administrators*—Members of this group have complete and unrestricted access to the domain and to servers and other resources within the domain. Administrators have the power to grant themselves any rights or permissions that they do not already have. Because the security context for members of the Administrators group is so high, the server and the network is vulnerable to attacks from Internet-related sources and email–related virus-infected attachments if accounts in the Administrators group are compromised. For these reasons, members of the Administrators group should log on using an administrative account only when necessary. The Runas command enables administrators to log on to the machine with their ordinary user accounts yet launch support tools under an administrative security context.

➤ *Backup Operators*—Members of this group can bypass security permissions on files and folders stored on NTFS drive volumes for data backup and restore purposes only.

➤ *Guests*—Members of this group can log on, run applications, and even shut down the system on computers that are not DCs. The Guest user account, which is disabled by default, and the Domain Guests global group are the default members of this group.

➤ *Incoming Forest Trust Builders*—Members of this group can establish incoming one-way trust relationships to the forest. No members belong to this group by default. This group only exists on DCs.

➤ *Network Configuration Operators*—Members of this group can make changes to TCP/IP settings, and they can release and renew automatically assigned IP addresses.

➤ *Performance Log Users*—Members of this group have permission to remotely monitor *logged* performance counters on DCs.

➤ *Performance Monitor Users*—Members of this group have permission to remotely monitor performance counters on DCs.

➤ *Pre-Windows 2000 Compatible Access*—Members of this group have read access for all users and groups within the domain. Members also retain permissions to access DCs from the network and to bypass traverse checking. This group is designed for backward compatibility with Windows NT 4.0 workstation computers.

➤ *Print Operators*—Members of this group can set up local and network printers as well as manage printers and print queues.

➤ *Remote Desktop Users*—Members of this group can remotely log onto Windows Terminal Services servers (including domain controllers) using the Terminal Services Client or the Remote Desktop Connection software.

➤ *Replicator*—This group is reserved for supporting file replication within a domain, and it has no members by default.

➤ *Server Operators*—Members of this group can log on interactively (locally at the system console) to domain controllers (DCs). These members can create shared folders, delete shared folders, start and stop some system services, back up and restore files, format hard drives, and shut down the server.

➤ *Terminal Server Users*—This group is a *special identity* group; membership in this group is assigned only by the operating system itself. Any users currently logged onto a server via Terminal Services (also known as Remote Desktop Connections) become a member of this special identity group for as long as they remain connected.

➤ *Users*—Members of this group perform actions such as running application programs and accessing local and network printers. By default, members of the Domain Users group, the Authenticated Users special identity group, and the Interactive special identity group are members of this group. Each domain user account that is created automatically becomes a member of this group. Members cannot make changes to their computer systems nor can they install application or utility programs.

Using the Run as Option

The Run as option gives administrators (and other users) the ability to run programs and system utilities under the security credentials of one user while being logged onto the server as a different user. For example, an administrator named DanB can be logged onto a server or a workstation with an ordinary user account that is only a member of the Domain Users group. While logged on as the ordinary user, DanB, he can right-click any MMC snap-in tool, such as ADUC (dsa.msc), and select Run as from the pop-up menu. The Run as dialog box appears with two options to run this program—Current User (with Restricted Access) and the Following User. By selecting the second option and typing in the appropriate administrative username and password (see Figure 7.1), DanB can log on using the alternate credentials without logging off of the machine.

Figure 7.1 Running a program as a different user with the Run as option.

You can use the Run as command for all types of programs, utilities, and even Control Panel applets. For using Run as on Control Panel tools, hold down the Shift key while you right-click a Control Panel icon to display the Run as option. You might need to hold down the Shift key while you right-click to access the Run as option for other applications as well. Using Run as is a more secure way for accessing security-sensitive utilities rather than always logging on to systems as a user who is a member of the Administrators group.

You can even use the Run as command to launch an instance of Windows Explorer under the security credentials of a different user. For example, if you are currently logged on as JoeUser, at a command prompt or at the Start, Run box, you can type `runas /noprofile /user:domain1\administrator explorer.exe` to launch an Explorer window under the security context of Domain1's Administrator account. Any folders or files that you access from *that* Explorer window are subject to the Access Control List (ACL) for the Administrator user account, not the ACL for JoeUser.

Using Run as from the Command Line

You can also use the Run as feature from the command line, both for GUI tools as well as for command-line tools. For example, you can run the Computer Management console as the administrator for the `Windows2003.local` domain by clicking Start, Run; typing `runas /user:windows2003\administrator "mmc %windir%\system32\compmgmt.msc"` in the Open box; and clicking OK. From a command prompt, you can type `runas /?` and press Enter to view the many options and syntax for this command. You can also open a command-prompt window as a different user—the administrator for a domain named `Windows2003.local`, for example—by clicking Start, Run; typing `runas /user:windows2003\administrator cmd.exe` in the Open box; and clicking OK. In addition, you can create shortcuts to administrative tools that require the administrator's password to run. For an example of how to create such a short-cut, follow these steps:

1. Right-click the Windows desktop and select New, Shortcut.

2. Type a command string such as `runas /user:windows2003\administrator "mmc %windir%\system32\compmgmt.msc"` in the Type the Location of the Item box.

3. Click Next.

4. Type a name for the shortcut in the Type a Name for This Shortcut box, such as `Admin Computer Mgmt`.

5. Click Finish.

When you double-click the shortcut, you are prompted for the administrator password. If you do not type in the correct password for the administrator user account, the program (Computer Management, in this example) does not run.

Using Server Management Tools Remotely

Server management tools such as Computer Management, Event Viewer, and other MMC snap-ins give you the ability to administer computers and servers remotely. For example, in the Computer Management console, you can right-click the Computer Management root node and select Connect to Another Computer. From the Select Computer dialog box, click the Another Computer option and either type the name of the remote computer or click Browse to locate it. Click OK to connect to the remote computer (see Figure 7.2). You can use Computer Management (and other support tools) to remotely manage different computers as long as you are running the MMC snap-in (or other utility) under a user account that has the proper permissions to access those remote computers. Most MMC snap-ins support remote administration. For other snap-ins and tools such as Event Viewer, Services, and DNS Management (among others), you can also right-click the root node and select Connect to Another Computer to remotely manage other machines.

Adding Snap-Ins to a Custom MMC for Remote Management

You can remotely manage servers and other computers by adding snap-ins that you need into an empty MMC shell. Many MMC snap-ins give administrators the option of local focus or remote focus when adding them to a console. Once you configure all the snap-ins, you can create a custom Microsoft Saved Console (.msc) file that you can use over and over again, without having to reconfigure the console every time you use it. To create a custom MMC for remotely managing one or more computers, follow these steps:

1. Click Start, Run; type mmc; and click OK. An empty MMC appears.

2. Click File, Add/Remove Snap-in or press Ctrl+M to display the Add/Remove Snap-in dialog box.

3. Click the Add button to add snap-ins to this MMC. The Add Standalone Snap-In dialog box appears, as shown in Figure 7.3.

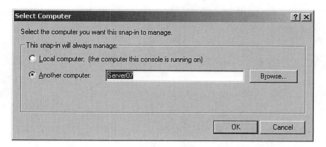

Figure 7.2   Connecting to a remote computer for the Computer Management console.

Figure 7.3   Selecting snap-ins to add to the MMC.

4. Select one of the snap-ins shown in the Available Standalone Snap-Ins list and click the Add button. If the snap-in supports remote management, a Select Computer dialog box appears, as shown in Figure 7.4 for the Disk Management snap-in.

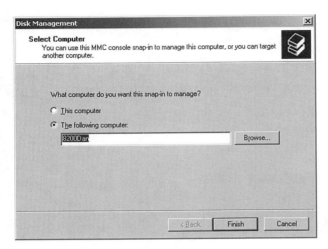

Figure 7.4 Selecting a remote computer to manage for the Disk Management MMC snap-in.

5. Click The Following Computer option button and type in the remote computer's name or click Browse to locate it.

6. Click Finish to add the snap-in.

7. Repeat steps 4 through 6 for each snap-in that you want to add.

8. Click Close to exit from the Add Standalone Snap-In dialog box. The snap-ins that you chose appear in the Add/Remove Snap-In dialog box, as shown in Figure 7.5.

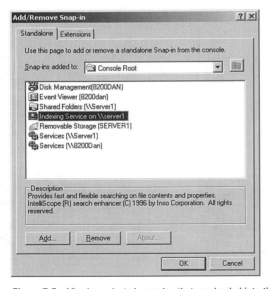

Figure 7.5 Viewing selected snap-ins that you loaded into the MMC for managing remote computers.

9. Click OK to close the Add/Remove Snap-In dialog box and return to the main MMC window with all the selected snap-ins loaded.

10. To save your customized console, click File, Save as; type in a filename for this MMC (*.msc) file; and click Save.

Using Remote Assistance for Remote Administration

Remote Assistance (RA) was designed primarily for help-desk personnel (or other trusted computer technicians) to assist users with general computer usage questions and to troubleshoot system problems for Windows XP Professional desktop computers. The RA feature is turned on by default on Windows XP Professional, but for security reasons, it is turned off by default on Windows Server 2003 computers.

To request remote assistance, both the RA requester and the RA provider computers must be running either Windows XP Professional or Windows Server 2003. You can make an RA request via an email message, via Windows Messenger, or by sending an RA invitation as a file. You can use RA between two computers over an Internet connection, over a local area network (LAN) connection, or through a firewall connection to the Internet, provided that TCP port 3389 is open on the firewall at each end. This port is the same TCP port that is used for Remote Desktop connections accessing Terminal Services.

NOTE You must be sure that TCP port 3389 is open for incoming traffic on the firewall for the requester as well as for outgoing traffic on the firewall for the provider; otherwise, RA will not work. If one location does not have a firewall for some reason, you don't need to worry about opening port 3389 for that location; all ports are open without a firewall present unless the Internet service provider (ISP) blocks certain ports.

Configuring Group Policy Settings for Remote Assistance

Windows Server 2003 Active Directory domains offer two distinct group policy object (GPO) settings for the RA feature. Both GPO settings appear in the Computer Configuration\Administrative Templates\System\Remote Assistance node. The Solicited Remote Assistance setting determines whether users can solicit help from other users via RA. When it is enabled, you must specify either Allow Helpers to Remotely Control the Computer or Allow Helpers to Only View the Computer (see Figure 7.6).

You must also specify the Maximum Ticket Time (Value), Maximum Ticket Time (Units), and the method for sending email invitations—Mailto or Simple MAPI. The Mailto option allows RA providers to reply to RA invitations via a hyperlink within the email message that connects the RA provider to the RA requester's computer. The Simple MAPI (SMAPI) option actually embeds the RA invitation file as an attachment within the email message. Double-clicking the RA invitation attachment connects the RA provider to the RA requester's computer.

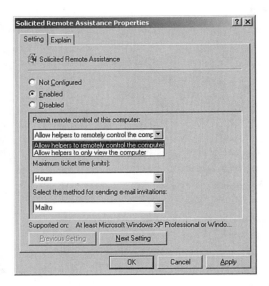

Figure 7.6   Enabling the Solicited Remote Assistance GPO setting and specifying its options.

The Offer Remote Assistance GPO setting determines whether another user, referred to as the "expert," is allowed to offer RA to the computer without the user requesting RA first. The expert user still cannot connect to the computer needing assistance without the user's permission, even if this GPO setting is enabled. If you enable this setting, you must select either Allow Helpers to Remotely Control the Computer or Allow Helpers to Only View the Computer from the Permit Remote Control of This Computer drop-down list box, just as with the Solicited Remote Assistance GPO setting. You must also specify the names of the users and groups that you want to grant permission for offering RA by clicking the Helpers: Show button (see Figure 7.7).

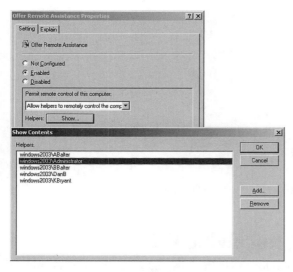

Figure 7.7 Enabling the Offer Remote Assistance GPO setting and specifying the authorized RA helpers.

Configuring Remote Assistance on the Client Side

In Windows Server 2003 and Windows XP Professional, if you right-click My Computer, select Properties, and click the Remote tab, you can configure the settings for RA from the client computer's perspective. As previously mentioned, RA is turned on by default for Windows XP, but it is turned off by default for Windows Server 2003. Make sure that the Turn on Remote Assistance and Allow Invitations to Be Sent from This Computer check box is marked if you want to use RA on the computer. If you click the Advanced button, you can configure the two option settings for RA, as shown in Figure 7.8. In the Remote Control section, you can clear the Allow This Computer to Be Controlled Remotely check box if you want to provide view-only access to RA personnel. In the Invitations section, you can change the default expiration time for RA invitations from the two drop-down list boxes. You can select from 1 to 99 and you can specify the time interval as Days, Hours, or Minutes. The default maximum time for invitations to remain open is 30 days.

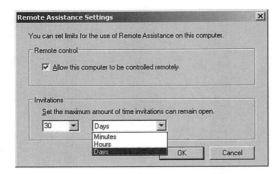

Figure 7.8 Specifying RA settings for an individual computer.

Requesting and Receiving RA

If you are working on a Windows XP Professional or even on a Windows Server 2003 computer, you can make a request for someone to assist you by launching the Windows Help and Support Center. From the main Help and Support Center page, find and click the Remote Assistance link. You see the Remote Assistance page where you can click the Invite Someone to Help You link, and then you can follow these steps:

1. After the RA feature loads within the Help and Support Center window, you must select how you want to contact the person whom you want to assist you—via Windows Messenger, via an email invitation, or using the advanced feature of saving the invitation as a file.

2. If you choose to save the RA invitation as a file, you must type the name that you want to appear on the invitation as the person requesting assistance in the From box.

3. Specify the Set the Invitation to Expire parameters; the default for saved invitations is one hour.

4. Click Continue.

5. Be sure to leave the Require the Recipient to Use a Password check box marked for security reasons.

6. Type a password for the person who will be assisting you and confirm it in the Type Password and the Confirm Password boxes.

7. Click the Save Invitation button.

8. When the Save as dialog box appears, choose a location on disk and accept the default filename of RAInvitation.msrcincident (unless you want to change it).

9. Click Save to save the RA invitation file.

10. In some manner (email, file transfer, copy it to a shared network location, and so on), send the invitation file to the person that you want to assist you.

11. When the assistant double-clicks the invitation file, he is prompted for the password for that invitation, as shown in Figure 7.9.

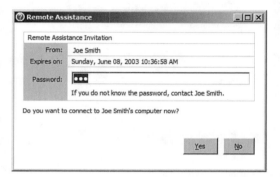

Figure 7.9 Initiating an RA session by responding to an RA invitation.

12. The person offering assistance must type the proper invitation password and click Yes to connect to the requester's computer.

13. On the requester's computer, a message box appears asking whether you want to grant permission to the requester to connect to your computer to view and interact with your Windows session (see Figure 7.10). Click Yes to allow the assistant to initiate the RA session.

Figure 7.10 Accepting an assistant's offer to launch an RA session.

14. Once the requester accepts the assistant's offer for help, the RA session is initiated, as shown in Figure 7.11. Either party can disconnect from the RA session by clicking the Disconnect button.

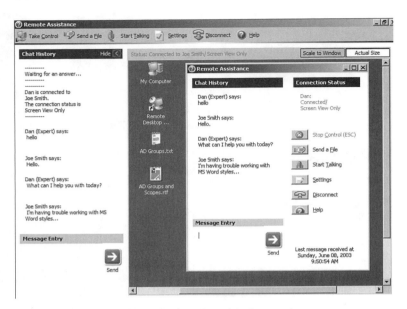

Figure 7.11   Viewing an RA session from the assistant's computer.

Using Terminal Services for Remote Administration

The concept of Windows Terminal Services (TS) was first introduced under the moniker Windows NT Server 4.0, Terminal Services Edition. The idea was to use screen emulation to pass mouse and keyboard input back and forth between the client and the server; it supported multiple, simultaneous remote session connections in which all the processing happened on the server computer, not on the workstations. This concept was a throwback to the days of mainframe computing, where all the processing power existed on the main ("server") computer and "dumb" terminals provided the output display and the keyboard input. You installed and configured application programs only once, on the mainframe computer.

Windows 2000 Server brought TS into the mainstream and introduced the concept of using TS for remote administration—at no extra charge! You can install TS on a Windows 2000 Server computer in Remote Administration mode. This option supports up to a maximum of two administrators logged on via TS simultaneously, and you can have one other administrator logged onto the console (working locally and interactively) at the same time. Windows Server 2003 works the same way for Remote Administration mode.

Generally, TS on the server side is referred to as a Terminal Server. On the client side, TS is referred to as Remote Desktop Connections in Windows XP or newer. The protocol TS uses is called the Remote Desktop Protocol (RDP): Windows Server 2003 implements RDP version 5.2. Windows XP uses RDP version 5.1 and Windows 2000 uses RDP version 5.0.

Windows Server 2003 takes TS to new heights by installing TS in Remote Desktop for Administration mode by default. As an option, Terminal Server is also available on every server to support multiple user connections using Application Server mode. To install this mode, go to Control Panel, Add and Remove Programs; click Add/Remove Windows Components; and mark the check box to install Terminal Server. Under Application Server mode, you need to set up a Terminal Server Licensing Server on your network within 120 days of the first client computer successfully logging onto a Terminal Server in Application Server mode. After this 120-day period, client computers are not allowed to connect to a Terminal Server without a proper Terminal Server Client Access License (TSCAL) issued to each computer that requests a TS connection. Unlike Windows 2000 Server, all Remote Desktop Connection client computers must be issued a TSCAL; there are no built-in TSCALs for connections coming from computers running Windows 2000, Windows XP, or Windows Server 2003.

Licensed users of Windows XP Professional computers are eligible for the Terminal Server 2003 Licensing Transition Plan. Microsoft customers who own licenses for Windows XP Professional on the date that Windows Server 2003 was publicly released in the United States (April 2003) can receive TSCALs for Windows Server 2003 for the number of Windows XP Professional licenses that they own. Microsoft volume licensing customers (Enterprise Agreement, Select, and Open) must enter their volume licensing agreement information into the Terminal Server licensing administration tool on the Microsoft Web site. Retail and original equipment manufacturer (OEM) customers must enter their Windows XP Professional product keys into the Terminal Server activation Web site to receive TSCALs for Windows Server 2003.

For Windows Server 2003 computers installed in the default configuration for TS Remote Desktop for Administration mode, no license server and no TSCALs are required.

Configuring TS on the Server

As previously mentioned, TS is installed automatically in Windows Server 2003. However, you must enable Remote Desktop connections to allow any RDP connections to the server. To turn on Remote Desktop Connections for a server, right-click My Computer, select Properties, and click the Remote tab. Mark the Allow Users to Connect Remotely to This Computer check box. You can click the Select Remote Users button to add or remove users who have permission to access the server using TS, as shown in Figure 7.12. Adding or removing users and groups with this dialog box is the same as adding or removing users and groups through the properties sheet for the Remote Desktop Users group itself, as shown in Figure 7.13. By default, the local and domain Administrator user accounts retain permission to log on using TS without being members of either the local or the domain Remote Desktop Users groups.

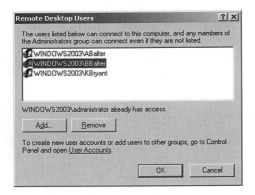

Figure 7.12   Enabling Remote Desktop connections and selecting Remote Desktop users.

If users will be connecting from Internet connections (without a VPN) to one or more Terminal Servers that are protected by a firewall, you must open TCP port 3389, the default port for TS traffic, on the firewall. You can use a different port for TS traffic to pass through the firewall, if desired. If you change the port on the firewall to TCP port 3393, for example, users need to specify the server name or IP address for the Terminal Server and append it with a colon (:) plus the nondefault port number in the Computer box for the RDC client—as in **server1:3393** or **209.144.100.50:3393**—instead of simply typing **server1** or **209.144.100.50** when using the default port. Connecting over a VPN connection does not involve going through the TCP port number on a firewall; the port on the firewall is bypassed using the VPN.

Figure 7.13   Viewing members of the Remote Desktop Users group.

Configuring RDP Settings

You can configure several parameters of the RDP using the TS Configuration utility. Click Start, (All) Programs, Administrative Tools, Terminal Services Configuration to launch this program. If you click the Server Settings node, you can view the settings that are listed and you can modify all but two of them from this window—Licensing and Permission Compatibility (see Figure 7.14). If you click the Connections node, you see the RDP-Tcp Connection listed as type Microsoft RDP 5.2 in the details pane. If you double-click this connection name, you display the properties sheet for the Remote Desktop protocol on the server. From the General tab, you can specify the Encryption Level setting. The default encryption level is Client Compatible where all data sent between client and server is encrypted. The High level and the FIPS Compliant level increase the encryption; however, the Low level only encrypts data going from the client computer to the server. The other tabs on the RDP-Tcp Properties window are as follows:

➤ *Logon Settings*—This tab lets you set specific logon information (username, domain, and password) for all users connecting to the server using RDP. You can also specify that the server must always prompt Terminal Server users for a password. The defaults: Use client-provided logon information and do not always prompt for a password.

➤ *Sessions*—This tab allows you to override user settings for session limits and client reconnections.

➤ *Environment*—This tab lets you override user settings for a startup application program at logon time.

➤ *Remote Control*—This tab allows you to override user settings for remote-control options.

➤ *Client Settings*—This tab lets you override user settings for device redirection and maximum color depth.

➤ *Network Adapter*—This tab allows you to specify one individual network adapter or all network adapters for use with remote desktop connections. You can also limit the number of RDP connections from this dialog box.

➤ *Permissions*—This tab lets you set access permissions for users and groups for connecting via RDP. By clicking the Advanced button, selecting a user or group, and clicking Edit, you can view and modify advanced permissions for the RDP, as shown in Figure 7.15.

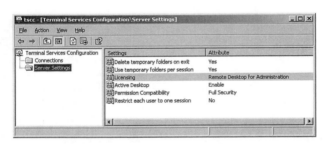

Figure 7.14   Viewing terminal settings.

Managing Terminal Server Sessions

If you click Start, (All) Programs, Administrative Tools, Terminal Services Manager, you can run the RDP session monitoring tool. From the Terminal Services Manager, you can view the users, sessions, and processes currently connected and running on each Terminal Server. As you can see in Figure 7.16, by right-clicking a user from the Users tab, you can connect to the current session, disconnect the user from the current session, send the user a message, remotely control the user's session, reset the session, view the current status of the session, and even log off the user from the current session. From the Sessions tab, you can view all the RDP sessions in progress. From the Processes tab, you can view all the processes that are currently active. If you right-click a process, you can select the End Process option to end that particular application or service.

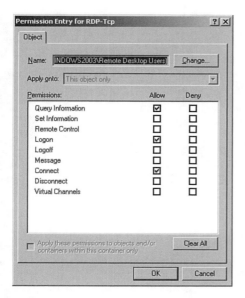

Figure 7.15 Viewing advanced permissions for the Remote Desktop Users group.

Figure 7.16 Monitoring user activity with the Terminal Services Manager tool.

Managing Group Policy Settings for Terminal Services

You can work with the many GPO settings for TS by opening the Group Policy Object Editor and navigating to the Computer Configuration\ Administrative Templates\Windows Components\Terminal Services node. If you are running Windows Server 2003, Enterprise Edition or Datacenter Edition, you can make available a session directory for Remote Desktop users. By enabling the Join Session Directory GPO setting, you can specify that TS should use a session directory for tracking user sessions, which allows a group of Terminal Servers to locate and connect users back to disconnected remote desktop sessions. To enable this setting, you must also enable the Session Directory Server setting and the Session Directory Cluster Name setting, as shown in Figure 7.17. In addition, the Terminal Services Session Directory service must be running on the Terminal Server computers running the Enterprise or Datacenter editions of Windows Server 2003.

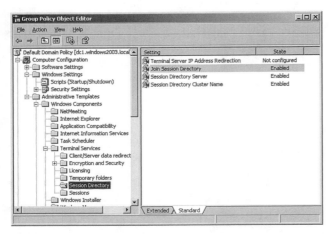

Figure 7.17 Specifying GPO settings for a TS session directory under Windows Server 2003, Enterprise Edition or Datacenter Edition.

Configuring Remote Desktop Connections on the Client

Windows Server 2003 and Windows XP ship with the Remote Desktop Connection (RDC) client software, and these two operating systems install the RDC software by default. The RDC client is a big improvement over its previous cousin, the Terminal Services Client, that shipped with Windows 2000 Server. The Terminal Services Client program had to be installed separately on each computer that needed to connect using TS and its feature set was somewhat limited. The RDC client supports a much richer feature set, including an enhanced color scheme for its display, support for the redirection of system sounds, and support for local printers and local disk drives for the remote client session. In addition, it enables you to use Windows keyboard combinations such as Alt+Tab within an RDC session, and you can easily save settings for each remote desktop connection for later use.

You can download a self-extracting installation file for the RDC client from Microsoft's Web site to install on previous Windows operating systems, such as Windows 95, Windows 98, Windows Me, Windows NT 4.0, and Windows 2000. The URL for the RDC client software is **http://www.microsoft.com/windowsxp/pro/downloads/ rdclientdl.asp**. Microsoft also offers a Macintosh RDC client that runs on the Mac OS 10.1 or higher; you can find it at **http://www.microsoft.com/mac/DOWNLOAD/MISC/ RDC.asp**.

On Windows Server 2003 and Windows XP computers, you can find the RDC client by clicking Start, (All) Programs, Accessories, Communications, Remote Desktop Connection. When you launch the RDC client, it displays as a small window, ready to connect to a Terminal Server as soon as you type a server name or IP address in the Computer box and click Connect. If you click the Options button, you can view the tabbed dialog box showing you the wide array of settings that you can specify for each RDC session:

➤ *General*—The General tab lets you specify the computer name to connect to, and optionally, you can type in a username, password, and
domain name and you can mark the Save My Password check box to
have the RDC client retain this information for subsequent connections.
By default, Windows Server 2003 user logon information is allowed to
pass through to the Terminal Server without your having to re-enter
user logon credentials. Current settings are saved by default; the filename is `default.rdp` located in the My Documents folder for each user
and you can open this file in any text editor, such as Notepad.

➤ *Display*—The Display tab lets you configure the resolution for the
remote desktop display. It also lets you specify the number of colors to
display and whether to display the connection bar when the session is in
full-screen mode. The connection bar lets you easily minimize and
restore the RDC window as well as disconnect the session by clicking
the close (X) icon.

➤ *Local Resources*—The Local Resources tab lets you redirect sound,
Windows keyboard combinations, local disk drives, local printers, and
even local serial ports to the RDC session (see Figure 7.18).

➤ *Programs*—The Programs tab lets you specify an application to run
when you connect to the Terminal Server. When you exit from the
application program, the RDC session ends. This option works well
when a user needs to access one specific program on the Terminal
Server and then wants to be returned to the local computer when she
exits that program.

➤ *Experience*—The Experience tab lets you customize the visual elements of the RDC session to the speed of the connection that you will be using for the RDC session (see Figure 7.19). You can select from modem speeds, broadband speeds, and LAN speed (10Mbps or higher), or you can mix and match the settings yourself (Custom).

Figure 7.18 Setting Local Resources redirection for the RDC client.

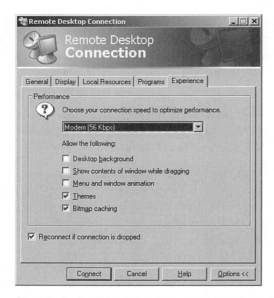

Figure 7.19 Specifying the user's visual experience for the RDC client based on connection speed.

Previously, pass-through of Windows 2000 user logon information to the Terminal Server was not allowed by default; users were required to re-enter their logon credentials at the Terminal Server logon dialog box. To change this setting, an administrator cleared the Always Prompt for Password check box on the Logon Settings tab for the RDP-Tcp properties sheet in the Terminal Services Configuration tool (see Figure 7.20).

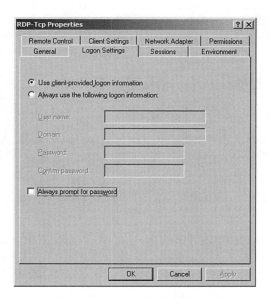

Figure 7.20 The Always Prompt for Password check box is cleared (disabled) by default under Windows Server 2003 for RDC logons.

Disconnected sessions are *still active!* If you click the close button on an RDC session window, a message box lets you know that programs continue to run while the session is disconnected (see Figure 7.21). Be sure to log out of a session if you are finished working, and you do not need to have the session continue to run while you are away. After two disconnected sessions, those administrators must reconnect to those sessions and then log off to make RDC sessions available to other administrators. Administrators can also log off users' sessions using Terminal Services Manager. Remember, the maximum number of RDC sessions for Remote Desktop for Administration is two.

Figure 7.21 The message box for disconnecting from an RDC session.

For Windows Server 2003 Terminal Servers, you can actually connect to a Terminal Server's console, as if you were physically there at the Terminal Server computer and logging on. Connecting to a console session allows you to get access to programs that are running within the console session, and it also lets you run applications that might not run within a normal Remote Desktop session. Simply create a shortcut to the RDC client program (**mstsc.exe**) and append the option **/console** to the target command line. For example, you can use this command line as your shortcut's target: **%systemroot%\system32\mstsc.exe /console**. To view all the other command-line options for the RDC client, click Start, Run; type **mstsc /?**; and click OK.

Using the Remote Desktops Snap-In

The Remote Desktops snap-in allows you to view multiple RDC sessions that can all be running simultaneously within one MMC window. This tool is great for centralizing remote administration using one utility for accessing multiple servers at the same time. To use the Remote Desktops snap-in and create a new connection, follow these steps:

1. Click Start, (All) Programs, Administrative Tools, Remote Desktops to launch the snap-in.

2. In the left pane, right-click the Remote Desktops node and select Add New Connection.

3. From the Add New Connection dialog box, type a server's name or IP address in the Server Name or IP Address box (see Figure 7.22). You can also click the Browse button to locate a server.

4. Type a name for this remote connection in the Connection Name box.

5. Clear the Connect to Console check box unless you want to remotely connect to a console session. Only one console session is permitted at a time: If an Administrator is currently logged onto the console, that person will be logged off when you successfully log on.

6. Type in logon information, if desired.

7. Click OK to create this new Remote Desktop connection.

 By default, when you connect to an RDC session from the Remote Desktops snap-in, you are connected to the *console* session. You must clear the Connect to Console check box in the properties sheet for each Remote Desktops connection to connect to nonconsole RDC sessions.

Figure 7.22   Adding a new connection to the Remote Desktops MMC snap-in.

To delete a connection, simply right-click the connection name and select Delete. To work with a connection's configuration settings, right-click the connection name and select Properties. Several options are only available *after* you create a connection—screen display settings, the option to run a program upon connection, and the option to redirect local disk drives to the remote session. Each connection's properties sheet displays three tabs—General, Screen Options, and Other. The General tab displays the same settings that you see when you create a new connection. The Screen Options tab offers you three different choices for configuring the remote display: Expand to Fill MMC Result Pane, Choose Desktop Size, or Enter Custom Desktop Size (see Figure 7.23). The Other tab lets you specify a startup program for the connection, and you can also mark the Redirect Local Drives When Logged on to the Remote Computer check box to make your local disk drives available within the RDC session (see Figure 7.24).

If you install the Remote Desktop Web Connection Windows component, users and administrators can connect to Remote Desktop sessions using their Web browsers. From the Add or Remove Programs applet in Control Panel, click Add/Remove Windows Components, select Application Server, and click Details. From the Application Server Components dialog box, select Internet Information Services, click Details, select the World Wide Web Service and click Details, and then mark the Remote Desktop Web Connection check box. Click OK for each of the preceding dialog boxes and click Next to install this component. After you install this feature on a server, users can access this server remotely by opening Internet Explorer and typing **http://***server_name***/tsweb** in the Address box to display the Remote Desktop Web Connection page, as shown in Figure 7.25.

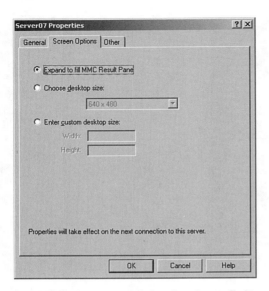

Figure 7.23 Setting screen options for a Remote Desktops connection.

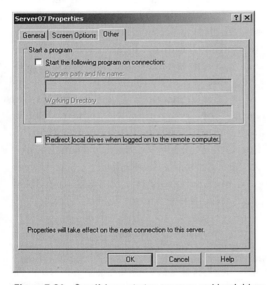

Figure 7.24 Specifying a startup program and local drives redirection.

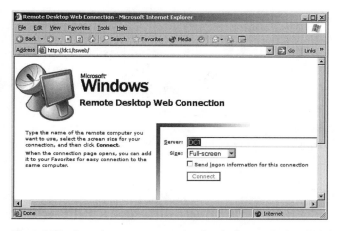

Figure 7.25 Accessing a server remotely using the Remote Desktop Web Connection.

Managing IIS

Microsoft greatly improved and enhanced version 6.0 of IIS under Windows Server 2003. Security is a major focus for this release. As a big departure from previous Windows server operating systems, IIS is *not* installed by default when you install Windows Server 2003. In fact, even simple Web browsing is limited by default in Windows Server 2003. IIS 6.0 is now actually a subcomponent of the main Application Server component for Windows Server 2003. IIS itself consists of several different components, including the File Transfer Protocol (FTP) service, Front Page Server Extensions, Internet Printing, the Network News Transfer Protocol (NNTP), the Simple Mail Transfer Protocol (SMTP), and the World Wide Web (WWW) service, among others. You can install each of these components individually, although certain components require that other components be installed, such as the Internet Information Services Manager. In this section, you learn how to install IIS components, how to manage a Web server, and how to properly administer security settings under IIS 6.0.

Administering a Web Server

Because IIS 6.0 is not automatically installed, you must use the Add or Remove Programs applet in the Control Panel to install the IIS components you require for each server. You do not need to install IIS components that you won't be using: for example, you do have to install the FTP service, the

NNTP service, or the SMTP service if the server won't be using those services. Microsoft renamed IIS in Windows Server 2003: When you launch the Add or Remove Programs dialog box and click Add/Remove Windows Components, this component is now referred to as "Application Server." To install the WWW service along with a minimal setup of IIS, follow these steps:

1. Go to the Control Panel, double-click Add or Remove Programs, and click the Add/Remove Windows Components button.

2. Select the Application Server component, but do not mark or clear its check box, and click the Details button.

3. Next, select Internet Information Services (IIS), but do not mark or clear its check box, and click the Details button.

4. Mark the World Wide Web Service check box and click OK (see Figure 7.26).

5. Click OK for the Application Server dialog box and then click Next for the Windows Components dialog box to start the installation and configuration process for the selected IIS components.

6. Click Finish when the Windows Components Wizard completes and then you can close the Add or Remove Programs dialog box.

 Even after you install the WWW service as an IIS component, the Web server is set up in a locked-down state by default. Features such as Active Server Pages (ASPs), ASP.NET, server-side includes, Web Distributed Authoring and Versioning (WebDAV) publishing, and FrontPage server extensions do not function unless you specifically install each of these IIS components. If anyone attempts to access a Web page hosted by IIS 6.0 that contains a feature that you have not yet installed, the user receives an HTTP Error 404 message.

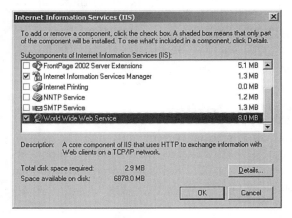

Figure 7.26 Installing the WWW service as a subcomponent of IIS 6.0.

Managing Web Servers with the IIS Manager Snap-In

You can manage a Web server from its local console or over a LAN connection using the IIS Manager snap-in. The IIS Manager snap-in file is `iis.msc` and it's in the `%systemroot%\system32\inetsrv` folder. You can launch this snap-in by adding the snap-in to an MMC window or by clicking Start, (All) Programs, Administrative Tools, Internet Information Services (IIS) Manager on computers where IIS 6.0 has already been installed and on computers that have the Windows Server 2003 administration tools installed. Clicking Start, Run; typing `inetmgr.exe`; and clicking OK launches the IIS Manager snap-in as well.

You can also program your own script files that perform administrative tasks on the IIS server or use the ones provided in the `%systemroot%\system32` folder. Script files such as `iisback.vbs` run automated routines such as backing up or restoring the IIS configuration database. Another included VB script file, `iisweb.vbs`, lists and manages IIS Web sites.

From the IIS Manager console, you can view the Web server computer that you are currently connected to as a root node in the left pane. Just below the Web Server node, you see the Application Pools subnode, the Web Sites subnode, and the Web Service Extensions subnode. Worker Process Isolation mode is the default processing method that IIS 6.0 uses for *clean* installations of Window Server 2003. IIS 5.0 Isolation mode is the default processing method that IIS 5.0 uses under Windows 2000 Server. You can choose to run IIS 6.0 in IIS 5.0 Isolation mode; however, you must choose to run IIS under only one mode. An IIS 6.0 Web server cannot run simultaneously under both modes. For computers that are upgraded to Windows Server 2003 from Windows 2000 Server, IIS 6.0 runs in the backward-compatible IIS 5.0 Isolation Mode by default. To switch to IIS 5.0 Isolation mode, follow these steps:

1. Open the IIS Manager snap-in.

2. Expand the Web server node that you want to work with, right-click the Web Sites subnode, and select Properties.

3. Click the Service tab.

4. Mark the Run WWW Service in IIS 5.0 Isolation Mode check box (see Figure 7.27).

5. Click OK to save the setting and click Yes when the IIS Manager message box prompts you to restart IIS.

For Web applications that are not compatible with IIS 6.0 Worker Process Isolation mode, you can configure the Web server to run under IIS 5.0 Isolation mode.

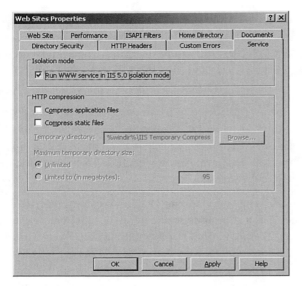

Figure 7.27   Configuring IIS 6.0 to run in IIS 5.0 Isolation mode.

 You can also set up HTTP compression from the Service tab in the Web Sites Properties dialog box.

From the Web Sites Properties dialog box, you can also configure Web site identification, connections settings, and Web site logging from the Web Site tab. You can specify bandwidth throttling and you can limit the number of Web site connections from the Performance tab. You can work with (ISAPI) filters settings and HTTP headers information from the ISAPI Filters and HTTP Headers tabs, respectively. You can set home directory permissions, at the global level, from the Home Directory tab, including setting global permissions for Read, Write, and Directory Browsing access. Directory security settings can be globally configured from the Directory Security tab, where you can edit authentication and access control settings and IP address and domain name restrictions, and you can enable or disable the Windows Directory Service Mapper. (It is disabled by default.) You can edit HTTP error messages from the Custom Errors tab and you can enable and specify default Web content pages from the Documents tab.

The Web Server root node located in the left pane of IIS Manager gives Web administrators some powerful options when managing Web services. If you right-click the Web Server node, and select All Tasks, Restart IIS, you can restart all Internet services, stop all Internet services, start all Internet services, or even restart the server computer itself, if you have the proper rights to do so (see Figure 7.28).

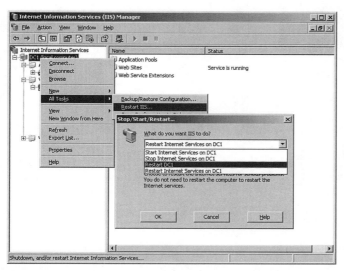

Figure 7.28 Stopping, starting, and restarting options for the Web server and its Internet services.

 You can also restart the Internet services or reboot the Web server using the **iisreset.exe** tool at a command prompt. For example, typing **iisreset webserver01 /restart** and pressing Enter at a command prompt restarts all Internet services on the computer. If you type the command **iisreset webserver01 /reboot** and press Enter, the Web server itself actually reboots, provided that you possess the appropriate rights and permissions to shut down the server. Type **iisreset /?** to view all the command-line options.

If you right-click the Web Server root node and select Properties, you can enable the "edit-while-running" mode for IIS's configuration database file, known as the *metabase*. The IIS metabase contains all the important configuration data for all the Internet services on the computer. The IIS 6.0 metabase now uses the XML file format. By default, the metabase file is stored in the `%systemroot%\system32\inetsrv` folder and uses the filename `metabase.xml`. If you turn on the edit-while-running mode, any configuration changes that you make to an IIS 6.0 server take effect immediately. Simply mark the Enable Direct Metabase Edit check box on the Web server's properties sheet, as shown in Figure 7.29. You must enable the metabase history feature to take advantage of the edit-while-running mode; however, the history feature is enabled by default. The Direct Metabase Edit feature is not turned on by default. You must restart the Internet services for this change to take effect.

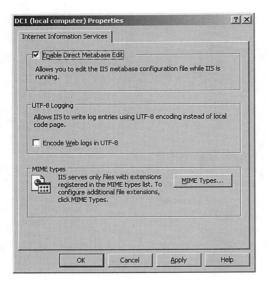

Figure 7.29 Enabling the Direct Metabase Edit feature.

Managing Web Servers with the Remote Administration Tool

There are several ways to manage IIS servers remotely. One way to manage IIS 6.0 Web server computers remotely is to use Windows TS. You can also manage Web servers remotely by installing the Windows Server 2003 administration tools on each computer where you'll be managing IIS 6.0 Web servers. IIS 6.0 is not compatible with the Windows 2000 Server administration utilities for IIS 5.0, so you must use the new version of the administration tools. Double-click the adminpak.msi file in the \I386 folder on the Windows Server 2003 CD-ROM to install the updated server administration tools on any Windows XP Professional with Service Pack 1 (SP1) or Windows Server 2003 computer.

Another way to manage Web servers remotely is with the IIS Manager MMC snap-in. From the IIS Manager snap-in, right-click the Internet Information Services root node and select Connect. Type the Web server's name in the Computer Name box, or click Browse to locate the Web server that you want to work with. To connect to the remote server using a different username and password, mark the Connect as check box and type in the appropriate user credentials. Finally, click OK to connect to the remote Web server. You can connect to Windows Web servers running IIS versions 5.0, 5.1, and 6.0 only from the IIS 6.0 Manager snap-in.

A third method for remotely managing a Web server, or any server, is to use the Remote Administration (HTML) tool. You can administer IIS 6.0 Web servers using a Web browser when the Remote Administration (HTML) tool is installed. To connect to an IIS 6.0 server using the Remote Administration Web site without installing a Secure Socket Layer (SSL) certificate, open a Web browser window and type `https://web_server_name:8098`. For example, you type `https://server05:8098` if the server's name is `server05` (see Figure 7.30). The Remote Administration (HTML) tool can help you to remotely manage many aspects of a server, such as configuring network settings, administering local users and groups, and performing maintenance chores such as viewing event logs and restarting the server. The Remote Administration tool is not limited to only working with IIS settings. To install the Remote Administration (HTML) tool, follow these steps on a Windows Server 2003 Web server:

1. Go to Control Panel, double-click Add or Remove Programs, and click Add/Remove Windows Components.

2. Select the Application Server component, but do not mark or clear its check box, and click Details.

3. Next, select the Internet Information Services (IIS) component, but do not mark or clear its check box, and click Details.

4. Select the World Wide Web Service component, but do not mark or clear its check box, and click Details.

5. Mark the Remote Administration (HTML) check box and click OK.

6. Click OK for the Internet Information Services dialog box and click OK for the Application Server dialog box.

7. Click Next for the Windows Components Wizard window and wait for the wizard to complete the installation of the Remote Administration (HTML) tool.

8. Click Finish to complete the Windows Component Wizard and then close the Add or Remove Programs dialog box.

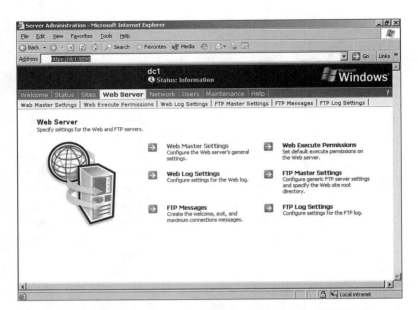

Figure 7.30 Managing a Web server with the Remote Administration (HTML) tool.

NOTE

As mentioned earlier, Web browsing under IE 6.0 on Windows Server 2003 computers is greatly restricted by default. You might want to change the default Internet Explorer Enhanced Security Configuration setting. To modify this setting, launch the Add or Remove Programs applet in Control Panel, click Add/Remove Windows Components, and select the Internet Explorer Enhanced Security Configuration component. You can completely remove this setting by clearing its check box. Alternatively, you can click the Details tab and specify whether members of Administrator groups get restricted access and whether all other users get restricted access to Web content. Click OK for the Internet Explorer Enhanced Security Configuration dialog box and then click Next to have the Windows Components Wizard save the new settings.

Backing Up and Restoring Web Server Configuration Settings

The IIS Manager snap-in has its own built-in backup and restore feature for safeguarding the important IIS configuration database file (metabase.xml) and the matching metabase schema file (mbschema.xml). This feature is intended to restore metabase backups to and from the same server. *You cannot restore a metabase from a previous version of IIS onto an IIS 6.0 Web server.* To transfer the setting from another IIS 6.0 server, you can use the export and import functions instead. IIS 6.0 automatically creates backups of the metabase on a periodic basis; these backups are called *history files* and this feature is enabled by default. To create a manual metabase backups for a Web server, perform the following steps:

1. Open the IIS Manager snap-in.

2. Right-click the Web server name in the left pane that you want to back up and select All Tasks, Backup/Restore Configuration.

3. Click Create Backup.

4. Type a name for this backup in the Configuration Backup Name box, as shown in Figure 7.31.

5. Mark the Encrypt Backup Using Password, if desired, and then type and confirm the password.

6. Click OK to create the backup; the metabase is locked while the back-up file is created.

7. Click Close to exit from the Configuration Backup/Restore dialog box.

Figure 7.31 Creating a manual backup of the IIS metabase.

You should perform IIS backups on each Web server to safeguard the IIS metabase for each computer. You can easily restore a backup of the metabase onto the same Web server where the backup was created, or you can use metabase backup files to restore to other IIS 6.0 computers. To transfer only metabase configuration elements between different Web servers, you can use the export and import procedures instead of the metabase backup feature. Before you import metabase elements into a Web server, however, you must be sure to remove all *machine-specific* and *system-specific* information that is stored within the metabase import file.

Restoring the metabase from a previous backup on the same computer is easy. Right-click the Web server name in IIS Manager and select All Tasks, Backup/Restore Configuration. Select one of the listed backups and click the Restore button. When you click the Restore button, a message box informs you that restoring the metabase from backup is a lengthy procedure that deletes all the current settings and stops all Internet services on the comput-er. After the restore process is finished, IIS restarts the services that were stopped. Click Yes for this message box to continue with the metabase restore. You are prompted for a password if the backup was encrypted using a password.

Exporting and Importing Metabase Configuration Elements

Because IIS 6.0 metabase backups are machine-specific and system-specific, you cannot restore a complete IIS 6.0 server using a backup file from a different IIS 6.0 computer nor can you restore from a metabase backup file after reinstalling Windows Server 2003. You can, however, import elements of the IIS metabase from one server to another. If you use one of the VBScript files that ship with Windows Server 2003 and IIS 6.0, `iisback.vbs` or `iiscnfg.vbs/copy`, you can import an entire IIS 6.0 metabase from one computer into another because these commands replace all the machine-specific and system-specific settings stored in metabase backup files. To ensure that all new settings are saved to the metabase file, you can right-click the Web server name in the left pane of IIS Manager and select Save Configuration to Disk. To import elements of the IIS metabase into another IIS 6.0 computer, follow these steps:

1. Open IIS Manager.

2. In the left pane, depending on which element that you want to import, do one of the following:

   ➤ Right-click the Web Sites node and select New, Web Site (from File).

   ➤ Right-click an existing Web Site subnode and select New, Web Site (from File) or New, Virtual Directory (from File).

   ➤ Right-click the Application Pools subnode, or an existing application pool subnode, and select New, Application Pool (from File).

3. From the Import Configuration dialog box, type the location and name of the metabase file to use for the import or click the Browse button to find it.

4. Click the Read File button to have IIS read the configuration settings stored in the metabase file.

5. Select the configuration element to import from the metabase file, as shown in Figure 7.32.

6. Click OK to import the settings. If, for example, a Web site being imported uses the same name as one that already exists, IIS asks you whether you want to create a new site or to replace the existing one.

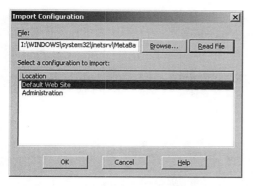

Figure 7.32 Importing metabase configuration elements.

 When you work with IIS metabase files, do not use the Encrypting File System (EFS) for security; the secure properties within the metabase files are already encrypted. Encrypting metabase files a second time is unnecessary and creates additional overhead for the server to unencrypt these files twice whenever they are accessed.

Administering Security for IIS

To properly secure computers running IIS 6.0, you need to work with both Windows security settings and IIS security settings. Windows security settings include such features as user and group accounts, NTFS permissions for folders and files, and local policy or group policy settings. IIS security settings include configuring permissions for content, specifying authentication methods, and setting operator permissions.

Learning About IIS 6.0 User and Group Accounts

The user and group accounts used by IIS 6.0 must conform to the Windows Server 2003 security model that offers local accounts only for standalone servers but a choice of local or domain accounts for servers that are members of an Active Directory domain. Servers that are DCs cannot use local accounts because no local accounts exist on a DC. It is not a preferred practice to use a DC as an IIS server for hosting public access to FTP or Web sites. You should configure IIS to use domain user and group accounts only if you need to give IIS users access to domain resources: This is a security risk because you are exposing domain resources to potential intruders. You can use local user and group accounts for standalone servers and for servers that are members of a domain to limit access for IIS users to the local computer only. The following user and group accounts are commonly used by IIS:

➤ *ASPNET*—This account is a local user account used by IIS and ASP.NET when IIS is configured to run in IIS 5.0 Isolation mode. By default, this account cannot log on to the computer via RDC.

➤ *IUSR_ServerName*—This user account allows users anonymous access to Internet Web and FTP sites hosted by IIS. This account appends the computer's name to IUSR_. This account must be active for users to access Internet sites without having to enter a valid username and password. If the server is part of a domain, this user account is a member of the Domain Users group and the Guests group.

➤ *IWAM_ServerName*—This user accounts grants the Log on as a Batch Job user right and is used for Web applications. This account appends the computer's name to IWAM_. When IIS runs in IIS 5.0 Isolation mode, out-of-process applications cannot run if this account is not active. If the server is part of a domain, this user account is a member of the Domain Users group and the IIS_WPG group.

➤ *IIS_WPG*—This group is created on the local computer and within the domain, if the computer is a member of a domain. The local group account includes the IWAM_*ServerName*, Local Service, Network Service, and System accounts by default.

➤ *Local Service*—This account permits access to the local system only and has limited rights. This accounts grants users the right to log on as a batch job.

➤ *Local System*—This account permits access to log on to the local computer interactively, as a batch job, or as a service. All users who access IIS or the Indexing service do so through the Local System account.

➤ *Network Service*—This account offers more permissions than the Local Service account, but it grants fewer permissions and rights than the Local System account. Applications or services that log on using this account can log on as a service and can access other servers on the network. By default, Web applications use this account when IIS 6.0 is running in Worker Process Isolation mode.

Configuring IIS User Authentication

IIS 6.0 offers four types of user-authentication methods. In addition to the four basic types of user authentication that are available in IIS 6.0, you can also configure client or server certificates, each of which use SSL encryption for secure communications. Client certificates allow the server to positively identify the client based on personal information contained in each client's certificate. Server certificates allow the client to positively identify the server based on specific information contained in each server's certificate. Each of the four basic authentication methods offers different functionality and security; therefore, you need to select an authentication method based on the functionality required for a particular application or purpose. The following authentication methods are available:

➤ *Basic authentication*—This method sends passwords in unencrypted clear text over the network (through an intranet or through the Internet). This authentication method is not secure.

➤ *Digest authentication for Windows domain servers*—This method works only with Active Directory user accounts, and it sends encrypted passwords over the network using hash values. It is considered a secure authentication method. It can work through proxy servers and through firewalls, and it works with Web Distributed Authoring and Versioning (WebDAV).

➤ *Integrated Windows authentication*—This method incorporates NTLM authentication protocol (also referred to as Windows NT Challenge/Response authentication), the Kerberos version 5 authentication protocol, and the Negotiate authentication method. This integrated approach provides secure authentication through firewalls and proxy servers, whereas Kerberos alone is generally blocked by firewalls and NTLM alone is generally blocked by proxy servers. With Kerberos and NTLM together, Integrated Windows authentication can traverse both firewalls and proxy servers. This authentication method is considered secure.

➤ *.NET Passport authentication*—This method uses the Microsoft .NET Passport user authentication service to identify and verify users. This method uses Internet standards such as SSL, HTTP redirects, cookies, JScript, and strong symmetric key encryption. It provides a single sign-in (logon) for users to access resources that are secured by the .NET Passport authentication method. It is considered a secure authentication method.

You can modify the way in which users are authenticated and granted access to Web sites under IIS either globally or individually for each Web site hosted by the IIS server. By default, Anonymous Access is enabled so that guest users do not need to enter a username or password to visit Web sites hosted by an IIS server. You can configure access and authentication settings at the Web Sites node level, the individual Web site level, the Web site virtual directory level, or at the individual file level within each virtual directory. To specify access and authentication settings for any of these levels, follow these steps:

1. Open IIS Manager.

2. Right-click the Web Sites node, one of the Web sites listed, a virtual directory, or a file within a virtual directory, and select Properties.

3. From the object's properties sheet, click the Directory Security tab (for a file, click the File Security tab).

4. For the Authentication and Access Control section, click the Edit button to display the Authentication Methods dialog box (see Figure 7.33).

5. You can make the following modifications to the Authentication Methods dialog box:

   ➤ To change the user account for anonymous access, type the user account and the password in the User Name and Password boxes.

   ➤ To disable anonymous access, clear the Enable Anonymous Access check box.

   ➤ To specify authenticated access methods, mark or clear the check box for each method that you want to enable or disable: Integrated Windows Authentication (default), Digest Authentication for Windows Domain Servers, Basic Authentication (Password Is Sent in Clear Text), and .NET Passport Authentication.

   ➤ For Digest Authentication, you can select or type the name of a realm in the Realm box.

   ➤ For Basic Authentication, you can select or type the name of a realm in the Realm box or the name of a default domain in the Default Domain box.

   ➤ For .NET Passport Authentication, you can select or type the name of a default domain in the Default Domain box.

6. When you're finished specifying authentication methods, click OK to save your settings.

7. Click OK to close the properties window.

Setting Web Server Permissions

In addition to any NTFS security permissions that you might apply to folders and files stored on disk, Web sites, virtual directories, and files stored in those virtual directories are assigned Web server permissions that apply to all users. Web server permissions also affect WebDAV permissions in terms of which actions are allowed for accessing documents using WebDAV-enabled applications. The WebDAV protocol gives users the ability to read, write, and create documents via Hypertext Transfer Protocol (HTTP) and its associated default TCP port, port 80. Windows 2000 and later operating systems along with Microsoft Office 2000, Office XP, and Office 2003 all support WebDAV.

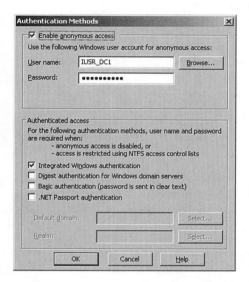

Figure 7.33   Specifying user access and authentication methods for IIS 6.0.

You can set Web server permissions both globally and locally. You apply global Web server permissions at the Web Sites (parent object) node level; these security settings are inherited by all of the Web sites, virtual directories, and files (child objects) that exist beneath the parent level. If you set Web server permissions locally for individual Web sites, virtual directories, or files, those settings can override the global permissions. If global and local settings conflict, IIS asks whether you want to apply the global settings and override the local settings or retain the local settings. To configure global Web server settings, follow these steps:

1. Open IIS Manager.

2. Right-click the Web Sites node and select Properties.

3. Click the Home Directory tab (see Figure 7.34).

4. Mark the check box for each permission that you want to enable and have child objects inherit; clear the check box for each permission that you want to disable and have child objects inherit:

   ➤ *Script Source Access*—This permission allows users to read the programming source code for scripts (such as ASP scripts) stored in the virtual directory if either the Read or Write permission is enabled. If the Write permission is enabled, the Script Source Access permission allows users to modify, delete, or add to script files in the virtual directory. You should use the Script Source Access permission *only in directories that require user authentication* because this permission exposes the Web site to potentially malicious attacks.

➤ *Read*—This permission allows users to access a virtual directory or to read and display a file. The Read permission also allows users to download files.

➤ *Write*—This permission allows users to create files within a virtual directory or to change the contents of a file. The Write permission also allows users to upload files. *Limit the Write permission for security purposes.*

➤ *Directory Browsing*—This permission allows users to view a list of files and subdirectories within the current virtual directory, if no default document exists in the directory. *Limit the Directory Browsing permission for security purposes.*

➤ *Log Visits*—This security setting specifies that IIS record users' visits to the virtual directory in a log file; logging must be enabled for the Web site for this setting to take effect. (Logging is enabled by default.)

➤ *Index This Resource*—This security setting allows the Microsoft Indexing Service to include the virtual directory as part of a full-text index for the Web site.

5. From the Execute Permissions drop-down list box, you can choose the application program's execution level allowed for this resource, if the resource is used as part of an IIS application:

➤ *None*—This execute permission level only allows static files to be accessed, such as `.html` files, `.gif` files, and `.jpg` files.

➤ *Scripts Only*—This execute permission level only allows script files to run, such as ASP script files; it does not permit binary executables to run, such as application program files (`*.com` or `*.exe` files).

➤ *Scripts and Executables*—This execute permission level allows both script files and executable files to run on the Web server.

6. Click OK to save the Web server security permissions settings.

Figure 7.34 Configuring global Web server permissions and application execution permissions under IIS 6.0.

To configure local Web server permissions for individual Web sites, virtual directories, and files, right-click one of these objects in IIS Manager and select Properties. The next option varies depending on the object that you're working with. For a Web site, click the Home Directory tab to configure IIS permissions for that Web site. For a virtual directory, click the Directory tab to configure IIS permissions for that virtual directory. For a file, click the File tab to configure IIS permissions for that file.

Exam Prep Questions

Question 1

You are logged on to a Windows Server 2003 member server as AlexisB and the user account you are logged on as is a member of the Domain Users group. The server is configured using default settings. How can you temporarily stop the fax service on the server without logging out and logging back on using the Administrator user account?

- ○ A. Click Start, Run; type **services.msc**; and click OK. Then, right-click the fax service and select stop.
- ○ B. Open a command prompt and type **net stop fax /user:windows2003. local\administrator**.
- ○ C. Open a command prompt, type **runas /user:windows2003.local\ administrator "net stop fax"**, and then type in the proper password when prompted.
- ○ D. Right-click My Computer and select Manage. Expand the Services and Applications node, right-click the Fax node, and select Stop.

Answer C is correct because only the Run as command allows you to run a system utility or a program as a different user other than the user you are currently logged on as. Answer A is incorrect because you must be at least a member of the Server Operators group to stop and start system services. Answer B is incorrect because the net stop and net start commands do not support the /user: option. Answer D is incorrect because, as just mentioned, you must be a member of the Server Operators or the Administrators group to stop and start system services.

Question 2

Which of the following Windows operating systems support the RA feature? (Choose two.)

- ❑ A. Windows XP Professional
- ❑ B. Windows Server 2003
- ❑ C. Windows Me
- ❑ D. Windows 2000 Professional
- ❑ E. Windows 2000 Server

Answers A and B are correct. The RA feature is only supported on Windows XP and Windows Server 2003 computers. Answers C, D, and E are incorrect because RA is not supported on these operating systems.

Question 3

Which of the following Windows operating systems support TS as a server? (Choose three.)

❑ A. Windows XP Professional

❑ B. Windows Server 2003

❑ C. Windows NT Server 4.0 Standard Edition

❑ D. Windows 2000 Professional

❑ E. Windows 2000 Server

❑ F. Windows Me

Answers A, B, and E are correct. Windows XP Professional supports one Remote Desktop console session, whereas Windows Server 2003 and Windows 2000 Server both support up to two simultaneous Remote Desktop connections as a server in Remote Administration mode. Answers C, D, and F are incorrect because TS as a server is not supported on these operating systems.

Question 4

Which tool do you need to use to specify settings, such as the encryption level between client and server computers, for TS on a Windows Server 2003 computer?

○ A. Terminal Services Manager

○ B. Terminal Services Configuration

○ C. Terminal Server Licensing

○ D. The Remote Desktops snap-in

Answer B is correct. Terminal Services Configuration allows you to select the Connections node and double-click the RDP-Tcp connection object to specify Terminal Server properties such as the encryption level. Answer A is incorrect because Terminal Services Manager lets you administer active TS sessions. Answer C is incorrect because Terminal Server Licensing lets you work with TS licenses when the server is set up in Application Server mode. Answer D is incorrect because the Remote Desktops snap-in connects you to other Terminal Servers; it does not configure TS settings.

Question 5

> How can you rebuild an entire IIS 6.0 Web server after reinstalling the Windows Server 2003 operating system?
>
> ○ A. Right-click the server name in IIS Manager on the new computer and select Backup/Restore Configuration. Restore all Web server content from a recent tape backup using the Windows Server 2003 Backup Utility.
>
> ○ B. Import a recent backup copy of the **metabase.xml** file from the old server that was created using the **iiscnfg.vbs /copy** command. Restore all Web server content from a recent tape backup using the Windows Server 2003 Backup Utility.
>
> ○ C. Replace the **metabase.xml** file on the new server with the **metabase.xml** file from the old server. Restore all Web server content from a recent tape backup using the Windows Server 2003 Backup Utility.
>
> ○ D. Use the Windows Server 2003 Backup utility to restore the System State for the old server onto the new server. Also, restore all Web server content from a recent tape backup using the Windows Server 2003 Backup Utility.

Answer B is correct because you cannot directly import the metabase.xml file from one server to another without first removing all machine-specific settings stored in the file. The iiscnfg.vbs /copy command removes all machine-specific settings from the import file. Answers A, C, and D are incorrect because you cannot directly import the metabase.xml file from one server to another without first removing all machine-specific settings stored in the file.

Question 6

> How can you connect to the console session using an RDC without any intervention from another user? (Choose two.)
>
> ❑ A. Add a new connection using the Remote Desktops snap-in and accept all default settings.
>
> ❑ B. Click Start, Run; type **mstsc.exe /console**; and click OK. In the Remote Desktop Connection dialog box, type in the remote computer name and click Connect.
>
> ❑ C. Use the RA feature.
>
> ❑ D. Use the TS client to connect to a Windows 2000 Server.
>
> ❑ E. Click Start, Run; type **mstsc.exe /f**; and click OK. In the Remote Desktop Connection dialog box, type in the remote computer name and click Connect.

Answers A and B are correct. If you add a new connection in the Remote Desktops snap-in, the default setting provides for connecting to the console session. The Windows Server 2003 version of the `mstsc.exe` command combined with the `/console` option connects the RDC client to the console session on Windows XP Professional and Windows Server 2003 computers. Answer C is incorrect because the RA feature requires a user to be at the console before permission can be granted to connect to the console. Answer D is incorrect because the legacy TS client cannot connect to the console session on any Windows computer. Windows 2000 Server does not support connecting to the console session remotely. Answer E is incorrect because the `mstsc.exe` command combined with the `/f` option connects the RDC client to a Terminal Server in full-screen mode; it does not connect to the console session.

Question 7

How can you administer a Web server remotely? (Choose two.)

- ❑ A. Use the IIS Manager snap-in that ships with Windows Server 2003.
- ❑ B. Install **adminpak.msi** from the Windows Server 2003 CD-ROM onto a Windows 2000 Professional computer after installing SP3 for Windows 2000.
- ❑ C. Install **adminpak.msi** from the Windows Server 2003 CD-ROM onto a Windows XP Professional computer without SP1 for Windows XP installed.
- ❑ D. Use the Internet Services Manager on a Windows 2000 Server computer and connect to the remote IIS 6.0 computer.
- ❑ E. Use the Internet Explorer Web browser, type in the URL **https:// server05:8098**, and enter a valid username and password when prompted.

Answers A and E are correct. Answer B is incorrect because the Windows Server 2003 support tools in the `adminpak.msi` do not install under Windows 2000 Server or Professional. Answer C is incorrect because the Windows Server 2003 support tools in the `adminpak.msi` do not install under Windows XP Professional unless SP1 or higher is installed. Answer D is incorrect because you cannot administer an IIS 6.0 server using a previous version of the IIS support utilities.

Question 8

> You are the network administrator for a company that has offices in three different geographic locations—New York, New York; Dallas, Texas; and San Francisco, California. You are in Dallas and you're trying to remotely administer a Windows Server 2003 computer named server07 in San Francisco. The San Francisco office has an Exchange Server computer installed that handles company email for the entire West Coast region. You have visited the San Francisco office before, and you've been able to access the server using an RDC within the office. From Dallas, you can send and receive SMTP and POP3 email over the Internet using the San Francisco Exchange Server. However, when you attempt to connect to server07 using an RDC and the IP address 207.107.17.77, you receive a message box that states: "The client could not connect to the remote computer. Remote connections might not be enabled for the computer or it might be too busy to accept new connections. It is also possible that network problems are preventing your connection." What is the most likely cause of this problem?
>
> ○ A. Remote Desktop connections are not enabled on server07. Mark the Allow Users to Connect to This Computer Remotely check box on the Remote tab of the System Properties window.
>
> ○ B. The Remote Desktop for Administration feature is not yet installed on server07.
>
> ○ C. The RA feature is not enabled on server07. Mark the Turn on Remote Assistance and Allow Invitations to Be Sent from This Computer check box on the Remote tab of the System Properties window.
>
> ○ D. TCP port 3389 is closed on the company's Internet firewall.

Answer D is correct. Because you have successfully logged on to server07 remotely within the San Francisco office, this attempt would indicate that the problem is from outside the LAN and that the firewall port 3389 is not open to allow RDP-TCP traffic. Answer A is incorrect because RDCs apparently work within the LAN. Answer B is incorrect because the Remote Desktop for Administration feature is installed by default under Windows Server 2003. Answer C is incorrect because RDCs do not depend upon the RA feature being enabled or disabled.

Question 9

How can you remotely view and interact with a user's Windows desktop who is working within a Remote Desktop Connection session without using RA?

○ A. Use Terminal Services Manager to "shadow" the user's console session by right-clicking the user's name and selecting Remote Control.

○ B. Use Terminal Services Manager to shadow the user's RDC session by right-clicking the user's name and selecting Remote Control.

○ C. Use Terminal Services Configuration to shadow the user's console session by right-clicking the user's name and selecting Remote Control.

○ D. Use the Remote Desktops snap-in to shadow the user's session by making sure that the Connect to Console check box is marked in the connection's properties sheet.

Answer B is correct. Answer A is incorrect because although you can use Terminal Services Manager to shadow users, you can only use Remote Control to connect to existing RDP sessions, not a console session where the user is logged on interactively. Answer C is incorrect because you cannot use Terminal Services Configuration to shadow a user's session. Answer D is incorrect because you cannot use the Remote Desktops snap-in to shadow a user's session, especially if you mark the Connect to Console check box.

Question 10

On which of the following operating systems can you install an edition of the Microsoft RDC client software? (Choose two.)

❑ A. Mac OS X 10.1 or higher

❑ B. Windows NT Workstation 4.0

❑ C. Windows NT Server 3.51

❑ D. Windows for Workgroups 3.11

❑ E. MS-DOS 6.22

Answers A and B are correct. Answer C is incorrect because Microsoft does not publish a version of the RDC client for Windows NT Server 3.51. Answer D is incorrect because Microsoft does not publish a version of the RDC client for the 16-bit Windows for Workgroups operating system. Answer E is incorrect because Microsoft does not publish a version of the RDC client for the legacy MS-DOS operating system.

Need to Know More?

 Holme, Dan, and Orin Thomas. *MCSA/MCSE Self-Paced Training Kit (Exam 70-290): Managing and Maintaining a Microsoft Windows Server 2003 Environment.* Redmond, Washington: Microsoft Press, 2003.

 Morimoto, Rand, et. al. *Microsoft Windows Server 2003 Unleashed.* Indianapolis, Indiana: SAMS Publishing, 2003.

 Stanek, William R. *Microsoft IIS 6.0 Administrator's Pocket Consultant.* Redmond, Washington: Microsoft Press, 2003.

 Search the Microsoft Product Support Services Knowledge Base on the Internet: http://support.microsoft.com. You can also search Microsoft TechNet on the Internet: http://www.microsoft.com/technet. Find technical information using keywords from this chapter, such as Run as, administration tools, MMC, Remote Assistance, Terminal Services, Remote Desktop, Internet Information Services, and IIS metabase.

Disaster Recovery Techniques and Procedures

Terms you'll need to understand:

✓ Disaster recovery
✓ Shadow Copies of Shared Folders
✓ Safe Mode
✓ Recovery Console
✓ Automated System Recovery (ASR)
✓ Last Known Good Configuration
✓ Headless servers
✓ In-band management
✓ Out-of-band management
✓ Special Administration Console (SAC)
✓ Emergency Management Services (EMS)

Techniques you'll need to master:

✓ Restoring data from shadow copies
✓ Creating a startup disk
✓ Troubleshooting Windows Server 2003 startup problems
✓ Using Safe Mode to troubleshoot server problems
✓ Using the Last Known Good Configuration
✓ Installing and using the Recovery Console
✓ Creating an Automated System Recovery (ASR) Backup
✓ Restoring a server using Automated System Recovery (ASR)
✓ Using the Special Administration Console (SAC) in Emergency Management Services (EMS)

A comprehensive, fully tested disaster recovery plan should be an integral part of any IT department's policies and procedures. Windows Server 2003 has a number of features to get the server up and running in the event of operating system (OS) file corruption or data loss. Emergency Management Services (EMS) allows you to perform out-of-band remote server management when you cannot access a server using a standard network connection.

Preparing for Disaster Recovery Situations

Reliable and up-to-date server backups are a critical part of any sound network maintenance and disaster recovery plan. A backup plan can only be judged "sound" in the context of the data-recovery requirements. For example, questions such as "What do you need to restore in the event of a catastrophe?" are appropriate to determine what kinds of precautions are necessary.

Even so, some measures are required and considered best practice in all environments. It is not considered optional to run daily backups on all servers. If the tape drive does not have the capacity to perform a daily full backup, consider weekly full backups and daily differential backups instead. Differential backups do not reset the archive bit, so it only takes two backup sets to perform a complete restore—one set with the full backup and one set with the latest differential backup. Shadow copies of shared folders can prevent the need to ever restore data files from a tape backup. In addition, creating a Windows Server 2003 startup disk, installing the Recovery Console, and configuring Emergency Management Services (EMS) before you have server startup problems can get you out of trouble if your server refuses to start. This chapter covers these and other backup-related concepts relevant to disaster recovery. Chapter 9, "Data Backup Techniques and Procedures," provides details on Windows Server 2003 backup and restore procedures.

What Are Shadow Copies of Shared Folders?

Shadow copies of shared folders is a new Windows Server 2003 feature. Shadow copies automatically creates backup copies of the data stored in shared folders on specific drive volumes at scheduled times. Restoring a damaged or deleted file from a shadow copy can increase productivity and save time by preventing the administrator from having to restore files from tape.

For more information on setting up and configuring shadow copies, refer to Chapter 5, "Managing Network Resources and Terminal Services."

Accessing Shadow Copies

After shadow copies are properly installed and configured on Windows Server 2003, make sure to install the Previous Versions Client software program on the workstations. This program allows Windows XP and Windows Server 2003 computers to access shadow copies stored on Windows Server 2003 computers. For more information on this client and its installation, you can also refer to Chapter 5. When a user selects a data file that has one or more shadow copies, the View Previous Versions option appears in the File and Folder tasks pane in Windows Explorer and My Computer. A Previous Versions tab is available when a user views the properties sheet for a data file that has one or more shadow copies, as shown in Figure 8.1.

Computers running Windows 2000 SP3 and Windows 98 are also supported for retrieving previous versions of folders and files from a shared network folder stored on a Windows Server 2003 computer where Shadow Copies is set up. You must download and install the Shadow Copy Client software at **http://www. microsoft.com/windowsserver2003/downloads/shadowcopyclient.mspx**. Windows 2000 SP3 computers and Windows 98 computers must have the Shadow Copy Client software installed on the Windows Server 2003 computer where the shadow copies are stored as well as have this software installed on the workstations.

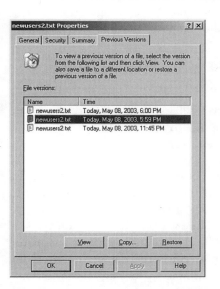

Figure 8.1   Viewing previous versions (shadow copies) of a file from its properties sheet.

If you are logged on locally to Windows Server 2003, you *must use* a Uniform Naming Convention (UNC) path to access shadow copies. For example, to access shadow copies on the C: drive, you can click Start, Run; type the command **\\server_name\share_name** (for instance, **\\server01\c$**); and click OK. You must use a UNC path because previous versions of folders and files can only be accessed via network shared folders on drive volumes where the Shadow Copies feature is configured. Remember that the name of this new feature is Shadow Copies of Shared Folders.

Booting Windows Server 2003 with a Startup Disk

In some cases, Windows Server 2003 computers might not start properly. Windows Server 2003 computers might fail to start when the boot record, or files required to start Windows Server 2003, somehow become corrupted or get deleted. Complete the following steps to create a startup disk for a Windows Server 2003 computer:

1. Format a blank floppy disk in a machine running the Windows Server 2003 operating system. In My Computer, right-click the floppy drive icon, select Format, mark the Quick Format check box, and click OK.

2. Copy the following files to the floppy disk: boot.ini, ntdetect.com, ntldr, plus bootsect.dos (if the machine is in a dual-boot configuration) and ntbootdd.sys, if these files exist on the computer that you want to use this startup disk on.

3. Make sure to test the startup disk by placing the disk in the floppy drive, restarting the server, and verifying that the server starts properly.

4. Label the disk as the Windows Server 2003 startup disk with the server name and date it was created. Make sure to update this disk if you change the disk configuration on the server.

If you did not create a startup disk ahead of time, you can copy the startup files from an existing Windows Server 2003 computer. You might need to make some adjustments to the boot.ini file if the server you are trying to repair starts from a different partition. The boot.ini file resides on the system drive on every Windows Server 2003 computer. This file contains the Advanced RISC Computing (ARC) path specifications that define where the operating-system partition (or volume) is physically located on the computer's hard drives. The boot.ini file handles single-boot, dual-boot, and multi-boot configurations. This file also determines which operating system is the default, when more than one operating system is installed, and the amount of time before the default operating system loads. Refer to Microsoft Knowledgebase article 317526, which you can find at http://support. microsoft.com/default.aspx?scid=kb;en-us;317526, for more information on editing boot.ini files.

Using Safe Mode to Recover a Server

If the server does not start after you install a device driver, new software, or a new service, you can use Safe Mode to start the server with a minimal amount of services and drivers. Once the server is running in Safe Mode, you can disable or remove the offending driver, software program, or service. Table 8.1 lists the available Safe Mode options for Windows Server 2003.

Table 8.1 Safe Mode Startup Options for Windows Server 2003	
Safe Mode Options	**When to Use**
Safe Mode	Remove offending program, driver, or service that prevents Windows Server 2003 from starting.
Safe Mode with Networking Support	Use to verify that network components are working properly.
Safe Mode with Command Prompt	Use to run command-line utilities only. After logon, only a command prompt appears. Try running this option if Safe Mode does not work.

Accessing Safe Mode

The Safe Mode options are installed by default on all Windows Server 2003 editions. If the server does not start after you install a service pack, install new hardware, or make some other change to the server, uninstall the service pack or hardware in Safe Mode. If the server starts up after you remove the offending files, then you can be confident that the item you removed was the source of the problem. To access Safe Mode, complete the following steps:

1. Restart the Server.

2. Before the Windows Server 2003 splash screen appears, press the F8 key.

3. Use the arrow keys to select one of the listed Safe Mode options and press Enter.

4. Log on to the server as the administrator; a message box will inform you that you have logged on using Safe mode, as shown in Figure 8.2.

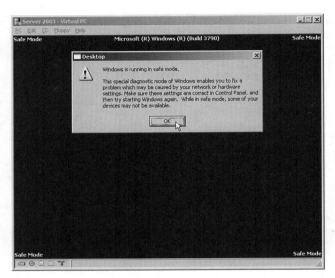

Figure 8.2 Logging on to Windows Server 2003 under Safe Mode.

 Whenever you make a major change to a server, restart the server to verify it starts properly. If it does not start, you can quickly reverse the changes using Safe Mode. If you do not verify that the server restarts, it will be more difficult to determine the cause of a startup problem at a (potentially much) later date when a server restart is mandatory.

Using Last Known Good Configuration

If you have difficulty starting the server, you can use the Last Known Good Configuration to restore the settings of the server, which were saved automatically by the server at the last successful logon. Using the Last Known Good Configuration restores information for the Registry subkey `HKEY_LOCAL_MACHINE\SYSTEM\CurrentControlSet`. Any updated drivers are restored to the previous version if you use the Last Known Good Configuration. Complete the following steps to start Windows Server 2003 with the Last Known Good Configuration:

1. Restart the Server.

2. Before the Windows Server 2003 splash screen appears, press the F8 key.

3. Select the Last Known Good Configuration and press Enter.

4. Use the arrow keys to select an operating system and press Enter, if the computer has multiple instances of an operating system installed.

 Although Microsoft recommends trying the Last Known Good Configuration before using Safe Mode, use Safe Mode first. Often the Last Known Good Configuration returns the server to a much earlier state than anticipated. Because Safe Mode does not update the Last Known Configuration registry key, you still have this option available if Safe Mode does not resolve the problem.

Working with the Recovery Console

If a startup disk, Safe Mode, and the Last Known Good Configuration all fail to start the server, use the Recovery Console. The Recovery Console in Windows Server 2003 provides a command-prompt–only environment that you can use for the following:

➤ Enabling or disabling services that prevent Windows Server 2003 from properly starting.

➤ Reading, writing, and copying files on a local drive. The Recovery Console enforces NTFS permissions.

➤ Formatting hard disks.

➤ Repairing a boot sector.

To use the Recovery Console, you must log onto the server using the local administrator account. You can either preinstall the Recovery Console or you can run it directly from the Windows Server 2003 CD-ROM. To install the Recovery Console, complete the following steps:

1. Insert the Windows Server 2003 CD into the computer's CD-ROM drive.

2. Click Start, Run; type cmd in the Open box; and click OK.

3. At the command prompt, type the letter of the CD-ROM drive and a colon (:), and press Enter. (For example, type R: and press Enter.)

4. Type cd\i386 and press Enter.

5. Type winnt32 /cmdcons and press Enter. Windows Server 2003 might check for any updates to the software before installing the Recovery Console.

6. After the installation is finished, click Yes, and then click OK.

To run the Recovery Console, restart Windows Server 2003 and select the Microsoft Windows Recovery Console from the Please Select the Operating System to Start screen.

Starting the Recovery Console from the Windows Server 2003 CD

As an alternative, you can start the Recovery Console by booting the server from the Windows Server 2003 CD-ROM. This step is useful if the Recovery Console was not previously installed or if the server does recognize the boot hard drive. Complete the following steps to start the Recovery Console from the Windows Server 2003 CD-ROM:

1. Insert the Windows Server 2003 CD-ROM into the CD drive.

2. If necessary, press a key to boot from the CD.

3. Press R to select the Repair/Recover option.

Logging On to the Recovery Console

Once the Recovery Console screen boots, you must specify which Windows Server installation that you want to log on to. On a multiboot server, you can log on to any of the available Microsoft operating systems that are compatible with the Recovery Console, such as Windows 2000, Windows XP, and Windows Server 2003. Complete the following steps to log onto the Recovery Console:

1. Type the number of the Windows installation you want (usually 1) and press Enter.

2. Type the password for the local administrator account and press Enter (see Figure 8.3).

Recovery Console Commands

Once you successfully log on to the Recovery Console, you can type `help` and press Enter at the command prompt to display a list of Recovery Console commands. Table 8.2 lists the available Recovery Console commands, their functions, and their command line syntax and options.

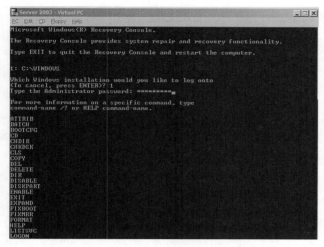

Figure 8.3 The Recovery Console screen showing available commands.

Table 8.2	Recovery Console Commands	
Command	**Function**	**Syntax and Options**
ATTRIB	Display and set file attributes.	**ATTRIB -RI+RI-SI+SI-HI+HI-CI+C *filename*** **+** Sets an attribute. **-** Clears an attribute. **R** Read-only file attribute. **S** System file attribute. **H** Hidden file attribute. **C** Compressed file attribute. To view attributes, use the **DIR** command.
BATCH	Execute commands in a text file.	**BATCH *InputFile* [*OutputFile*]** ***InputFile*** Specifies the text file that contains the list of commands to be executed. ***OutputFile*** If specified, contains the output of the specified commands. If not specified, the output appears onscreen.

Table 8.2   Recovery Console Commands *(continued)*

Command	Function	Syntax and Options
BOOTCFG	Repair boot configuration and recovery.	**BOOTCFG /ADD** **BOOTCFG /REBUILD** **BOOTCFG /SCAN** **BOOTCFG /LIST** **BOOTCFG /DISABLEEMS** **BOOTCFG /EMS [PORT BAUDRATE]I[useBiosSettings]** **/SCAN** Scans all disks for Windows installations and displays the results. **/ADD** Adds a Windows installation to the boot list. **/REBUILD** Iterates through all Windows installations and allows the user to choose which to add. **/DEFAULT** Sets the default boot entry. **/LIST** Lists the entries already in the boot list. **/DISABLEEMS** Disables redirection in the boot loader. **/EMS** Enables redirection in the boot loader with the specified configuration. Example: **bootcfg /ems com1 115200 bootcfg /ems useBiosSettings**
CD (CHDIR)	Display the name of the current directory or change to another directory.	**CD [path]** **CD [..]** **CD [drive:]** **CD ..** Specifies that you want to change to the parent directory. **CD drive:** Displays the current directory in the specified drive. **CD** Without parameters, displays the current drive and directory. The **CD** command treats spaces as delimiters. Use quotation marks around a directory name containing spaces. For example **cd "\windows\profiles\username\programs"** **CD** operates only within the system directories of the current Windows installation, removable media, the root directory of any hard disk partition, or the local installation sources.

Table 8.2 Recovery Console Commands *(continued)*		
Command	**Function**	**Syntax and Options**
CHKDSK	Check a disk and display a status report.	**CHKDSK** [*drive:*] [/P] [/R] [*drive:*] Specifies the drive to check. /P Checks even if the drive is not flagged dirty. /R Locates bad sectors and recovers readable information (implies /P). You can use **CHKDSK** without any parameters, in which case the current drive is checked with no switches. You can specify the listed switches. **CHKDSK** requires the **AUTOCHK.EXE** file. **CHKDSK** automatically locates **AUTOCHK.EXE** in the startup (boot) directory. If it cannot be found in the startup directory, **CHKDSK** attempts to locate the Windows installation CD. If the installation CD cannot be found, **CHKDSK** prompts for the location of **AUTOCHK.EXE**.
CLS	Clear the screen.	**CLS**
COPY	Copy a single file to another location.	**COPY** *source* [*destination*] *source* Specifies the file to be copied. *destination* Specifies the directory and filename for the new file. The *source* can be removable media, any directory within the system directories of the current Windows installation, the root of any drive, the local installation sources, or the **cmdcons** directory. The *destination* can be any directory within the system directories of the current Windows installation, the root of any drive, the local installation sources, or the **cmdcons** directory. The *destination* cannot be removable media. If a *destination* is not specified, it defaults to the current directory. **COPY** does not support replaceable parameters (wildcards). **COPY** prompts if the destination file already exists. A compressed file from the Windows installation CD is automatically decompressed as it is copied.
DEL (DELETE)	Delete one or more files.	**DEL** [*drive:*][*path*]*filename* [*drive:*][*path*]*filename* Specifies the file to delete. **DELETE** operates only within the system directories of the current Windows installation, removable media, the root directory of any hard disk partition, or the local installation sources.

Table 8.2	Recovery Console Commands *(continued)*	
Command	**Function**	**Syntax and Options**
DIR	Display a list of files and subdirectories in a directory.	**DIR** [*drive*:][*path*][*filename*] [*drive*:][*path*][*filename*] Specifies drive, directory, and files to list. **DIR** lists all files, including hidden and system files. Files can have the following attributes: **D** Directory **R** Read-only **H** Hidden file **A** Files ready for archiving **S** System file **C** Compressed **E** Encrypted **P** Reparse point **DIR** operates only within the system directories of the current Windows installation, removable media, the root directory of any hard disk partition, or the local installation sources.
DISABLE	Disable a system service or device driver.	**DISABLE** *servicename* *servicename* The name of the service or driver to be disabled. **DISABLE** prints the old *start_type* of the service before resetting it to **SERVICE_DISABLED**. You should make a note of the old *start_type*, in case you need to enable the service again. The *start_type* values that the **DISABLE** command displays are **SERVICE_DISABLED** **SERVICE_BOOT_START** **SERVICE_SYSTEM_START** **SERVICE_AUTO_START** **SERVICE_DEMAND_START**
DISKPART	Manage partitions on your hard drive.	**DISKPART** [/ADD|/DELETE] [*device-name*| *drive-name*|*partition-name*] [*size*] **/ADD** Creates a new partition. **/DELETE** Deletes an existing partition. *device-name* Device name for creating a new partition. You can get the name from the output of the **MAP** command.

Table 8.2	Recovery Console Commands *(continued)*	
Command	**Function**	**Syntax and Options**
		An example of a good device name is **\Device\HardDisk0**.
		drive-name A drive letter-based name for deleting an existing partition.
		An example of a good drive name is **D:**.
		partition-name A partition-based name for deleting an existing partition; can be used in place of the *drive-name* argument.
		An example of a good partition name is **\Device\HardDisk0\Partition1**.
		Note: If you use the **DISKPART** command with no arguments, a user interface for managing your partitions appears.
ENABLE	Enable a system service or device driver.	**ENABLE** *servicename* [*start_type*]
		servicename The name of the service or driver to be enabled.
		start_type Valid values are
		SERVICE_BOOT_START
		SERVICE_SYSTEM_START
		SERVICE_AUTO_START
		SERVICE_DEMAND_START
		ENABLE prints the old *start_type* of the service before resetting it to the new value. You should make a note of the old value, in case it is necessary to restore the *start_type* of the service.
		If you do not specify a new *start_type*, **ENABLE** prints the old *start_type* for you.
		The *start_type* values that the **DISABLE** command displays are
		SERVICE_DISABLED
		SERVICE_BOOT_START
		SERVICE_SYSTEM_START
		SERVICE_AUTO_START
		SERVICE_DEMAND_START
EXIT	Exit Recovery Console and re-start the computer.	**EXIT**

Table 8.2	Recovery Console Commands *(continued)*	
Command	**Function**	**Syntax and Options**
EXPAND	Expand a compressed file.	**EXPAND** *source* [/F:*filespec*] [*destination*] [/Y] **EXPAND** *source* [/F:*filespec*] /D *source* Specifies the file to be expanded. May not include wildcards. *destination* Specifies the directory for the new file. Default is the current directory. /Y Do not prompt before overwriting an existing file. /F:*filespec* If the source contains more than one file, this parameter is required to identify the specific files to be expanded. May include wildcards. /D Do not expand; only display a directory of the files that are contained in the source. The *destination* may be any directory within the system directories of the current Windows installation, the root of any drive, the local installation sources, or the **cmdcons** directory. The destination cannot be removable media. The *destination* file cannot be read-only. Use the **ATTRIB** command to remove the read-only attribute. **EXPAND** prompts if the destination file already exists unless /Y is used.
FIXBOOT	Write a new boot sector onto the system partition.	**FIXBOOT** [*drive*:] [*drive*:] Specifies the drive to which a boot sector will be written, overriding the default choice of the system boot partition. **FIXBOOT** is supported only on x86-based computers.
FIXMBR	Repair the master boot record of the partition boot sector.	**FIXMBR** [*device-name*] *device-name* Optional name that specifies the device that will be updated with a new master boot record (MBR). If this is left blank, then the boot device is used. **FIXMBR** is supported only on x86-based computers.
FORMAT	Format a disk.	**FORMAT** [*drive*:] [/Q] [/FS:*file-system*] [*drive*:] Specifies the drive to format. /Q Performs a quick format. /FS:*file-system* Specifies the file system to use (**FAT**, **FAT32**, or **NTFS**).

Table 8.2	Recovery Console Commands *(continued)*	
Command	**Function**	**Syntax and Options**
HELP	Display list of Recovery Console commands.	**HELP**
LISTSVC	List all available services and drivers on the computer.	**LISTSVC**
LOGON	Log onto the Recovery Console for a different installation of Windows Server 2003 on the same computer.	**LOGON**
MAP	Display drive letter mappings.	**MAP [arc]** The **arc** parameter tells MAP to use ARC paths instead of Windows device paths.
MD (MKDIR)	Create a directory.	**MD [*drive*:]*path*** **MD** operates only within the system directories of the current Windows installation, removable media, the root directory of any hard disk partition, or the local installation sources.
MORE	Display a text file to screen.	**MORE *filename*** or **TYPE *filename***
RD (RMDIR)	Remove a directory.	**RD [*drive*:]*path*** **RD** operates only within the system directories of the current Windows installation, removable media, the root directory of any hard disk partition, or the local installation sources.
REN (RENAME)	Rename a single file.	**REN [*drive*:][*path*]*filename1 filename2*** You cannot specify a new drive or path for your destination file. **RENAME** operates only within the system directories of the current Windows installation, removable media, the root directory of any hard disk partition, or the local installation sources.
SYSTEMROOT	Set the current folder to the **systemroot** folder.	**SYSTEMROOT**
TYPE	Display a text file to screen.	**TYPE *filename***

The Automated System Recovery Feature

Automated System Recovery (ASR) is a new feature in Windows XP and Windows Server 2003. ASR is integrated within the Windows Backup Utility (NTBackup.exe), and you can use it to recover a system that does not start. You can think of it as a system restore CD that commonly ships with many new OEM computers from vendors such as Dell, HP, and IBM. The ASR has two parts—backup and recovery. Restoring an ASR backup brings the server back to the state at the point in time when the ASR set was originally created. Whenever you perform an operation that is potentially damaging to the operating system (installing service packs, driver upgrades, hardware upgrades, and so on), consider creating an ASR backup set. If anything goes wrong, you can quickly restore the server back to its original configuration without much trouble.

 Note that *ASR only saves the Windows Server 2003 operating-system configuration!* It saves the system state, system services, and the operating-system components, but it *does not back up any user data files.* Any data files that are stored on the operating-system drive volume (**%systemdrive%**) are destroyed during an ASR restore. ASR creates a boot floppy, which contains backup information and disk configuration settings. ASR gives administrators the ability to quickly reinstall Windows Server 2003, if necessary, with all the required drivers already in place. You can then perform a restore operation from a full system backup, if needed.

Creating an ASR Backup Set

You must use the Windows Server 2003 Backup Utility to create ASR backup sets. You cannot perform an ASR restore unless you have first created an ASR backup set. It's a good idea to periodically create updated ASR backup sets to ensure that the ASR backup is as current as possible should you ever need to use it. Complete the following steps to create an ASR backup setup:

1. Click Start, (All) Programs, Accessories, System Tools, Backup.

2. Click the Advanced Mode link on the Welcome window.

3. Click the Automated System Recovery button on the Backup Utility Advanced Mode page to start the ASR Wizard.

4. Click Next for the Welcome to the Automated System Recovery Preparation Wizard window.

5. Select the Backup Media Type in the drop-down list box and then select the backup media or type the backup file name in the dialog box on the Backup Destination page (see Figure 8.4).

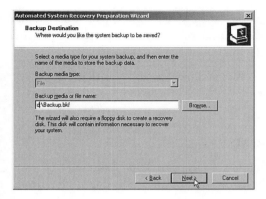

Figure 8.4 Selecting the backup destination using the ASR Wizard.

6. Click Next. If you are backing up to file, make sure not to store the backup file on the same drive as the operating system (usually the `c:\` drive).

7. Click Finish to complete the media backup portion of the ASR backup procedure. After the ASR media backup finishes, you are prompted to create a boot disk to complete the ASR backup (see Figure 8.5). Make sure to label the disk with the backup filename, creation date, and time.

Figure 8.5 Creating the boot floppy for ASR.

The ASR backup procedure actually generates a shadow copy to create a snapshot of the necessary operating-system information. During the restore process, ASR formats the operating-system drive volume and then copies the original default operating-system files onto it. You must have your ASR backup files stored somewhere other than the system partition. *If you save the ASR backup file on the* ***%systemdrive%*** *volume (usually the* ***C:*** *drive) and later perform an ASR restore, it will fail because ASR will format the* ***%systemdrive%*** *volume and destroy your ASR backup file.*

Restoring a Server Using ASR

Use the ASR to restore the entire operating system on a server that does not start. *When you restore a backup set using ASR, the system will format and destroy any data contained on the operating-system drive, referenced by the system environment variable* `%systemdrive%`*!* (This drive volume is usually drive `c:\`.) Any other drive volumes on the server that do not contain operating-system files are not formatted. ASR only restores the operating system and related files.

If you have any other data on the operating system drive, you will lose this data and will have to restore the data from another backup method. To use an ASR restore set, you must have the following:

➤ An ASR backup set created as a file on a hard disk (other than the system volume) or on a backup tape.

➤ Floppy disk created by the ASR.

➤ Windows Server 2003 CD-ROM.

➤ Optional, but highly recommended: a recent backup of all non-operating–system data files that are stored on the operating system drive (usually c:).

 If you have a tape drive or other mass-storage device where the ASR backup set was created, and, if its device driver is not included on the Windows Server 2003 CD-ROM, make sure to have this driver available on a floppy disk or some other accessible location. Without the driver, your ASR restore process will fail because Windows will not be able to read the data on the device.

Assuming you have all the necessary components for an ASR restore, you can begin the restore process. To restore an ASR backup set, complete the following steps:

1. Insert the Windows Server 2003 CD-ROM into the CD-ROM drive.

2. Restart the server. If prompted, press a key to boot from the CD.

3. If you have a third-party SCSI or RAID driver, press the F6 key, when prompted.

4. Press the F2 key to run the ASR restore, when prompted.

5. Insert the ASR disk into the disk drive and press any key on the keyboard. The ASR restore loads the necessary files to restore your operating system.

6. If you installed a third-party SCSI or RAID driver, press the F6 key again, when prompted, after the system restarts.

7. When the server reboots, remove the ASR disk, but leave the Windows Server 2003 CD in the drive (see Figure 8.6). When the server reboots, make sure the server does not start from the CD.

8. If you installed a third-party SCSI or RAID driver, after the system restarts, press the F6 key when prompted.

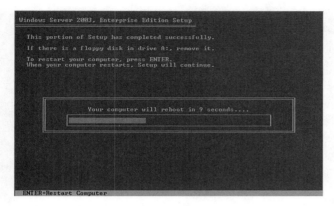

Figure 8.6   Restarting the computer after the character-based phase of an ASR restore.

9. When prompted, select the backup file that you want to restore from the Data Recovery Source window. The ASR Wizard then displays a summary window listing the ASR restore settings (see Figure 8.7).

Figure 8.7   Viewing the ASR Wizard summary window before launching the media restore using the Windows Backup Utility.

10. Click Finish to begin the ASR restore using the Windows Backup Utility media. After this restore procedure is complete, the system will restart.

The ASR floppy disk that gets created contains three files—**asr.sif**, **asrpnp.sif**, and **setup.log**. If you misplace the ASR floppy disk, you can use the Windows Server 2003 Backup Utility on a different Windows Server 2003 computer to restore the **asr.sif** and **asrpnp.sif** files from the ASR media backup set onto a blank floppy disk. You can then use that floppy disk as the ASR floppy disk during the ASR restore operation.

Emergency Management Services

Emergency Management Services (EMS) is a new feature in Windows Server 2003. EMS allows an administrator to perform remote management and system recovery tasks when the server is not available. It includes support for headless servers and out-of-band management. Headless servers are servers that do not have a local keyboard, mouse, and video monitor directly connected to the server. Out-of-band management support allows an administrator to remotely access a server though a connection other than the normal network (Ethernet) connection or system console. Typically, you perform out-of-band management via a modem or serial port.

Out-of-Band Management

Out-of-band management is useful when the server is not accessible via the regular network port or the system console. The primary goal of out-of-band management is to restore the state of the server to a point where you can use in-band management. The functionality of EMS is partially dependent upon the hardware or firmware support of the server where EMS is installed. The server must support Serial Port Console Redirection (SPCR) for EMS to work. Check with your server vendor to verify the extent of SPCR support. SPCR redirects video output to and accepts keyboard input from a serial port. The server is remotely accessed via terminal emulation (VT100, VT100+, and VT-UTF8 terminal emulation modes are supported) through two consoles: Special Administration Console (SAC) and !Special Administration Console (!SAC).

EMS with New Installations of Windows Server 2003

If your server supports SPCR, EMS is enabled by default during the installation of Windows Server 2003. EMS configures itself by reading the settings in the SPCR table. At the end of the text mode setup, you are prompted to allow setup to automatically configure your system with no user intervention (using unattend.txt and winnt.sif files) or to enter the GUI mode setup. For more information on unattend.txt, winnt.sif, and Remote Installation Services (RIS), refer to http://support.microsoft.com/default. aspx?scid=kb;en-us;308662.

The unattend.txt and winnt.sif files are necessary to perform a remote installation of Windows Server 2003. You can change two EMS parameters in these files to modify the behavior of EMS. These parameters appear in Table 8.3.

Table 8.3 EMS Parameters in **unattend.txt** and **winnt.sif** Files	
[Data] Parameter	**Possible Values**
EMSPort={com1|com2|useBiosSettings}	**Com**x (where x specifies serial port 1 or 2). This option is valid for x86-based systems only.
	UseBiosSettings instructs the operating system to detect firmware that supports EMS and uses SPCR settings. If an SPCR table is not present, EMS is not enabled, which is the default setting for Advanced Configuration and Power Interface (ACPI) systems.
EMSBaudRate=_value_	9600 baud is the default, with other values of 19200, 57600, and 115200 possible, depending on the capabilities of the serial port. You must use this parameter with **EMSPort=,** or the parameter is ignored.

EMS with Existing Installations of Windows Server 2003

On x86-based systems, you can also enable, configure, or disable EMS on an existing Windows Server 2003 computer using the BOOTCFG command. The bootcfg.exe command allows you to add or change the EMS headless redirection settings for EMS. Table 8.4 displays the list of available commands that appear when you type the command bootcfg /ems /?.

Table 8.4 Available EMS Command-Line Options for **bootcfg.exe**		
Parameter List	**Value**	**Description**
/EMS	_value_	**ON**, **OFF**, **EDIT**
		Note: **EDIT** changes the current settings, you cannot use **/ID** with **EDIT**.
/S	_system_	Specifies the remote system to connect to.
/U	[_domain_]_user_	Specifies the user context under which the command should execute.
/P	[_password_]	Specifies the password for the given user context. Prompts for input if omitted.
/PORT	_port_	Specifies the COM port for redirection. Valid ports are **COM1**, **COM2**, **COM3**, **COM4**, and **BIOSSET** (EMS uses BIOS settings).

Table 8.4	Available EMS Command-Line Options for **bootcfg.exe** *(continued)*	
Parameter List	**Value**	**Description**
/BAUD	*baudrate*	Specifies the baud rate for redirection. Valid baud rates are **9600**, **19200**, **57600**, and **115200**.
/ID	**Booted**	Specifies the boot entry ID to add the EMS option. This parameter is required when the EMS value is **ON** or **OFF**.

The /ID switch is required for the /EMS ON or /EMS OFF options. The following examples show how you can use bootcfg.exe with the /EMS ON or /EMS OFF command-line options for enabling or disabling EMS and specifying the boot entry identifier:

➤ BOOTCFG /EMS ON /PORT COM1 /BAUD 19200 /ID 1

➤ BOOTCFG /EMS ON /PORT BIOSSET /ID 3

➤ BOOTCFG /EMS OFF /S *system* /ID 2

➤ BOOTCFG /EMS EDIT /PORT com2 /BAUD 115200

➤ BOOTCFG /EMS OFF /S *system* /U *domain\user* /P *password* /ID 2

Special Administration Console

The Special Administration Console (SAC) is a set of command-line utilities that allows you to perform out-of-band management for a Windows Server 2003 computer. The SAC is the primary interface for EMS. Table 8.5 lists some of the available SAC commands.

Table 8.5	SAC Commands
Command	**Description**
ch	Lists all channels.
Cmd	Creates Windows command-prompt channels. To use a command-prompt channel, you must provide valid logon credentials. You must log on to each command-prompt instance.
Crashdump	Manually generates a Stop error message and forces a memory dump file to be created.
restart	Restarts the computer.
S	If no parameters are passed, this command displays the current date using the 24-hour clock format. You can set the system time by providing the date and, optionally, the time in this format: *mm/dd/yyyy hh:mm*.

Table 8.5	SAC Commands *(continued)*
Command	**Description**
shutdown	Shuts down the computer. Do not use this command unless you can be physically present at the computer when you are ready to restart it.
T	Lists the processes and threads that are currently running.
? or **help**	Lists the available commands.

!Special Administration Console

The !Special Administration Console (!SAC) is separate from both the SAC and Windows Server 2003 command-line utilities. You should use it when the SAC is unavailable. !SAC contains a subset of the SAC command-line options. Some of the available !SAC commands appear in Table 8.6.

Table 8.6	!SAC Commands
Command	**Description**
restart	Restarts the server immediately.
D	Displays all log entries (screen pauses at each page of information).
Id	Displays computer identification.
Q	Quits !SAC and resumes normal out-of-band port operation.
? or **Help**	Lists available commands.

Summary of Disaster Recovery Options

Windows Server 2003 offers you several options for restoring data files and troubleshooting server startup problems. You should create an ASR backup set after you complete the installation and configuration of every Windows Server 2003 computer. You should also create a new, updated ASR backup set prior to making any major OS, hardware, service pack, or device driver changes to the system. Make sure not to save the ASR backup file on the same drive as the operating system, if you don't save the ASR backup to tape or some other media besides a local disk. To fully leverage ASR, only store operating-system files on the system drive volume (%systemdrive%).

Administrators and users can restore data using the shadow copies of shared folders feature along with the Previous Versions Client software that you can install only on Windows XP and Windows Server 2003 computers. If a file is corrupted, damaged, or accidentally deleted, you can use shadow copies to restore the file. You must properly configure shadow copies on a Windows Server 2003 computer and install the Previous Version Client on a workstation to access the shadow copy versions of files. The following list details the different disaster recovery techniques that you can choose when a Windows Server 2003 computer does not restart.

➤ *Boot the server using a startup disk*—You should create a startup boot disk after Windows Server 2003 is finalized and prior to any startup problems. In general, the startup disk only works if `boot.ini`, `ntdetect.com`, `ntldr`, or the MBR is damaged on the server, but the hard disk that contains the Windows Server 2003 operating system files must be available.

➤ *Boot the server using Safe Mode*—Use this option when you suspect that the server is not booting because of a recently installed program, service pack, or driver.

➤ *Boot the server using Safe Mode with Networking Support*—Use this option to verify that networking components are working properly.

➤ *Boot the server using Safe Mode with Command Prompt*—This option gives you a command-prompt–only environment. Use this option if the other Safe Mode options fail to start the server.

➤ *Boot the server using the Last Known Good Configuration*—Use this option after trying all of the Safe Mode options. Booting with this option might return the server to an earlier state than anticipated, so be careful.

➤ *Boot the Recovery Console*—Use this option after trying the Last Known Good Configuration. The Recovery Console is especially useful for copying files to a local drive. You can also use it to access NTFS volumes and partitions from previous Windows Server versions, such as Windows NT and Windows 2000.

➤ *Use the EMS SAC and !SAC utilities*—Use these options to restore the server to a point where you can use in-band management. Use these features if the server does not start or if you do not have local or network access to the server. Make sure that EMS is properly configured and that your hardware supports console redirection *before* you use these techniques.

➤ *Perform an ASR restore*—Use this option as a last resort. An ASR restore destroys all files on the operating-system drive volume (`%systemdrive%`). It only restores operating-system files, not data files. Make sure you have an ASR backup set, the Windows Server 2003 CD-ROM, and the ASR-created disk *prior* to attempting an ASR restore.

Exam Prep Questions

Question 1

> Which one of the following is not true about shadow copies? (Choose two.)
>
> ❑ A. Shadow copies can create a backup of files at scheduled intervals.
>
> ❑ B. You can directly access shadow copies on Windows Server 2003 without Common Internet File Sharing (CIFS).
>
> ❑ C. To access shadow copies from a workstation, you must have a Previous Version Client installed on the workstation.
>
> ❑ D. You can view shadow copies of a file under the Previous Versions tab of a file's properties sheet.
>
> ❑ E. You can store shadow copies on a Windows 2000 Server computer.

Answers B and E are correct. To access shadow copies on Windows Server 2003, you must access the data files using CIFS. You must store shadow copies on Windows Server 2003 or higher; shadow copies are not available on Windows 2000 Server. Answer A is incorrect because shadow copies can create backups of files at scheduled intervals. Answer C is incorrect because you must install the Previous Versions Client to access shadow copy files from a workstation. Answer D is incorrect because you can view a file's previous versions from its properties sheet.

Question 2

> When will booting a Windows Server computer from a startup disk not work?
>
> ○ A. When the **boot.ini** file is corrupted
>
> ○ B. When the boot hard drive that stores the operating-system files has a hardware failure
>
> ○ C. When the **ntdetect.com** file is corrupted
>
> ○ D. When the **ntldr** file is corrupted
>
> ○ E. When the CD-ROM drive is not working

Answer B is correct. To use a Windows Server 2003 startup disk, the hard drive that stores the operating-system files must be functioning. Answer A is incorrect because a startup disk can normally boot the server when the boot.ini file is corrupted. Answer C is incorrect because a startup disk can normally boot the server when the ntdetect.com file is corrupted. Answer D is incorrect because a startup disk can normally boot the server when the ntldr file is corrupted. Answer E is incorrect because a startup disk does not use the CD-ROM during the boot process.

Question 3

What strategies can you use to troubleshoot a server that does not start properly? (Choose four.)

❑ A.   Use a Windows Server 2003 startup disk to try to boot the server.

❑ B.   Use Safe Mode to try to start the server.

❑ C.   Perform an Automated System Recovery (ASR) backup.

❑ D.   Implement shadow copies on the server.

❑ E.   Use the Last Known Good Configuration to try to start the server.

❑ F.   Run the Recovery Console on the server and run the **DISABLE** command to prevent a service from loading upon startup.

❑ G.   Install the Previous Versions software on the server.

Answers A, B, E, and F are correct. A Windows Server 2003 Startup disk can start a server that has a damaged boot.ini, ntdetect.com, or ntldr file or damaged master boot record. All Safe Modes are useful to troubleshoot server startup problems. Using the Last Known Good Configuration can start a server when the last successful logon is a good configuration. Using the Recovery Console to disable one or more services that might be preventing Windows Server 2003 from starting is a valid method for troubleshooting server startup problems. Answer C is incorrect because performing an ASR backup cannot be done on a server that will not start; performing an ASR restore would help, however. Answer D is incorrect because shadow copies allow users to restore files when the server is up and running. Answer G is incorrect because the Previous Versions software only serves to restore data files from shared folders stored on drive volumes where shadows copies are enabled.

Question 4

Which of the following commands will format the operating-system drive? Assume that the operating system drive is **C:** (Choose two.)

❑ A.   The Recovery Console using the command **format c:**

❑ B.   Booting the server using a Windows Server 2003 startup floppy disk

❑ C.   Using the Last Known Good Configuration to start the server

❏ D. Using Safe Mode to start the server

❏ E. Restoring a file from a shadow copy

❏ F. An ASR restore

Answers A and F are correct. The format c: command formats the operating-system drive, and an ASR restore formats the operating-system drive as part of the restore process. Answer B is incorrect because booting the server with a startup floppy disk does not format the operating-system drive. Answer C is incorrect because booting the server using the Last Known Good Configuration startup option does not format the operating-system drive. Answer D is incorrect because booting the server using Safe Mode does not format the operating-system drive. Answer E is incorrect because restoring a file from a shadow copy version does not format the operating-system drive.

Question 5

Which of the following is not true about the Recovery Console? (Choose two.)

❏ A. The Recovery Console can be preinstalled and run directly from the hard drive.

❏ B. You can run the Recovery Console from the Windows Server 2003 CD-ROM.

❏ C. The Recovery Console does not enforce NTFS permissions.

❏ D. The Recovery Console can repair a boot sector on the hard drive with the **FIXBOOT** command.

❏ E. The Recovery Console command **LISTSVC** lists all available services and drivers running on the computer.

❏ F. You must install the Recovery Console to perform an ASR restore.

Answers C and F are correct. The Recovery Console does enforce NTFS permissions, and you can perform an ASR restore without first installing the Recovery Console. Answer A is incorrect because it is true that the Recovery Console can be preinstalled and run directly from the hard drive. Answer B is incorrect because it is true that you can run the Recovery Console from the Windows Server 2003 CD-ROM. Answer D is incorrect because it is true that the Recovery Console can repair a boot sector on the hard drive with the FIXBOOT command. Answer E is incorrect because it is true that the Recovery Console command LISTSVC lists all available services and drivers running on the computer.

Question 6

Which of the following will prevent a successful ASR restore? (Choose three.)

☐ A. Storing the ASR Backup file on the same drive as the operating system

☐ B. Losing the ASR floppy disk

☐ C. A boot-sector virus on the operating system drive

☐ D. A failed CD-ROM drive

☐ E. A missing or damaged **ntdetect.com** file on the operating-system drive volume

☐ F. A missing **ntldr** file on the operating-system drive

Answers A, B, and D are correct. If you store the ASR backup file on the operating-system drive, you will be unable to complete the ASR process because an ASR restore formats the operating-system drive as part of the ASR restore process. If you do not have the ASR floppy, or an ASR floppy disk that you created by restoring the files from backup media, you cannot start the ASR restore process. The ASR restore procedure copies files from the Windows Server 2003 CD-ROM to complete the restore process, so you must have the CD available. Answer C is incorrect because an ASR restore formats the operating-system drive; therefore, it does not matter what is currently contained on the drive before the ASR restore starts. Answer E is incorrect because a missing or damaged ntdetect.com file does not affect an ASR restore. Answer F is incorrect because a missing ntldr file does not affect an ASR restore.

Question 7

Which of the following utilities can you use to restart a server remotely? (Choose two.)

☐ A. Use the restart command in the SAC under EMS.

☐ B. Use the restart command in the Recovery Console.

☐ C. Use the restart command with shadow copies.

☐ D. Use the restart command in ASR during the restore process.

☐ E. Use the restart command in the !SAC under EMS.

Answers A and E are correct. Answer B is incorrect because you cannot perform remote management using the Recovery Console, and there is no restart command in the Recovery Console. Answer C is incorrect because there is no restart command with the shadow copies of shared folders feature. Answer D is incorrect because there is no restart command in ASR restore process.

Question 8

> Which communication channels can you use to perform out-of-band management on a headless server under EMS? (Choose two.)
>
> ❑ A. Primary network connection
> ❑ B. Serial port
> ❑ C. Modem
> ❑ D. USB port
> ❑ E. Parallel port (lpt)
> ❑ F. SCSI port

Answers B and C are correct. Both serial ports and modems are supported in Windows Server 2003 for remote out-of-band management. Answer A is incorrect because managing a server with a primary network connection is considered in-band management. Answers D and E are incorrect because USB ports and parallel ports (lpt) are not supported for out-of-band management. Answer F is incorrect because SCSI ports are not supported for out-of-band management.

Question 9

> Which one of the following commands do you use to enable console redirection for EMS?
>
> ○ A. **Bootcfg /EMS UseBiosSettings** in the !SAC
> ○ B. Safe Mode with Command Prompt issuing the **bootcfg /InstallEMS** command
> ○ C. **Bootcfg /EMS UseBiosSettings** in the Recovery Console
> ○ D. **Bootcfg /EMS UseBiosSettings** in the SAC
> ○ E. Safe Mode with Networking Support issuing the **bootcfg /InstallEMS** command
> ○ F. Safe mode issuing the **bootcfg /InstallEMS** command

Answer C is correct. Answer A is incorrect because there is no `bootcfg` command in either the SAC or !SAC consoles. Answer B is incorrect because there is no `/InstallEMS` option with the `bootcfg` command. Answer D is incorrect because there is no `bootcfg` command in either the SAC or !SAC consoles. Answers E and F are incorrect because there is no `bootcfg /InstallEMS` command under Safe Mode.

Question 10

Which Safe Mode option should you use when the other Safe Mode options fail?

○ A. Safe Mode

○ B. Safe Mode with Command Prompt

○ C. Safe Mode with Networking Support

○ D. Safe Mode with EMS Support

○ E. Safe Mode with SAC Support

Answer B is correct. The Safe Mode with Command Prompt option only starts the command-line utilities. Answers A and C are incorrect because these two Safe Mode options require more resources to start than the Safe Mode with Command Prompt option. Answers D and E are incorrect because there is no Safe Mode option with EMS or SAC support.

Need to Know More?

Boswell, William. *Inside Windows Server 2003*. Boston, Massachusetts: Addison-Wesley, 2003.

Honeycutt, Jerry. *Introducing Microsoft Windows Server 2003*. Redmond, Washington: Microsoft Press, 2003.

Jones, Don, and Mark Rouse. *Microsoft Windows Server 2003 Delta Guide*. Indianapolis, Indiana: SAMS Publishing, 2003.

Search the Microsoft Product Support Services Knowledge Base on the Internet: `http://support.microsoft.com`. You can also search Microsoft TechNet on the Internet: `http://www.microsoft.com/technet`. Find technical information using keywords from this chapter, such as Shadow Copies of Shared Folders, Safe Mode, Automated System Recovery, Emergency Management Services, Recovery Console, and Last Known Good Configuration.

Data Backup Techniques and Procedures

. . . .

Terms you'll need to understand:

✓ The Windows Backup Utility
✓ **NTBackup.exe**
✓ Copy backups
✓ Daily backups
✓ Normal backups
✓ Incremental backups
✓ Differential backups

✓ System State backups
✓ **NTDSUTIL.exe**
✓ Primary restores
✓ Authoritative restores
✓ Nonauthoritative restores
✓ Directory Services Restore Mode

Techniques you'll need to master:

✓ Performing different types of backups
✓ Performing a restore operation
✓ Verifying backup jobs
✓ Backing up the System State
✓ Restoring the System State
✓ Scheduling automatic backups
✓ Managing backup storage media

✓ Performing backups from the command line
✓ Using the **NTDSUTIL** command-line tool
✓ Performing primary restores
✓ Performing authoritative restores
✓ Performing nonauthoritative restores
✓ Using Directory Services Restore Mode

The process of backing up valuable data files and folders simply involves copying that data to one or more different locations where you can retrieve it later, if you need it. You might need to restore data from backup because of a hardware failure or because someone accidentally or intentionally ruins or deletes some data. Reliable, up-to-date backups of user and system data are the cornerstone of any sound data protection and preservation policy. Numerous third-party data backup products on the market offer all sorts of fancy features, but the Windows Backup Utility does a fine job of safeguarding and restoring server data, as long as you use it properly. In this chapter, you'll look at how to properly use the built-in backup tool that ships with Windows Server 2003. You'll explore the different types of backup routines that you can implement and what impact those backup procedures have on restoring server data. You'll also learn how to schedule server backups and how to recover the Active Directory database on a domain controller (DC) and mark it as authoritative.

Managing Backup Procedures

How frequently you need to back up your organization's data depends on how often it gets updated and how important that data is to the organization. Which data should get backed up is an easier question: If you or someone in the company needs the information that certain data files contain, or if you need it for archival or legal purposes, it needs to get backed up. For these reasons, most organizations employ consistent, regularly scheduled backup operations for all computers that store valuable data. The new Shadow Copies of Shared Folders feature is a nice way to supplement regular backup procedures, but shadow copies should never be a replacement for a regularly scheduled backup routine. Shadow Copies of Shared Folders is covered in both Chapter 5, "Managing Network Resources and Terminal Services," and Chapter 8, "Disaster Recovery Techniques and Procedures."

 It's always a good idea to set up a rotating system for server data backups. Your organization might want or need data backups to be maintained over a period of several weeks or more. At a minimum, keep at least one week's worth of backups before overwriting previous backup sets. Keeping at least two weeks' worth of previous backup sets is an even better idea. In addition, you might want to archive data by taking a backup set out of the normal rotation and keeping it in a safe location, off the premises. You might decide to keep one backup set per month as an archive so that you can retrieve older data after several months, if necessary. Keeping recent backups offsite as part of your normal backup rotation is a very important thing to do. Catastrophes such as fire, theft, acts of nature, or acts of violence can completely destroy an entire data center; offsite backups provide invaluable insurance against such unexpected events.

Backing Up Data Files

The Windows Server 2003 Backup Utility offers several different types of backups that you can use for backing up data files. The various types of backups determine which files get backed up and whether each backed-up file's archive bit gets cleared (turned off) or left alone. Each and every file stored on Windows– and MS-DOS–based computers retains at least four attributes that you can manipulate: R (Read-Only), S (System), H (Hidden), and A (Archive). The archive attribute (or bit) specifies whether the file has been modified since that last backup or since the last time the archive bit was cleared. Both normal backups and incremental backups clear (turns off) the archive bit for each file that gets backed up. As soon as a file that was previously backed up (archive bit off) gets modified, its archive bit gets set (turned on) to indicate that the file needs to be backed up again because its data has changed. The Windows Backup Utility offers five backup types to choose from when you perform a data backup:

➤ *Normal*—All files that are selected for backup are backed up and each backed-up file's archive bit is cleared.

➤ *Copy*—This setting backs up all selected files, but each backed-up file's archive bit is not changed; files that have their archive bits set remain that way. In this way, a copy backup that is performed will not interfere with your regular backup procedures, but it allows you to back up your files onto a tape (or other media), which will not be included with your normal backup sets. This procedure is often used to produce month-end or year-end data archives.

➤ *Differential*—This setting only backs up files that have their archive bits set (turned on) to indicate that they have been modified since the last normal or incremental backup. Each backed-up file's archive bit is not changed; in this way, you can perform other types of backups on these files at a later time.

➤ *Incremental*—This setting only backs up files that have their archive bits set (turned on) to indicate that they have been modified since the last normal or incremental backup. However, each backed-up file's archive bit is cleared (turned off) to indicate that it has been backed up.

➤ *Daily*—This setting only backs up files that have been modified or created on the same day as the backup is run (today). Each backed-up file's archive bit is not changed. Daily backups can be convenient when you are performing normal backups each night, but you want to have some added insurance by creating a backup set that contains all the data that was modified during the current day. Before you do something to the server such as add memory or install one or more additional hard drives, you can run a daily backup fairly quickly as compared to a normal backup. If all goes well, you can discard the daily backup; if things don't go so well, you have the daily backup to restore from in addition to your regularly scheduled backups.

NOTE Be sure that no NT File System (NTFS) disk quotas are in effect for the users responsible for backing up data on the server's drive volumes. NTFS disk quotas can prohibit backup operations by restricting a user's access to a drive volume. Chapter 5 discusses NTFS disk quotas.

To back up server data, you must be logged on to the computer as a member of the Backup Operators group, a member of the Server Operators group (in a domain environment), or a member of the Administrators group. From the Backup Utility, you can back up files and folders that are stored on the local computer, or you can back up files and folders that are stored on remote computers over the network, assuming that the user account you are logged on with has the proper permissions for backing up the remote computer. To perform a data backup, follow these steps:

1. Click Start, (All) Programs, Accessories, System Tools, Backup, or click Start, Run; type `NTBackup.exe`; and click OK.

2. At the Welcome to the Backup or Restore Wizard window, click the Advanced Mode link to switch to Advanced Mode. (The default is Wizard Mode.)

3. From the Welcome tab (in Advanced Mode), click the Backup tab instead of using the Backup Wizard (Advanced) for even more control over the backup process.

4. From the Backup tab, expand the drive volumes to select the folders and files that you want to back up (see Figure 9.1). Marking a check box for a parent container automatically selects all child objects within the container. You can select local drives, mapped network drives, and network shared folders on remote computers without local drive letter mappings.

5. From the drop-down list box, select the Backup Destination—such as tape or file. Backup files get the filename extension `.bkf`, as in `backup.bkf`. Be sure not to back up to a file stored on the same server as the server that you are backing up, or else copy the backup file to different media or to a network location immediately after the backup finishes.

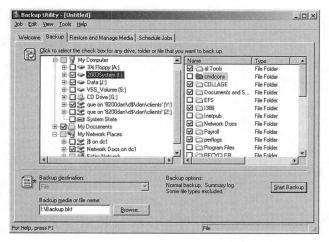

Figure 9.1 Selecting files to be backed up with the Windows Server 2003 Backup Utility.

6. If backing up to a file, type the full path and filename, or click Browse to navigate to a location for the backup file.

7. Click Start Backup to enter descriptions and choose various options for the Backup Job Information dialog box, as shown in Figure 9.2.

Figure 9.2 Adding descriptions and choosing options in the Backup Job Information dialog box.

8. Type a description in the Backup Description box or accept the default text.

9. Select either the Append This Backup to the Media option or the Replace the Data on the Media with This Backup option, if the media already has stored backups on it.

10. Type a label description in the If the Media Is Overwritten, Use This Label to Identify the Media box, or accept the default text.

11. For tape backups, you can mark the Allow Only the Owner and the Administrator Access to the Backup Data check box, if you want.

12. Click the Advanced button to configure Advanced Backup Options, as shown in Figure 9.3.

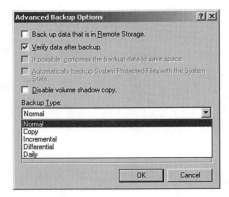

Figure 9.3 Configuring Advanced Backup Options.

13. Mark the check box labeled Back Up Data That Is in Remote Storage, if desired.

14. Mark the check box labeled Verify Data After Backup, if desired. As a best practice, you should always verify backup jobs; the default setting has Verify turned off.

15. For tape backups, you can mark the check box labeled If Possible, Compress the Backup Data to Save Space.

16. For System State backups, you can mark the Automatically Backup System Protected Files with the System State.

17. You can mark the Disable Volume Shadow Copy check box, but this move is not recommended. (See the note following these steps.)

18. Select the type of backup to perform from the Backup Type drop-down list box.

19. Click OK to save your Advanced Backup Options and return to the Backup Job Information dialog box.

20. Click the Start Backup button to begin the backup operation for this backup job. The Backup Progress window appears.

21. The Backup Utility notifies you when the backup operation is finished (see Figure 9.4).

22. You can click the Report button to view and print the Backup Report log file for the completed backup job (see Figure 9.5).

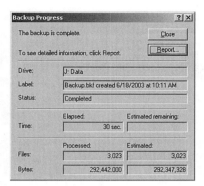

Figure 9.4   Viewing the Backup Progress window after the backup job finishes.

Figure 9.5   Viewing the Backup Status report log after the backup job finishes.

23. Close the report log (Notepad) window when you are finished viewing the report, and then click the Close button to finish the backup job.

By default, the Windows Server 2003 Backup Utility saves its backup logs to the **%systemdrive%\documents and settings\%*username*%\local settings\ application data\microsoft\windows nt\ntbackup\data** folder. The **%*username*%** folder is based on the user account under which the backup job was performed. If a backup operator runs the Backup Utility under the security credentials of a different user with the **runas** command, the backup log is saved under the **%*username*%** folder of the username used for the **runas** command. Only the last 10 backup logs are retained; older report logs are overwritten one at a time, from the oldest to the newest.

By default, Windows XP Professional and Windows Server 2003 computers first create a shadow copy of the files that you select for backup. The files are then copied (or backed up) from the shadow copy "snapshot," rather than copied directly from the files themselves. This procedure allows files that are open or locked to be backed up instead of being skipped because they cannot be backed up while they are in use.

Backing Up the System State

A computer's System State data contains most of the operating system's vital configuration settings, important databases, and critical files for Windows 2000, Windows XP, or Windows Server 2003. These vital software components include the Windows Registry, the COM+ Class Registration database, boot files and system files such as ntldr and ntdetect.com, the Certificate Services database (if the computer runs Certificate Services), the Active Directory database and the sysvol folder contents (if the computer is a DC), operating-system files that are protected by Windows File Protection, the Internet Information Services (IIS) metabase (if IIS is installed), and cluster service information (if the computer is part of a cluster).

You can only back up the System State for the local computer; you cannot remotely back up a server's System State data with the native tools. Also, you cannot select individual components of the System State to be backed up separately. You must either back up the entire System State data or none of the System State data.

As a separate operation from your full system backup procedures, you should also back up each server's System State data on a frequent and regular basis because this information is critical to the successful operation of a Windows Server 2003 computer. To back up a computer's System State, simply follow the steps outlined in the previous section, "Backing Up Data Files," and mark the System State check box as the item that you want to back up in the Windows Server 2003 Backup Utility (see Figure 9.6). You can back up the System State to tape or to a file, just like any other data backup. If you back up the System State to a file, you can copy the backup file to some other media, such as a CD-R/CD-RW or writable DVD.

Using the Windows Backup Utility from the Command Line

You can use the same executable program for the graphical Backup Utility program from the command line. You can use the NTBackup.exe program at a command prompt to run backup operations only; you cannot perform restores from the command line. You can also use NTBackup.exe in batch files to create an entirely customized backup routine that you can schedule to run at various times using the Task Scheduler and the Scheduled Tasks folder. If you type NTBackup.exe without any parameters after it, the graphical Backup Utility program runs. To see the entire list of available command-line options that you can use with NTBackup.exe, type NTBackup.exe /? at a command prompt. If you use the NTBackup.exe program at a command prompt, it only backs up entire folders. Instead, you can use wildcard characters (such as ? and *) to select groups of files to back up, such as using *.doc to indicate that all files with the .doc extension should be backed up. An example of using NTBackup.exe to back up the E: drive on the local computer, assigning the backup job name "Sample Backup of E" and using a file backup to the file named "SampleBackup.bkf" on drive N:, is NTbackup backup E: /j"Sample Backup of E" /f"N:\SampleBackup.bkf."

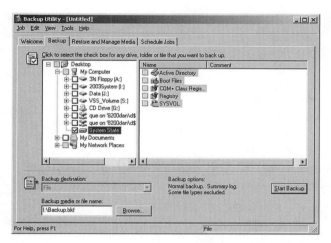

Figure 9.6   Selecting the System State check box to back up System State data.

Setting Backup Utility Defaults

You can set global default options for all backup and restore jobs using the graphical Backup Utility interface. These customizable default settings include whether to perform verifications of backup jobs; whether to replace files that already exist on the computer during a restore operation; which backup type should be the default; the level of logging that you want for backup jobs; and which files, if any, that you want excluded from all backup jobs. To configure default settings for backup and restore operations, follow these steps:

1. Run the Backup Utility in graphical Advanced Mode.

2. Click Tools, Options from the menu bar.

3. From the General tab, mark or clear the check box for each option that you want to turn on or off as a global program default. The

options on this tab include Verify Data After the Backup Completes and Back Up the Contents of Mounted Drives (see Figure 9.7).

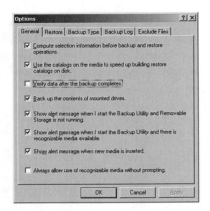

Figure 9.7   Specifying global default options from the General tab.

4. Click the Restore tab to specify which action that the Backup Utility should take when restoring a file that already exists in the same folder where the file is supposed to be restored:

   ➤ Do Not Replace the File on My Computer (Recommended).

   ➤ Replace the File on Disk Only if the File on Disk Is Older.

   ➤ Always Replace the File on My Computer.

5. Click the Backup Type tab to indicate the default backup type for backup jobs to use—normal, copy, differential, incremental, or daily.

6. Click the Backup Log tab to specify the level of logging that you want enabled by default:

   ➤ *Detailed*—Logs All Information, Including the Names of All the Files and Folders

   ➤ *Summary*—Logs Only Key Operations, Such as Loading a Tape, Starting the Backup, or Failing to Open a File

   ➤ *None*—Do Not Log

7. Click the Exclude Files tab to specify any files that you do not want backed up by default. (You can use wildcards to specify groups of files by filename extension.) Several files are already listed by default (see Figure 9.8). You can specify files to exclude from backup jobs for all users, and you can specify files to exclude from backup jobs only for members of the Administrators group. Excluded files for Administrator

users are only excluded when someone logs onto the computer as a member of the Administrators group to perform a backup.

Figure 9.8 Specifying files to exclude from backups by default for all users and for members of the Administrators group.

8. Click OK to save your global default settings.

Scheduling Backup Jobs

You can easily schedule backup jobs to run automatically at predetermined times using the graphical Backup Utility as well as by specifying the proper parameters for the NTBackup.exe program on the command line. For the Backup Utility, you can schedule a backup job to run when you create the backup job or you can click the Add Job button in the bottom-right corner of the Schedule Jobs tab to launch the Backup Wizard to set up a new scheduled backup job (see Figure 9.9).

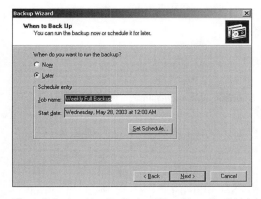

Figure 9.9 Invoking the Backup Wizard from the Add Job button on the Schedule Jobs tab.

To schedule a new backup job that you set up from the Backup tab, take these steps:

1. Follow the steps listed in the section titled "Backing Up Data Files," and click the Schedule button when you get to the Backup Job Information dialog box, after you configure any advanced backup options for the job.

2. Click Yes when you are prompted to save the backup selections. The backup job's settings are saved to a file with the .bks extension.

3. At the Set Account Information dialog box, type the user account name or accept the logged-on user account name (default), type the user account's password, and confirm the password.

4. Click OK.

5. At the Scheduled Job Options dialog box, type a name for this backup job in the Job Name box.

6. Click the Backup Details tab to view a summary of the name for this backup job, the backup device or file that is to be used, and a description of the options configured for this backup job (see Figure 9.10).

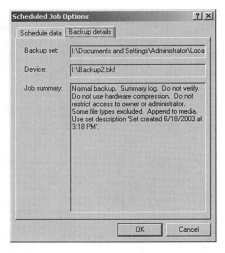

Figure 9.10 The Backup Details tab for the Scheduled Options window.

7. Click back on the Schedule Data tab and then click the Properties button to schedule the backup job (see Figure 9.11).

8. Click OK to save the schedule settings. The scheduled backup job appears on the calendar for the Scheduled Jobs tab for each time that it is scheduled to run.

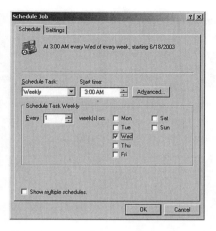

Figure 9.11   The Schedule Job dialog box for scheduling times for a backup job to run automatically.

Managing Backup Storage Media

The Removable Storage Manager (RSM) in Windows Server 2003 is responsible for managing storage media that you can use for backup and restore
operations. The RSM provides removable storage services for applications
and network administrators that enhance the sharing and management of
removable media hardware such as backup tape devices, optical disc drives,
and automated (robotic) media-pool libraries. Removable storage and media
support in Windows Server 2003 precludes the need for third-party software
developers to write custom application programs to support each different
type of removable media device. In addition, removable storage services
allow organizations to leverage their investment in expensive removable-
storage equipment by having multiple removable-storage applications share
these devices.

NOTE

You cannot back up data files directly to CD-R, CD/RW, DVD-R, DVD-RW, DVD+R, or
DVD+RW media using the Windows Server 2003 Backup Utility. However, you can
back up data to a file, instead of backing up to tape, and you can copy the backup file
to recordable media of this type. During a restore operation, the Backup Utility does
support reading a backup file from these recordable media types, so you can restore
from recordable and rewritable CDs and DVDs without a problem.

The Windows Server 2003 Removable Storage service implements a set of
APIs that enable third-party software solutions to catalog all removable
media, such as CDs, DVDs, tapes, and optical discs. You can catalog both
offline (shelved) as well as online (housed in a library) media. The
Removable Storage service organizes media using *media pools*. These media

pools control access to the removable media, categorize the media according to each type, and permit the media to be shared by applications. The Removable Storage service tracks the application programs that share the removable media. The Removable Storage feature is logically structured into five basic components: media units, media libraries, media pools, work queue items, and operator requests (see Figure 9.12). You can manage removable storage from the Computer Management console or from the Microsoft Management Console (MMC) snap-in named Removable Storage.

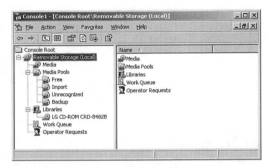

Figure 9.12   Managing backup storage media with the Removable Storage snap-in.

Configuring Security for Backup Operations

By default, all user accounts retain the appropriate rights and permissions to back up their own folders and files, but ordinary users cannot back up folders and files that are owned by other users. Only members of the Backup Operators group, the Server Operators group, and the Administrators group have the ability to back up and restore all files stored on a server regardless of which users own those folders and files. Members of these three groups retain both the Back Up Files and Directories user right and the Restore Files and Directories user right on standalone servers, member servers, and domain controllers.

Local or group policy settings are responsible for controlling user rights assignments. For standalone and member server Windows Server 2003 computers, the Backup Operators group and the Administrators group are assigned these backup and restore rights by default in the Local Security Settings MMC snap-in. For DCs, the Backup Operators group, the Server Operators group, and the Administrators group are assigned these backup and restore rights in the Default Domain Controller Security Settings MMC snap-in (see Figures 9.13 and 9.14). The location for these two policy settings is `Computer Configuration\Windows Settings\Security Settings\ Local Policies\User Rights Assignment`.

Figure 9.13   Viewing the default members of the Back Up Files and Directories security policy setting for a DC.

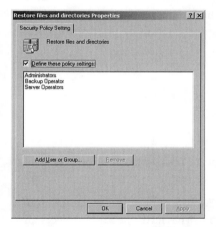

Figure 9.14   Viewing the default members of the Restore Files and Directories security policy setting for a DC.

For increased security, you might consider removing the Backup Operators group (in domain and standalone environments) and the Server Operators group (in domain environments) from both the Back Up Files and Directories user rights assignment policy and from the Restore Files and Directories user rights assignment policy. In their place, you can create two different groups, such as "Backup Admins" and "Restore Admins." You can then add the appropriate user accounts to these custom groups, and you can add the Backup Admins group to the Back Up Files and Directories policy setting, while adding only the Restore Admins group to the Restore Files and Directories policy setting. In this way, you are separating the backup and restore user rights into two distinct groups, which enables you to allow only certain users to back up data and only certain other users to restore that data.

 For even more protection, users can mark the Allow Only the Owner and the Administrator Access to the Backup Data check box from the Backup Job Information dialog box. However, this additional security measure is only available if you select the Replace the Data on the Media with This Backup option instead of the Append This Backup to the Media option. When you enable this security option, only a member of the Administrators group or the user who created the backup set can restore the files and folders contained within the backup set.

Restoring Backup Data

Restoring data from a backup set using the Backup Utility is a fairly straight-forward process. You cannot restore backup data from a command prompt using the NTBackup.exe command-line program; you must use the Backup Utility GUI. By default, you must be a member of the Backup Operators group, the Server Operators group (in a domain environment), or the Administrators group to perform a restore operation. To restore backup data, follow these steps:

1. Run the Backup Utility program.

2. Click the Advanced Mode link, if the program is not already in Advanced Mode.

3. Click the Restore and Manage Media tab.

4. Expand the media item that you want to restore from and then expand the backup set that you want to restore from.

5. Mark the check box for each drive letter, folder, or individual file that you want to restore. Marking a parent drive letter or folder selects all the child folders and files contained within it. Clear each item that you do not want to restore (see Figure 9.15).

6. From the Restore Files to drop-down list box, select where you want the restored files to be copied to—Original Location, Alternate Location, or Single Folder. If you select Alternate Location or Single Folder, type in the path (drive letter and folder name) or click the Browse button to select the restore path for the Alternate Location box.

7. Click the Start Restore button to begin the restore operation.

8. When the Confirm Restore message box appears, click the Advanced button to specify advanced restore options.

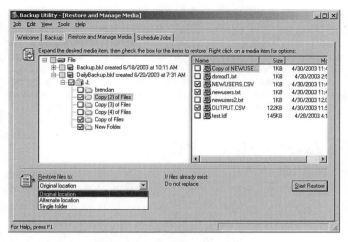

Figure 9.15   Selecting folders and files to restore.

9. From the Advanced Restore Options dialog box (see Figure 9.16), make sure that the Restore Security check box is marked, which is the default. This option restores all NTFS security settings for the restored files and folders, if you are restoring onto an NTFS drive volume. Other options include restoring junction points and preserving existing mount points.

Figure 9.16   Setting advanced restore options.

10. Click OK to save the advanced restore options settings and then click OK to begin restoring the data.

11. The Restore Progress window keeps you updated on the progress of the restore job and it notifies you when the restore is finished. Click the Report button to view the Restore Report log.

12. Click the Close button to finish the restore operation.

You can back up data files from FAT, FAT32, and NTFS drive volumes with the Windows Server 2003 Backup Utility. However, when you restore the data files, you should restore them onto the same file system as they were stored on originally. This concept is especially critical if you attempt to restore files that were backed up from an NTFS drive volume onto a FAT or FAT32 drive volume: NTFS security permissions, NTFS disk quotas, NTFS data compression attributes, and Encrypting File System (EFS) data encryption attributes all become lost for the restored data files when they are restored onto a FAT or FAT32 drive volume.

Restoring System State Data

You can easily restore a backup of a computer's System State data using the Windows Server 2003 Backup Utility in much the same way as you perform a restore operation for user data. However, a System State restore operation for a DC is more complex than a System State restore operation for a member server or a standalone server. Performing a restore operation for a DC is covered in the following section, "Restoring the System State for DCs." To restore a computer's System State, follow these steps:

1. Run the Backup Utility program.

2. Click the Advanced Mode link, if the program is not already in Advanced Mode.

3. Click the Restore and Manage Media tab.

4. Expand the media item that you want to restore from and then expand the backup set that you want to restore from.

5. Mark the check box for the System State item (see Figure 9.17).

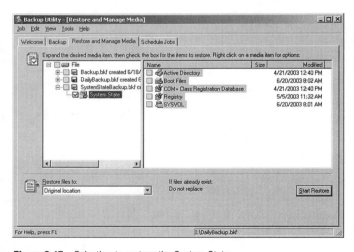

Figure 9.17   Selecting to restore the System State.

6. From the Restore Files to drop-down list box, select the Original Location option.

7. Click the Start Restore button to begin the restore operation.

8. Click OK for the Warning message box that appears, informing you that "Restoring the System State will always overwrite current System State unless restoring to an alternate location."

9. Next, the Confirm Restore message box appears. Click OK to begin the restore operation, or click Advanced to specify Advanced Restore Options and then begin the restore.

10. The Restore Progress window keeps you updated on the progress of the restore job and it will notify you when the restore is finished. Click the Report button to view the Restore Report log.

11. Click the Close button to finish the System State restore process.

12. For a System State restore, you might be prompted to restart the computer. Click Yes to restart the computer immediately, or click No and you can restart it later.

Restoring the System State for DCs

Windows Server 2003 computers that act as DCs store Active Directory data within the sysvol folder and within the Active Directory database (ntds.dit) file. The objects contained within the sysvol folder and the Active Directory database are always open and being accessed by the directory service. The shadow copy service cannot help with this condition for Active Directory files because the data is always in a state of flux due to replication of the data between DCs. Therefore, you must reboot a DC and select Directory Services Restore Mode from the Windows Advanced Options startup menu (see Figure 9.18) to perform a restore of its System State and the DC's Active Directory database. You still use the Windows Server 2003 Backup Utility to perform the System State restore, but the restore operation must occur while the computer is in Directory Services Restore Mode.

Because Active Directory uses multimaster replication to synchronize all the DC databases throughout an Active Directory domain, performing a normal restore is not sufficient when objects such as user accounts, groups, or organizational units get accidentally deleted or incorrectly modified. All objects in Active Directory are assigned Update Sequence Numbers (USNs) that determine which objects are the most up to date when replication occurs between DCs. After you perform a normal, or nonauthoritative, restore, the restored objects retain their previous USNs; objects that had been deleted with older USNs will become deleted again when the DC is restarted in normal mode and replication takes place.

Figure 9.18 Restarting a DC in Directory Services Restore Mode to restore the System State.

> **NOTE**
>
> If a DC goes down completely and you have to rebuild it from scratch, you can perform a normal restore. After the DC comes back online, Active Directory replication synchronizes the DC with the most recent updates from the other DCs in the domain. For such a scenario, an authoritative restore is not necessary. Authoritative restores should always be done with great caution and only in coordination with the responsible administrative personnel who manage the other DCs within the same domain.

To ensure that the restored Active Directory objects do not get deleted again via replication, you must use the ntdsutil.exe command-line tool to mark the restored Active Directory objects as authoritative while the computer is still in Directory Services Restore Mode. An authoritative restore marks and updates the USNs for each object that is marked as authoritatively restored; Active Directory objects with newer USNs appear newer than objects on other DCs that have older USNs. Objects with older USNs are discarded and the objects with newer USNs are replicated throughout the domain or forest.

To run ntdsutil.exe, open a command prompt, type ntdsutil, and press Enter. At any NTDSUTIL: prompt, you can type help to view a list of available commands. In the following step-by-step example, the entire Active Directory database is marked as authoritative to demonstrate how to perform an authoritative restore. In the real world, you would be more likely to mark an object or a subtree as authoritative, not the entire database. To restore the System State and Active Directory database on a Windows Server 2003 DC, follow these steps:

1. Restart the computer, press the F8 key during the startup process, select Directory Services Restore Mode from the Windows Advanced Options startup menu, and then press Enter.

2. Log on to the DC as the administrator under Safe Mode (Directory Services Restore Mode). You must log on with the administrator password that was created for Directory Services Restore Mode at the time that the computer was promoted to a DC using the Active Directory Installation Wizard (dcpromo.exe).

3. Perform the System State restore operation using the Backup Utility, as outlined in the previous section, "Restoring System State Data."

4. After the System State restore operation is successful and finished, open a command prompt.

5. At a command prompt, type ntdsutil and press Enter.

6. At the NTDSUTIL: prompt, type authoritative restore and press Enter.

7. At the Authoritative Restore: prompt, you can type help to view a list of available commands for marking Active Directory objects as "authoritative."

8. To mark the *entire restored Active Directory database as authoritative*, type restore database at the Authoritative Restore: prompt and press Enter (see Figure 9.19).

Figure 9.19   Using the **ntdsutil.exe** tool to mark a restored Active Directory database as authoritative.

9. Click Yes when the confirmation dialog box appears. Be extremely cautious and make sure that you understand all of the ramifications of this action before you attempt to mark the entire Active Directory database as authoritative. Changes made to Active Directory objects on other DCs might be lost when you mark one DC's database as authoritative and replication takes place.

10. You are notified when the authoritative restore is complete by the ntdsutil program.

11. Type quit for the authoritative restore prompt.

12. Type `quit` at the NTDSUTIL: prompt to exit the utility and return to the Windows Server 2003 command prompt.

13. Restart the computer under Windows Server 2003 normally.

If you have only one DC in the domain, or, if you need to rebuild an entire domain from backup when all DCs have been lost, you should perform a primary restore. A primary restore lets you restore the domain's first replica set as well as letting you restore Active Directory and the SYSVOL folder on a standalone DC or on the first DC within a forest.

To perform a primary restore of Active Directory from a System State backup, you still must boot the computer into Directory Services Restore Mode; however, you do not need to use the NTDSUTIL program. After you select the System State item for the restore in the Windows Backup Utility, click Start Restore, click OK for the Warning dialog box, and then click the Advanced button to specify advanced restore options. You must mark the When Restoring Replicated Data Sets, Mark the Restored Data as the Primary Data for All Replicas check box to specify that the restore operation is a primary restore (see Figure 9.20). After selecting this option, start the restore job; you boot Windows normally after the restore job finishes.

Figure 9.20   Using the Advanced Restore Options dialog box to mark restored Active Directory data as primary.

Exam Prep Questions

Question 1

> Which type of backup can you perform using the Windows Server 2003 Backup Utility if you only want to back up files that have their archive bits set and you want the backup job to clear each file's archive bit after each file has been backed up?
>
> ○ A. Incremental
> ○ B. Differential
> ○ C. Normal
> ○ D. Copy

Answer A is correct. Incremental backups only back up files that have their archive bit set and each backed up file has its archive bit cleared. Answer B is incorrect because differential backups do not clear each file's archive bit. Answer C is incorrect because normal backups back up all files, not just files that have their archive bits set. Answer D is incorrect because a copy backup backs up all files and does not clear each backed-up file's archive bit.

Question 2

> Alexis is a member of the Backup Operators group on a Windows Server 2003 computer. The server's data drive volume contains more than 25GB of data files that need to be backed up. Alexis's user account is currently subject to a 500MB NTFS disk-quota entry and disk quotas are enabled on the drive volume. What must the network administrator do to allow Alexis to back up the entire data volume without unnecessarily compromising security?
>
> ○ A. Make Alexis a member of the Administrators group.
> ○ B. Make Alexis a member of the Server Operators group.
> ○ C. Grant Alexis the Backup Files and Directories user right on the server.
> ○ D. Assign Alexis an unlimited disk-quota entry for the data volume.

Answer D is correct. Assigning an unlimited disk-quota entry for Alexis allows her to back up all the data files on the volume. Answer A is incorrect because even though members of the Administrators group have unlimited disk quotas by default, the network administrator would be granting much more authority to Alexis than she needs to do her job. Answer B is incorrect because making Alexis a member of the Server Operators group would not solve her disk-quota restriction. Answer C is incorrect because Alexis already has this user right by being a member of the Backup Operators group.

Question 3

> How can you back up files that might be open as well as files that might be open and locked in memory during the backup operation?
>
> ○ A. Use third-party backup software that supports backing up open or locked files.
> ○ B. Disable the Volume Shadow Copy service (VSS).
> ○ C. Be sure that all users are logged off before you begin a backup job.
> ○ D. Run the Windows Server 2003 Backup Utility with default settings.

Answer D is correct. By default, the Windows Server 2003 Backup Utility generates a shadow-copy snapshot of all the files that it is going to back up; the shadow-copy snapshot enables the Backup Utility to back up files that are open or locked. Answer A is incorrect because although you always have the option of purchasing third-party backup software, you do not need third-party software to back up open files. Answer B is incorrect because disabling the VSS does not allow the Backup Utility to back up open files. Answer C is incorrect because you do not need to have all users log off before you begin a backup job on a Windows Server 2003 computer.

Question 4

> In which of the following ways can you perform a restore operation using the Windows Server 2003 Backup Utility? (Choose three.)
>
> ❏ A. From backup tape
> ❏ B. From DVD recordable or rewritable media
> ❏ C. From an external USB hard drive
> ❏ D. By using the **NTBackup.exe** tool from a command prompt
> ❏ E. By restoring a remote computer's System State over the network
> ❏ F. By selecting Advanced Restore Options to mark the restored data as authoritative for Active Directory

Answers A, B, and C are correct. You can restore from backup tape, from DVD recordable or rewritable media, and from any type of external hard drive. Answer D is incorrect because you cannot use the NTBackup.exe command-line tool to perform a restore. Answer E is incorrect because you cannot restore a computer's System State remotely. Answer F is incorrect because you cannot mark restored System State data as authoritative from the Backup Utility; you must use NTDSUTIL for that purpose. You can, however, use the Backup Utility to mark restored System State data as primary for Active Directory objects.

Question 5

Which of the following backup types instructs the Backup Utility to back up all selected folders and files?

- ○ A. Copy
- ○ B. Daily
- ○ C. Incremental
- ○ D. Complete

Answer A is correct. The copy backup type backs up all files, similar to a normal backup, except that it does not clear each backed-up file's archive bit. Answer B is incorrect because a daily backup only backs up files that have been created or modified on the same day as when the backup occurs. Answer C is incorrect because an incremental backup only backs up files that have their archive bits set. Answer D is incorrect because there is no such backup type named complete in the Windows Server 2003 Backup Utility.

Question 6

Which is the best way to restrict a tape backup set from being restored by just any member of the Backup Operators group?

- ○ A. Apply appropriate NTFS security permissions on the backup set.
- ○ B. Remove all users from the Backup Operators group.
- ○ C. Revoke the Restore Files and Directories user right from the Backup Operators group.
- ○ D. Mark the Allow Only the Owner and the Administrator Access to the Backup Data check box for the Backup Job Information dialog box when you run a backup job.

Answer D is correct. Answer A is incorrect because you cannot apply NTFS permissions on a tape backup set. Answer B is incorrect because removing all users from the Backup Operators group allows only administrators to create backups. Answer C is incorrect because revoking the Restore Files and Directories user right from the Backup Operators group means that only administrators can perform restores for any backup sets.

Question 7

> How can you manage removable storage media, media pools, and libraries?
>
> - ○ A. By using the Remote Storage MMC snap-in
> - ○ B. By using the Computer Management console
> - ○ C. By clicking the Removable Storage button on the Hardware tab of the System Properties window
> - ○ D. By clicking the Restore and Manage Media tab in the Backup Utility

Answer B is correct. The Removable Storage snap-in is a default component of the Computer Management console. Answer A is incorrect because there is no Remote Storage MMC snap-in that ships with Windows Server 2003. Answer C is incorrect because there is no Removable Storage button on the Hardware tab of the System Properties window. Answer D is incorrect because you cannot manage removable-storage items from the Restore and Manage Media tab in the Backup Utility.

Question 8

> Which of the following restore operations results in a loss of security permissions and other advanced features for the restored files?
>
> - ○ A. Restoring files onto an NTFS drive volume when the files were originally stored on a FAT drive volume
> - ○ B. Restoring files onto an NTFS drive volume from a backup (**.bkf**) file stored on a FAT32 drive volume
> - ○ C. Restoring files onto a FAT32 drive volume when the files were originally stored on an NTFS drive volume
> - ○ D. Restoring files onto an NTFS drive volume when the files were originally stored on a FAT32 drive volume

Answer C is correct. If you restore files onto a FAT or FAT32 drive volume when the files were originally stored on an NTFS drive volume, the files lose all of their security permissions, disk quotas, NTFS compression attributes, and EFS encryption attributes. Answer A is incorrect because files do not lose any security permissions or features when they are restored onto an NTFS drive volume from a FAT drive volume. Answer B is incorrect because it does not matter where a Backup Utility file (.bkf) is stored: It has no effect on the restored files. Answer D is incorrect because files do not lose any security permissions or features when they are restored onto an NTFS drive volume from a FAT32 drive volume.

Question 9

On a DC, which of the following types of restores can you perform without first booting the computer into Directory Services Restore Mode? (Choose three.)

❑ A. Performing a System State restore to an alternate location

❑ B. Performing a System State restore to a single folder

❑ C. Performing a System State restore to the original location

❑ D. Performing a restore of user data

❑ E. Performing a primary restore of Active Directory

❑ F. Performing an authoritative restore of Active Directory

Answers A, B, and D are correct. Answers C, E, and F are incorrect because when you perform a System State restore to the original location on a DC, you must be in Directory Services Restore Mode for the restore job to run. Answer C, E, and F all require Directory Services Restore Mode whether you are performing a normal (nonauthoritative), primary, or authoritative restore of Active Directory.

Question 10

How can you specify that certain files should be excluded during backup jobs when a member of the Administrators group performs a backup operation using the Backup Utility?

○ A. At the Advanced Backup Options dialog box for a backup job

○ B. At the Options dialog box from the Tools, Options menu

○ C. At the Advanced Restore Options dialog box for a backup job

○ D. At the Restore Options dialog box for a backup job

Answer B is correct. Answer A is incorrect because there is no option for excluding files from the Advanced Backup Options dialog box. Answer C is incorrect because there is no Advanced Restore Options dialog box for a backup job. Answer D is incorrect because there is no Restore Options dialog box for a backup job.

Need to Know More?

 Minasi, Mark, et. al. *Mastering Windows Server 2003*. Alameda, California: Sybex Inc., 2003.

 Holme, Dan, and Orin Thomas. *MCSA/MCSE Self-Paced Training Kit (Exam 70-290): Managing and Maintaining a Microsoft Windows Server 2003 Environment*. Redmond, Washington: Microsoft Press, 2003.

 Scales, Lee, and John Michell. *MCSA/MCSE 70-290 Training Guide: Managing and Maintaining a Windows Server 2003 Environment*. Indianapolis, Indiana: Que Publishing, 2003.

 Search the Microsoft Product Support Services Knowledge Base on the Internet: http://support.microsoft.com. You can also search Microsoft TechNet on the Internet: http://www.microsoft.com/technet. Find technical information using keywords from this chapter, such as Backup Utility, NTBackup, backup types, System State, authoritative restore, verifying backups, scheduling backups, NTDSUTIL, and Directory Services Restore Mode.

Practice Exam 1

Now it's time to put to the test the knowledge that you've learned from reading this book! Write down your answers to the following questions on a separate sheet of paper. You will be able to take this sample test multiple times this way. After you answer all the questions, compare your answers with the correct answers in Chapter 11, "Answers to Practice Exam 1." The answer keys for both exams immediately follow each Practice Exam chapter. When you can correctly answer at least 54 of the 60 practice questions (90%) in each Practice Exam, you are ready to start using the PrepLogic Practice Exams CD-ROM at the back of this *Exam Cram 2*. Using the Practice Exams for this *Exam Cram 2*, along with the PrepLogic Practice Exams, you can prepare yourself quite well for the actual 70-290 Microsoft certification exam. Good luck!

Question 1

What Windows 2003 Server utility program can you use as a nonadministrator to troubleshoot hardware that is not functioning correctly?

○ A. Hardware Troubleshooter

○ B. Add or Remove Programs

○ C. Add New Hardware Wizard

○ D. **msconfig.exe**

Question 2

As an administrator, you want to be sure no unsigned drivers are installed on your computer. What steps can you take?

○ A. Choose Block and also mark the Make This Action the System Default check box in the Driver Signing Options dialog box from the System Properties window.

○ B. Choose the Ignore option and also mark the Make This Action the System Default check box in the Driver Signing Options dialog box from the System Properties window.

○ C. Choose Ignore in the Driver Signing Options dialog box from the System Properties window.

○ D. Choose Block in the Driver Signing Options dialog box from the System Properties window.

Question 3

Morgan is trying to install a new network scanner on the company's Windows Server 2003 computer, but it is not allowing her to begin the installation. The scanner driver was not included with Windows, but it has a Designed for Windows logo, and she has the CD containing the signed driver. What is the most likely cause of the installation problem?

○ A. She is not a member of the Power Users group.

○ B. She is not a member of the Administrators group.

○ C. The scanner is not approved by Microsoft.

○ D. The software was written for Windows 3.1.

Question 4

Gina has been given the task of bringing another Active Directory domain online in her corporate network. She does not have enough time to purchase a new server, but she does have several computers running Windows Server 2003, Web Edition, that are underutilized at the moment. She decides to use one of them as a domain controller (DC) for the new domain but cannot promote it. Why not?

- ○ A. The computer does not have enough RAM to become a DC.
- ○ B. The paging file is not on the boot drive, which is a requirement for DCs.
- ○ C. Only Windows Server 2003, Enterprise Edition, can be a DC.
- ○ D. Windows Server 2003, Web Edition, cannot be a DC.

Question 5

Your company's server is beginning to experience slowdowns that you associate with having only a single processor. To alleviate the problems, you install a second processor in the computer. What application can you run in Windows Server 2003 to enable the second processor?

- ○ A. **procup.exe** in the **\support** directory of the Windows Server 2003 CD-ROM
- ○ B. Device Manager from the System Control Panel
- ○ C. Processor MMC in the Computer Management MMC
- ○ D. **setup.exe** from the Windows Server 2003 CD-ROM, choosing the Upgrade to Multiple Processors option

Question 6

A Windows Server 2003 computer in your office has a special video-editing card installed in a PCI slot. This card is vital to the operation of your company. You've been having some minor problems with the card, and you installed a new set of drivers that the manufacturer just released. Unfortunately, the card is now corrupting all the data it processes. What is the best way to solve this problem?

- ○ A. In Device Manager, go into the properties of the device, choose the Drivers tab, and select Roll Back Driver.
- ○ B. Reinstall the original driver from the CD-ROM included with the device.
- ○ C. Download and install the latest beta driver from the manufacturer's Web site.
- ○ D. Manually delete the files associated with the new driver.

Question 7

Mike works in a small company that has recently acquired a new server prein-stalled with Windows Server 2003, Standard Edition. The server was purchased with a CD/RW drive so that all employees could copy project data files to the server and then burn archive CDs. They made sure that the drive was on the Hardware Compatibility List when purchasing the server. Mike is attempting to burn an archive CD, but when he right-clicks on the server's CD/RW drive, he does not see Write These Files to CD as a choice. What does he need to do to enable CD burning on Windows Server 2003?

○ A. Select CD Burning from Add/Remove Windows Components inside the Add/Remove Programs Control Panel.

○ B. Enable CD burning in the local security policy of the Windows Server 2003 computer.

○ C. Enable the IMAPI CD-Burning COM Service in the Services MMC snap-in to start automatically.

○ D. Update the burner's firmware to a version compatible with Windows Server 2003.

Question 8

While updating your Windows Server 2003 computer, you decide to install a new video driver. Upon rebooting, your monitor reports "Signal out of range." You want to maintain the new driver, but you need to access the display. How can you gain access to the display again so you can change the video settings to functional settings for your environment?

○ A. Hold down Ctrl+Alt+Tab and press 1 to force the computer to switch to 640 x 480 resolution.

○ B. While booting the machine, press F8 to gain access to the advanced boot menu. Choose Enable VGA Mode to boot into 640 x 480 with 16 colors so you can fix the video settings.

○ C. While booting the machine, press F8 to gain access to the advanced boot menu. Choose Safe Mode so you can roll the driver back to the previous version.

○ D. Hold down V on the keyboard as the computer boots to enable VGA mode.

Question 9

Johanna has a maintenance program that she needs to run on her Windows Server 2003 computer once per month. The application is extremely resource intensive, and Johanna would like to have as few applications and services loaded as possible when she runs the application. What feature of Windows Server 2003 will help Johanna configure her server to have very few services and devices loaded when she needs to run her application?

- ○ A. Hardware profiles
- ○ B. User profiles
- ○ C. Hardware configuration
- ○ D. Device selection

Question 10

A catastrophic failure causes you to lose two drives in your eight-drive RAID-5 volume. Choose all the tasks related to recovering the data and regaining fault tolerance. (Choose two.)

- ❑ A. Replace one drive and allow the rebuild process to begin.
- ❑ B. Replace the two failed drives.
- ❑ C. Move the remaining drives into a dedicated recovery server and rebuild the array.
- ❑ D. Restore the information from your most recent tape.
- ❑ E. In Logical Disk Management, right-click the failed volume and choose Restore from Shadow Copy.

Question 11

Windows Server 2003 supports legacy file-system types, such as FAT and FAT32, as well as the latest NTFS file system. Which partition schemes does Windows Server 2003 support on a single IDE hard drive, if you have one extended partition on the same drive? (Choose two.)

- ❑ A. Two primary partitions
- ❑ B. Four primary partitions
- ❑ C. Three simple volumes
- ❑ D. One simple volume and one extended partition
- ❑ E. Three primary partitions

Question 12

> After upgrading your Windows NT 4.0 Server to Windows Server 2003, you no
> longer can access your stripe set with parity. How can you access the data
> stored on your stripe set with parity on Windows Server 2003?
>
> ○ A. Use the **ftonline.exe** utility in the **\Support\Tools** folder on the
> Windows Server 2003 CD-ROM.
>
> ○ B. Convert the stripe set to a RAID-5 volume using Disk Management in
> the Computer Management console.
>
> ○ C. Reboot the computer into Windows NT 4.0 Server and copy the data to
> an existing dynamic volume.
>
> ○ D. Use the **stripetoraid.exe** utility in the **\Support\Tools** folder on the
> Windows Server 2003 CD.

Question 13

> Which of the following is not a true statement about striped volumes in
> Windows Server 2003?
>
> ○ A. Striped volumes provide no fault tolerance for data stored on them.
>
> ○ B. Striped volumes may be created onto a maximum of 32 disks.
>
> ○ C. Striped volumes may be extended to add more storage space.
>
> ○ D. Striped volumes provide better performance than simple volumes.

Question 14

> On a multiboot computer with Windows Server 2003, Windows XP
> Professional, and Windows NT 4.0 Server with SP6, what types of storage vol-
> umes are natively accessible to all of these operating systems? (Choose three.)
>
> ❑ A. Primary partition formatted with FAT
>
> ❑ B. Extended partition formatted with FAT32
>
> ❑ C. Extended partition formatted with NTFS
>
> ❑ D. Simple volume formatted with FAT32
>
> ❑ E. Stripe set formatted with NTFS
>
> ❑ F. RAID-5 volume formatted with NTFS
>
> ❑ G. Logical drive formatted with FAT

Question 15

What is the preferred method for running the Disk Defragmenter utility on Windows Server 2003?

○ A. Log onto the computer as a user with local administrative privileges and run Disk Defragmenter.

○ B. Log onto a different computer as a domain administrator and launch the defragmenter remotely to ensure the least performance impact.

○ C. Log onto the computer as a user without administrative privileges, right-click the Disk Defragmenter icon and choose Run as, and type in the credentials of a user account with administrative privileges.

○ D. Log onto the computer as an administrative user using Terminal Services and launch Disk Defragmenter.

Question 16

Which of the following defines the system partition in Windows Server 2003?

○ A. A simple volume on a dynamic disk that contains the **\Windows** folder

○ B. A spanned volume on a basic disk that contains the boot files such as **ntldr**, **ntdetect.com**, and **boot.ini**

○ C. A partition on a basic disk that contains the boot files such as **ntldr**, **ntdetect.com**, and **boot.ini**

○ D. A partition on a dynamic disk that contains the **\Windows** folder

Question 17

After moving a hard disk that contains data from an old Windows Server 2003 computer to a new one, it is listed as Foreign in Disk Management. What can you do to make the data accessible in the new server?

○ A. In Disk Management, right-click on the disk and choose Import Foreign Disks.

○ B. In Device Manager, enter the properties of the disk and choose Activate This Disk.

○ C. In Disk Management, right-click on the disk and choose Activate This Disk.

○ D. In Device Manager, enter the properties of the disk and choose Import Foreign Disks.

Question 18

You believe that one of the drives in your mirrored volume is beginning to fail. You want to break the mirror and replace the failing drive. The mirrored volume consists of the physical disks numbered 2 and 3 in Disk Management. The drive letter assigned to the volume is H:. You want to be sure that Disk 3 retains the H: drive letter designation because it is the good disk and it will be retained. You also want to retain the data on the possibly failing disk as a failsafe option in case problems arise during the replacement process. How can you accomplish this? (Choose three.)

- ❑ A. Right-click Disk 3 and choose Remove Mirror.
- ❑ B. Right-click Disk 3 and choose Break Mirrored Volume.
- ❑ C. Right-click Disk 2 and choose Break Mirrored Volume.
- ❑ D. Right-click the remaining H: drive, choose Add Mirror, and then choose a dynamic disk with enough unallocated space.
- ❑ E. Ensure the new mirrored volume reports a status of Healthy.
- ❑ F. Right-click Disk 2 and choose Remove Mirror.
- ❑ G. Right-click on the remaining H: drive and choose Add Mirror, choosing another simple volume that is the same size or larger than the volume you are mirroring.

Question 19

Which of the following command-line tools can you use to remove a user from Active Directory?

- ○ A. **dsquery**
- ○ B. **dsrm**
- ○ C. **dsmove**
- ○ D. **dsadd**
- ○ E. **dsget**
- ○ F. **net user**

Question 20

In an Active Directory domain, what does name mapping allow you to do?

○ A. Map a user profile to a network share.

○ B. Map a user to his home folder.

○ C. Log on to a non-Windows Kerberos realm.

○ D. Log on to a Windows 2000 child domain.

Question 21

Which networking components must be present on the network to install Active Directory? (Choose two.)

❑ A. Windows Internet Name Service (WINS)

❑ B. Domain Name System (DNS)

❑ C. Kerberos

❑ D. Remote Procedure Call (RPC)

❑ E. Transmission Control Protocol/Internet Protocol (TCP/IP)

❑ F. NetBIOS

Question 22

You plan to raise the functional level of your Active Directory forest to Windows Server 2003. What must you do to fulfill the requirements necessary to do this upgrade? (Choose two.)

❑ A. Upgrade all the workstations to Windows 2000 Professional or Windows XP Professional.

❑ B. Upgrade all Windows NT 4.0 member servers to Windows Server 2003.

❑ C. First upgrade the forest to Windows 2000 native mode.

❑ D. Make sure all DCs are running Windows 2003 Server.

❑ E. Raise the domain functional level on all DCs to at least Windows 2003 native mode.

❑ F. Raise the domain functional level of all the domains in the forest to at least Windows 2000 native mode.

Question 23

How can you identify a prestaged computer account in Active Directory? (Choose two.)

❑ A. By its fully qualified domain name (FQDN)

❑ B. By its TCP/IP address

❑ C. By its computer name

❑ D. By its globally unique identifier (GUID)

❑ E. By its security identifier (SID)

❑ F. By its universally unique identifier (UUID)

Question 24

You have reset the computer account password, but now the user can no longer log on to the domain. What must you do to fix it?

○ A. Reset the user account password.

○ B. Rejoin the computer to the domain.

○ C. Reboot the workstation.

○ D. Reset the security identifier.

Question 25

Users on Windows 98 computers who log on to a Windows NT Server 4.0 domain need to be able to access shared folders and printers within a Windows Server 2003 Active Directory environment. What must be in place for this access to occur?

○ A. A one-way trust

○ B. The **dsclient.exe** utility installed on all Windows 98 computers

○ C. The Kerberos authentication protocol

○ D. DNS configured on the Windows 98 computers

Question 26

For a domain set at the Windows 2000 mixed domain functional level, which type of group scope can contain accounts and global groups from any domain in the forest?

- ○ A. Universal groups
- ○ B. Domain local groups
- ○ C. Security groups
- ○ D. Global groups

Question 27

A user complains that she is not able to access a resource that she once could. You suspect that it is a group-policy issue. What is the best way to determine whether group policy is the problem?

- ○ A. Check the group policy for the OU the user is in.
- ○ B. Use **dsquery**.
- ○ C. Use **dsget**.
- ○ D. Run the RSoP wizard.

Question 28

MartyB belongs to the Domain Admins group within the CORINTH.LOCAL domain. The Domain Admins group is a group that belongs to the local Administrators group on Windows XP workstations, which are also joined to the CORINTH domain. Which **runas** command (or commands) does MartyB need to run to execute the Computer Management console with domain administrative credentials? (Choose two.)

- ❑ A. **runas /user:MARTYB "mmc %windir%\system32\compmgmt.msc"**
- ❑ B. **runas /user:CORINTH\MARTYB "mmc %windir%\system32\ compmgmt.msc"**
- ❑ C. **runas /user:MARTYB@CORINTH.LOCAL "mmc %windir%\system32\compmgmt.msc"**
- ❑ D. **runas /user:LOCAL\MARTYB "mmc %windir%\system32\ compmgmt.msc"**
- ❑ E. **runas /user:Administrator\MARTYB "mmc %windir%\system32\ compmgmt.msc"**

Question 29

You are a network administrator for a clothing manufacturer that is headquartered in Sacramento, California. The manufacturing facilities are located in Reno, Nevada, and St. Paul, Minnesota. Both manufacturing facilities are connected to the corporate office by a VPN tunnel over the Internet. You are working from the Sacramento location and you were sent an email request for Remote Assistance (RA) from the local technician in St. Paul. When you attempted to make an RA connection to a Windows 2003 server located in St. Paul, the connection fails. What are two possible reasons for the failure? (Choose two.)

❑ A. The RA invitation has expired.

❑ B. RA has not been enabled on the server.

❑ C. TCP port 3389 is blocked on the firewall.

❑ D. UDP port 3389 is blocked on the firewall.

❑ E. You do not have administrative permissions on the server.

Question 30

You are a Windows Server 2003 network administrator running Terminal Services in Application Server mode. After a period of 120 days, your Terminal Server users complain that they can no longer access the Terminal Server. Upon examination of the problem, you realize that you have additional steps to finish. Each correct step is only a portion of the solution. (Choose two.)

❑ A. Upgrade each client computer to Windows XP Professional or Windows 2000 Professional with SP3.

❑ B. Install the proper number of Terminal Server Client Access Licenses (TSCALs).

❑ C. Reboot the Terminal Server every four months.

❑ D. Install a Terminal Server License Server on your network.

❑ E. Uninstall Terminal Services and restore the System State from backup. Reinstall Terminal Services and ensure that the users can connect.

Question 31

Which port needs to be open on the firewall that will enable an external user to connect to an internal Terminal Server that is listening on the default port?

- ○ A. TCP port 21
- ○ B. TCP port 8000
- ○ C. TCP port 3398
- ○ D. TCP port 3389

Question 32

You manage two network administrators. Each administrator has left for the day, and you receive a call that a remote Windows 2003 Web server is not responding to HTTP requests. You attempt to establish a connection to this server, but you receive a message that the maximum number of connections has been reached. Through investigation, you realize that your two network administrators left their sessions running. What Terminal Services tool can you use to disconnect one of the sessions so that you can use Terminal Services to connect to the remote Web server?

- ○ A. Terminal Services Manager
- ○ B. Terminal Services Configuration
- ○ C. Terminal Services Licensing
- ○ D. Managing Your Server—Terminal Services Edition

Question 33

Which Terminal Services administration tool would you use to view users, sessions, and processes for current connections running on each Terminal Server?

- ○ A. Active Directory Users and Computers
- ○ B. Terminal Services Configuration
- ○ C. Terminal Services Manager
- ○ D. Terminal Services Licensing

Question 34

You realize you have just sent off an RA invitation by email to the wrong technician. You want the invitation to expire immediately. What steps do you need to perform to ensure that the invitation expires before the default of one hour?

- ○ A. Open the Help and Support Center, click the View Invitation Status option, select the proper Invitation, and then click the Expire button.

- ○ B. Open the Help and Support Center, click the Invite Someone to Help You option, select the proper invitation, and then click the Expire button.

- ○ C. Open the Help and Support Center, click the Invite Someone to Help You option, select the proper invitation, and then click the Delete button.

- ○ D. Open the Control Panel, click the View Invitation Status option, select the proper invitation, and then click the Expire button.

Question 35

Under which Registry subkey will you find the Group Policy Object (GPO) settings for the Remote Assistance feature?

- ○ A. User Configuration\Administrative Templates\System\Remote Assistance

- ○ B. Computer Configuration\Administrative Templates\System\Remote Assistance

- ○ C. Computer Configuration\Windows Settings\Security Settings\Remote Assistance

- ○ D. Computer Configuration\Security Settings\System\Remote Assistance

Question 36

As the network administrator, to better protect your network from data loss through accidental overwrites and deletions, you come up with the following strategies for Server1:

- ➤ Incremental backups of the server at 8:00 p.m. nightly

- ➤ Full backups of the server on Sundays at 12 noon

- ➤ Shadow Copies of Shared Folders scheduled to run twice daily at 10:00 a.m. and 3:00 p.m. for the E: drive

On Thursday, you are working on a document that you stored in the **E:\SpecialDocs** folder on the server. It contains sensitive information, so instead of sharing the folder, you connect to it using a Remote Desktop Connection to work on the file. You realize that you deleted some information from the file last Monday morning that you now need. Where can you find the latest copy of the document that has the information you need?

❑ A. On Monday night's incremental backup tape

❑ B. In the Previous Versions tab on the properties sheet for the file, as long as you connect over the network using the UNC path **\\server1\e$\specialdocs**

❑ C. On Sunday's full backup tape

❑ D. In the Previous Versions tab on the properties for the file by logging onto the server locally or via Remote Desktop Connection

Question 37

Which three files are required if you need to boot a Windows Server 2003, Web Edition, computer from a floppy disk? (Choose three.)

❑ A. **ntldr**

❑ B. **io.sys**

❑ C. **boot.ini**

❑ D. **ntdetect.com**

❑ E. **boot.sys**

❑ F. **bootsect.dos**

Question 38

Which options are presented to you when you boot the server and press the F8 key to enter the Advanced Startup Options menu? (Choose three.)

❑ A. Safe Mode with Recovery Console

❑ B. Safe Mode with Networking Support

❑ C. Safe Mode with Command Prompt

❑ D. Recovery Console

❑ E. Automated System Recovery (ASR)

❑ F. Last Known Good Configuration

Question 39

While you are working with another operating system on a Windows Server 2003 computer configured for dual-booting, a system-level command overwrites the boot sector. Now, whenever you boot the computer, it boots straight into the other operating system without giving you a chance to even select Windows Server 2003. You want to restore the Windows Server 2003 boot menu for choosing which operating system to run. What steps must you take? (Choose two.)

❏ A. Use the Windows Server 2003 CD-ROM to boot the computer into the Recovery Console.

❏ B. After booting into Windows Server 2003, be sure the operating-system selection timeout is greater than zero in the System applet in the Control Panel.

❏ C. Execute **fixboot** from the Recovery Console prompt.

❏ D. Boot with an MS-DOS–based startup disk and execute **fdisk /mbr** to repair the master boot record.

❏ E. Perform an ASR to repair the boot sector.

Question 40

Marty wants to create an ASR backup of his company's Windows Server 2003 computer. He has a variety of media that he could create the backup set on. Which media will allow him to successfully recover his server with the fewest configuration changes or questions?

○ A. A SCSI hard drive that stores both the system and boot volumes

○ B. A tape drive that requires a special driver from the manufacturer

○ C. A write once, read many (WORM) optical drive that requires a manufacturer-provided device driver that is connected to the server via a SCSI cable

○ D. An IDE hard drive used for data storage only

Question 41

What must your server hardware support to utilize Emergency Management Services (EMS) in Windows Server 2003?

○ A. SPCR (Serial Port Console Redirection)

○ B. OOBM (Out-of-Band Management)

○ C. NTFS (New Technology File System)

○ D. IPv6 (TCP/IP version 6)

Question 42

Which disaster-recovery tools allow you to disable a service that you believe is causing your Windows Server 2003 computer to crash on a regular basis? (Choose three.)

❑ A. Recovery Console

❑ B. Safe Mode with Networking Support

❑ C. ASR

❑ D. EMS Special Administration Console (SAC)

❑ E. Safe Mode

❑ F. Directory Services Restore Mode

Question 43

Vinnie is troubleshooting a startup problem on his Windows Server 2003 computer. He is able to start the computer using Safe Mode but not Safe Mode with Networking. What assumption can Vinnie make about the problem his server is having?

○ A. A recently installed video driver is causing the problems.

○ B. A recently updated network driver is causing the problems.

○ C. A corrupted shared folder is causing the problems.

○ D. A corrupted boot sector is causing the problems.

Question 44

You want to implement Shadow Copies of Shared Folders on all your data drive volumes to help protect your users' data from accidental deletion and overwrites. You have two Windows Server 2003, Standard Edition, computers, each configured with NTFS drive volumes; you also have one Windows Server 2003, Enterprise Edition, server configured with FAT32 volumes. Additionally, you have one Windows 2000 Advanced Server computer, configured with FAT32 drive volumes, and you have one Windows Server 2003, Web Edition, computer, configured with dynamic disks, running NTFS. Which computers are capable of creating shadow copies? (Choose two.)

❑ A. The Windows Server 2003, Standard Edition, computers

❑ B. The Windows Server 2003, Enterprise Edition, computer

❑ C. The Windows 2000 Advanced Server computer

❑ D. The Windows 2000 Advanced Server computer after you install the Previous Versions client

❑ E. The Windows Server 2003, Web Edition, computer

Question 45

Using the Windows 2003 Backup Utility, which type of backup should you perform if you only want to back up those files that have their archive bits set and you do not want to have them cleared?

- ○ A. Incremental
- ○ B. Copy
- ○ C. Normal
- ○ D. Daily
- ○ E. Differential

Question 46

Vireya is a system administrator for a large automobile manufacturer. She administers a Windows Server 2003 Active Directory domain. Both the domain and the forest are running at the Windows Server 2003 functional level. On a Thursday at 6:00 p.m., one of the member servers that controls an assembly-line robot experienced a catastrophic hard-disk crash. The server must be restored from tape backup. Based on the following backup schedule, which backup tapes does Vireya need to use to restore the server as quickly as possible?

Backup Schedule:

Monday—Incremental backup at 12:30 a.m.

Tuesday—Incremental backup at 12:30 a.m.

Wednesday—Incremental backup at 12:30 a.m.

Thursday—Incremental backup at 12:30 a.m.

Friday—Normal backup at 12:30 a.m.

- ○ A. Friday, Monday, Tuesday, Wednesday, Thursday
- ○ B. Monday, Tuesday, Wednesday, Thursday
- ○ C. Friday, Thursday
- ○ D. Friday, Wednesday
- ○ E. Monday, Thursday

Question 47

You are the administrator of a Windows Server 2003 domain. You have a Windows Server 2003 member server that contains a large number of shared folders and has the following backup schedule:

Sunday—Normal backup at 1:45 a.m.

Monday—Differential backup at 1:45 a.m.

Tuesday—Differential backup at 1:45 a.m.

Wednesday—Differential backup at 1:45 a.m.

Thursday—Differential backup at 1:45 a.m.

Friday—Differential backup at 1:45 a.m.

Saturday—Differential backup at 1:45 a.m.

Thursday afternoon, you experience a hard-disk failure. Which backup tapes do you need to quickly restore this server?

○ A. Sunday, Monday, Tuesday, Wednesday, Thursday

○ B. Thursday only

○ C. Sunday and Thursday only

○ D. Friday, Saturday, Sunday, Monday, Tuesday, Wednesday, Thursday

Question 48

Robert is the network administrator of Clamberto Enterprises, a large financial firm in Hastings, Minnesota. One Windows Server 2003 computer that Robert is responsible for runs a vital financial transaction-processing application. For disaster recovery, he uses the Windows Server 2003 Backup Utility to back up his server early each morning. Saturday night at 11 p.m., Robert receives a call from the police department informing him that his data center has been broken into. Upon Robert's inspection, he sees that his financial server is missing. For Robert, the first order of business is to get this financial server up and running as quickly as possible. He has identical hardware so that he can recreate the missing server, and fortunately, no backup tapes are missing. Robert's routine backup schedule is as follows:

Sunday—Normal backup at 1:45 a.m.

Monday—Differential backup at 1:45 a.m.

Tuesday—Incremental backup at 1:45 a.m.

Wednesday—Differential backup at 1:45 a.m.

Thursday—Incremental backup at 1:45 a.m.

Friday—Incremental backup at 1:45 a.m.

Saturday—Differential backup at 1:45 a.m.

Which backup tapes does Robert need to restore the data as quickly as possible?

- ○ A. Sunday, Tuesday, Thursday, Friday, and Saturday
- ○ B. Sunday, Monday, Wednesday, and Saturday
- ○ C. Sunday and Saturday
- ○ D. Sunday, Monday, Wednesday, and Saturday
- ○ E. Sunday, Monday, Tuesday, Wednesday, Thursday, Friday, and Saturday

Question 49

You are the network administrator for a Windows Server 2003 standalone server. You are creating a backup routine that will allow for the shortest possible time to restore from the backup. You are not worried about the amount of time it takes to back up the files and folders. Assume that this server is using a Sunday through Saturday backup schedule. Which routine guarantees the quickest restore if a failure occurs on a Friday?

- ○ A. A normal backup on Sunday followed by differential backups Monday through Saturday
- ○ B. A normal backup on Sunday followed by incremental backups Monday through Saturday
- ○ C. A daily backup on Sunday followed by differential backups Monday through Saturday
- ○ D. A daily backup on Sunday followed by incremental backups Monday through Saturday
- ○ E. All normal backups each day

Question 50

Which default groups allow backing up and restoring of files and folders on a Windows 2003 Server? (Choose three.)

- ❏ A. Administrators
- ❏ B. Account Operators
- ❏ C. Backup Operators
- ❏ D. Print Operators
- ❏ E. Users
- ❏ F. Server Operators

Question 51

You are executing **NTBackup.exe** from the command line on a computer named Server01. Your goal is to do a normal backup of Server01 that includes the C$ administrative share and backs it up to the d$ administrative share. You want to ensure that backup verification is enabled and that access is restricted to the administrator and to you, the person performing the backup operation. What command-line entry will accomplish this goal?

- ○ A. **ntbackup backup \\server01\c$ /J "Command Line Backup" /F \\ server01\d$\backup.bkf /R:no /M normal**

- ○ B. **ntbackup backup \\server01\c$ /J "Command Line Backup" /F \\ server01\d$\backup.bkf**

- ○ C. **ntbackup backup \\server01\c$ /J "Command Line Backup" /F \\ server01\d$\backup.bkf /M normal /R:yes /V:yes**

- ○ D. **ntbackup backup \\server01\c$ /J "Command Line Backup" /F \\ server01\d$\backup.bkf /V:yes /M copy**

Question 52

Orin is unsure which components are included in a backup of the Windows 2003 System State. He made five lists of those components he believes are backed up. Which lists are correct? (Choose two.)

- ❏ A. COM+ class registration database, **SYSVOL**, Active Directory database, C$ administrative share

- ❏ B. COM+ class registration database, **SYSVOL**, Active Directory database, **%systemroot%\system32** folder

- ❏ C. Active Directory database, COM+ class registration database, **SYSVOL**, Certificate Services database

- ❏ D. COM+ class registration database, **SYSVOL**, Active Directory database, Certificate Services database, Windows Registry, **%systemdrive%** folder

- ❏ E. COM+ class registration database, **SYSVOL**, Active Directory database, operating-system files that are protected by Windows File Protection, Windows Registry, IIS metabase

Question 53

For Windows Server 2003 DCs, which additional event logs are added to Event Viewer? (Choose two.)

❑ A. System performance

❑ B. Directory Service

❑ C. File Replication Service

❑ D. Security

❑ E. Application

❑ F. DNS server

Question 54

Event Viewer only opens saved files using which file format?

○ A. **.doc**

○ B. **.evt**

○ C. **.csv**

○ D. **.txt**

○ E. **.pdf**

Question 55

What metric within the default configuration of System Monitor indicates good performance for Memory:Pages/Sec on a Windows Server 2003 computer?

○ A. Between 0 and 2

○ B. Between 10 and 30

○ C. Between 0 and 20

○ D. Between 20 and 40

Question 56

To get the most accurate results when measuring a computer's performance, which best practice should you implement?

○ A. Use Task Manager.

○ B. Use System Monitor in default mode.

○ C. Log the information.

○ D. Monitor the computer remotely.

Question 57

Which default group allows members to manage performance counters, logs, and alerts on the local computer or, on servers within the domain, both interactively (locally) and remotely?

○ A. Performance Monitor Users group

○ B. Power Users group

○ C. Performance Log Users group

○ D. Local Administrators group

Question 58

You use the Event Viewer primarily for viewing what type of data?

○ A. Network data

○ B. Performance data

○ C. Logged data

○ D. Real-time data

Question 59

You want to run an application after an event exceeds your predefined threshold. Which monitoring component should you use?

○ A. Performance Monitor

○ B. Counter log

○ C. Trace log

○ D. Alert

Question 60

As a network administrator, you are responsible for ensuring a high level of performance for the network and the servers for all the users in your company. What must you do first to be able to document changes in the future that might degrade the performance of your network over time?

○ A. Save the event logs in the **.csv** format.

○ B. Establish a baseline.

○ C. Set up performance logs at peak usage times.

○ D. Set up trace logs.

Answers to Practice Exam 1

1. C	**21.** B, E	**41.** A
2. A	**22.** D, F	**42.** A, B, E
3. B	**23.** D, F	**43.** B
4. D	**24.** B	**44.** A, E
5. B	**25.** A	**45.** E
6. A	**26.** B	**46.** A
7. C	**27.** D	**47.** C
8. B	**28.** B, C	**48.** A
9. A	**29.** A, C	**49.** E
10. B, D	**30.** B, D	**50.** A, C, F
11. A, E	**31.** D	**51.** C
12. A	**32.** A	**52.** C, E
13. C	**33.** C	**53.** B, C
14. A, C, G	**34.** A	**54.** B
15. C	**35.** B	**55.** C
16. C	**36.** B, C	**56.** D
17. A	**37.** A, C, D	**57.** C
18. B, D, E	**38.** B, C, F	**58.** C
19. B	**39.** A, C	**59.** D
20. C	**40.** D	**60.** B

Question 1

Answer C is correct. The Add New Hardware Wizard launched from the Control Panel gives users the ability to look at a device that is already installed, attempting to find a quick fix or suggesting further steps as necessary. Answer A is incorrect because the Hardware Troubleshooter only makes suggestions based on user input and is an extension of the Windows Server 2003 Help and Support Center. Answer B is incorrect because the Add or Remove Programs applet does not diagnose or fix hardware problems. Answer D is incorrect because the msconfig utility must be run by a member of the Administrators group, and it manages system-configuration settings, not hardware and device drivers.

Question 2

Answer A is correct. On the Hardware tab of the System Control Panel, you click the Driver Signing button to get into Driver Signing options. Your choices at this point are Ignore, meaning allow any driver; Warn, which is the default; and Block, which stops all nonsigned driver installation. Also, making it the system default imposes your choice on all the other users of the computer. Answer B is not correct because Ignore allows all drivers. Answer C is not correct because the location of the Driver Signing options is incorrect. Answer D is not correct, because Make This Action the System Default is not chosen; the next user to log on could change the setting herself.

Question 3

Answer B is correct. Drivers that are signed by Microsoft typically install for any user without problem, except in a few special cases. If the drivers are not already on the computer or extra configuration is necessary, for instance, you must be a member of the Administrators group to complete the installation. Answer A is not correct because the Power Users group does not give you the proper permissions for installing hardware. Answer C is not correct because the question states that it is. Answer D is not correct because the logo program and signed drivers are recent developments. If the software were truly developed for Windows 3.1, then it is a true statement that would stop the installation because software developed for Windows 3.1 will not run on Windows Server 2003.

Question 4

Answer D is correct. Microsoft does not allow Windows Server 2003, Web Edition, to act as a domain controller (DC); it can be a member server, but not a DC. Answer A is not correct because if the computer has enough RAM to run Windows Server 2003, it has enough RAM to be a DC, although busy DCs can benefit from more RAM. Answer B is not correct because there is no requirement for the placement of the paging file. Answer C is not correct because Standard Edition can also be a DC.

Question 5

Answer B is correct. To enable multiple processors in Windows Server 2003, you must update the hardware abstraction layer (HAL) to utilize the new processors. You can change the HAL by changing the "computer driver" in the Device Manager from uniprocessor to multiprocessor. Answer A is not correct because such an application does not exist. Answer C is not correct because although you can access the Device Manager from Computer Management, there is no Processor Microsoft Management Console. Answer D is not correct because you do not need to rerun Windows Server 2003 installation at all for the upgrade to be successful.

Question 6

Answer A is correct. Windows Server 2003 includes the Roll Back Driver function first introduced in Windows XP. It gives you the ability to get back to a previous version of the driver simply by clicking a button. Answer B is not correct because, although it might work, it is not the best solution. Complications could arise from installing the old driver over the new driver that will not arise from simply rolling back. Answer C is not correct because in a production environment, beta drivers are never the best solution and might introduce more problems than they solve. You should definitely communicate your problems with this latest driver to the manufacturer, however, so it can work on a solution. Answer D is not correct because of the extreme danger it poses to completely disabling your device, if not your server. Device drivers are too intertwined with the core operating system and Registry to attempt manual removal.

Question 7

Answer C is correct. On Windows Server 2003, the CD-burning service is disabled by default because most environments won't attempt to burn from a server. For those computers that do need this ability, simply enable the service, start it, and use the burner. Answer A is not correct because burning is installed by default, just not enabled; it actually is not available as a component to add or remove. Answer B is not correct because burning is not controlled via the local security policy. Answer D is not correct because the machine was preinstalled with Windows Server 2003, and the drive is on the Hardware Compatibility List, so compatibility is not an issue.

Question 8

Answer B is correct. VGA Mode is the lowest common denominator supported by virtually all computers, video cards, and monitors. By booting into VGA Mode, you can set a resolution, color depth, and refresh rate applicable to your hardware and reboot using the new settings. Answer A is not correct because the key combination does not function. Answer C is not correct because it does not allow you to maintain the new driver, which is a requirement of the question. Answer D is not correct because holding down V does not enable VGA mode.

Question 9

Answer A is correct. Hardware profiles give you the ability to choose a "set" of drivers and services to load at boot time. If your server is configured with multiple hardware profiles, and it cannot determine which profile is correct at boot time, it prompts you to choose. Johanna can create a new hardware profile, boot into it, disable all services and devices her application and the server do not rely on, reboot in the regular profile, and then just reboot into the "slim" profile once a month when she needs to run her application. Answer B is not correct because user profiles do not afford you the ability to disable services and devices at boot time. Johanna would have to manually turn off all services she did need and then restart them when her application was done. Answer C is not correct because although configuring your hardware by disabling it in Device Manager might release resources, it is a manual process that you must do each time the application needs to run. Answer D is not correct because Windows Server 2003 does not have such a feature.

Question 10

Answers B and D are correct because two drives in the RAID-5 set died. That means the redundancy information is lost. At this point, restoring from backup is the only solution. Answer A is not correct because two drives have failed, so replacing one has no effect. Answer C is not correct because even if you have a dedicated "recovery" server, it cannot recover the redundancy information lost from losing two drives. Answer E is not correct because Windows Server 2003 does not maintain enough information elsewhere to recover from two failed drives in a RAID 5 array.

Question 11

Answers A and E are correct. The drive is a basic disk because it already has an extended partition on it. It only supports primary and extended partitions. With a maximum of four partitions—one of which can be extended—only the answers containing two or three primary partitions are correct. Answer B is not correct because you cannot have five partitions on a basic disk. Answer C is incorrect because simple volumes only appear on dynamic disks, and the question deals with a basic disk. Similarly, Answer D is incorrect because it mixes volumes and partitions, which cannot exist on the same physical disk.

Question 12

Answer A is correct because it is the tool provided by Microsoft to mount fault-tolerant volumes created in Windows NT 4.0 Server. By default, Windows Server 2003 does not mount fault-tolerant volumes from Windows NT 4.0 Server, but this tool allows them to mount as a temporary solution so you can copy the data elsewhere. Answer B is not correct because the stripe set with parity cannot be converted to a dynamic RAID-5 volume. Answer C is not correct because assuming you left Windows NT 4.0 Server as a bootable operating system, you cannot access dynamic disks from it. Answer D refers to a utility that does not exist.

Question 13

Answer C is the correct choice because you cannot extend a striped volume—one of the main limitations of using striped volumes. Answer A is not correct because fault tolerance is not available on a striped volume. Answer B is not correct because 32 disks are the maximum you can use in a striped volume. Answer D is not correct because the performance of a striped volume is better than a simple volume; the data is written to and read from multiple drives at the same time.

Question 14

Answers A, C, and G are correct because all three operating systems support these combinations of drive configurations and file systems. Answer B is not correct because Windows NT 4.0 Server does not support FAT32 natively. Likewise, you can rule out Answers D and F because Windows NT 4.0 Server does not support dynamic disks, and therefore, it does not support dynamic volumes. Answer E is not correct because Windows Server 2003 does not *natively* support stripe sets, which would have been created on Windows NT 4.0 because of the name, "stripe set." Windows Server 2003 can *use* stripe sets but only after mounting them with an additional tool found on the Windows Server 2003 CD-ROM.

Question 15

Answer C is correct because it provides the ability to run Disk Defragmenter without compromising the security of the computer by logging on as an administrative user. Answer A is not correct because it is not recommended to use the computer while logged on with administrative credentials. Answer B is not correct because you must run Disk Defragmenter locally on a computer. Answer D is not correct because it exposes the computer to risks by using it as a user with administrative privileges as well as adding the overhead of the Terminal Services session to the computer.

Question 16

Answer C is correct because the question asks about the system *partition*. Partitions exist only on basic disks, and the system partition contains the files necessary to boot the computer. Answer A is not correct because it refers to the boot volume, which contains the operating system. Answer B is not correct for several reasons. A spanned volume and a basic disk are mutually exclusive: Spanned volumes exist only on dynamic disks. Also, the system volume—and boot volume—must be on a simple volume rather than on a spanned volume or on any other volume. Answer D is incorrect because partitions and dynamic disks are mutually exclusive, and the \Windows folder is the boot volume or partition rather than the system volume or partition.

Question 17

Answer A is correct because a dynamic disk moved from one Windows 2000, Windows XP Professional, or Windows Server 2003 computer to a different computer is listed with a status of Foreign in Disk Management. You can simply right-click the disk and import it to make it available in the new computer. Answer B is not correct because Device Manager is not the appropriate tool to use. Answer C is not correct because Activate This Disk is not a valid choice to render the foreign disk operable. Answer D is not correct, again because Device Manager is not the correct tool to use.

Question 18

Answers B, D, and E are correct because they explain the procedure for breaking and replacing a mirrored volume. You must right-click on Disk 3 and break the mirror from there for Disk 3 to retain the existing drive letter. Also, when creating a mirror, you must choose a dynamic disk with enough unallocated space, and you want to be sure the status of the new mirrored volume is Healthy. Answer A is incorrect because it removes the volume completely from Disk 3. Answer C is not correct because it gives Disk 2 the H: drive letter. Answer F is incorrect because, although Disk 3 retains the H: drive letter, the volume is removed completely from Disk 2, which does not meet the objective of retaining the data. Answer G is not correct because to add a mirror to an existing simple volume, you must choose another dynamic disk with enough unallocated space. You cannot create a mirror from two existing simple volumes.

Question 19

Answer B is correct. You can use the `dsrm` command for removing objects in Active Directory. Answer A is incorrect because you use `dsquery` for performing search operations. Answer C is incorrect because you use the `dsmove` command to move or rename objects in Active Directory. Answer D is incorrect because you use `dsadd` for adding objects to Active Directory. Answer E is incorrect because you use `dsget` for displaying properties of objects in Active Directory. You use the `net user` command for adding users and for viewing user information.

Question 20

Answer C is correct. Domain mapping allows an administrator to configure the account to be able to log on to a non-Windows Kerberos realm. Answer A is incorrect because name mapping is not used to map a user profile to a network share. Answer B is incorrect because name mapping is not used for mapping a user to his home folder. Answer D is incorrect because name mapping is not necessary for a computer to log on to a child domain.

Question 21

Answers B and E are correct. Both the Domain Name System and TCP/IP are network components that you must install to install Active Directory. Answer A is incorrect because Windows 2000 domains use DNS not WINS for the domain name-resolution protocol so it does not have to be present to install Active Directory. Answer C is incorrect. Kerberos is the default protocol for logon authentication in Active Directory, but you do not install it. It becomes part of the Active Directory installation, but it does not have to be present before you can install Active Directory. Answer D is incorrect because Remote Procedure Call (RPC) does not need to be present before you can install Active Directory. Answer F is incorrect because NetBIOS does not need to be present to install Active Directory.

Question 22

Answers D and F are correct. To raise the function level for your forest to Server 2003, you must have all the DCs running Windows 2003 Server and all domains in the forest must be at least in Windows 2000 native mode. Answer A is incorrect because the workstation operating system is not a factor in raising the function level of the forest. Answer B is incorrect because you do not need to upgrade your servers, just the DCs. Answer C is incorrect because there is no Windows 2000 native mode for forests. Answer E is incorrect because there is no Windows 2003 domain native mode in a Windows Server 2003 Active Directory forest, only the interim and Windows 2003 levels.

Question 23

Answers D and F are correct. You prestage computer accounts in Active Directory to have more control over which computers will be able to contact a Remote Installation Services (RIS) server to download the operating system for each computer. You identify that computer using its GUID or UUID. Answer A is incorrect. Although a computer's fully qualified domain name (FQDN) must be unique within the forest, it is not used for prestaging computer accounts. Answer B is incorrect because the TCP/IP address is not used for prestaging computer accounts. Answer C is incorrect because computer names are not used for prestaging computer accounts. Answer E is incorrect because security identifiers (SIDs) are not used for prestaging computer accounts.

Question 24

Answer B is correct. Computer accounts in Active Directory must have a password to communicate with Active Directory. If the password on the computer gets out of sync with the password in Active Directory, the computer can no longer be authenticated by Active Directory. To fix this problem, you must reset the computer account and then rejoin the computer to the domain. Answer A is incorrect because the user account password has nothing to do with the computer account. Answer C is incorrect because rebooting the computer does not rejoin the computer to the domain. Answer D is incorrect because SIDs are what Active Directory uses to identify an object's permission level; they do not allow the user to log back on to the network in this situation.

Question 25

Answer A is correct. A one-way trust must be in place between a Windows NT 4.0 domain and a Windows Server 2003 domain before users who are running Windows 98 on their computers can access resources in the Active Directory domain. Answer B is incorrect because you only use `dsclient.exe` for Windows 98 computers that need to access Active Directory features, such as querying Active Directory objects, within the same domain. Answer C is incorrect because although Kerberos is the authentication protocol for Active Directory, it is not used by Window 98 computers. Answer D is incorrect because DNS is used for locating computers, not for authentication.

Question 26

Answer B is correct. Domain local groups can contain user accounts and global groups from any domain in the forest. Answer A is incorrect because universal groups are not available in a domain set at the Windows 2000 mixed level. Answer C is incorrect because security groups refer to a type of group where you can apply permissions to the members in the group; it is not a group scope. Answer D is incorrect because in a Windows 2000 mixed-mode domain, global groups can only contain accounts from the same domain.

Question 27

Answer D is correct. In the Active Directory Users and Computers console, when you right-click any user and select All Tasks, you find the Resultant Set of Policy (Logging) option. This option lets you view policy settings for a particular computer. Answer A is incorrect because although you might be able to determine the problem by going through the Group Policy Object Editor, you have to search through all the nodes to find the one that might be causing the problem. Answer B is incorrect because you use `dsquery` for searching for computers, groups, and organizational units (OUs)—not for group policies. Answer C is incorrect because you use `dsget` for displaying the properties of computers, servers, and OUs—not for displaying group policy.

Question 28

Answers B and C are correct because the syntax of the /user option should be in the form of USER@DOMAIN or DOMAIN\USER. Answers A, D, and E are incorrect because these answers do not provide domain administrative credentials when running the Computer Management console.

Question 29

Answers A and C are correct. The default setting is for a Remote Assistance (RA) invitation to remain active for one hour. If the invitation expires, you cannot make a connection to the requesting computer. Also, if TCP port 3389 is blocked at the firewall, you cannot make a connection either. Answer B is incorrect because an RA invitation could not have been generated if RA were disabled. Answer D is incorrect because RA listens on TCP port 3389, not UDP port 3389. Answer E is incorrect because user permissions are not considered during an invitation response—which is why it is imperative that you fully trust the person from whom you are requesting assistance.

Question 30

Answers B and D are correct because Terminal Services (TS) stops accepting connection requests after 120 days if it does not find a TS License Server with the correct number of Terminal Server Client Access Licenses (TSCALs). Answer A is incorrect because the client operating-system version is irrelevant in this case. Answer C is incorrect because rebooting the server does not reset the 120-day period. Answer E is incorrect because the Terminal Server in this case is not corrupted.

Question 31

Answer D is the correct choice because TS listens on TCP port 3389 by default. Answers A, B, and C are incorrect because the question states that the Terminal Server is listening on the default port.

Question 32

Answer A is correct because the Terminal Services Manager provides the ability to disconnect or log off Terminal Server sessions from any Windows Server 2003 or Windows XP computer. Answer B is incorrect because you cannot terminate sessions from Terminal Services Configuration. Answer C is incorrect because you cannot terminate sessions from TS Licensing. Answer D is incorrect because there is no such TS tool.

Question 33

Answer C is correct. There you find options to view user statistics, session information, processes held by individual users, and processes held by the server. You can disconnect users as well as remotely control their sessions. Answer A is incorrect because Active Directory Users and Computers is for doing general user tasks (adding, deleting, moving, and so on) in Active Directory. Answer B is incorrect because Terminal Services Configuration allows you to set or modify Terminal Server configuration settings. Answer D is incorrect because Terminal Services Licensing is for adding TSCALs and activating or deactivating the license servers.

Question 34

Answer A is correct because by launching the Help and Support Center and selecting the View Invitation Status option, you can force the invitation to expire immediately. Answers B and C are incorrect because you will not find the Expire or Delete button within the Invite Someone to Help You option. Answer D is incorrect because the Control Panel does not contain any options for RA.

Question 35

Answer B is correct because the RA configuration settings are stored in the Computer Configuration\Administrative Templates\System\Remote Assistance Registry subkey. Answers A, C, and D are incorrect because those Registry keys do not exist.

Question 36

Answers B and C are correct. Because all drive letters have hidden administrative shares created automatically, you can retrieve the unmodified document from a previous version using the Shadow Copies of Shared Folders feature. In this case, you have to specify the network UNC path of \\server1\ e$\specialdocs to access the previous versions; up to 64 previous versions are retained. Because you made the modification on Monday, Sunday's full backup was the last time the unmodified document was backed up onto backup media. Answer A is not correct because you modified the document on Monday. On Monday night, the modified document, minus the information you need, was backed up during the incremental backup. Answer D is not correct because you need to connect to the file over the network to work with shadow copies.

Question 37

Answers A, C, and D are correct. These three files are necessary for any 32-bit Windows Server 2003 computer to boot. You also need to make sure that the boot.ini file is correct for the computer that you are using the disk on. Answer B is not correct because it is an MS-DOS file, and you do not need it to start Windows Server 2003. Answer E is not correct because this file, although it might exist, is not a Windows Server 2003 system or boot file at all. Answer F is not correct because, although it might be needed on some Windows Server 2003 boot disks, it is not one of the required files for all installations.

Question 38

Answers B, C, and F are correct. These options all appear when you enter the advanced startup menu. Answer A is not correct because the Recovery Console is not part of Safe Mode. Answer D is not correct because you cannot launch the Recovery Console from this menu. Answer E is not correct because you start Automated System Recovery (ASR) by booting from the Windows Server 2003 CD-ROM and choosing the appropriate option.

Question 39

Answers A and C are correct. You need to boot into the Recovery Console; even if you have it installed, you cannot get to the boot menu in this case, so booting off the CD-ROM is the only practical method to launch the Recovery Console. Once in the Recovery Console, the `fixboot` command repairs the boot sector. Answer B is not correct because the question stated that you are unable to boot into Windows Server 2003 in the first place. Answer D is not correct because it creates an MS-DOS master boot record and boot sector on the hard drive, which does not allow booting Windows Server 2003. Answer E is not correct because an ASR overwrites the entire computer instead of fixing this one problem.

Question 40

Answer D is correct. You can make an ASR backup to any media supported by the Windows Server 2003 backup program, which includes files on hard drives, tapes, and other removable media. When performing the restore, however, bear in mind that Windows Server 2003 needs to be able to access the device that the backup was made on. If that device requires a third-party driver, that driver must be installed for the ASR to restore the server successfully. Answer A is not correct because part of the ASR recovery is to format the boot volume, which destroys the ASR backup. Answers B and C are not correct because the need for the manufacturer's device driver software presents an added step that other solutions do not require.

Question 41

Answer A is correct. Serial Port Console Redirection (SPCR) is a standard that must be supported by the hardware vendor for Windows Server 2003 to utilize it. SPCR redirects video output and accepts keyboard input using the serial port. Answer B is not correct because it is not a standard. Answer C is not correct because NTFS deals with storage on hard drives, not emergency management of the server. Answer D is not correct because Emergency Management Services (EMS) gets access to a server specifically because it is not accessible via the network.

Question 42

Answers A, B, and E are correct. The Recovery Console gives you the ability to enable and disable services using a command line. If you can get into Safe Mode or Safe Mode with Networking Support, you can easily go into the Services snap-in and disable the service that you believe is causing the problem. Answer C is not correct because ASR totally restores your server, wiping out data on the system volume in the process. Answer D is not correct because the EMS Special Administration Console (SAC) does not allow you to disable services directly. Answer E is incorrect because Directory Services Restore Mode is not a recovery tool for troubleshooting operating system services; it is used for restoring the Active Directory database on DCs.

Question 43

Answer B is correct because Safe Mode works, but enabling networking components causes the computer to stop working. Therefore, some component in the network subsystem is probably causing the problem. Answer A is not correct because if it were a video driver issue, Safe Mode itself might not function, but you would not see the different behavior in the two Safe Mode options. Answer C is not correct because although some type of corruption in networking components is likely causing the problem, the best assumption is that it is at a lower level than shared folders. Answer D is not correct because a corrupted boot sector would not allow the computer to boot even into Safe Mode.

Question 44

Answers A and E are correct. All editions of Windows Server 2003 have the capability to create shadow copies, as long as the volumes configured for shadow copies are running NTFS. In fact, if they are running FAT or FAT32, the Shadow Copies tab does not even appear. Answer B is not correct because the computer is running FAT32. Answers C and D are not correct because shadow copies are not available for creation on any edition of Windows 2000 Server. Also, the Previous Versions client has nothing to do with the creation of shadow copies, only with their restoration, and the Previous Versions client that comes with Windows Server 2003 will not install on Windows 2000. Note as well that even if Windows 2000 Server did support shadow copies, the server is running FAT32, which does not support shadow copies.

Question 45

Answer E is correct. The differential backup backs up only those files that have their archive bits set, indicating they have been modified since the last normal or incremental backup. Additionally, the archive bits are not cleared after the files are backed up during a differential backup. Answer A is incorrect because the archive bits are cleared after an incremental backup. Answer B is incorrect because a copy backup backs up all files and leaves the archive bits just as they are. Answer C is incorrect because the archive bits are cleared during a normal backup. Answer D is incorrect because a daily backup only backs up those files created or modified on the day when the backup takes place, and it does not modify the archive-bit settings on the backed-up files.

Question 46

Answer A is correct. A normal backup (also known as a full backup) copies all selected files and clears the archive bit. An incremental backup backs up files that have their archive bits set, which indicates they have been modified since the last normal or incremental backup. Once an incremental backup is performed, those files' archive bits are cleared. If you are performing a combination of normal and incremental backups, you need the last normal backup as well as all the incremental backups since the last normal backup will be needed for the restore. Answer B is incorrect because you would not have the files and folders modified on Friday available to be restored. Answers C, D, and E are incorrect because with incremental backups, you need each incremental backup tape leading up to the most recent normal backup tape.

Question 47

Answer C is correct. Because a differential backup backs up those files that have changed since the last normal backup and it does not clear the archive bits, you need only the Sunday (normal) and the Thursday (differential) tapes. Answer A is incorrect because the Monday, Tuesday, and Wednesday backups contain the same backed-up files as the Thursday backup tape. Answer B is incorrect because Thursday's differential backup alone is not sufficient—Thursday's backup only contains files whose data had changed since the last normal or incremental backup. The balance of the data would be missing from that backup set. Answer D is incorrect because you generally want to start a restore with a normal or full backup, not with a differential backup.

Question 48

Answer A is correct. With this backup routine, you need the Sunday normal; the Tuesday, Thursday, and Friday incremental; and Saturday's differential backups to restore from. It is important to remember, differential backups do *not* clear the archive bits, but the incremental backups do. Therefore, Answer B is incorrect because you do not need any differential backups except for Saturday's. The Tuesday, Thursday, and Friday incremental backups contain all the data stored on the Monday and Wednesday differential backups. Answer C is incorrect because the Sunday backup does not contain any data from Monday through Friday and the Saturday backup is only a differential backup. Answer D is incorrect because again, not enough data is being restored. Answer E is incorrect because you don't need the differential backups from Monday or Wednesday. The data from the Monday and Wednesday differential backups is contained on the incremental backups that follow those differentials.

Question 49

Answer E is correct. As with all normal backups, you only need to restore from one backup tape, which in this case is the Friday tape. Answer A is incorrect because you need to restore from two tapes, the Sunday and Friday tapes. Answer B is incorrect because you need to restore from six tapes. Answers C and D are incorrect because a daily backup backs up only the data that is new or that has been changed on the same day that the backup is performed. You need to start with a normal backup to guarantee that all data is restored.

Question 50

Answers A, C, and F are correct. By default, these groups have the proper permissions to back up and restore files and folders. Answers B, D, and E are incorrect because they do not have the proper permissions to back up and restore files.

Question 51

Answer C is correct. The /V:yes switch verifies the backup, the /R:yes switch only allows access to the owner and the administrator, and the /M normal switch specifies a normal backup. Answers A, B, and D are incorrect because they don't specify the correct switch settings.

Question 52

Answers C and E are correct. The files that are included in a System State backup include the Windows Registry, the COM+ class registration database, boot and system files, the Certificate Services database (if Certificate Services is installed), the Active Directory database, the SYSVOL folder (if the computer is a DC), operating-system files protected by Windows File Protection (WFP), the Internet Information Services (IIS) metabase (if IIS is installed), and cluster service information (if the server is part of a cluster). Answer A is incorrect because the C$ administrative share is not included in a System State backup. Answer B is incorrect because the %systemroot%\system32 folder is not included in a System State backup. Answer D is incorrect because the %systemdrive% folder is not included in a System State backup.

Question 53

Answers B and C are correct. When a Windows 2003 Server is promoted to a DC, the Directory Service and the File Replication Service event logs are automatically added to help monitor critical services that deal with Active Directory. Answer A is incorrect because system performance is not available through the Event Viewer. Answers D and E are incorrect because these logs are installed automatically with the default installation of Windows Server 2003. Answer F is incorrect because the DNS Server event log is not necessarily added when a server is promoted to a DC. The DNS Server event log appears only if the DNS service is installed on the DC. DNS might be hosted on other Windows servers or on UNIX servers.

Question 54

Answer B is correct. You can save log files in several different formats in Event Viewer, such as .evt, .csv, and .txt. But only log files saved as .evt can be viewed using Event Viewer. Answer A is incorrect because you cannot save Event Viewer log files as a Word document. Answer C is incorrect because you cannot open .csv files with Event Viewer. You have to use a program such as Excel to open the file. Answer D is incorrect because you can open a log file saved as .txt only with a program like Notepad. Answer E is incorrect because Event Viewer cannot save a log as a .pdf file.

Question 55

Answer C is correct. Hard page faults occur when a process requests a page from RAM (Random Access Memory) and the system cannot find it, so it must then be retrieved from the hard drive. As long as the value remains between 0 and 20, performance on the server should not suffer. Answer A is incorrect because this metric is too low. As long as the metric stays below 20, you will still have good performance on your server. Answers B and D are incorrect because these metrics indicate too many page faults; therefore, performance might suffer.

Question 56

Answer D is correct. Because the performance monitoring tool requires system resources to run, if you run the tool locally, the readings will not be as accurate as they could be. The readings would include not only the server's performance as a result of its workload, but also the load on the system's resources from the monitoring tool. Answers A and B are incorrect because although you use both Task Manager and System Manager for monitoring performance, the question asks how you get the most accurate results. Answer C is incorrect because you need to log the information so that it can be viewed and evaluated later; this fact does not answer the question of how to obtain the most accurate results.

Question 57

Answer C is correct. Performance Log Users group is a new group created by default that allows members to manage performance counters, logs, and alerts. Answer A is incorrect because members of the Performance Monitor Users group only have permissions to *monitor* performance counters. Answer B is incorrect because members of the Power Users group would not have the proper level of permissions to manage performance information on servers. Answer D is incorrect because members of the local Administrators group do not have permission to monitor other servers remotely.

Question 58

Answer C is correct. Events are recorded into log files by the Event Log service, which is configured to run at system startup by default. You use Event Viewer to view these log files. Answer A is incorrect because you use the Networking tab in Task Manager to view networking performance. Answer B is incorrect because you use Performance Monitor and Task Manager to view computer performance data. Answer D is incorrect because you use Event Viewer to view events that have already occurred, not events as they happen in real time.

Question 59

Answer D is correct. When an alert is triggered based on its settings, it can perform several actions, including creating an entry in the application event log, sending a network message to someone, initiating logging for a specific performance log, and running an application program. Answer A is incorrect because Performance Monitor is the monitoring program, but it is the Alert log where you can set up an action to be triggered based on a condition or event. Answers B and C are incorrect because neither of these types of logs can be configured to perform the action required.

Question 60

Answer B is correct. To be able to document what changes might have occurred to degrade system and network performance, you need to establish a performance baseline. In this way, you can compare the baseline-performance history with the current performance measurements to diagnose the problem. Answer A is incorrect because the Event Viewer does not show information that deals with server performance. Answer C is incorrect because to establish a baseline, you need to monitor server performance during normal usage workloads, not during high-usage workloads. Answer D is incorrect because you do not use trace logs to measure server performance.

Practice Exam 2

Question 1

How can you allow users to have their unique desktop settings follow them no matter which workstation they log on to but not save whatever changes they make to their desktop settings?

- ○ A. On each workstation in the domain, delete the **%systemdrive%\Documents and Settings\Default User** folder.

- ○ B. Rename the file named **system** in the **%systemroot%\system32\config\system** folder to **system.man**.

- ○ C. Configure a roaming profile for each user in the domain. Create a shared profile folder on a server, such as **\\server1\profiles**. On server1, rename the **ntuser.dat** file within each user's profile to **ntuser.man**.

- ○ D. Create a GPO named RoamProfile. Assign the RoamProfile GPO to the domain. Configure the RoamProfile GPO to delete the local copy of each user's profile when each user logs off.

Question 2

You have RIS running so that you can easily install the operating system for your domain. What can you do to prevent users from installing the operating system on unauthorized computers?

- ○ A. Upgrade all Windows 98 and Windows NT 4.0 workstation computers to Windows 2000 or Windows XP Professional so that users can log on using only the Kerberos authentication protocol.

- ○ B. In the ADUC console, add new computers to the RIS default container.

- ○ C. Create a group called Remote Installation Users and add only those users whom you want to grant permission to add computer accounts to the domain.

- ○ D. Specify that only prestaged computer accounts can be installed by RIS.

Question 3

Ellen, a network administrator in your New York office, has just added a child OU named Specialties to the existing Sales OU. The Sales OU is a child OU within the Northeast OU. John, a network administrator in Chicago, has just accidentally deleted the Sales OU, after Ellen added the Specialties OU. The organization has only one Active Directory domain, and there are DCs at each physical location. You go to recover the Specialties OU in the Lost and Found container. You check the ADUC console and cannot see any Lost and Found container. What must you do to fix this?

⭘ A. Add yourself to the Enterprise Admins group.

⭘ B. Click the View menu and select Advanced Features.

⭘ C. Go to Control Panel, click Add or Remove Programs, and then click Add Windows Components.

⭘ D. Go to the ADUC console, right-click the domain name, and then click the Show Hidden Container option.

Question 4

For which of the following domain functional levels can administrators nest groups within other groups and change the scope of groups? (Choose two.)

❑ A. Windows 2000 native

❑ B. Windows 2000 mixed

❑ C. Windows Server 2003

❑ D. Windows Server 2003 interim

❑ E. Windows Server 2003 mixed

Question 5

A user reports that she cannot log on to her Windows 2000 Professional computer because she gets the following error message: "NETLOGON Event ID 3210: Failed to authenticate with \\DC07, a Windows NT domain controller for domain CORPSALES." What must you do so that the user can log on?

⭘ A. Reset the computer account.

⭘ B. Reset the user account's password.

⭘ C. Delete and then re-create the user account.

⭘ D. Move the computer account into the Computers container and press the F5 function key to refresh the account.

Question 6

Which of the following **dsadd.exe** commands creates a universal distribution group called Sales Reps in the Sales OU that is within the East Coast OU within the Windows2003.local domain?

- ○ A. **dsadd group cn=sales reps,ou=sales,ou=east coast,dc= windows2003,dc=local –secgrp no -scope l**

- ○ B. **dsadd group "cn=sales reps ou=sales ou=east coast dc= windows2003 dc=local" –secgrp -scope u**

- ○ C. **dsadd group "cn=sales reps,ou=sales,ou=east coast,dc= windows2003,dc=local" –secgrp no -scope u**

- ○ D. **dsadd group "cn=sales reps,ou=sales,ou=east coast,dc= windows2003,dc=local" –secgrp yes -scope u**

Question 7

You have all the account information for 148 new users in an Excel worksheet. Which command-line utility can you use to import all these users into Active Directory?

- ○ A. **dsadd.exe**
- ○ B. **ldifde.exe**
- ○ C. **dsget.exe**
- ○ D. **csvde.exe**

Question 8

In the Windows 2000 mixed domain functional level, which group can contain global groups from any domain in the forest?

- ○ A. Universal groups
- ○ B. Security groups
- ○ C. Global groups
- ○ D. Domain local groups

Question 9

Windows Server 2003, like Windows XP, implements much stricter permissions by default. What are the default permissions for an NTFS boot partition or boot volume for the Everyone group?

- ○ A. Allow Full Control
- ○ B. Deny Full Control and Allow Read
- ○ C. Allow Read and Execute without inheritance
- ○ D. Allow Read and Execute with inheritance

Question 10

Jean has a legacy application on the D: drive that her department relies on to complete its daily tasks. The application does not function correctly with the NTFS file system. Unfortunately, during the upgrade of the departmental server to Windows Server 2003, the central IT department converted all disks to dynamic disks and all volumes to NTFS. Jean must convert the D: drive back to FAT. What steps must she take to ensure the conversion happens without losing any data? (Choose three.)

- ❑ A. Run the command **convert D: /fs:fat32**.
- ❑ B. Run the command **convert D: /fs:fat**.
- ❑ C. Back up all data to another location.
- ❑ D. Reformat the D: drive using the Disk Management console.
- ❑ E. Reformat the D: drive using Windows Explorer.
- ❑ F. Convert the disk to a basic disk.
- ❑ G. Restore the data to the reformatted volume.

Question 11

Shadow Copies relies on the Previous Versions client software that comes with Windows Server 2003. Where is this client located?

- ○ A. In the **\support\tools** folder of the Windows Server 2003 CD-ROM
- ○ B. In the **%systemroot%\system32\clients\twclient** directory on the Windows Server 2003 computer
- ○ C. In the **%systemroot%\system32\clients\tsclient** directory on the Windows Server 2003 computer
- ○ D. In the default shared folder named **PVClient** on the Windows Server 2003 computer

Question 12

Which of the following statements are true regarding NTFS data compression? (Choose three.)

❏ A. NTFS compression is vital when using quotas because it allows a user to store more physical data than the quota allows.

❏ B. Compressing a volume compresses all new files and folders created on that volume.

❏ C. NTFS compression allows individual files and folders to be compressed as an attribute of the file or folder.

❏ D. If a folder is compressed, all the files created or copied into the folder are compressed as well.

❏ E. You must be a member of the Administrators group to have your files or folders compressed.

❏ F. You must be a member of the Power Users group to have your files or folders compressed.

Question 13

Jane wants to be able to administer her Windows Server 2003 member server using Remote Desktop for Administration. She does not want to log on to the computer as the administrator for security reasons. What must she do to ensure that her user account can log on to the server using the Remote Desktop Connection client? (Choose three.)

❏ A. Mark the Allow Users to Connect Remotely to This Computer check box on the Remote tab of the System Properties window.

❏ B. Mark the Turn on Remote Assistance and Allow Invitations to Be Sent from This Computer check box on the Remote tab of the System Properties window.

❏ C. Ensure that her user account does not have a blank password.

❏ D. Make sure she is a member of the Terminal Services Users group.

❏ E. Make sure she is a member of the Remote Desktop Users group.

❏ F. Ensure her password is at least 12 characters long.

Question 14

Harvey has decided to implement NTFS disk quotas on the data volume of his Windows Server 2003 computer. He enables quotas in the properties of the data drive volume. He wants to set the limit for all members of the Research group to 50MB each but no limits for anyone else currently. How can he accomplish this goal?

- ○ A. By setting the quotas for each user individually to 50MB
- ○ B. By setting the quotas for the Research group to 50MB
- ○ C. By choosing each user in ADUC and selecting Quotas from the All Tasks menu
- ○ D. By executing the command **fsutil quota modify d: 0 50 research** at a command prompt

Question 15

What are the benefits of using FAT32 as a file system in Windows Server 2003? (Choose two.)

- ❑ A. You ensure security for the Windows system files.
- ❑ B. You retain the ability to access files with an MS-DOS–based boot disk.
- ❑ C. You gain the ability to create fault-tolerant volumes.
- ❑ D. You retain compatibility with previous operating systems that might coexist on the server.
- ❑ E. You have the ability to compress files and folders at the file-system level.

Question 16

Which applications let you publish a shared folder to Active Directory? (Choose two.)

- ❑ A. The **net share** command from the command line
- ❑ B. The Shared Folders console in Computer Management
- ❑ C. The Sharing tab in the properties of a folder
- ❑ D. Windows Explorer
- ❑ E. The ADUC console

Question 17

Arthur receives a frantic call at 2 a.m. from the auditing department of his company. They need to access files that are stored in the **E:\reports** folder on the server, but the folder is currently not shared. Arthur's computer at his home runs Windows 95 and does not have a Remote Desktop Connection client installed on it. The server at the office temporarily has the Telnet service enabled, and the firewall is forwarding all Telnet traffic to the server. How can Arthur share the **E:\reports** directory for the auditing department without having to go in to the office?

- ○ A. Dial in directly to the server and use the Windows Server 2003 shared folder snap-in over the dial-up connection.
- ○ B. Connect to the server using Telnet and run the command **net share reports=e:\reports**.
- ○ C. Connect to the server using Telnet and use the Windows Server 2003 shared folder snap-in.
- ○ D. Dial in directly to the server and run the command **net view \\server\ reports add**.

Question 18

Max is trying to modify a file stored on a share on his Windows Server 2003 computer. He is a member of the Users and Accounting groups. The permissions that are currently in effect are as follows:

- ➤ Share permissions—Everyone:Allow Full Control
- ➤ Max's NTFS permissions—Allow Read and Execute
- ➤ Users group NTFS permissions—Allow Modify
- ➤ Accounting group NTFS permissions—Deny Write

Why isn't Max able to save his changes to the file?

- ○ A. The share permissions are too restrictive.
- ○ B. The combination of share permissions and the User group's permissions is causing the problem.
- ○ C. The combination of Max's and the User group's permissions is too restrictive.
- ○ D. Max's membership in the Accounting group is causing the problem.

Question 19

Uma has read about Shadow Copies of Shared Folders in Windows Server 2003 and wants to enable this feature on her server. She currently has two physical disks with two volumes each. Drive D:, on physical disk 1, has four shares, but only one share needs Shadow Copies enabled. Drives E: and F:, on physical disk 2, have several shares each, but only the shares on drive E: need Shadow Copies enabled. Where should Uma enable shadow copies for these shares? (Choose two.)

- ❑ A. On physical disk 1
- ❑ B. On physical disk 2
- ❑ C. On drive D:
- ❑ D. On drive E:
- ❑ E. On drive F:
- ❑ F. Only on the shares that need the Shadow Copies service

Question 20

A user who is no longer with your company encrypted some important files that you now need to access. How can you gain access to these files?

- ○ A. Copy the files from the NTFS volume to a FAT32 volume. They will be unencrypted by virtue of the fact that FAT32 does not support encryption.
- ○ B. Back up the files to tape as an administrator and restore them to another server.
- ○ C. Use the designated data recovery agent (DRA) to decrypt the files.
- ○ D. Disable encryption using group policies to force all encrypted files to become unencrypted.

Question 21

Alison is a user in the NorthAmerica Active Directory domain and she is a member of several different groups. As the network administrator, you need to give her access permissions to read and write to files in the **E:\Common\Sales\VPs** shared folder. You believe that by making Alison a member of the VP Assistants group, she should have the proper access permissions to the VPs folder, but she reports that she can't save documents in that folder. In diagnosing the problem, you narrow it down to an NTFS permissions issue. How can you quickly troubleshoot this problem so that you can solve it?

- ○ A. Make Alison a member of the Administrators group.
- ○ B. Grant Alison's user account the Allow:Modify permission for this folder only.
- ○ C. Grant Alison's user account the Allow:Full Control permission for this folder only.
- ○ D. Check the NTFS Effective Permissions for Alison.

Question 22

When viewing the Effective Permissions dialog box to find the effective permissions that actually apply to a user, what are you actually looking at?

- ○ A. Permissions granted explicitly to the user
- ○ B. Permissions combined from the user and the groups that the user is a member of
- ○ C. Permissions combined from the user and groups that the user is a member of, as well as permissions inherited from the parent object
- ○ D. Permissions granted to the Everyone group

Question 23

You notice that your E: drive, which stores all your company's data files, is starting to fill up rapidly. You want to implement disk quotas on the drive, limiting all users to 100MB of space. You will then make individual changes as necessary. You enable quotas on the E: drive, you set the default quota limit to 100MB, and then you deny space to users exceeding that limit. One of your users, Amy, compresses her folder using NTFS compression in the hope that she'll be able to store more data on drive E: and get around the disk space quota. What happens when Amy has used 97MB of disk space on drive E: and she then attempts to copy a 5MB file into her compressed folder?

- ○ A. Windows Server 2003 allows the file to be copied into that folder because NTFS compression is enabled.
- ○ B. Windows Server 2003 displays a warning message box to Amy regarding her disk-quota limit, but it allows her to copy the file into the compressed folder.
- ○ C. Windows Server 2003 allows the file to be copied, but it will not allow any more files to be stored on drive E: for Amy unless she moves or deletes her existing files to comply with her disk quota.
- ○ D. Windows Server 2003 does not allow the file to be copied into the folder because Amy would then be exceeding her disk-quota limit.

Question 24

Which of the following are features of the NTFS file system? (Choose three.)

❑ A. NTFS compresses files and folders by creating a special file to fill the drive and mounting it as a virtual drive.

❑ B. NTFS offers the ability to encrypt files.

❑ C. NTFS offers the ability to apply permissions to files and folders.

❑ D. You can use NTFS on floppy disks.

❑ E. NTFS has a disk-quota system built in that lets you implement disk-space restrictions.

❑ F. You can format CD-R, CD/RW, DVD+R, DVD-R, DVD+RW, and DVD-RW media as NTFS.

Question 25

Henrietta wants to use permissions to ensure that users' access to resources is consistent, whether they are sitting locally at the server or accessing resources remotely over the network. What permissions should Henrietta utilize to achieve this goal in the easiest manner possible?

○ A. NTFS permissions, setting share permissions to Everyone:Allow Full Control

○ B. NTFS permissions, leaving share permissions at their default values

○ C. Share permissions, settings NTFS permissions to Everyone:Allow Full Control

○ D. Share permissions, leaving NTFS permissions at their default values

Question 26

What are the default share permissions in Windows Server 2003?

○ A. Users:Allow Full Control

○ B. Everyone:Allow Full Control

○ C. Users:Allow Read and Execute

○ D. Everyone:Allow Read

Question 27

After successfully migrating your Windows 2000 Server IIS 5.0 Web server to Windows Server 2003 and IIS 6.0, your CIO asks you what mode the Web site is currently running. Perplexed, you use Remote Access to access your IIS server to find out. Where should you look to determine the mode in which the Web site is running, and what answer will you give to your CIO? (Choose two.)

❑ A. In the IIS Manager snap-in, expand the Web server node that you want to work with and right-click the Web Site subnode. Select Properties and click the Services tab. There you find the Isolation Mode option.

❑ B. In the IIS Manager snap-in, expand the Web server node that you want to work with and right-click the Web Site subnode. Select Properties and click the Web Site tab. There you find the Isolation Mode option.

❑ C. In the IIS Manager snap-in, expand the Web server node that you want to work with and right-click the Web Site subnode. Select Properties and click the Directory Security tab. There you find the Isolation Mode option.

❑ D. You will inform your CIO that the Web site is running in IIS 5.0 Isolation Mode.

❑ E. You will inform your CIO that the Web site is running in Worker Process Isolation Mode.

Question 28

You have installed the default components of IIS 6.0 on server02, a Windows Server 2003 computer. You open IE 6.0 on server02 and type **https://server02:8098** in the address box. You receive a Page Cannot Be Displayed error message. What is the most likely reason that you are receiving this error?

○ A. The firewall is blocking TCP port 8098.

○ B. You did not select the Remote Administration option when installing IIS 6.0.

○ C. You must start the Internet services on server02.

○ D. You do not have administrative permissions on the domain.

Question 29

You are a Windows 2003 Server administrator. You want to be able to browse the Web without receiving an Internet Explorer Enhanced Security Configuration alert message. However, you only want this option disabled for administrators. What must you do to disable this feature for administrators only?

- ○ A. In Internet Explorer 6.0, click Tools, Internet Options, and click the Advanced Tab. Scroll down to the Security settings and clear the Warn If Changing Between Secure and Not Secure Mode check box.

- ○ B. Open Control Panel, double-click Add or Remove Programs, click Add/Remove Windows Components, select Internet Explorer Enhanced Security Configuration, click the Details button, and make sure both check boxes are marked.

- ○ C. In Internet Explorer 6.0, click Tools, Internet Options, and click the Security tab. Click the Internet Zone and set the slider for the Security Level for This Zone to Low.

- ○ D. Open Control Panel, double-click Add or Remove Programs, click Add/Remove Windows Components, select Internet Explorer Enhanced Security Configuration, click the Details button, and clear the appropriate check box.

Question 30

Which utility allows you to change the way users are authenticated or granted access to a Web site? (Choose two.)

- ❑ A. Active Directory Users and Computers
- ❑ B. Internet Information Services (IIS) Manager
- ❑ C. IIS 6.0 Remote Administration (HTML)
- ❑ D. Internet Authentication Service
- ❑ E. Component Services

Question 31

Which default user allows anonymous access to a Web site on the Web server named SERVER-WEB1?

- ○ A. IUSR_ANONYMOUS
- ○ B. IWAM_SERVER-WEB1
- ○ C. IUSR_SERVER-WEB1
- ○ D. IIS_WPG
- ○ E. ASPNET

Question 32

You are a network administrator managing an internal Windows Server 2003 intranet Web server. You want to give your developers the ability to modify the various scripts stored on the Web server and save those modifications back to the Web server. What permissions must you enable? (Choose three.)

☐ A. Write permission

☐ B. Read permission

☐ C. Directory browsing

☐ D. Index this resource

☐ E. Log visits

☐ F. Script source access

Question 33

You need to configure a Windows Server 2003 Web server's permissions that would allow users to view the files for one Web site only. Which steps allow you to do such a task?

○ A. Open Internet Information Services Manager. Right-click the Web site and select Properties. Click the Home Directory tab and mark the Directory Browsing check box.

○ B. Open Internet Information Services Manager. Right-click the Web site and click Properties. Click the Home Directory tab and remove all permissions to enable Directory browsing.

○ C. Open Internet Information Services Manager. Right-click the Web site and click Properties. Click the Web Site tab and mark the Directory Browsing check box.

○ D. Open Internet Information Services Manager. Right-click the Web Sites subnode and click Properties. Click the Home Directory tab and mark the check box for Directory Browsing.

Question 34

Your Windows Server 2003 Web server suffers a catastrophic failure. Part of the solution is to reinstall the operating system and reinstall IIS 6.0. You have reliable backups of the **metabase.xml** and **mbschema.xml** files. You decide to import the entire IIS 6.0 metabase using the scripts provided. Which two scripts provide for this functionality? (Choose two.)

❑ A. **iisback.vbs**

❑ B. **iisext.vbs**

❑ C. **iiscnfg.vbs**

❑ D. **iisapp.vbs**

❑ E. **iisweb.vbs**

Question 35

While working on a critical CAD drawing, a user accidentally deletes a major section of the drawing and saves the file. After realizing the mistake, he contacts you asking whether you can get the file back to its previous state. The file is stored in **D:\CADD**, which is shared as **\\SERVER\CADD**. You know that you had a successful differential backup last night and a successful full backup two nights ago. You also configured Shadow Copies of Shared Folders for the drive hosting the CADD share to run every two hours. You are currently working on the console of the server. What is the fastest way to recover the drawing for the user?

○ A. Restore the server from the full backup and then perform a restore from the differential backup.

○ B. In Windows Explorer, navigate to **D:\CADD**; right-click on the file; choose Properties, Previous Versions; and restore the most recent shadow copy.

○ C. Restore the file from the differential backup or from the full backup if it isn't on the differential.

○ D. In Windows Explorer, navigate to **\\SERVER\CADD**, right-click the file, choose Properties, click the Previous Versions tab, and restore the most recent shadow copy.

Question 36

After installing a new RAID array driver on your Windows Server 2003 computer, you experience a STOP error and you have to reboot the computer. The server does not start successfully, so you want to remove the driver you just installed. Unfortunately, the manufacturer has a program that you must run to revert back to the previous driver, and it is stored on a remote computer. Your server does not have a floppy drive or any other type of removable storage that you can use to load the program. All drives on the server are using NTFS. What can you do?

- ○ A. Boot the computer using the Safe Mode with Networking option and then copy the previous driver from the remote computer and run the driver reversion program.
- ○ B. Boot the computer with an MS-DOS network boot disk and copy the file from the remote computer first; then, boot into Safe Mode.
- ○ C. Boot the computer with the Windows Server 2003 CD-ROM and choose Automated System Recovery.
- ○ D. Boot the computer with the Recovery Console and roll back the driver.

Question 37

How do you install the Recovery Console so that it becomes an option that you can pick while booting your server?

- ○ A. Choose Recovery Console from the Add Windows Components section of Add or Remove Programs in the Control Panel.
- ○ B. Boot from the Windows Server 2003 CD-ROM and choose the Install Recovery Console option from the Repair menu.
- ○ C. Execute the command **\i386\winnt32.exe /cmdcons** from the Windows Server 2003 CD-ROM.
- ○ D. Download and install it from Windows Update Web site.

Question 38

When you create an Automated System Recovery (ASR) backup set, what components are backed up? (Choose two.)

- ❑ A. User data
- ❑ B. Shadow copies of all shares
- ❑ C. System State
- ❑ D. Operating-system files
- ❑ E. Data that you specify stored on the boot volume

Question 39

Gina needs to launch an ASR of her Windows Server 2003 computer. How does she begin the restore phase of an ASR?

- ○ A. By booting from the Windows Server 2003 CD-ROM and pressing the F2 key when prompted
- ○ B. By running **NTBackup.exe** and choosing Automated System Recovery under the Restore tab
- ○ C. By booting from the Windows Server 2003 CD-ROM and pressing the F6 key when prompted
- ○ D. By booting into the Recovery Console and typing **ASRRESTORE** at the Recovery Console prompt

Question 40

Jane has connected to an unresponsive Windows Server 2003 computer via Emergency Management Services. She wants to execute a command using the Special Administration Console to cause the server to write the contents of memory to a file on the hard disk. Which command should she execute?

- ○ A. **writemem**
- ○ B. **!sac**
- ○ C. **crashdump**
- ○ D. **dumpmem**

Question 41

Which of the following statements is not true regarding Windows Server 2003's Emergency Management Services?

- ○ A. It allows you to manage a server via a serial port.
- ○ B. It gives you the ability to reboot a server immediately.
- ○ C. It requires no special hardware support.
- ○ D. It uses a process known as out-of-band management.

Question 42

Norma is upgrading drivers on her new Windows Server 2003 computer, preparing it for production use in the marketing department of her company. As part of the update process, she is rebooting after every driver installation. After she installs the updated network card driver, the server crashes immediately after presenting the logon dialog box. What is the quickest method of undoing the changes Norma just made?

- ○ A. Boot using the Last Known Good Configuration.
- ○ B. Initiate an ASR restore.
- ○ C. Boot using Safe Mode and perform a driver rollback.
- ○ D. Boot into the Recovery Console and disable the Workstation service.

Question 43

You are the administrator for eight Windows 2003 Server computers. You are creating a backup scheme that will use the Windows Server 2003 Backup Utility. You want to make sure that the backup scheme includes the Registry, the **SYSVOL** folder, the Active Directory database, and the boot and system files. You are not concerned about the COM+ components being backed up. Which solution presents the best choice?

- ○ A. From the command prompt, execute the Windows 2003 Backup Utility in System State Restore mode.
- ○ B. Reboot the server, press the F8 key at the boot loader prompt, and select the Backup System State option.
- ○ C. Run the Windows Server 2003 Backup Utility and expand the System State node. Select all System State components but deselect the COM+ component.
- ○ D. Run the Windows Server 2003 Backup Utility and select the option to back up the System State data.

Question 44

Pete, a network administrator on your domain, accidentally deleted the Sales OU. You need to recover this OU as quickly as possible so that your Sales staff can perform their duties. You check the backup logs and see that the System State was backed up on each domain controller (DC) the previous night. On a randomly selected DC, you restore the System State. You breathe a sigh of relief to see the OU reappear on the DC on which you performed the restore. Thirty minutes later, you inspect another DC and see that the OU does not appear there. Concerned, you go back to the DC that you restored the System State onto and you see that the OU does not appear there either.

Why did this happen, and what should you do to ensure the permanent recovery of the Sales OU?

- ○ A. You can only perform System State restores on the DC that holds the Flexible Single Master Operation (FSMO) role of Schema Master. You must repeat the restore operation on this DC.

- ○ B. You did not perform an authoritative restore. Restart the server, press the F8 key at the boot loader menu, select Directory Services Restore Mode, perform the restore operation again, and then run the **NTDSUtil.exe** utility to mark the restored Sales OU as authoritative.

- ○ C. Only members of the Administrators, Backup Operators, and Server Operators groups can restore the System State. Log back on with an account that belongs to one of these groups.

- ○ D. When you restored the System State, the backed-up data was more than 60 days old. Find a newer backup set and repeat the System State restore.

Question 45

You are attempting to perform an authoritative restore. You restart a DC, press the F8 key when prompted, and select Directory Services Restore Mode. When prompted for the administrator's password, you enter it, but you immediately receive an error. You know that you are entering the domain administrator's password correctly. What is the most likely reason for your problem?

- ○ A. You have not performed a System State restore on a DC yet. Restore the System State and then perform the authoritative restore.

- ○ B. To perform this function, the DC must be the PDC Emulator. Locate the DC that holds the PDC Emulator role and then perform the authoritative restore.

- ○ C. You must log on with the Directory Services Restore Mode administrator's password. Locate that password and log on again.

- ○ D. A domain-level GPO setting is disabling the Administrator account. Modify the GPO setting to enable the Administrator account and log on again.

Question 46

You are a network administrator responsible for the three DCs that host a single domain. All DCs were lost when a water main broke over the server room. Given this scenario of having to rebuild the entire domain, which restore method is most recommended for the first DC?

- ○ A. Authoritative restore
- ○ B. Nonauthoritative restore
- ○ C. Primary restore
- ○ D. Normal restore

Question 47

You are a senior network administrator for a large medical-appliance distributor. James, your junior administrator, informed you that he accidentally deleted the OU that contains the user accounts for 12 senior-level management staff. In his attempt to fix the problem, he performed a System State restore from last night's DC System State backup. He was relieved to see the OU restored on the DC. However, that relief was short-lived. James realized he needed to seek your help immediately. After giving him a thorough reprimand about the dangers of deleting Active Directory objects and swimming within an hour of eating, you verify that the complete set of backup tapes and the ASR set are in hand. Your task is to immediately restore the OU and the senior-level management user accounts.

Which of the following do you not need in the procedure to restore the OU and user accounts? (Choose two.)

- ❑ A. ASR set
- ❑ B. The backup tapes
- ❑ C. The **NTDSUtil** utility
- ❑ D. An authoritative restore
- ❑ E. A user who is a member of the Enterprise Admins group

Question 48

William, your number-one network administrator, accidentally deletes the OU for the Marketing department. He immediately realizes what he has done and decides to pull the DC offline before it has a chance to replicate with other DCs. What two steps must William perform to restore the OU to its original state? (Choose two.)

- ❑ A. Perform a System State restore on all the DCs in the forest.
- ❑ B. The restore must be nonauthoritative.
- ❑ C. Perform a System State restore on the DC from which the OU was deleted.
- ❑ D. Perform a System State restore on all DCs in the domain.
- ❑ E. The restore must be authoritative.
- ❑ F. Perform a primary restore on the PDC Emulator and then bring the affected DC back online.

Question 49

You are having a discussion with a co-worker about the default settings for the Windows Server 2003 Backup Utility. Stacey, your co-worker, makes the following list and presents it to you as fact. Being the astute systems administrator you are, you politely point out her errors. Which answers on Stacey's list are not correct? (Choose two.)

- ❑ A. Default setting—Backup type is Normal.
- ❑ B. Default setting—Verify Data After Backup is enabled.
- ❑ C. Default setting—Information reported in the backup log is summarized.
- ❑ D. Default setting—Replace the File on Disk Only If the File on Disk Is Older.
- ❑ E. Default setting—Files to be restored to their original locations.

Question 50

You are a senior network administrator performing a security audit on the corporate servers. Part of your audit leads you to determine how files are restored and who can restore them. In your investigation, you find that any backup operator can restore extremely sensitive corporate Merger and Acquisition information. The corporate policy is that only those members of the Administrators group and the owner of the files must be able to restore this information. What recommendations will you give to those who are responsible for administering the tape backups for these servers?

- ○ A. Delete the Backup Operators group.
- ○ B. Recommend that the Administrators account take ownership of the Merger and Acquisition folders and files and remove all users from the Backup Operators group.
- ○ C. Enable the Allow Only the Owner and the Administrator Access to the Backup Data option.
- ○ D. After you create the backup, add the Backup Operators to the NTFS security permissions for the folders and mark the Deny option for Full Control.

Question 51

You are getting error message 202 stating that your Windows Server 2003 computer is out of licenses. When you go to the Licensing tool in the Administrative Tools folder on the Start menu, the information does not appear. What must you do to view this information?

- ○ A. Start the License Logging service.
- ○ B. Enable licensing on the DC.
- ○ C. Look in the default licensing group.
- ○ D. Enable licensing in the Active Directory Sites and Services console.

Question 52

You are running out of room on the drive volume that contains the server's print spooler. You move the print spooler to a different drive volume that has more disk space. The users tell you that nothing will print. What do you need to do to correct the problem?

○ A. Reinstall the drivers on the print server computer.

○ B. Stop and restart the spooler service.

○ C. Make sure that the users have full control permissions.

○ D. Stop and restart the printer service.

Question 53

The Accounting department is printing large documents that are monopolizing the printers, and no one else can print. What is the best solution to this problem?

○ A. Get the Accounting department its own printer.

○ B. Change the Accounting department's print-queue priority to 99.

○ C. Set up a logical printer for the Accounting department and tell the accountants to use it for large print jobs.

○ D. Change the Accounting department print-queue priority to 2.

Question 54

Management tells you that users are complaining that printing takes too long. You need to gather statistics about the company's printers and print jobs. How will you gather this information?

○ A. Use System Monitor.

○ B. Save the system log files from the Event Viewer.

○ C. Use the advanced properties of the print server.

○ D. Use Performance Logs and Alerts.

Question 55

> Your company has decided to start using SUS. You are chosen to head the project. You do a clean install of Windows Server 2003 on a Pentium 700Mhz computer with 1GB of RAM installed. After installing the SUS version 1.0 with Service Pack 1 (SP1) on the computer, you test the service and it does not work. What must you do to fix the problem?
>
> ○ A. Make sure that you have at least 3GB of disk space available.
>
> ○ B. Upgrade to Internet Explorer 6.0.
>
> ○ C. Install IIS 6.0.
>
> ○ D. Enable Remote Procedure Calls (RPCs).

Question 56

> Which of the following Microsoft operating systems and service-pack levels are not able to use SUS? (Choose three.)
>
> ❏ A. Windows NT 4.0 Workstation with SP5
>
> ❏ B. Windows 2000 Professional
>
> ❏ C. Windows 2000 Server with SP3
>
> ❏ D. Windows XP Professional
>
> ❏ E. Windows XP Home with SP1
>
> ❏ F. Windows Server 2003

Question 57

> While looking through the Event Viewer, you see an entry in the System log: Disk Event ID 36. What does this signify?
>
> ○ A. The server is running out of space for the paging file.
>
> ○ B. Disk space is running low on the drive volume.
>
> ○ C. %Disk Time is greater than 50%.
>
> ○ D. A user has exceeded his or her disk quota.

Question 58

In monitoring your server, you notice a steady increase in nonpaged bytes without a corresponding increase in server load. What is the probable cause of this performance decrease?

- ○ A. One of the RAM modules on the motherboard is going bad.
- ○ B. A program is causing a memory leak.
- ○ C. A process is causing excessive paging.
- ○ D. A process is using a disproportional amount of RAM.

Question 59

How can you perform an ASR restore operation if you have lost the ASR floppy disk?

- ○ A. Make your own Windows Server 2003 boot disk.
- ○ B. Use an ASR floppy disk created on a different computer that runs Windows XP Professional.
- ○ C. Use the Backup Utility on a different Windows Server 2003 computer to restore the **asr.sif** and **asrpnp.sif** files from the ASR media backup set onto a blank floppy disk. Use the floppy disk as the ASR floppy disk during the ASR restore operation.
- ○ D. You cannot perform an ASR restore without the original ASR floppy disk.

Question 60

What is the easiest and fastest way that you can restore a previously installed video driver after you install a new video driver, restart the computer, and see that the video display is completed garbled and you cannot log on to the computer?

- ○ A. Do not log on, restart the computer again, press the F8 key during startup, and choose the Last Known Good Configuration startup option.
- ○ B. Do not log on, restart the computer again, press the F8 key during startup, and choose the Safe Mode startup option.
- ○ C. Do not log on, restart the computer again, press the F8 key during startup, and choose the Recovery Console startup option.
- ○ D. Do not log on, restart the computer again, press the F8 key during startup, and choose the Enable VGA Mode startup option.

Answers to Practice Exam 2

1. C	**21.** D	**41.** C
2. D	**22.** C	**42.** A
3. B	**23.** D	**43.** D
4. A, C	**24.** B, C, E	**44.** B
5. A	**25.** A	**45.** C
6. C	**26.** D	**46.** C
7. D	**27.** A, D	**47.** A, E
8. D	**28.** B	**48.** C, E
9. C	**29.** D	**49.** B, D
10. C, E, G	**30.** B, C	**50.** C
11. B	**31.** C	**51.** A
12. B, C, D	**32.** A, B, F	**52.** B
13. A, C, E	**33.** A	**53.** C
14. A	**34.** A, C	**54.** D
15. B, D	**35.** D	**55.** C
16. B, E	**36.** A	**56.** A, B, E
17. B	**37.** C	**57.** D
18. D	**38.** C, D	**58.** B
19. C, D	**39.** A	**59.** C
20. C	**40.** C	**60.** A

Question 1

Answer C is correct. For users to be able to log on to any computer in the domain and have their desktop settings follow them, you need to configure each user with a roaming user profile. Configure the user account's profile setting to point to a network path that will contain the user settings. As each user logs on to any workstation in the domain, the user profile is downloaded from the server that stores the roaming user profiles. If you rename the `ntuser.dat` to `ntuser.man`, the user profile does not allow any changes to be saved to it. Answer A is incorrect because deleting the local default profile only makes it such that when a new user logs on to the computer, there is no default profile to load. Answer B is incorrect because the system file has nothing to do with the user profile. Answer D is incorrect because deleting the local profile does not allow the users' desktop settings to follow them from workstation to workstation.

Question 2

Answer D is correct. A prestaged computer account is one that has been created in advance. By specifying under Remote Installation Services (RIS) to only accept prestaged requests, you prevent any unauthorized installations. Answer A is incorrect because although Kerberos is a more secure authentication protocol than what was used by NT 4.0, it is does not control who can connect to a RIS server. Answer B is incorrect because there is no default RIS container. Answer C is incorrect. Even though you restrict which users can install with RIS, any of those users still have the ability to install unauthorized operating systems.

Question 3

Answer B is correct. By clicking the View menu and selecting Advanced Features, you can view the Lost and Found Container along with the NTDS Quotas, Program Data, and System containers. Answer A is incorrect because adding yourself to the Enterprise Admins group does not bring the Lost and Found container into view. Answer C is incorrect because the Lost and Found container is not a Windows component that you can add. Answer D is incorrect because there is no option named Show Hidden Containers in the Active Directory Users and Computers (ADUC) console.

Question 4

Answers A and C are correct. Administrators can nest groups and change the scope of groups for the Windows 2000 native and the Windows Server 2003 domain functional levels. Answer B is incorrect because administrators cannot nest groups nor change the scope of groups under the Windows 2000 mixed domain functional level. Answer D is incorrect because administrators cannot nest groups nor change the scope of groups under the Windows Server 2003 interim domain functional level. Answer E is incorrect because the Windows Server 2003 mixed level does not exist.

Question 5

Answer A is correct. Computers that are members of a domain communicate with a domain controller (DC) computer using a secure channel and a password that is automatically generated. This password is changed every 30 days. If the password that is stored on the DC is not synchronized with the password on the member computer, you get the error message. To fix this problem, you need to reset the computer account. Answer B is incorrect because the error is a computer password problem, not a user password problem. Answer C is incorrect as well because the error is not a user account problem. Answer D is incorrect because the F5 function key refreshes only the screen display, not the computer account.

Question 6

Answer C is correct. This command line creates a distribution group called Sales Reps in the Sales organizational unit (OU) within the East Coast OU in the Windows2003.local domain. Answer A is incorrect because there are no quotes around the LDAP distinguished name, which you need for names with embedded spaces such as "East Coast." Answer B is incorrect because the command-line option "secgrp" does not specify "no." Answer D is incorrect because it creates a security group, not a distribution group.

Question 7

Answer D is correct. Programs like Microsoft Excel can read and write to .csv files. The csvde.exe command-line tool is Microsoft's preferred method for bulk-importing users into Active Directory. Answer A is incorrect; you use the dsadd.exe command for creating a single user at a time, not for importing and exporting .csv files. Answer B is incorrect because you use ldifde.exe for importing and exporting data in the LDAP format, not the comma-separated values format. Answer C is incorrect because you use the dsget.exe command for displaying the properties of computers, OUs, and other objects within Active Directory; it is not used for importing or exporting data.

Question 8

Answer D is correct. In the Windows 2000 mixed domain mode, domain local groups can contain global groups from any domain in the forest. Answer A is incorrect because universal groups are not available in a Windows 2000 mixed mode domain. Answer B is incorrect because there are two types of Active Directory groups—security and distribution. However, there are no groups that have a group scope of "Security" in an Active Directory domain. Answer C is also incorrect. In a Windows 2000 mixed domain, global groups can contain only user accounts from the same domain.

Question 9

Answer C is correct. Microsoft has started locking down its operating systems by default, which is drastically different from earlier products. Instead of expecting end users to understand how to secure everything, Microsoft now expects the end users to *unlock* those resources they need to use. Answer A is not correct because Full Control is not what is granted to the Everyone group under Windows Server 2003, unlike previous operating systems. Answer B is not correct because deny permissions override allow permissions, meaning the Everyone group would have *no* permissions at all on the boot partition or volume. Answer D is not correct because the default permissions do not inherit to lower levels in the boot drive volume folder structure—which ensures that someone who misconfigures the root drive volume does not affect other critical system folders, such as the \Windows folder.

Question 10

Answers C, E, and G are correct. There is no direct path to convert from NTFS back to FAT. You must reformat the volume, and if there was any data on it, you must restore it from backup. Of course, that assumes that you backed up the data before reformatting the volume. Answer A is not correct because there is no command-line utility for converting from NTFS to FAT32 or FAT (FAT16). The same is true for Answer B. In fact, the convert command requires the /FS switch but only accepts NTFS as a valid parameter. Answer D is not correct because the Disk Management console does not let you format a volume with the FAT file system if the disk is dynamic. Answer F is not correct because there is no requirement for the drive to be basic.

Question 11

Answer B is correct. Answer A is incorrect because the client software does not reside in the \support\tools folder on the Windows Server 2003 CD-ROM. Answer C does exist, but it is the Remote Desktop client included with Windows Server 2003, not the Previous Versions client. Answer D is incorrect because there is no default shared folder named PVClient under Windows Server 2003.

Question 12

Answers B, C, and D are correct. Compression is an attribute of the volume and the files and folders stored on that volume. If an entire volume is compressed, then all new files and folders created on it are compressed as well. The same can be said for folders that are compressed. And compression is simply a check box in the attributes of a file. Even on a compressed volume, you can choose to not compress a file by turning compression off for that file. Answer A is not correct because compression is not a workaround for exceeding quota limits. The quota engine looks at the actual file size, not the amount of disk space it is using. Answers E and F are not correct because as long as you have the ability to write files to a compressed volume, your files are compressed regardless of your group membership.

Question 13

Answers A, C, and E are correct. By default, Remote Desktop for Administration is not enabled and must be turned on. Once it is on, the default restrictions stop anyone with a blank password from connecting. Users must also be a member of the Remote Desktop Users group to connect. Answer B is not correct because that option is for Remote Assistance, not Remote Desktop connections. Answer D is not correct because it is not the group that she needs to be a member of. Answer F is not correct because although you cannot have a blank password, there is no other default restriction on the type of password required to connect via Remote Desktop connections.

Question 14

Answer A is correct because you must set the quotas individually if you do not want to affect all users equally. Answer B is not correct because you cannot set a quota on a group. Answer C is not correct because quotas are not available through the ADUC console. Answer D is not correct because, again, quotas cannot be set on groups, and in addition, the 50 should be actually be 50000000 to approximate 50MB.

Question 15

Answers B and D are correct because FAT32 is accessible by most previous Microsoft operating systems and many other non-Microsoft operating systems as well. Answer A is not correct because FAT32 has no native method of applying permissions to files and folders. Answer C is not correct because NTFS gives you this ability and is a better choice for fault tolerance than FAT32. Answer E is not correct because NTFS, not FAT32, gives you the ability to compress files at the file-system level.

Question 16

Answers B and E are correct. The Shared Folders console allows you to publish a shared folder into Active Directory, either while the share is being created or after the fact from the properties of the share. ADUC allows you to create a shared-folder object that points to a physical shared folder on a server. Answer A is not correct because the net share command does not let you publish to Active Directory. Answer C is not correct because the standard properties of the folder, accessed from the Windows Explorer, offer nothing in terms of publishing to Active Directory. Only the properties accessed from the Shared Folders snap-in have the elusive Publishing tab. Answer D is not correct because Windows Explorer does not offer that option, as previously discussed.

Question 17

Answer B is correct because Telnet lets you execute only command-line programs. The correct command line to run is the net share command as specified; however, leaving the Telnet port open on a firewall is not a recommended practice due to the security vulnerability that it creates. Answer A is not correct because the question does not state that dialing into the server is an option, and Windows 95 cannot support the Windows Server 2003 administration tools. Answer C is not correct because a Telnet session does not let you run GUI utilities. Answer D is not correct because the command line listed is wrong.

Question 18

Answer D is correct because the Accounting group has been denied the write permission to the folder. Answer A is not correct because the share permissions are wide open. Answer B is not correct because the User group allows modify, which includes write. Answer C is not correct because the combination of just Max and the User group allows modify, which also includes write.

Question 19

Answers C and D are correct because Shadow Copies of Shared Folders is enabled at the drive volume (or drive letter) level. Answers A and B are not correct because you do not work with Shadow Copies at the disk level. Answer E is not correct because drive F: does not need shadow copies. Answer F is not correct because you cannot enable Shadow Copies only for specific shares.

Question 20

Answer C is correct because the designated data recovery agent (DRA) is the user whose encryption certificate is allowed to decrypt files. Answer A is not correct because you are not allowed to copy the encrypted files unless you have access to them. Answer B is not correct because the file is backed up in an encrypted state and restored in an encrypted state. Answer D is not correct because once a file is encrypted, it can only be unencrypted by the owner of the file or by the DRA.

Question 21

Answer D is correct. By right-clicking the E:\Common\Sales\VPs folder, you can select the Security tab, click the Advanced button, and then click the Effective Permissions tab to determine Alison's effective NTFS permissions for the folder. Answer A is not correct because if you make Alison a member of the Administrators group, you are giving her far more permission than she needs. Answers B and C are not correct because you should not assign NTFS permissions directly to user accounts; you should add users to the appropriate groups and then grant those groups the proper permissions.

Question 22

Answer C is correct because the Effective Permissions dialog box takes into account all user permissions and group permissions, both for the local computer and for the domain, as it calculates the effective permissions granted to a user. Answer A is not correct because it is only a subset of the actual effective permissions. Answer B is not correct because it does not include inherited permissions in the list. Answer D is not correct because it does not take user and other group permissions into account.

Question 23

Answer D is correct because NTFS disk quotas apply only to the uncompressed disk-space sizes of files. When Amy attempts to copy a 5MB file onto drive E: when her used quota amount is already 97MB, she would exceed her disk quota, so the file copy operation is not allowed and a message box appears. Answer A is not correct because disk quotas disregard NTFS compressed file sizes. Answer B is incorrect because NTFS disk quotes are based on the uncompressed size of files—any user who exceeds his/her disk quota cannot use more disk space than the specified quota if you select the option to deny users space when they exceed their quota limits. Answer C is not correct because NTFS disk quotas are enforced by not allowing users to exceed their disk-quota limits, even by just a little bit; there are no "grace periods."

Question 24

Answers B, C, and E are correct because they are all features of NTFS and some of the most compelling reasons to use it over FAT or FAT32. Answer A is not correct because this behavior describes the method used to compress a drive in earlier versions of MS-DOS. NTFS compresses on a file-by-file basis, giving better performance and functionality. Answer D is not correct because you cannot format floppy disks with the NTFS file system. Answer F is incorrect because you cannot format DVD recordable/rewritable or CD recordable/rewritable media as NTFS. CD media generally use the CD-ROM File System (CDFS) format and DVD media generally use the UDFS format.

Question 25

Answer A is correct because this option allows one set of permissions to essentially take effect for everyone, whether they log on locally or remotely. By setting share permissions to allow full control, they allow wide-open access, meaning that NTFS permissions are what actually enforces any restrictions. Because NTFS permissions take effect whether a user is local or remote, it is exactly what Henrietta has in mind. Answer B is not correct because the default share permissions allow only read access to a share, which could be more restrictive than NTFS permissions—which is not consistent with local file access. Answer C is not correct because share permissions affect only remote file access. Answer D is not correct because share permissions affect only remote file access—which means that someone sitting locally at the server is not affected by share permissions at all!

Question 26

Answer D is the correct choice because Windows Server 2003 tightened the defaults. First introduced in Windows XP, Everyone:Allow Read is the default permission for all new shares. Answer A is not correct because that is not the default permission. Answer B is not correct because the Everyone group is not granted Allow Full Control by default. Answer C is incorrect because it actually lists an NTFS permission rather than a share permission.

Question 27

Answers A and D are correct. Answer A is correct because you will find the setting for Isolation Mode under the Services tab for the Web site's properties. Answer D is correct because this server was upgraded from Windows 2000 Server and IIS 5.0. Because it was an upgrade from IIS 5.0, it operates in IIS 5.0 Isolation Mode to maintain compatibility with existing applications. Answers B and C are incorrect because you configure Isolation Mode under the Services tab on the Web site properties window. Answer E is incorrect because when you upgrade to IIS 6.0 from IIS 6.0, IIS maintains IIS 5.0 Isolation Mode.

Question 28

Answer B is correct. By default, no components or services are installed when IIS 6.0 is installed. Under a default installation, you must manually select the Remote Administration (HTML) option if you want remote-administration capabilities. Answer A is incorrect because you are opening IE 6.0 locally on server02; no firewall is involved. Answer C is incorrect because you do not need to restart the Internet services when you add components. Answer D is incorrect because you have not yet logged on to the Remote Administration Web site.

Question 29

Answer D is correct. For only the administrator to not receive the Explorer Enhanced Security Configuration error message, you must clear the For Administrator Groups check box in the Internet Explorer Enhanced Security Configuration option in Add/Remove Windows Components. Answers A and C are incorrect because the option to disable this feature is in Add/Remove Windows Components on the server. Answer B is incorrect because having both options selected enables this feature for all groups who can browse from the server.

Question 30

Answers B and C are both correct. You can set authentication requirements and you can specify the users to be granted access with both of these utilities. Answers A, D, and E are incorrect because you do not use these utilities to configure settings for IIS.

Question 31

Answer C is correct. IUSR_*ServerName* is the name of the local or domain account, depending on whether the Web server is a member of a domain. This user account gives Web-site users the ability to access the Web site without having to enter a valid username and password. Answer A is incorrect because there is no such user account by default. Answer B is incorrect because this user account grants the Log On as a Batch Job user right and is used for Web applications. Answer D is incorrect because it is actually a group that contains the IWAM_*ServerName* and various other groups for running Web applications.

Question 32

Answers A, B, and F are correct. You must have write permissions to save the changes back to the Web server. You must have read permissions to "read" the file, and you must have script source access to modify, delete, or add to the script files in the virtual directory. Answer C is incorrect because Directory Browsing is not required for modifying scripts. Answer D is incorrect because the Index This Resource permission is not required for modifying scripts. Answer E is incorrect because the Log Visits permission is not required for modifying scripts.

Question 33

Answer A is correct. You can only enable Directory Browsing for an entire Web site. Answer B is incorrect because removing all permissions disables anyone from reading, writing, or browsing the Web site. Answer C is incorrect because the Web Site tab does not contain the Directory Browsing option. Answer D is incorrect because this option enables Directory Browsing for all the Web sites that this server is hosting.

Question 34

Answers A and C are correct. Answer B is incorrect because `iisext.vbs` enables and lists applications; adds and removes application dependencies; enables, disables, and lists Web service extensions; and adds, removes, enables, disables, and lists individual files. Answer D is incorrect because `iisapp.vbs` lists applications that are running. Answer E is incorrect because `iisweb.vbs` creates, deletes, and lists Web sites that are being hosted on servers running Windows Server 2003. The `iisweb.vbs` script starts, stops, and pauses a Web site as well.

Question 35

Answer D is correct. To use the Shadow Copies capability, you must connect to the file using a network path. Answer A is not correct because restoring the server from tape is definitely not the fastest way to recover this drawing. Answer B is not correct because you cannot utilize Shadow Copies by connecting to a physical drive path. Answer C is not correct because restoring the file from tape is not as fast as restoring the shadow copy that was created no longer than two hours ago.

Question 36

Answer A is correct because you need networking support to copy the file from the remote computer. Safe Mode should allow the computer to start well enough to run the reversion program and get the server working again. Answer B is not correct because not only does the server not have a floppy disk, but all drives are NTFS, so MS-DOS cannot access them. Answer C is not correct because ASR is meant to restore a server quickly from bare metal, not simply recover from one driver problem. Answer D is not correct because the Recovery Console does not give you network support or the ability to roll back a driver.

Question 37

Answer C is correct because you must execute `winnt32 /cmdcons` to install the Recovery Console as a boot option. Answer A is not correct because there is no choice to install the Recovery Console from Add or Remove Programs.

Answer B is not correct because you can launch the Recovery Console when you boot from the Windows Server 2003 CD-ROM, but you cannot install the Recovery Console from the CD-ROM. Answer D is not correct because you will not find the Recovery Console on the Windows Update Web site.

Question 38

Answers C and D are correct. The ASR process backs up the system state, the operating-system files, the drive configuration, the service configuration, and other critical information about the configuration of the operating system. Answer A is incorrect because ASR does not back up user data. Answer B is incorrect because ASR does not back up the shadow copies of all shared folders. Answer E is not correct because you cannot specify any extra data to back up during an ASR backup.

Question 39

Answer A is correct. F2 is the correct key to press when booting from the Windows Server 2003 CD-ROM. Answer B is not correct because you launch an ASR restore when you cannot boot into Windows Server 2003, which means you could not run NTBackup.exe. Answer C is not correct because pressing the F6 key prompts you to install a mass storage device driver; it does not launch ASR. Answer D is incorrect because that command does not exist in the Recovery Console, and you cannot launch an ASR restore from the Recovery Console.

Question 40

Answer C is correct. *Crashdump* is the term Microsoft uses to refer to the process of writing memory to a file when a STOP error occurs on your server. It chose to use this same term in reference to forcing a crashdump to happen. Answers A and D provide commands that do not exist. Answer B refers to the special administration console that you can access if all other avenues of gaining control of your server fail.

Question 41

Answer C is correct because there is a requirement for hardware support. Serial Port Console Redirection (SPCR) must be supported by the hardware before Emergency Management Services (EMS) can function. Answer A is not correct because it does give you the ability to manage basic tasks via the serial port. Answer B is not correct because you can reboot a server if necessary. Answer D is not correct because the service does utilize out-of-band management, which means managing the server through non-normal channels.

Question 42

Answer A is correct because Norma's last boot and logon before installing the new network card driver was successful. That configuration was saved as the last known good. She can boot into the Last Known Good Configuration and be at a point right before she installed the bad network card driver. Answer B is not correct because ASR restores the state of the operating system on the server to the point when an ASR backup was made. Answer C is not correct because, although it might get the server back to a stable operating state, it is not the quickest method of undoing Norma's changes. Answer D is not correct because disabling the Workstation service does not undo the problems caused by the new network card driver.

Question 43

Answer D is correct. You simply need to choose the System State check box in the Backup Utility to ensure that all System State components are backed up. Answer A is incorrect because there is no ability to restore from the command prompt; besides, the question asks how to create a backup scheme. Answer B is incorrect because the boot loader menu does not offer an option named Backup System State. Answer C is incorrect because you cannot selectively choose which System State components are to be backed up.

Question 44

Answer B is correct. You did not perform an authoritative restore. You must use the NTDSUtil.exe utility to perform the authoritative restore. Answer A is incorrect because you can restore the system state on any DC in the domain. Answer C is incorrect because Pete had the required permissions to restore the system state. However, Pete did not perform an authoritative restore. Answer D is incorrect because the age of the backup set is not relevant.

Question 45

Answer C is correct. You must know the Directory Services Restore Mode administrator's password that was created when the server was promoted using dcpromo to a DC. It is a separate account from the domain administrator's account. Answer A is incorrect because it is not the cause of the administrator not being able to log on. Answer B is incorrect because you can do an authoritative restore on any DC in the domain. Answer D is incorrect because a Group Policy Object (GPO) setting has no effect on the administrative logon under Directory Services Restore Mode.

Question 46

Answer C is correct. You want to use a primary restore on the first DC and a normal (nonauthoritative) restore on the other DCs. Answers A, B, and D are incorrect because a primary restore should be the restore method on the first DC.

Question 47

Answers A and E are not needed. The ASR set is not needed for an Active Directory authoritative restore, and the person performing the restore must know the password for the Directory Services Restore Mode administrator. Answers B, C, and D are needed to resolve this problem.

Question 48

Answers C and E are correct. You can do the restore from this DC, however, it must be an authoritative restore. Answers A and D are incorrect because you need to perform the restore only on the DC that had the OU deleted. Answer B is incorrect because it must be an authoritative restore for the restored data to replicate. Answer F is incorrect because performing a primary restore will not solve the problem.

Question 49

Answers B and D are correct. Data is not verified and "Do not replace the file on my computer (recommended)" are both the defaults. Answers A, C, and E are all correctly defined as defaults.

Question 50

Answer C is correct. You want to enable this option to prevent unauthorized access to these files and folders. Answer A is incorrect because it would unnecessarily affect other backup operators from performing their jobs. Answer B is incorrect because of the sensitive nature of these files. It would be inappropriate for the administrator to arbitrarily take ownership of those folders and files. Also, if you remove all users from the Backup Operators group, only administrators could back up those files. Answer D is incorrect because if you performed this step, only the administrators would be able to back up the files and folders.

Question 51

Answer A is correct. The License Logging service is installed by default but not started. To work with licensing, you must start the Licensing Logging service. Answer B is incorrect because you do not enable licensing on a DC. Answer C is incorrect because there is no default licensing group. Answer D is incorrect because although you can view the license site settings in Active Directory Sites and Services, you cannot see any information on the actual licenses themselves.

Question 52

Answer B is correct. When you move the print spooler to a different drive volume, you need to stop and restart the spooler service before the change to the new spooler folder takes effect. Answer A is incorrect because reinstalling the printer drivers does not make the print-spooler service restart. Answer C is incorrect because the problem is not a permissions issue. Answer D is incorrect because there is no printer service in the Services snap-in.

Question 53

Answer C is correct. By setting up a logical printer for the Accounting department, you can have large print jobs print after hours and not tie up the printer for all the other users. Answer A is incorrect because although it provides a solution, it is a costly one so it is not the best solution to the problem. Answer B is incorrect because changing the priority to 99 gives the Accounting department's print jobs a lower priority, but when it prints large jobs, it still ties up the printer for the other users. Answer D is incorrect because setting the priority of 2 gives the Accounting department's print jobs a higher priority and ties up the printer, which is opposite of what you are trying to do.

Question 54

Answer D is correct. Performance Logs and Alerts allow you to monitor many aspects of printing and printer performance, including job errors, not-ready errors, and out-of-paper errors. Answer A is incorrect because System Monitor does not allow you to gather information on printing. Answer B is incorrect because system log in the Event Viewer does not contain information on printer performance. Answer C is incorrect because the advanced print server properties contain no information on printer performance.

Question 55

Answer C is correct. For Software Update Services (SUS) to work correctly, IIS 5.0 or higher must be installed. With Windows Server 2003, IIS 6.0 is not installed by default, so in this instance, you must install it separately. Answer A is incorrect because you need to have at least 6GB of disk space available. Answer B is incorrect because the Internet Explorer version on Windows 2003 is already IE 6.0. Answer D is incorrect because enabling Remote Procedure Calls (RPCs) is not part of the procedure to enable SUS.

Question 56

Answers A, B, and E are correct. For computers to be able to receive automatic updates through SUS, they must have the Automatic Updates software installed. Windows NT 4.0 does not have Automatic Updates installed and neither does Windows 2000 Professional without Service Pack 3. Windows XP Home cannot be a member of a domain, so it cannot use SUS. Answers C, D, and F are incorrect because all the computers mentioned have the Automatic Updates service installed and therefore could use SUS.

Question 57

Answer D is correct. The Event ID 36 indicates that a user who is being monitored for disk-storage space has exceeded his or her allowable amount, which shows up in the System log. Answer A is incorrect because this Event ID refers to disk quotas, not the paging file. Answer B is incorrect because Event ID 36 does not refer to a low disk-space warning. Answer C is incorrect because the Event ID 36 deals with disk quotas, not disk time for performance monitoring.

Question 58

Answer B is correct. An increase in nonpaged bytes without a corresponding increase in server load indicates that one or many programs have not released their allocated memory back to the server's memory pool—which is referred to as a memory leak. Answer A is incorrect because the stated problem is not an indication of a RAM module going bad. Answer C is incorrect because excessive paging is measured in page faults, not in nonpaged bytes. Answer D is incorrect because nonpaged bytes have nothing to do with a process using a disproportional amount of RAM.

Question 59

Answer C is correct. Both the `asr.sif` file and the `asrpnp.sif` file are stored in the `%systemroot%\repair` folder by default. By restoring these files from the ASR backup media set, you can copy these files onto a floppy disk to use as the ASR floppy disk. Answer A is incorrect because you cannot use a Windows Server 2003 boot disk in place of the ASR floppy disk. Answer B is incorrect because using an ASR floppy disk that was created on another computer is not supported, especially if the other computer is not running Windows Server 2003. Answer D is incorrect because you can perform an ASR restore without the original ASR floppy disk, if you restore both the `asr.sif` file and the `asrpnp.sif` files from backup to a new floppy disk.

Question 60

Answer A is correct. Selecting the Last Known Good Configuration startup option is the fastest and easiest way to roll back the video driver to the previous version. Answer B is incorrect because the new video driver would not necessarily work under the Safe Mode option, and even if it did, you'd still have to go to the Display Properties and change the driver. Answer C is incorrect because you cannot select the Recovery Console by pressing the F8 key, and it is a more involved procedure than simply using the Last Known Good Configuration. Answer D is incorrect because you need to log on under VGA Mode, change the video driver, and then restart the computer again before you resolve the problem; the Last Known Good Configuration option is faster and easier to implement.

Suggested Readings and Resources

Because *Exam Cram 2* books focus entirely on Microsoft certification exam objectives, you can broaden your knowledge of Windows Server 2003 by taking advantage of the plethora of technical material that's available. Books, Web sites, and even the Windows Server 2003 built-in help system offer a wealth of technical insight for network and system administrators. In the following pages, we present a list of valuable resources that you can check out at your leisure.

Microsoft Windows Server 2003 Help and Support

Your first source for help with any aspect of Microsoft Windows Server 2003 should be the user-assistance features that Microsoft ships with its server products:

➤ *Help and Support*—This option is available within the Manage Your Server interface, as well as through the Start menu, and provides access to the Help and Support Center, where you can search through the online help files installed with your server.

➤ *List of Common Administrative Tasks*—This option is available within the Manage Your Server interface and provides access to a list of the more common administrative tasks you might be expected to use, along with examples of each task.

Books

The following are some useful books on Windows Server 2003:

➤ Boswell, William. *Inside Microsoft Windows Server 2003.* Boston, Massachusetts: Addison-Wesley Professional, 2003.

➤ Honeycutt, Jerry. *Introducing Microsoft Windows Server 2003.* Redmond, Washington: Microsoft Press, 2003.

➤ Minasi, Mark, et al. *Mastering Windows Server 2003.* Alameda, California: Sybex, 2003.

➤ Morimoto, Rand, et al. *Microsoft Windows Server 2003 Unleashed.* Indianapolis, Indiana: Sams Publishing, 2003.

➤ Scales, Lee, and John Michell. *MCSA/MCSE 70-290 Training Guide: Managing and Maintaining a Windows Server 2003 Environment.* Indianapolis, Indiana: Que Publishing, 2003.

➤ Stanek, William R. *Microsoft Windows Server 2003 Administrator's Pocket Consultant.* Redmond, Washington: Microsoft Press, 2003.

➤ Stanek, William R. *Windows Server 2003.* Redmond, Washington: Microsoft Press, 2003.

Web Sites

The following are useful Internet resources for Windows Server 2003:

➤ The Microsoft Windows Server 2003 site (many documents and technical references for this product line)—http://www.microsoft.com/windowsserver2003/

➤ The Microsoft Server 2003 MSDN site (access to any technical references and downloads)—http://msdn.microsoft.com/library/default.asp?url=/nhp/default.asp?contentid=28001691

➤ The MSDN Windows Script site (extensive information on scripting)—http://msdn.microsoft.com/library/default.asp?url=/nhp/Default.asp?contentid=28001169

➤ The Microsoft download site for the Group Policy Management Console (GPMC), including additional details on this free download (gpmc.msi)—http://www.microsoft.com/downloads/details.aspx?FamilyID=f39e9d60-7e41-4947-82f5-3330f37adfeb&DisplayLang=en

➤ The Microsoft download site for the Remote Control add-in to the Windows Server 2003 Active Directory Users and Computers MMC— http://www.microsoft.com/downloads/details.aspx?FamilyID=0a91d2e7-7594-4abb-8239-7a7eca6a6cb1&DisplayLang=en

➤ The Windows Server 2003 Terminal Services Technology site— http://support.microsoft.com/default.aspx?scid=fh;EN-US;winsvr2003term

➤ The Software Update Service home page— http://www.microsoft.com/downloads/details.aspx?FamilyId=A7AA96E4-6E41-4F54-972C-AE66A4E4BF6C&displaylang=en

➤ The Automatic Update Client for the SUS service, along with additional information on the Automatic Update process— http://www.microsoft.com/windows2000/downloads/recommended/susclient/

➤ The Windows Update site, which allows an automated evaluation of hotfixes and service packs—http://windowsupdate.microsoft.com

➤ Microsoft Software Update Services, Flash demo site— http://www.microsoft.com/windows2000/windowsupdate/sus/flashpage.asp

➤ Software Update Services components and features— http://www.microsoft.com/windows2000/windowsupdate/sus/suscomponents.asp

➤ What's New in Internet Information Services 6.0— http://www.microsoft.com/windowsserver2003/evaluation/overview/technologies/iis.mspx

➤ *MCP Magazine*—IIS 6.0 Mature at Last: Microsoft's Internet Information Server—http://mcpmag.com/features/article.asp?editorialsid=330

➤ White paper: Technical overview of management services— http://www.microsoft.com/windowsserver2003/docs/Manageover.doc

➤ Microsoft TechNet Windows Server 2003 Resources— http://www.microsoft.com/technet/treeview/default.asp?url=/technet/prodtechnol/windowsserver2003/

➤ Microsoft Training and Certifications site— http://www.microsoft.com/traincert/

➤ Microsoft Preparation Guide for Exam 70-290— http://www.microsoft.com/traincert/exams/70-290.asp

➤ The Shadow Copies of Shared Folders client—http://www.microsoft.com/windowsserver2003/downloads/shadowcopyclient.mspx

➤ Technical Overview of Windows Server 2003—http://www.microsoft.com/
windowsserver2003/techinfo/overview/

➤ Introduction to Shadow Copies of Shared Folders—http://www.
microsoft.com/windowsserver2003/techinfo/overview/scr.mspx

➤ An overview of the new features for Windows Server 2003 DNS—http://
www.microsoft.com/technet/treeview/default.asp?url=/technet/prodtechnol/
windowsserver2003/proddocs/standard/sag_DNS_ovr_NewFeatures.asp

➤ Microsoft TechNet Security information for DNS—http://www.
microsoft.com/technet/treeview/default.asp?url=/technet/prodtechnol/
windowsserver2003/proddocs/standard/sag_DNS_ovr_topnode.asp

➤ Microsoft TechNet information on managing Windows Server 2003—
http://www.microsoft.com/technet/treeview/default.asp?url=/technet/
prodtechnol/windowsserver2003/proddocs/standard/sag_DNS_imp_
ManagingServers.asp

➤ Microsoft TechNet security administration tasks—
http://www.microsoft.com/technet/treeview/default.asp?url=/technet/
prodtechnol/windowsserver2003/proddocs/entserver/comexp/
adsecuretasks_6dkj.asp

➤ Microsoft TechNet security overview—http://www.microsoft.com/
technet/treeview/default.asp?url=/technet/prodtechnol/windowsserver2003/
proddocs/standard/sag_SEconceptsSecModel.asp

➤ Microsoft TechNet site for the Security Configuration Manager—
http://www.microsoft.com/technet/treeview/default.asp?url=/technet/
prodtechnol/windowsserver2003/proddocs/standard/seconcepts_SCM.asp

➤ White paper: Windows Server 2003 security guide—
http://microsoft.com/downloads/details.aspx?FamilyId=8A2643C1-0685-4D89-
B655-521EA6C7B4DB&displaylang=en

What's on the CD-ROM

This appendix provides a brief summary of what you'll find on the CD-ROM that accompanies this book. For a more detailed description of the *PrepLogic Practice Exams, Preview Edition* exam simulation software, see Appendix C, "Using the *PrepLogic Practice Exams, Preview Edition* Software." In addition to the *PrepLogic Practice Exams, Preview Edition* software, the CD-ROM includes an electronic version of the book, in the Portable Document Format (PDF).

The *PrepLogic Practice Exams, Preview Edition* Software

PrepLogic is a leading provider of certification training tools. Trusted by certification students worldwide, PrepLogic is the best practice-exam software available. In addition to providing a means of evaluating your knowledge of this book's material, *PrepLogic Practice Exams, Preview Edition* features several innovations that help you improve your mastery of the subject matter.

For example, the practice tests allow you to check your score by exam area or domain to determine which topics you need to study further. Another feature allows you to obtain immediate feedback on your responses in the form of explanations for the correct and incorrect answers.

PrepLogic Practice Exams, Preview Edition exhibit all the full-test simulation functionality of the Premium Edition but offer only a fraction of the total questions. To get the complete set of practice questions, visit http://www. preplogic.com and order the Premium Edition for this book and other exam training guides.

For a more detailed description of the features of the *PrepLogic Practice Exams, Preview Edition* software, see Appendix C.

An Exclusive Electronic Version of the Text

As mentioned previously, the CD-ROM that accompanies this book also contains an electronic PDF version of this book. This electronic version comes complete with all figures as they appear in the book. You can use Adobe Acrobat's handy search capability for study and review purposes.

Using the *PrepLogic Practice Exams, Preview Edition* Software

This book includes a special version of the PrepLogic Practice Exams software, a revolutionary test engine designed to give you the best in certification-exam preparation. PrepLogic offers sample and practice exams for many of today's most in-demand and challenging technical certifications. A special Preview Edition of the PrepLogic Practice Exams software is included with this book as a tool to use in assessing your knowledge of the training-guide material while also providing you with the experience of taking an electronic exam.

This appendix describes in detail what *PrepLogic Practice Exams, Preview Edition* is; how it works; and what it can do to help you prepare for the exam. Note that although the Preview Edition includes all the test-simulation functions of the complete retail version, it contains only a single practice test. The Premium Edition, available at http://www.preplogic.com, contains a complete set of challenging practice exams designed to optimize your learning experience.

The Exam Simulation

One of the main functions of *PrepLogic Practice Exams, Preview Edition* is exam simulation. To prepare you to take the actual Microsoft certification exam, PrepLogic is designed to offer the most effective exam simulation available.

Question Quality

The questions provided in *PrepLogic Practice Exams, Preview Edition* are written to the highest standards of technical accuracy. The questions tap the content of this book's chapters and help you review and assess your knowledge before you take the actual exam.

The Interface Design

The *PrepLogic Practice Exams, Preview Edition* exam-simulation interface provides you with the experience of taking an electronic exam. It enables you to effectively prepare to take the actual exam by making the test experience familiar. Using this test simulation can help eliminate the sense of surprise or anxiety you might experience in the testing center because you will already be acquainted with computerized testing.

The Effective Learning Environment

The *PrepLogic Practice Exams, Preview Edition* interface provides a learning environment that not only tests you using a computerized format, but also teaches the material you need to know to pass the certification exam. Each question includes a detailed explanation of the correct answer, and most of these explanations provide reasons for why the other answers are incorrect. This information helps reinforce the knowledge you already have and also provides practical information you can use on the job.

Software Requirements

PrepLogic Practice Exams requires a computer with the following minimum requirements:

➤ Microsoft Windows 98, Windows Me, Windows NT 4.0, Windows 2000, Windows XP, or Windows Server 2003

➤ A 166MHz or faster processor

➤ 32MB of RAM

➤ 10MB of hard-drive space

As with any Windows application, the more memory, the better the performance.

Installing *PrepLogic Practice Exams, Preview Edition*

You install *PrepLogic Practice Exams, Preview Edition* by following these steps:

1. Insert the CD-ROM that accompanies this book into your CD-ROM drive. The Autorun feature of Windows should launch the software. If you have Autorun disabled, click Start, Run. Click Browse to navigate to the root folder on the CD-ROM and select setup.exe. Click Open, and then click OK for the Run dialog box to launch the program.

2. The Installation Wizard copies the *PrepLogic Practice Exams, Preview Edition* files to your hard drive. It then adds the *PrepLogic Practice Exams, Preview Edition* shortcut icon to your desktop and the Program menu. Finally, it installs test-engine components to the appropriate system folders.

Removing *PrepLogic Practice Exams, Preview Edition* from Your Computer

If you decide to remove the *PrepLogic Practice Exams, Preview Edition* you can use the included uninstallation procedure to ensure that it is removed from your system safely and completely. Follow these instructions to remove *PrepLogic Practice Exams, Preview Edition* from your computer:

1. Click Start, Settings, Control Panel.

2. Double-click the Add/Remove Programs icon. You see a list of software programs that are installed on your computer.

3. Select the *PrepLogic Practice Exams, Preview Edition* title you want to remove. Click the Add/Remove button. The software is then removed from your computer.

How to Use the Software

PrepLogic is designed to be user friendly and intuitive. Because the software has a smooth learning curve, your time is maximized because you start practicing with it almost immediately. *PrepLogic Practice Exams, Preview Edition* has two major modes of study: Practice Exam and Flash Review.

Using Practice Exam mode, you can develop your test-taking abilities as well as your knowledge through the use of the Show Answer option. While you are taking the test, you can expose the answers along with detailed explanations of why each answer is correct or incorrect. This process helps you better understand the material presented.

Flash Review mode is designed to reinforce exam topics rather than quiz you. In this mode, you are shown a series of questions but no answers are available to choose from. You can click a button that reveals the correct answer to each question and a full explanation for that answer.

Starting a Practice Exam Mode Session

Practice Exam mode enables you to control the exam experience in ways that actual certification exams do not allow. To begin studying in Practice Exam mode, you click the Practice Exam option button from the main exam customization window. It displays the following options:

➤ *Enable Show Answer*—Clicking this button activates the Show Answer button, which allows you to view the correct answers and full explanation for each question during the exam. When this option is not enabled, you must wait until after your exam has been graded to view the correct answers and explanation for each question.

➤ *Enable Item Review*—Clicking this button activates the Item Review button, which allows you to view your answer choices. This option also facilitates navigation between questions.

➤ *Randomize Choices*—By clicking this button, you can randomize answer choices from one exam session to the next. This process makes memorizing question choices more difficult, thereby keeping questions fresh and challenging for a longer period of time.

On the left side of the main exam customization window, you see the option of selecting the preconfigured practice test or creating your own custom test. The preconfigured test has a fixed time limit and fixed number of questions. Custom tests allow you to configure the time limit and the number of questions in your exam.

The Preview Edition on this book's CD-ROM includes a single preconfigured practice test. You can get the complete set of challenging PrepLogic Practice Exams at http://www.preplogic.com to make certain you're ready for the big exam.

You click the Begin Exam button to begin your exam.

Starting a Flash Review Mode Session

Flash Review mode provides an easy way to reinforce topics covered in the practice questions. To begin studying in Flash Review mode, you click the Flash Review option button from the main exam customization window. Then, you select either the preconfigured practice test or create your own custom test.

You click the Begin Exam button to begin a Flash Review mode session.

Standard *PrepLogic Practice Exams, Preview Edition* Options

The following list describes the function of each of the buttons you see across the bottom of the screen:

> Depending on the options, some of the buttons might be grayed out and inaccessible, or some buttons might be missing completely. Buttons that are appropriate for each situation are active.

➤ *Exhibit*—This button is visible if an exhibit is provided to support the question. An *exhibit* is an image that provides supplemental information that is necessary to answer a question.

➤ *Item Review*—This button leaves the question window and opens the Item Review window, from which you can see all questions, your answers, and your marked items. You can also see correct answers listed here, when appropriate.

➤ *Show Answer*—This option displays the correct answer, with an explanation about why it is correct. If you select this option, the current question is not scored.

> *Mark Item*—You can check this box to flag a question that you need to review further. You can view your marked items by clicking the Item Review button (if it is enabled). When your exam is being scored, you are notified if you have any marked items remaining.

> *Previous Item*—You can use this option to view the previous question.

> *Next Item*—You can use this option to view the next question.

> *Grade Exam*—When you finish your exam, you can click Grade Exam to end your exam and view your detailed score report. If you have unanswered or marked items remaining, you are asked whether you want to continue taking your exam or view the exam report.

Seeing Time Remaining

If your practice test is timed, the time remaining is displayed on the upper-right corner of the practice exam window. The timer counts down the minutes and seconds remaining to complete the test. If you run out of time, you are asked whether you want to continue taking the test or end your exam.

Getting Your Examination Score Report

The Examination Score Report window appears when the Practice Exam mode ends, whether as a result of time expiring, completing all the questions, or making the decision to stop the exam early.

This window provides a graphical display of your test score with a breakdown of scores by topic domain. The graphical display at the top of the window compares your overall score with the PrepLogic Exam Competency Score. The *PrepLogic Exam Competency Score* reflects the level of subject competency required to pass this particular Microsoft certification exam. Although this score does not directly translate to a passing grade, consistently matching or exceeding this score does suggest that you possess the knowledge needed to pass the actual certification exam.

Reviewing Your Exam

From the Your Score Report window, you can review the exam that you just finished by clicking the View Items button. You can navigate through the items and view the questions, your answers, the correct answers, and the explanations for those questions. You can return to your score report by clicking the View Items button.

Contacting PrepLogic

If you want to contact PrepLogic to obtain information about its extensive line of certification practice tests, or for any reason, you can visit the company online at http://www.preplogic.com.

Customer Service

If you have a damaged product and need to contact customer service, please call 800-858-7674.

Product Suggestions and Comments

PrepLogic values your input! Please email your suggestions and comments to feedback@preplogic.com.

License Agreement

YOU MUST AGREE TO THE TERMS AND CONDITIONS OUT-LINED IN THE END USER LICENSE AGREEMENT ("EULA") PRESENTED TO YOU DURING THE INSTALLATION PROCESS. IF YOU DO NOT AGREE TO THESE TERMS, DO NOT INSTALL THE SOFTWARE.

Glossary

A (address) resource record

A resource record that is used to map a Domain Name System (DNS) domain name to a host Internet Protocol (IP) address on the network.

Accelerated Graphics Port (AGP)

An interface specification developed by Intel that was released in August 1997. AGP is based on peripheral connection interface (PCI) but is designed especially for the throughput demands of 3D graphics. Rather than use the PCI bus for graphics data, AGP introduced a dedicated point-to-point channel so that the graphics controller can directly access main memory. The AGP channel is 32 bits wide and runs at 66MHz, which translates into a total bandwidth of 266Mbps, as opposed to the PCI bandwidth of 133Mbps. AGP also supports two optional faster modes, with throughputs of 533Mbps and 1.07Gbps. In addition, AGP allows 3D textures to be stored in main memory rather than in video memory. AGP has a couple of important system requirements: The chipset must support AGP, and the motherboard must be equipped with an AGP bus slot or must have an integrated AGP graphics system.

access control entry (ACE)

An entry in an access control list (ACL). An ACE contains a set of access rights and a security identifier (SID) that identifies a user or group for whom the rights are allowed, denied, or audited.

account lockout

A Windows Server 2003 security feature that locks a user account if a certain number of failed logon attempts occur within a specified amount of time, based on security-policy lockout settings. Locked accounts cannot log on.

Active Directory

The directory service that is included with Windows Server 2003. Active Directory is based on the X.500 standards and those of its predecessor, Lightweight Directory Access Protocol (LDAP). It stores information about objects on a network and makes this information available to applications, users, and network administrators. Active Directory is also used for authentication to network resources, using a single logon process. It provides network administrators a hierarchical view of the network and a single point of administration for all network objects.

Active Directory partition

The information area that begins at a branch of a directory tree and continues to the bottom of that tree or to the edges of new partitions controlled by subordinate Directory System Agents (DSAs). An Active Directory partition is a contiguous subtree of the directory that forms a unit of replication.

Active Directory Users and Computers (ADUC) snap-in (console)

An administrative tool designed to perform daily Active Directory administration tasks, including creating, deleting, modifying, moving, and setting permissions on objects stored in the Active Directory database. These objects include organizational units (OUs), users, contacts, groups, computers, printers, and shared file objects.

Address Resolution Protocol (ARP)

A protocol that translates an IP address into a physical address, such as a Media Access Control (MAC) address (hardware address). A computer that wants to obtain a physical address sends an ARP broadcast request onto the TCP/IP network. The computer on the network that has the IP address in the request then replies with its physical hardware address.

Advanced Configuration and Power Interface (ACPI)

A power-management specification developed by Intel, Microsoft, and Toshiba that enables Windows Server 2003 to control the amount of power given to each device attached to the computer. With ACPI, the operating system can turn off peripheral devices, such as CD-ROM players, when they are not in use. As another example, ACPI enables manufacturers to produce computers that automatically power up as soon as you touch the keyboard.

Advanced Power Management (APM)

An application programming interface (API) developed by Intel and Microsoft that allows developers to include power management in the Basic Input/Output System (BIOS). APM defines a layer between the hardware and the operating system that effectively shields programmers from hardware details. ACPI has replaced APM.

AGP

See *Accelerated Graphics Port.*

ARP

See *Address Resolution Protocol.*

ARPANet

A wide area network (WAN) that was created in the 1960s by the U.S. Department of Defense (DoD) Advanced Research Projects Agency for the free exchange of information between universities and research organizations. ARPANet was the precursor to what we know as the Internet today.

Asynchronous Transfer Mode (ATM)

A networking technology that transfers data in cells (that is, data packets of a fixed size). Cells used with ATM are small compared to packets used with older technologies. The relatively small, constant cell size allows ATM hardware to transmit video images, audio, and computer data over the same network as well as ensures that no single type of data consumes all the connection's available bandwidth. Current implementations of ATM support data transfer rates from 25Mbps to 622Mbps. Most Ethernet-based networks run at 100Mbps or below.

attribute

A single property that describes an object, such as the make, model, or color that describes a car. In the context of directories, an attribute is the main component of an entry in a directory, such as an email address.

auditing

The process that tracks the activities of users by recording selected types of events in the security log of a server or workstation.

authentication ticket

A permission to indirectly access resources that a Kerberos Key Distribution Center (KDC) grants to clients and applications.

authoritative restore

A type of restore for Active Directory objects on a domain controller (DC) that updates the objects' update sequence numbers (USNs) to indicate that those objects should be replicated to other DCs throughout the forest. You must use the `ntdsutil.exe` utility to mark Active Directory objects as "authoritative."

authorize

To register a Remote Installation Services (RIS) server or a Dynamic Host Configuration Protocol (DHCP) server with Active Directory.

Auto Private IP Addressing (APIPA)

A client-side feature of Windows 98 and 2000 DHCP clients. If the client's attempt to negotiate with a DHCP server fails, the client computer automatically selects an IP address from the `169.254.0.0` Class B range.

Automated System Recovery (ASR)

A feature in Windows Server 2003 and Windows XP Professional that allows you to create a recovery backup set using the Windows Backup Utility that consists of a media backup of the system and boot drive volumes and the System State along with a backup ASR floppy disk. As a disaster-recovery option, you can restore the entire system drive volume, boot drive volume, and the computer's System State using the ASR feature. ASR formats the system drive, reinstalls Windows Server 2003 on that drive, and then restores all the configuration settings and files that existed on the system drive at the time that the ASR backup was created.

Automatic Update

A service that checks with the Windows Update Web site for critical updates and automates the process of downloading and installing the critical updates.

backup domain controller (BDC)

In Windows NT 4 Server, a server that receives a copy of the domain's directory database (which contains all the account and security policy information for the domain). BDCs can continue to participate in an Active Directory domain when the domain is configured in mixed mode.

Backup Utility

A Windows Server 2003 utility that helps you plan for and recover from data loss by allowing you to create backup copies of data as well as restore files, folders, and System State data (which includes the Registry) manually or on a schedule. The Windows Server 2003 Backup Utility allows you to back up data to a variety of media types besides tape. You can also run backups from the command line using ntbackup.exe and specifying the appropriate command-line options.

baselining

The process of measuring system performance so that you can ascertain a standard or expected level of performance.

basic disk

A term that indicates a physical disk, which can have primary and extended partitions. A basic disk can contain up to three primary partitions and one extended partition, or it can have up to four primary partitions. A basic disk can also have a single extended partition with logical drives. You cannot extend a partition stored on a basic disk unless it is formatted as NTFS, and you must use the diskpart.exe command-line tool to extend a basic partition.

BDC

See *backup domain controller*.

BIOS (Basic Input/Output System)

Built-in software that determines what a computer can do without accessing programs from a disk. On PCs, the BIOS contains all the code required to control the keyboard, display screen, disk drives, serial communications, and a number of miscellaneous functions. A BIOS that can handle Plug and Play devices is known as a Plug and Play BIOS. A Plug and Play BIOS is always implemented with Flash Memory rather than read-only memory (ROM). Windows Server 2003 benefits if a computer has the latest ACPI-compliant BIOS.

boot partition

The partition that contains the Windows Server 2003 operating system and its support files.

CD-R

A recordable CD-ROM technology using a disc that can be written only once.

CD-RW

A rewritable CD-ROM technology. You can also use CD-RW drives to write CD-R discs, and they can read CD-ROMs. Initially known as CD-E (for CD-Erasable), a CD-RW disk can be rewritten hundreds of times.

Challenge Handshake Authentication Protocol (CHAP)

An authentication protocol used by Microsoft remote access as well as network and dial-up connections. By using CHAP, a remote access client can send its authentication credentials to a remote access server in a secure form. Microsoft has modified the original CHAP, as specified in RFC 1334. These versions are Windows specific, such as Microsoft CHAP (MS-CHAP) and MS-CHAP 2.

CLI (command-line interface)

A software tool or utility that runs from the command line rather than from the graphical user interface (GUI).

client-side caching (CSC)

See *offline files*.

compression

The process of making individual files and folders occupy less physical disk space. You can compress data using NT File System (NTFS) compression or through third-party utilities.

See also *NTFS data compression*.

computer account

An account that a domain administrator creates and that uniquely identifies the computer on the domain. The Windows Server 2003 computer account matches the name of the computer that joins the domain.

container

An object in a directory that contains other objects.

convert.exe

A Windows Server 2003 command-line utility that turns a FAT or FAT32 drive volume into an NTFS drive volume without having to reformat or delete any data that is stored on the drive. The command-line syntax is convert.exe X: /FS:NTFS, where X: represents the drive letter that you want to convert to NTFS. There is no equivalent command to convert from NTFS to FAT or FAT32.

copy backup

A backup type that backs up all selected files, but each backed-up file's archive bit is not changed.

counter

A metric that provides information about particular aspects of system performance.

DACL

See *discretionary access control list*.

daily backup

A backup of files that have changed today which does not mark them as being backed up.

data compression

The process of making individual files and folders occupy less physical disk space. You can compress data using NTFS compression or through third-party utilities.

See also *NTFS data compression*.

data recovery agent (DRA)

A Windows Server 2003 administrator who has been issued a public-key certificate for the express purpose of recovering user-encrypted data files that have been encrypted with Encrypting File System (EFS). *Data recovery* refers to the process of decrypting a file without having the private key of the user who encrypted the file. A DRA might be necessary if a user loses his or her private key for decrypting files or if a user leaves an organization without decrypting important files that other users need.

default gateway

An address that serves an important role in Transmission Control Protocol/Internet Protocol (TCP/IP) networking by providing a default route for TCP/IP hosts to use when communicating with other hosts on remote networks. A router (either a dedicated router or a computer that connects two or more network segments) generally acts as the default gateway for TCP/IP hosts. The router maintains its own routing table of other networks within an internetwork. The routing table maps the routes required to reach the remote hosts that reside on those other networks.

Device Manager

The primary tool that is used in Windows Server 2003 to configure and manage hardware devices and their settings.

DHCP server
See *Dynamic Host Configuration Protocol server*.

dial-up access
A type of access in which a remote client uses a public telephone line or Integrated Services Digital Network (ISDN) line to create a connection to a Windows Server 2003 remote access server.

differential backup
A backup that copies files created or changed since the last normal or incremental backup. A differential backup does *not* mark files as having been backed up. (In other words, the archive attribute is not cleared.) If you are performing a combination of normal and differential backups, when you restore files and folders, you need the last normal backup as well as the last differential backup.

digital signature
Public-key cryptography that authenticates the integrity and originator of a communication.

Direct Memory Access (DMA)
A technique for transferring data from main memory to a device without passing it through the CPU. Computers that have DMA channels can transfer data to and from devices more quickly than can computers without DMA channels. It is useful for making quick backups and for real-time applications. Some expansion boards, such as CD-ROM cards, can access the computer's DMA channel. When

you install the board, you must specify the DMA channel to be used, which sometimes involves setting a jumper or dual in-line package (DIP) switch.

Directory Services Restore Mode
A startup option for DCs only. When restoring the System State and Active Directory objects from backup, you must restart the server under Directory Services Restore Mode.

discretionary access control list (DACL)
A list of ACEs that lets administrators set permissions for users and groups at the object and attribute levels. This list represents part of an object's security descriptor that allows or denies permissions to specific users and groups.

disk group
In Windows Server 2003, a collection of multiple dynamic disks that are managed together. All dynamic disks in a computer are members of the same disk group. Each disk in a disk group stores replicas of the same configuration data, and this configuration data is stored in a 1MB region at the end of each dynamic disk.

Disk Management
A Windows Server 2003 Microsoft Management Console (MMC) snap-in that you use to perform all disk maintenance tasks, such as formatting, creating partitions, deleting partitions, and converting a basic disk to a dynamic disk.

disk quota

A control that you use in Windows Server 2003 to limit the amount of hard-disk space available for all users or an individual user. You can apply a quota on a per-user, per-volume basis only.

diskpart.exe

A command-line utility that you use for managing disk storage, including creating and deleting partitions and volumes and formatting partitions and volumes.

distribution group

A group that can contain users and other groups which cannot be assigned an access control list (ACL); no security permissions may be assigned to a distribution group. It is used as a distribution list for email purposes.

DMA

See *Direct Memory Access*.

DNS

See *Domain Name System*.

domain

The fundamental administrative unit of Active Directory. A domain stores information about objects in the domain's partition of Active Directory. You can give user and group accounts in a domain privileges and permissions to resources on any system that belongs to the domain.

domain controller (DC)

A computer running Windows Server 2003 that hosts Active Directory and manages user access to a network, including logons, authentication, and access to the directory and shared resources.

domain forest

A collection of one or more Active Directory domains in a noncontiguous DNS namespace that share a common schema, configuration, and global catalog and that are linked with two-way transitive trusts.

domain functional level

The level at which a Windows Server 2003 Active Directory domain is operating—Windows 2000 mixed, Windows 2000 native, Windows Server 2003 interim, or Windows Server 2003.

domain local group

A group within Active Directory that you can only use to specify permissions on resources within a single domain.

Domain Name System (DNS)

DNS is used primarily for resolving fully qualified domain names (FQDNs) to IP addresses. DNS is the standard naming convention for hosts on the Internet, which have both domain names (such as `blastthroughlearning.com`) and numeric IP addresses (such as `192.168.2.8`).

domain tree

A set of domains that form a contiguous DNS namespace through a set of hierarchical relationships.

DRA

See *data recovery agent*.

driver rollback

A feature in Windows Server 2003 and Windows XP that allows a user to revert back to a previous device driver when a newly installed device driver does not work properly.

driver signing

A method for marking or identifying driver files that meet certain specifications or standards. Windows Server 2003 uses a driver-signing process to make sure drivers are certified to work correctly with the Windows Driver Model (WDM) in Windows Server 2003.

DVD (digital versatile disc or digital video disc)

An improved type of compact disc that holds a minimum of 4.7GB, enough for a full-length movie. The DVD specification supports discs with capacities from 4.7 to 17GB and access rates of 600Kbps to 1.3Mbps. One of the best features of DVD drives is that they are backward compatible with CD-ROMs. This means that DVD players can play old CD-ROMs, CD-I disks, video CDs, and new DVDs. Newer DVD players can also read CD-R disks. DVD uses Moving Picture Experts Group (MPEG)-2 to compress video data.

DVD-R

A write-once optical disk used to master DVD-Video and DVD-ROM discs. DVD-Rs are the DVD counterpart to CD-Rs and use the same recording technology to "burn" the disc.

DVD-RAM

A rewritable DVD technology that is best used for data storage. You cannot play recorded movies on most consumer DVD players.

DVD-RW

A rewritable DVD technology. Information can be written to and erased multiple times. DVD-RW primarily is used for movies and is compatible with most of the DVD players on the market.

DVD+RW

A rewritable DVD technology. You can use DVD+RW for both data and movies, and it is compatible with most of the DVD players on the market.

dynamic disk

A physical disk in a Windows Server 2003 computer that does not use partitions or logical drives. It has dynamic volumes that you create by using the Disk Management console. A dynamic disk can contain any of five types of volumes. In addition, you can extend a volume on a dynamic disk. A dynamic disk can contain an unlimited number of volumes, so you are not restricted to four volumes per disk as you are with a basic disk.

Dynamic Host Configuration Protocol (DHCP) server

A computer that dynamically assigns IP addresses to clients. The DHCP server can also provide direction toward routers, Windows Internet Name Service (WINS) servers, and DNS servers.

Dynamic Update

Works with Windows Update to download critical fixes and drivers needed during the setup process. Dynamic Update provides important updates to files required to minimize difficulties during setup.

dynamic volume

The only type of volume you can create on dynamic disks. There are five types of dynamic volumes: simple, spanned, mirrored, striped, and Redundant Array of Independent Disks (RAID)-5. Only computers running Windows Server 2003, Windows XP Professional, and any version of Windows 2000 can directly access dynamic volumes. Windows XP Professional and Windows 2000 Professional computers *cannot* host but *can* access mirrored and RAID-5 dynamic volumes that are stored on remote Windows Server 2003 and Windows 2000 Server computers.

EFS

See *Encrypting File System*.

Emergency Management Services (EMS)

Services that can be performed on headless servers and on servers whose network connections are not currently functioning. These services offer out-of-band management through a modem or a serial port connection using the Special Administration Console or the !Special Administration Console.

emergency repair disk (ERD)

A disk created by the Windows Backup utility, for Windows 2000 and earlier operating systems, that contains information about the current Windows system settings. You can use this disk to attempt to repair a computer if it does not start or if the system files are damaged or erased.

emergency repair process

A process that helps you repair problems with system files, the startup environment (in a dual-boot or multiple-boot system), and the partition boot sector on a boot volume. Before you use the emergency repair process to repair a system, you must create an emergency repair disk (ERD). You can do so by using the Windows Backup utility. Even if you have not created an ERD, you can still try to use the emergency repair process; however, any changes you made to the system—for example, service-pack updates—might be lost and might need to be reinstalled.

Encrypting File System (EFS)

A subsystem of NTFS that uses public keys and private keys to provide encryption for files and folders on computers using Windows Server 2003. Only the user who initially encrypted the file and a DRA can decrypt encrypted files and folders.

Event Viewer

An MMC snap-in that displays the Windows Server 2003 event logs for system, application, security, directory services, DNS server, and File Replication Service log files.

FAT (file allocation table) or FAT16

A 16-bit table that many operating systems use to locate files on disk. The FAT keeps track of all the pieces of a file. The FAT file system for older versions of Windows 95 is called virtual file allocation table (VFAT); the one for Windows 95 (OEM Service Release [OSR] 2) and Windows 98 is called FAT32. Windows Server 2003 can use the FAT file system; however, it is often not used on Windows Server 2003, Windows XP, Windows 2000, and Windows NT computers because the NTFS file system is preferred. FAT retains larger cluster sizes and is unable to scale to larger volume sizes. The FAT file system has no local security.

FAT32

A 32-bit version of FAT that is available in Windows 95 OSR 2 and Windows 98. FAT32 increases the number of bits used to address clusters and reduces the size of each cluster. The result is that FAT32 can support larger disks (up to 2TB) and better storage efficiency (less slack space) than the earlier version of FAT. The FAT32 file system has no local security. Windows Server 2003 can use and format partitions as FAT, FAT32, or NTFS.

fault tolerance

The capability of a computer or an operating system to ensure data integrity when hardware failures occur. Within the Windows 2000 Server and Windows Server 2003 product lines, mirrored volumes and RAID-5 volumes are fault tolerant.

fax service management console

An MMC snap-in that allows you to administer the settings for sending and receiving faxes using the fax service.

FireWire or IEEE (Institute of Electrical and Electronics Engineers) 1394

A newer, very fast external bus standard that supports data transfer rates of up to 400Mbps. Products that support the IEEE 1394 standard have different names, depending on the company. Apple originally developed the technology and uses the trademarked name FireWire. Other companies use other names, such as i.link and Lynx, to describe their 1394 products. You can use a single 1394 port to connect up to 63 external devices. In addition to its high speed, 1394 supports time-dependent data, delivering data at a guaranteed rate. This support makes it ideal for devices, such as video devices, that need to transfer high levels of data in real time. Although it is extremely fast and flexible, 1394 is expensive. Like universal serial bus (USB), 1394 supports both Plug and Play and hot plugging, and it provides power to peripheral devices. The main difference between 1394 and USB is that 1394 supports faster data transfer rates and is more expensive. For these reasons, it is used mostly for devices that require large throughputs, such as video cameras, whereas USB is used to connect most other peripheral devices.

forest functional level

The level at which an Active Directory forest running under Windows Server 2003 is operating—Windows 2000, Windows Server 2003 interim, or Windows Server 2003.

forward lookup

In DNS, a query process in which the friendly DNS domain name of a host computer is searched to find its IP address.

forward lookup zone

A DNS zone that provides host name–to–TCP/IP address resolution. In DNS Manager, forward lookup zones are based on DNS domain names and typically hold host (A) address resource records.

Frame Relay PVC (permanent virtual circuit)

A protocol in which messages are divided into packets before they are sent. Each packet is then transmitted individually, and the packets can even follow different routes to their destinations. When all the packets that form a message arrive at the destination, they are recompiled into the original message. Several WAN protocols, including Frame Relay, are based on packet-switching technologies. Ordinary telephone service is based on circuit-switching technology, in which a dedicated line is allocated for transmission between two parties. Circuit switching is best suited for data that must be transmitted quickly and must arrive in the same order in which it is sent. Most real-time data, such as live audio and video, requires circuit-switching technology. Packet switching is more efficient and robust for data that can withstand some delays (latency) in transmission, such as email messages and Web content.

global group

A group that can be granted rights and permissions and can become a member of domain local groups in its own domain and trusting domains. However, a global group can contain user accounts from its own domain only. Global groups provide a way to create sets of users from inside the domain that are available for use both in and out of the domain.

globally unique identifier (GUID)

A 16-byte value generated from the unique identifier on a device, the current data and time, and a sequence number. A GUID identifies a specific device or component.

group policy

A mechanism for managing change and configuration of systems, security, applications, and user environments in an Active Directory domain.

Group Policy Editor (GPE)

A Windows Server 2003 snap-in that allows customers to create custom profiles for groups of users and computers.

Group Policy Management Console (GPMC)

A downloadable tool from Microsoft for Windows Server 2003 that lets administrators manage group policy for multiple domains and sites within one or more forests, all in a simplified user interface with drag-and-drop support. Highlights include functionality such as backup, restore, import, copy, and reporting of group policy objects (GPOs). These operations are fully scriptable, which lets administrators customize and automate management. Together, these advantages make group policy easier to use and help you manage your enterprise more cost-effectively.

group policy object (GPO)

An object that is created by the GPE snap-in to hold information about a specific group's association with selected directory objects, such as sites, domains, or OUs.

GUID

See *globally unique identifier*.

Hardware Abstraction Layer (HAL)

A component of an operating system that functions something like an API. In strict technical architecture, HALs reside at the device level, a layer below the standard API level. HAL allows programmers to write applications and game titles with all the device-independent advantages of writing to an API but without the large processing overhead that APIs normally demand.

hardware profile

A profile that stores configuration settings for a collection of devices and services. Windows Server 2003 can store different hardware profiles so that users' needs can be met even though their computers might frequently require different device and service settings, depending on circumstances. The best example is a laptop or portable computer used in an office while in a docking station and then undocked so that the user can travel with it. The two environments require different power-management settings, possibly different network settings, and various other configuration changes.

Hash Message Authentication Code Message Digest 5 (HMAC-MD5)

A hash algorithm that produces a 128-bit hash of the authenticated payload.

headless server

A server that has no local mouse, keyboard, or video monitor directly connected to it.

hibernation

A power option in Windows Server 2003, Windows 2000 Server, Windows XP Professional, and Windows 2000 Professional portable computers that helps conserve battery power. Hibernation is a complete power-down while maintaining the state of open programs and connected hardware. When you bring the computer out of hibernation, the desktop is restored exactly as you left it, in less time than it takes for a complete system restart. However, it does take longer to bring the computer out of hibernation than out of standby. It's a good idea to put a computer in hibernation when you will be away from the computer for an extended time or overnight.

hidden shares

Shares that do not show up in the network browse list. Shared folders have a dollar sign ($) appended to their share names, such as admin$, c$, d$, and so on. Windows Server 2003 creates certain hidden shares by default. Administrators can create their own hidden shares.

home directory

A location for a user or group of users to store files on a network server. The home directory provides a central location for files that users can access and back up.

HOSTS file

A local text file in the same format as the 4.3 Berkeley Software Distribution (BSD) Unix /etc/hosts file. This file maps hostnames to IP addresses. In Windows Server 2003, this file is stored in the \%SystemRoot%\System32\Drivers\Etc folder.

IIS metabase

The database that holds all the configuration settings for Internet Information Services (IIS), stored in the XML file format—metabase.xml.

See also *Internet Information Services*.

in-band management

Access to a server via a regular network connection as opposed to a modem or serial port connection.

incremental backup

A backup that backs up only files created or changed since the last normal or incremental backup. It marks files as having been backed up. (In other words, the archive attribute is cleared.) If you use a combination of normal and incremental backups, you need to have the last normal backup set as well as all incremental backup sets to restore data.

Infrared Data Association (IrDA) device

A device that exchanges data over infrared waves. Infrared technology lets devices "beam" information to each other in the same way that a remote control tells a TV to change the channel. You could, for example, beam a document to a printer or another computer instead of having to connect a cable. The IrDA standard has been widely adopted by PC and consumer electronics manufacturers. Windows Server 2003 supports the IrDA standard.

input locale

The specification of the language in which you want to type.

integrated zone storage

Storage of DNS zone information in an Active Directory database rather than in a text file.

Internet Connection Firewall (ICF)

A built-in service that monitors all aspects of the traffic that crosses the network interface, which includes inspecting the source and destination addresses, for further control.

Internet Connection Sharing (ICS)

A feature that is intended for use in a small office or home office in which the network configuration and the Internet connection are managed by the computer running Windows Server 2003, where the shared connection resides. ICS can use a dial-up connection, such as a modem or an ISDN connection to the Internet, or it can use a dedicated connection such as a cable modem or Digital Subscriber Line (DSL) connection. It is assumed that the ICS computer is the only Internet connection—the only gateway to the Internet—and that it sets up all internal network addresses.

Internet Information Services (IIS)

A group of services that host Internet and intranet-related features on Windows Server 2003 computers such as File Transfer Protocol (FTP) and the World Wide Web (WWW) service under IIS version 6.0. Each of these services must be installed individually; none of these features are installed by default.

Internet Printing Protocol (IPP)

A standard that allows network clients the option of entering a uniform resource locator (URL) to connect to network printers and manage their network print jobs, using a Hypertext Transfer Protocol (HTTP) connection in a Web browser. Windows Server 2003 fully supports IPP. The print server is either a Windows Server 2003 computer or a Windows XP Professional computer running IIS 5, or it can be a Windows 2000 Professional system running Personal Web Server (PWS). PWS is the "junior" version of IIS. You can view all shared IPP printers at `http://servername/printers` (for example, `http://Server2/printers`).

Interrupt Request (IRQ)

A hardware line over which a device or devices can send interrupt signals to the microprocessor. When you add a new device to a PC, you sometimes need to set its IRQ number. IRQ conflicts used to be a common problem when you were adding expansion boards, but the Plug and Play and ACPI specifications have helped remove this headache in many cases.

I/O (input/output) port

Any socket in the back, front, or side of a computer that you use to connect to another piece of hardware.

IP (Internet Protocol)

One of the protocols of the TCP/IP suite. IP is responsible for determining whether a packet is for the local network or a remote network. If the packet is for a remote network, IP finds a route for it.

IP (Internet Protocol) address

A 32-bit binary address that identifies a host's network and host ID. The network portion can contain either a network ID or a network ID and a subnet ID.

ipconfig

A command that allows you to view, renegotiate, and configure IP address information for a Windows NT or 2000 computer.

IPSec (Internet Protocol Security)

A TCP/IP security mechanism that provides machine-level authentication, as well as data encryption, for virtual private network (VPN) connections that use Layer 2 Tunneling Protocol (L2TP). IPSec negotiates between a computer and its remote tunnel server before an L2TP connection is established, which secures both passwords and data.

ISDN (Integrated Services Digital Network)

An international communications standard for sending voice, video, and data over digital telephone lines or normal telephone wires. ISDN supports data transfer rates of 64Kbps. Most ISDN lines offered by telephone companies provide two lines at once, called B channels. You can use one line for voice and the other for data, or you can use both lines for data, giving you data rates of 128Kbps.

Kerberos version 5

A distributed authentication and privacy protocol that protects information on a network between devices and enables single sign-on (SSO). Kerberos version 5 is used in the Windows Server 2003 security model.

language group

A Regional Options configuration that allows you to type and read documents composed in languages of that group (for example, Western Europe, United States, Japanese, and Hebrew).

Last Known Good Configuration

A setting that starts Windows Server 2003 by using the Registry information that Windows saved at the last successful logon. You should use this setting only in cases when you have incorrectly configured a device or driver. Last Known Good Configuration does not solve problems caused by corrupted or missing drivers or files. Also, when you use this setting, you lose any changes made since the last successful logon.

Layer 2 Tunneling Protocol (L2TP)

An industry-standard Internet tunneling protocol that provides the same functionality as Point-to-Point Tunneling Protocol (PPTP). Unlike PPTP, L2TP does not require IP connectivity between the client workstation and the server. L2TP requires only that the tunnel medium provide packet-oriented point-to-point connectivity. You can use L2TP over media such as ATM, Frame Relay, and X.25.

local group

A group account that is stored in the Security Accounts Manager (SAM) of a single system. You can give a local group access to resources only on that system.

local user

A user account that is stored in the SAM of a single system. A local user can belong only to local groups on the same system and can be given access to resources only on that system.

logical drive

A simple volume or partition indicated by a drive letter that resides on a Windows Server 2003 basic disk.

logon script

A file that you can assign to one or more user accounts. Typically a batch file, a logon script runs automatically every time the user logs on. You can use it to configure a user's working environment at every logon, and it allows an administrator to influence a user's environment without managing all aspects of it.

metabase

See *IIS metabase*.

Microsoft Challenge Handshake Authentication Protocol (MS-CHAP)

A special version of CHAP that Microsoft uses. The encryption in MS-CHAP is two-way and consists of a challenge from the server to the client that consists of a session ID. The client uses a Message Digest 4 (MD4) hash to return the username to the server.

Microsoft Management Console (MMC)

A set of Windows Server 2003 utilities that allow authorized administrators to manage the directory remotely. The MMC provides a framework for hosting administrative tools, called consoles.

mirrored volume

A fault-tolerant set of two physical disks that contain an exact replica of each other's data within the mirrored portion of each disk. Mirrored volumes are supported only on Windows Server computer versions.

mixed-mode domain

A migration concept that provides maximum backward compatibility with earlier versions of Windows NT. In mixed-mode domain, DCs that have been upgraded to Active Directory services allow servers running Windows NT versions 4 and earlier to exist within the domain.

mounted drive, mount point, or mounted volume

A pointer from one partition to another. Mounted drives are useful for increasing a drive's size without disturbing it. For example, you could create a mount point to drive E: as C:\CompanyData. Doing so makes it seem that you have increased the size available on the C: partition, specifically allowing you to store more data in C:\CompanyData than you would otherwise be able to.

MPEG (Moving Picture Experts Group)

A family of digital video-compression standards and file formats. MPEG generally produces better-quality video than competing formats. MPEG files can be decoded by special hardware or by software. MPEG achieves a high compression rate by storing only the changes from one frame to another, instead of storing each entire frame. There are two major MPEG standards: MPEG-1 and MPEG-2. The MPEG-1 standard provides a video resolution of 352×240 at 30 frames per second (fps), which is video quality slightly below that of conventional VCR tapes. A newer standard, MPEG-2, offers resolutions of 720×480 and 1,280×720 at 60fps, with full CD-quality audio. This standard is sufficient for all the major TV standards, including National Television Standards Committee (NTSC) and even High Definition Television (HDTV). DVD-ROMs use MPEG-2. MPEG-2 can compress a two-hour video into a few gigabytes. Currently, work is being done on a new version of MPEG called MPEG-4 (there is no MPEG-3), which will be based on the QuickTime file format.

Multilink

An extension to Point-to-Point Protocol (PPP) that allows you to combine multiple physical connections between two points into a single logical connection. For example, you can combine two 33.6Kbps modems into one logical 67.2Kbps connection. The combined connections, called *bundles*, provide greater bandwidth than a single connection.

Multiple Processor Support (MPS) compliant

Compatible with Windows Server 2003 Symmetric Multiprocessing (SMP). Windows Server 2003 provides support for single or multiple CPUs. If you originally installed Windows Server 2003 on a computer with a single CPU, you must update the HAL on the computer so that it can recognize and use multiple CPUs. Windows XP Professional and Windows 2000 Professional both support up to a maximum of two processors.

name resolution

The process of mapping a computer name—either a FQDN or a NetBIOS name—to an IP address.

namespace

The hierarchical structure of objects in a group of cooperating directories or databases.

native-mode domain

A migration concept in which all DCs are running Windows Server 2003 and Windows 2000 Server Active Directory. A native-mode domain uses only Active Directory services multimaster replication between DCs, and no Windows NT DCs can participate in the domain through single-master replication.

network directory

A file or database where users or applications can get reference information about objects on the network.

network interface card (NIC), network adapter, or adapter card

A piece of computer hardware that physically connects a computer to a network cable.

normal backup

A backup that copies all files and marks those files as having been backed up (in other words, clears the archive attribute). A normal backup is the most complete form of backup.

NTBackup or NTBackup.exe

See *Backup Utility*.

ntdsutil.exe

A command-line utility for managing Active Directory, including marking Active Directory objects as "authoritative" after restoring them from backup.

NTFS (NT File System) 5

An advanced file system that is designed for use specifically within the Windows Server 2003 operating system. It supports file-system recovery, extremely large storage media, and long filenames.

NTFS data compression

The process of making individual files and folders occupy less disk space with the NTFS version 5.0 file system in Windows Server 2003. Compressed files can be read and written to over the network by any Windows- or DOS-based program *without* having to be decompressed first. Files decompress when opened and recompress when closed. The NTFS 5 file system handles this entire process. Compression is simply a file attribute that you can apply to any file or folder stored on an NTFS 5 drive volume.

NTFS data encryption

See *Encrypting File System.*

NTFS disk quota

See *disk quota.*

NTFS permission

A rule associated with a folder, file, or printer that regulates which users can gain access to the object and in what manner. The object's owner allows or denies permissions. The most restrictive permissions take precedence if conflicting permissions exist between share permissions and NTFS permissions on an object.

object

In the context of performance monitoring and optimization, a system component that has numerous counters associated with it. For example, objects include processor, memory, system, logical disk, and paging file.

offline files

A feature in Windows Server 2003, Windows XP, and Windows 2000 that allows users to continue to work with network files and programs even when they are not connected to the network. When a network connection is restored or when users dock their mobile computers, any changes that were made while users were working offline are updated to the network. When more than one user on the network has made changes to the same file, users are given the option of saving their specific version of the file to the network, keeping the other version, or saving both. Also known as client-side caching (CSC).

optimization

The process of tuning performance for a particular system component.

organizational unit (OU)

A type of container object that is used within the LDAP/X.500 information model to group other objects and classes together for easier administration.

OSI (Open Systems Interconnect) model

A layer architecture developed by the International Organization for Standardization (ISO) that standardizes levels of service and types of interaction for computers that are exchanging information through a communications network. The OSI model separates computer-to-computer communications into seven layers, or levels, each of which builds on the standards contained in the levels below it.

out-of-band management

Terminal-emulation support via modem or serial port for the Special Administration Console and the !Special Administration Console for EMS.

pagefile

See *paging file*.

paging file

A system file that is an extension of random access memory which is stored on the disk drive as a kind of virtual memory.

partition

A section on a basic disk that is created from free space so that data can be stored on it. On a basic disk, you can create up to four primary partitions or up to three primary partitions and one extended partition.

Password Authentication Protocol (PAP)

A protocol that allows clear-text authentication.

PC Card

See *PCMCIA*.

PCI (peripheral component interconnect)

A local bus standard developed by Intel. Most modern PCs include a PCI bus in addition to a more general Industry Standard Architecture (ISA) expansion bus. Many analysts believe that PCI will eventually replace ISA entirely. PCI is a 64-bit bus, although it is usually implemented as a 32-bit bus. It can run at clock speeds of 33MHz or 66MHz. Although Intel developed it, PCI is not tied to any particular family of microprocessors.

PCMCIA (Personal Computer Memory Card International Association)

An organization of some 500 companies that developed a standard for small, credit-card–sized devices called PC cards. Originally designed for adding memory to portable computers, the PCMCIA standard has been expanded several times and is suitable for many types of devices. There are in fact three types of PCMCIA cards, along with three types of PC slots the cards fit into: Type I, II, and III.

Performance MMC snap-in

A utility for monitoring, tracking, and displaying a computer's performance statistics, both in real time and over an extended period for establishing a system baseline. This console includes the System Monitor node and the Performance Logs and Alerts node.

ping (packet Internet groper) utility

A utility that determines whether a specific IP address for a network device is reachable from an individual computer. ping works by sending a data packet to the specified address and waiting for a reply. You can use ping to troubleshoot network connections in the TCP/IP network protocol.

Plug and Play

A standard developed by Microsoft, Intel, and other industry leaders to simplify the process of adding hardware to PCs by having the operating system automatically detect devices. The intent of the standard is to conceal unpleasant details, such as IRQs and DMA channels, from people who want to add new hardware devices to their systems. A Plug and Play monitor, for example, can communicate with both Windows Server 2003 and the graphics adapter to automatically set itself at the maximum refresh rate supported for a chosen resolution. Plug and Play compliance also ensures that devices are not driven beyond their capabilities.

Point-to-Point Protocol (PPP)

A method of connecting a computer to a network or to the Internet. PPP is more stable than the older Serial Line Internet Protocol (SLIP) and provides error-checking features. Windows XP Professional and Windows 2000 Professional are both PPP clients when dialing in to any network.

Point-to-Point Tunneling Protocol (PPTP)

A communication protocol that tunnels through another connection, encapsulating PPP packets. The encapsulated packets are IP datagrams that can be transmitted over IP-based networks, such as the Internet.

policy

A configuration or setting that is specified for one or more systems or users. Policies are refreshed at startup, at logon, and after a refresh interval, so if a setting is manually changed, the policy refreshes the setting automatically. Policies provide for centralized management of change and configuration.

prestaging computer accounts

A method for creating computer accounts within Active Directory in advance of installing the computers and then joining them to the domain using RIS.

primary domain controller (PDC)

In a Windows NT Server 4 or earlier domain, the computer running Windows NT Server that authenticates domain logons and maintains the directory database for a domain. The PDC tracks changes made to accounts of all computers on a domain. It is the only computer to receive these changes directly. A domain has only one PDC.

primary master

An authoritative DNS server for a zone that you can use as a point of update for the zone. Only primary masters can be updated directly to process zone updates, which include adding, removing, and modifying resource records that are stored as zone data. Primary masters are also used as the first sources for replicating the zone to other DNS servers.

primary monitor

The monitor designated as the one that displays the logon dialog box when you start a computer. Most programs display their windows on the primary monitor when you first open them. A Windows Server 2003 computer can support multiple monitors or displays.

primary restore

A type of restore for Active Directory objects that you should perform when there is only one DC in the domain or when you need to rebuild an entire domain from backup because all DCs have been lost.

privilege or user right

The capability to perform a system behavior, such as changing the system time, backing up or restoring files, or formatting the hard drive.

public-key cryptography

An asymmetric encryption scheme that uses a pair of keys to code data. The public key encrypts data, and a corresponding secret (private) key decrypts it. For digital signatures, the sender uses the private key to create a unique electronic number that can be read by anyone who has the corresponding public key, thus verifying that the message is truly from the sender.

RADIUS (Remote Authentication Dial-in User Service)

A protocol used by Internet Authentication Services (IAS) to enable the communication of authentication, authorization, and accounting to the homogeneous and heterogeneous dial-up or VPN equipment in the enterprise.

RAID (Redundant Array of Independent Disks)-5 volume or striped set with parity volume

A fault-tolerant collection of equal-sized partitions on at least three physical disks, in which the data is striped and includes parity data. The parity data helps recover a member of the striped set if the member fails. Neither Windows XP Professional nor Windows 2000 Professional can host a RAID-5 volume, but Windows Server 2003 and Windows 2000 Server computers can.

Recovery Console

A command-line interface (CLI) that provides a limited set of administrative commands that are useful for repairing a computer. For example, you can use the Recovery Console to start and stop services, read and write data on a local drive (including drives formatted to use NTFS), repair a master boot record (MBR), and format drives. You can start the Recovery Console from the Windows Server 2003 CD-ROM, or you can install the Recovery Console on the computer using the `winnt32.exe` command with the `/cmdcons` switch.

Remote Assistance (RA)

A built-in service that enables another user, typically a help-desk or IT employee, to remotely help the end user with an issue that she is experiencing on her Windows XP Professional or Windows Server 2003 computer.

Remote Desktop Connection

Client software that enables you to access a Terminal Services session that is running on a remote computer while you are sitting at another computer in a different location. This process is extremely useful for employees who want to work from home but need to access their computers at work.

Remote Desktops MMC snap-in

An MMC snap-in that allows administrators to log on to multiple Remote Desktop sessions simultaneously from a single management console.

Remote Installation Services (RIS)

A server that provides Windows Server 2003, Windows XP Professional, and Windows 2000 Professional operating-system images that can be downloaded and installed by network clients using network adapters that comply with the preboot execution environment (PXE) boot read-only memory (ROM) specifications. RIS requires Active Directory, DHCP, and DNS to serve clients.

Removable Storage

Allows applications to access and share the same media resources. This service is used for managing removable media. Different types of media include floppy disks, Zip disks, CD-ROMs, CD-Rs, CD-RWs, DVD media, and tape backup devices. Some include removable hard drives as removable storage.

Resultant Set of Policy (RSoP)

A term for the resulting (effective) group policies that are applied to a computer and user. With multiple group policies at sites, domains, and OUs, it is very complex to determine the final, resulting policies that are applied and how those policies affect the user and the computer.

reverse lookup zone

A DNS zone that provides TCP/IP address-to-hostname resolution.

route

A Windows Server 2003 command-line utility that manipulates TCP/IP routing tables for the local computer.

runas

A Windows Server 2003 GUI and command-line tool that allows a user or an administrator to run a program or to open a file under a different user's security credentials using the appropriate user account name and password.

Safe Mode startup options

The options you get at startup when you press the F8 function key while in Safe Mode. Safe Mode helps you diagnose problems. When started in Safe Mode, Windows Server 2003 uses only basic files and drivers (mouse, monitor, keyboard, mass storage, base video, and default system services but no network connections). You can choose the Safe Mode with Networking option, which loads all the preceding files and drivers plus the essential services and drivers to start networking. Or you can choose the Safe Mode with Command Prompt option, which is exactly the same as Safe Mode except that you get a command prompt instead of the Windows Server 2003 graphical user interface (GUI). You can also choose Last Known Good Configuration, which starts the computer by using the Registry information that Windows Server 2003 saved at the last shutdown. If a symptom does not reappear when you start in Safe Mode, you can eliminate the default settings and minimum device drivers as possible causes. If a newly added device or a changed driver is causing problems, you can use Safe Mode to remove the device or reverse the change. In some circumstances, such as when Windows system files required to start the system are corrupted or damaged, Safe Mode cannot help you. In such a case, an ERD might be of use.

sampling interval or update interval

The frequency with which a performance counter is logged. A shorter interval provides more detailed information but generates a larger log.

scalability

A measure of how well a computer, a service, or an application can grow to meet increasing performance demands.

scheduled tasks

A system folder that stores scheduled jobs that run at predefined times. Administrators can create scheduled jobs.

Scheduled Tasks Wizard

A series of dialog boxes that simplify the process of creating scheduled task jobs.

Security Accounts Manager (SAM)

The database of local user and local group accounts on a Windows Server 2003 member server, Windows XP Professional, or Windows 2000 Professional computer.

security group

A group that can contain users and other groups that can be assigned an ACL with ACEs to define security permissions on objects for the members of the group.

security identifier (SID)

A unique number that represents a security principal such as a user or group. You can change the name of a user or group account without affecting the account's permissions and privileges because the SID is what is granted user rights and resource access.

Serial Line Internet Protocol (SLIP)

An older remote access communication protocol that is used in Windows Server 2003 for outbound communication only. This protocol is commonly used for connecting to Unix servers.

Setup Manager

A utility program that ships on the Windows Server 2003 CD-ROM and that is used to create answer files for unattended installations. Setup Manager can create answer files for unattended, sysprep, or RIS installations.

Shadow Copies of Shared Folders

A new feature in Windows Server 2003 that creates "snapshots," or copies, of original data volumes at various scheduled intervals and during data backup operations. You can retrieve previous versions of files and folders from Shadow Copies by installing the Previous Versions Client software on Windows XP workstations and by installing the Shadow Copy Client software on Windows 2000 and previous operating systems.

share permission

A rule that is associated with a folder to regulate which users can gain access to the object over the network and in what manner.

shared folder

A folder that is shared for use by remote users over the network.

Shiva Password Authentication Protocol (SPAP)

A protocol that third-party clients and server typically use. The encryption for SPAP is two-way, but it is not as good as that for CHAP.

simple volume

In Windows Server 2003, the disk space on a single physical disk. A simple volume can consist of a single area on a disk or multiple areas on the same disk that are linked together. You can extend a simple volume within the same disk or among multiple disks. If you extend a simple volume across multiple disks, it becomes a spanned volume.

slipstreaming

The process of integrating a Windows Server 2003 service pack (SP) into an existing Windows Server 2003 installation share. Subsequent installations of Windows Server 2003 do not require separate SP installation because the updated SP files are included (slipstreamed) into the installation share.

smart card

A credit-card–sized device that is used to securely store public and private keys, passwords, and other types of personal information. To use a smart card, you need a smart card reader attached to the computer and a personal identification number (PIN) for the smart card. In Windows Server 2003, you can use smart cards to enable certificate-based authentication and SSO to the enterprise.

smart card reader

A small external or internal device, or even a built-in slot, into which you insert a smart card so that it can be read.

Software Update Services (SUS)

An add-on program that you can download from Microsoft's Web site that allows an organization to centrally manage and deploy software patches and updates for Microsoft operating systems. It works in a similar fashion to the Microsoft Windows Update Web site.

spanned volume

In Windows Server 2003, the disk space on more than one physical disk. You can add more space to a spanned volume by extending it at any time. In NT 4 and earlier operating systems, a spanned volume is called a volume set.

Special Administration Console and !Special Administration Console

A set of command-line utilities that allow you to perform out-of-band management on a Windows Server 2003 computer.

spooler service

The primary Windows Server 2003 service that controls printing functionality.

SRV (service) record

A resource record that is used in a zone to register and locate well-known TCP/IP services. The SRV resource record is specified in Request for Comments (RFC) 2052 and is used in Windows Server 2003 or later to locate DCs for Active Directory service.

standard zone storage

Storage of zone information in a text file rather than in an Active Directory database.

standby mode

A power-saving option in Windows Server 2003, Windows XP, and Windows 2000 computers in which a computer switches to a low-power state where devices, such as the monitor and hard disks, turn off and the computer uses less power. When you want to use the computer again, it comes out of standby quickly, and the desktop is restored exactly as you left it. Standby is useful for conserving battery power in portable computers. Standby does not save the desktop state to disk; if you experience a power failure while in standby mode, you can lose unsaved information. If there is an interruption in power, information in memory is lost.

static pool

A range of IP addresses configured on the remote access server that allows the server to allocate IP addresses to the remote access clients.

striped volume

A volume that stores data in stripes on two or more physical disks. Data in a striped volume is allocated alternately and evenly (in stripes) to the disks of the striped volume. Striped volumes are not fault tolerant. Striped volumes can substantially improve the speed of access to the data on disk. You can create them on Windows Server 2003, Windows XP Professional, Windows 2000 Professional, and Windows 2000 Server computers. Striped volumes with parity, also known as RAID-5 volumes, can be created only on Windows Server 2003 and Windows 2000 Server computers. In Windows NT 4 and earlier, a striped volume is called a striped set.

subnet mask

A filter that is used to determine which network segment, or subnet, an IP address belongs to. An IP address has two components: the network address and the host (computer name) address. For example, if the IP address 209.15.17.8 is part of a Class C network, the first three numbers (209.15.17) represent the Class C network address, and the last number (8) identifies a specific host (computer) on that network. By implementing subnetting, network administrators can further divide the host part of the address into two or more subnets.

suspend mode

A deep-sleep power-saving option that does use some power.

symmetric multiprocessing (SMP)

A computer architecture that provides fast performance by making multiple CPUs available to complete individual processes simultaneously (that is, multiprocessing). Unlike with asymmetric processing, with SMP you can assign any idle processor any task as well as add additional CPUs to improve performance and handle increased loads. A variety of specialized operating systems and hardware arrangements support SMP. Specific applications can benefit from SMP if their code allows multithreading. SMP uses a single operating system and shares common memory and disk I/O resources. Windows Server 2003 supports SMP.

sysprep

A tool that prepares a Windows Server 2003, Windows XP Professional, or a Windows 2000 Professional computer to be imaged by using third-party disk image software. It does so by removing unique identifiers such as computer name and SIDs. sysprep modifies the target operating system's Registry so that a unique local domain SID is created when the computer boots for the first time after the disk image is applied.

System Access Control List (SACL)

An ACL that specifies the security events to be audited for a user or group.

System Monitor

A node in the Performance MMC snap-in for monitoring and logging computer performance statistics using performance objects, counters, and instances.

System State

In the Windows Backup utility, a collection of system-specific data that you can back up and restore. For all Windows Server 2003, Windows XP, and Windows 2000 operating systems, the System State data includes the Registry, the Component Object Model (COM)+ Class Registration database, and the system boot files. For Windows Server 2003 and Windows 2000 Server, the System State data also includes the Certificate Services database (if the server is operating as a certificate server). If the server is a DC, the System State data also includes the Active Directory database and the sysvol directory.

sysvol

A shared directory that stores the server copy of the domain's public files, which are replicated among all DCs in the domain.

Task Manager

A utility program that displays the current application programs and processes that are running on the computer. It also monitors the system's recent processor usage, recent memory usage, current network utilization, and currently logged-on users.

Terminal Server

A computer that is running Terminal Services. A Windows Server 2003 computer installs Terminal Services in Remote Desktop for Administration mode by default. You must set up Terminal Services in Application Server mode separately.

Terminal Services

A built-in service that enables you to use the Remote Desktop Connection software to connect to a session that is running on a remote computer while you are sitting at another computer in a different location. This process is extremely useful for employees who want to work from home but need to access their computers at work.

ticket

A feature of the Kerberos security model by which clients are granted access to objects and resources only indirectly, through services. Application servers use the service ticket to impersonate the client and look up its user or group SIDs.

tracert

A Windows Server 2003 command-line utility that follows the path of a data packet from a local computer to a host (computer) somewhere on the network (or internetwork). It shows how many hops the packet requires to reach the host and how long each hop takes. You can use tracert to figure out where the longest delays are occurring for connecting to various computers.

universal group

A security or distribution group that you can use anywhere in a domain tree or forest; universal groups are only available when the domain's functional level is set at Windows 2000 native or Windows Server 2003. A universal group can have members from any Active Directory domain in the domain tree or forest. It can also include other universal groups, global groups, and accounts from any domain in the domain tree or forest. Universal groups can be members of domain local groups and other universal groups but cannot be members of global groups. Universal groups appear in the global catalog and should contain primarily global groups.

universally unique identifier

See *globally unique identifier*.

USB (universal serial bus)

An external bus standard (released in 1996) that supports data transfer rates of 12Mbps. You can use a single USB port to connect up to 127 peripheral devices, such as mice, modems, and keyboards. USB also supports Plug and Play installation and hot plugging. It is expected to completely replace serial and parallel ports.

user account

An object within Active Directory that contains information about a user, including the user logon name, password, and group memberships. Also, an object with a local computer's SAM database that contains information about a user, including the user logon name, password, and group memberships.

User Datagram Protocol (UDP)

A connectionless protocol that runs on top of IP networks. Unlike TCP/IP, UDP provides very few error-recovery services and does not guarantee delivery of data. UDP is a direct way to send and receive datagrams over an IP network. It's used primarily for sending broadcast messages over an IP network.

user locale

A group of settings that control the date, time, currency, and numbers on a per-user basis. All applications use these settings, and you can configure them via the Regional and Language Options applet in the Control Panel.

user profile

A collection of desktop and environmental settings that define the work area of a local computer.

user right

See *privilege*.

User State Migration Tool (USMT)

A CLI set of tools that stores user data and settings for an upgrade or reinstallation of the computer. The tools include scanstate and loadstate, which extract the information and restore the information, respectively.

UUID

Universally unique identifier; see *globally unique identifier*.

video adapter

The electronic component that generates the video signal that is sent through a cable to a video display. The video adapter is usually located on the computer's main system board or on an expansion board.

virtual private network (VPN)

A private network of computers that is at least partially connected using public channels or lines, such as the Internet. A good example of a VPN is a private-office local area network (LAN) that allows users to log in remotely over the Internet (an open, public system). VPNs use encryption and secure protocols such as PPTP and L2TP to ensure that unauthorized parties do not intercept data transmissions.

volume

A section on a dynamic disk that is created from unallocated space so that data can be stored on it. You can only create simple volumes, striped volumes, spanned volumes, mirrored volumes, and RAID-5 volumes on dynamic disks.

Volume Shadow Copy Service (VSS)

A new service in Windows Server 2003 and Windows XP that creates "snapshots," or copies, of original data volumes at various scheduled intervals and during data backup operations. Under Windows Server 2003, you can retrieve previous versions of files and folders from Shadow Copies; under Windows XP, Shadow Copies are used only for taking snapshots of data for backup operations.

WDM (Windows or Win32 Driver Model)

A 32-bit layered architecture for device drivers that allows for drivers that Windows Server 2003, Windows XP, Windows 2000, Windows NT, and Windows 98 computers can use. It provides common I/O services that all operating systems understand. It also supports Plug and Play; USB; IEEE 1394; and various devices, including input, communication, imaging, and DVD.

Windows Installer Service package

A file with the .msi extension that installs applications. Such files contain summary and installation instructions as well as the actual installation files. You can install Windows Installer Service packages locally or remotely through Windows Server 2003 group policies.

Windows Internet Name Service (WINS)

A service that dynamically maps NetBIOS names to IP addresses.

Windows Management Instrumentation (WMI)

An initiative supported in Windows Server 2003 that establishes architecture to support the management of an enterprise across the Internet. WMI offers universal access to management information for enterprises by providing a consistent view of the managed environment. This management uniformity allows you to manage the entire business rather than just its components. You can obtain more detailed information regarding the WMI Software Development Kit (SDK) from the Microsoft Developer Network (MSDN).

Windows Messenger

The new application built into the operating system that allows for chatting, notifications, voice communication, file transfer, and sharing of applications.

Windows Update

Offers device-driver support that supplements the extensive library of drivers available on the installation CD. Windows Update is an online extension, providing a central location for product enhancements.

winnt32 /cmdcons

The command and switch used to install the Recovery Console on a Windows Server 2003 computer. This command uses winnt32 on the installation media or in the distribution source.

workgroup

A peer-to-peer network in which user accounts are decentralized and stored on each individual system.

ZAP file

A file that you use to allow applications without an .msi file to be deployed via Active Directory group policy.

zone

In DNS standards, the namespace partition formed by each domain within the global namespace or within an enterprise namespace. Each zone is controlled by an authoritative DNS server, or in the case of Active Directory services, by a group of DCs.

zone transfer

Copying of DNS database information from one DNS server to another.

Index

How can we make this index more useful? Email us at indexes@quepublishing.com

How can we make this index more useful? Email us at indexes@quepublishing.com

E

F

How can we make this index more useful? Email us at indexes@quepublishing.com

How can we make this index more useful? Email us at indexes@quepublishing.com

How can we make this index more useful? Email us at indexes@quepublishing.com

informIT

www.informit.com

Your Guide to Information Technology Training and Reference

Que has partnered with **InformIT.com** to bring technical information to your desktop. Drawing on Que authors and reviewers to provide additional information on topics you're interested in, **InformIT.com** has free, in-depth information you won't find anywhere else.

Articles

Keep your edge with thousands of free articles, in-depth features, interviews, and information technology reference recommendations – all written by experts you know and trust.

Online Books

Answers in an instant from **InformIT Online Books'** 600+ fully searchable online books. Sign up now and get your first 14 days **free**.

POWERED BY
Safari

Catalog

Review online sample chapters and author biographies to choose exactly the right book from a selection of more than 5,000 titles.